Preserving the Old Dominion
Historic Preservation and Virginia Traditionalism

Preserving the Old Dominion

Historic Preservation and Virginia Traditionalism

James M. Lindgren

University Press of Virginia

Charlottesville and London

The University Press of Virginia
Copyright © 1993
by the Rector and Visitors
of the University of Virginia

First published 1993

Library of Congress Cataloging-in-Publication Data
Lindgren, James Michael, 1950–
    Preserving the Old Dominion : historic preservation and Virginia
traditionalism / James M. Lindgren.
        p.   cm.
    Includes bibliographical references (pp. 293–304) and index.
    ISBN 0-8139-1450-7
        1. Historic preservation—Virginia—History—20th century.
    2. Historic preservation—Virginia—History—19th century.
    3. Association for the Preservation of Virginia Antiquities—
History.   I. Title.
    F227.L55   1993
    363.6'9'09755—dc20   92-46301
                                                                          CIP

Printed in the United States of America

To My Parents

Contents

Illustrations

following page 136

Acknowledgments

T HIS PROJECT is literally a case of historic preservation itself. It began in a seminar in 1979 and culminated five years later with a Ph.D. dissertation at the College of William and Mary in which I studied the major historic preservation movements in Virginia and New England during the late nineteenth and early twentieth centuries. At a crucial fork in my intellectual road, and as newer approaches opened in the study of history, I realized that cultural history, and not simply the typical chronology of an organization's work, would reveal the most about the preservation movement, its sense of locale and identity, and the meaning it imparted to the "history" it preserved. I passed one milestone, *Preserving the Old Dominion,* and marched toward another, *Preserving Historic New England.* Both studies analyze preservation movements in the time, place, and circumstances that defined them.

As is customary, and especially fitting for a book on traditions, I want to thank my mentors at the College of William and Mary. When I first applied for admission to a doctoral program, I already had a dissertation in mind. No school better received my ideas than did those faculty members in Williamsburg who eventually served on my dissertation committee. I benefited not simply from their suggestions but from their tolerance and patience. Richard B. Sherman served as chair and worked most ably with Edward P. Crapol, Thad W. Tate, M. Boyd Coyner, and Shomer Zwelling. At the same time other faculty members encouraged me to consider different angles on my research: James Axtell on ethnohistory, George Rudé on cultural hegemony, and William Appleman Williams on the definition of history and society. James P. Whittenburg, then Director of the Graduate Program, helped me secure funding for some of this study. Subsequent research was funded in part by grants from the New York State / United University Professions PDQWL program.

Many scholars have read this study in a variety of revisions. I credit the strengths of this book, but not the weaknesses, to their suggestions and insights. I principally wish to thank Michael Kammen of Cornell University, Alan Trachtenberg of Yale University, Cary Carson of the Colonial Williamsburg Foundation, Charles B. Hosmer, Jr., of Principia College, T. J. Jackson Lears of Rutgers University, Michael Wallace of John Jay College (CUNY), Gary Kulik of the National Museum of American History, and Anita Rapone of SUNY/Plattsburgh. My thinking was further cleared when the gist of my work was presented in papers delivered before the Southern Historical Association, the American Studies Association, and the Colonial Williamsburg Foundation.

Aspects of this book have been developed in various journals. A very short introduction to my general argument was presented in " 'For the Sake of Our Future': The Association for the Preservation of Virginia Antiquities and the Regeneration of Traditionalism," *Virginia Magazine of History and Biography* 97 (1989): 47–74; " 'Virginia Needs Living Heroes': Historic Preservation in the Progressive Era," *Public Historian* 13 (1991): 9–24; " 'Whatever Is Un-Virginian Is Wrong': The APVA's Sense of the Old Dominion," *Virginia Cavalcade* 38 (1989): 112–23; and "APVA: Uniting Town and Gown," *William and Mary Magazine* 57 (Summer 1989): 30–31. I was honored when my essay in the *Public Historian* was awarded the G. Wesley Johnson Prize for 1991 by the National Council on Public History. A grateful hand is extended to the editors of those journals, as it is to those in the APVA who encouraged my work. Robert A. Murdock, then executive director, accommodated my investigations not only by opening his file cabinets and storage closets but by encouraging me to develop my research further. His most recent successor, Peter D. Grover, helped in the last stages of publication. Spotswood Hunnicutt Jones, an APVA board member, graciously helped most of all by facilitating the publication of my work in Virginia journals, reviewing this manuscript, and never failing to help in other matters.

In the past years many others have generously helped me to resolve nagging questions about the APVA's history and its preservationists: Frances S. Pollard of the Virginia Historical Society; Margaret Cook and Laura Parrish of the University Archives at the College of William and Mary; Robert T. Armistead, Helene S. Ward, and Parke Rouse, Jr., of Williamsburg; George Yetter and Carl Lounsbury of the Colonial Williamsburg Foundation; John S. Salmon of the Virginia Division of Historic Resources; Edward D. C. Campbell, Jr., of the Virginia State Library; Gregg D. Kimball of the Valentine Museum; David L. Moffitt of the Colonial National Historical Park; Peggy A. Haile of the Norfolk Public Library; Arthur S. Link of the Woodrow Wilson Papers; James I. Robertson, Jr., of Virginia Polytechnic Institute and State University; Daniel E. Sutherland of the University of

Arkansas; Thomas L. Connelly of the University of South Carolina; Gaines M. Foster of Louisiana State University; Carolyn F. Travers of Plimoth Plantation; Ellie Reichlin of the Society for the Preservation of New England Antiquities; and the staff of the Manuscripts Division at the Library of Congress, Duke University Archives, the University of Virginia Archives, and the Valentine Museum. Access to materials was never easy from afar, but Craig Koste and Mary Turner of the interlibrary loan department at SUNY/Plattsburgh helped me through the obstacle course. At the University Press of Virginia, Nancy C. Essig gave me encouraging words about my project.

The customary words of thanks to my family fails to describe their patience as this project evolved from mental musings to rough scribbles to printed pages. My spouse Mary Ann Weiglhofer cleared my sometimes foggy thinking and first taught me the mysteries of word processing. From their first days in a bassinet to those summer months of slugging baseballs, Brian and Charlie have grown with this project and wonder what a vacation would be without visiting old buildings and historic grounds.

Preserving the Old Dominion
Historic Preservation and Virginia Traditionalism

PROLOGUE

The Gospel of Preservation

T HE EYES OF most Americans in 1895 could hardly ignore signs of social
breakdown—national depression, popular-class revolt, and unsettling
rapid change. Such evident distress and anxiety may well have made the
pageantry and fanfare at Jamestown on 13 May seem all the more quixotic.
On that day the Association for the Preservation of Virginia Antiquities
assembled some four thousand reverent but buoyant Virginians at the site
of the nation's first permanent English settlement, which the APVA had
acquired two years earlier, to commemorate the landing of John Smith and
his company of adventurers in 1607. Seven hundred of "the best people of
Richmond" sailed the broad expanse of the James River aboard the brightly
decorated *Pocahontas*. When the steamer arrived at the island's rickety wharf,
it was greeted by a small flotilla of ships, the smartly dressed Surry Troop,
and nearly one thousand kindred souls from the hamlet of Williamsburg.
The Richmond Howitzers' Band then played, and the crowd sang patriotic
songs, including a version of "America" especially written for that day to
tout Virginia's priority in the United States. Pilgrims walked the sacred
grounds, inspected the ancient ruins, shared their memories of the past, and
planted four willow trees in the churchyard to be symbols of
the continuing vitality of Jamestown's soil.[1]

Those present on the podium for the day's ceremony revealed the
official sanction that the APVA had won only six years after its organization.
Honored seats were occupied not only by the wives of past and present
governors but many of the state's cultural and economic elite. They listened
to stirring orations by John Lesslie Hall and Lyon Gardiner Tyler of the
College of William and Mary. Both reminded the audience that the primitive ruins of this seventeenth-century settlement symbolized the advent and
primacy of Anglo-Saxon, Protestant culture in the United States. "This island is to us," said Professor Hall, "what those scared spots were to the older

nations. It is at once our Acropolis, our Palatine Hill, and our isle of Thanet. Let us ever love it and preserve it." The threats against Jamestown in 1895 came from many quarters. While wind and wave eroded its material legacy, its memory was obscured by the lure of the modern age and the falsehoods of its schoolbooks. One of the Old Dominion's foremost traditionalists, Joseph Bryan, used his Richmond *Times* the next day to challenge particularly the story of the Pilgrim Fathers, which had been cast as the nation's founding tradition by generations of Yankees. Rejecting the claims associated with Plymouth Rock, he asked Virginians to preserve what remained of their pioneer colony and prevent it from being "supplanted by any pretensions for other States or places."[2]

What the APVA inaugurated in 1895 as Virginia Day, it repeated year after year when elite, tradition-minded Virginians visited the island's ruins to pay homage to their forebears. Of all historic sites in the Old Dominion, Jamestown became the metaphor for Virginia traditionalism, and the APVA spotlighted it by building monuments, holding pilgrimages, and popularizing its history. Preservationists held solemn public ceremonies there—full of pomp, ritual, and oration—that renewed traditionalism, observed Protestantism, and commemorated the civil religion. The APVA literally invented a tradition through its memorials, pilgrimages, and celebration of Virginia Day. Its promotion of Jamestown with colorful pageantry and historical reinterpretation of the settlement contradicted the evident fact that Jamestown had been almost forgotten in the nineteenth century. From a desolate island, Jamestown became the birthplace of the republic. The APVA's rites brought thousands to the island. As one Richmond paper later acknowledged, "For many years, the pilgrimages—they are that, not 'excursions'—offered about the only opportunity extended the people of Richmond to visit the cradle of the race." Pilgrims immersed themselves in the vicarious but much romanticized thrills of early Virginians. All the while, they learned about the cultural traditions that, according to the APVA, had shaped the Old Dominion. "Once visiting it," a preservationist declared, "interest in all that it stands for in our national life; all that is lasting and beneficent that has eminated from it must be imperishably implanted in the hearts of even the average tourist."[3] Nothing better illustrates the APVA's work than its transformation of this barren island into a powerful symbol, but it is only appropriate to ask, Just what did Jamestown stand for? *Preserving the Old Dominion* examines this question and explores the cultural meaning of historic preservation in the late nineteenth and early twentieth centuries.

Throughout history, preservation movements have been closely tied to the cultural politics of their day. As in the case of the APVA in the late nineteenth century, its rituals and work are neither quixotic nor escapist; they closely draw their meaning from the day's cultural contests. The association is significant in many ways. It was the first statewide preservation agency in the United States; and within twenty years of its establishment, a wide range of preservation groups organized on the national and state level. More importantly, it played a crucial role in the resurgence of conservatism in the Old Dominion after the traumatic defeat of the Confederacy and the unsettling rise of popular-class radicalism. To be a proper Virginian meant joining the APVA.

All the while, preservationists disputed the claims of African-Americans and popular-class radicals who demanded that Virginia alter its ancient ways. Preserved history became a means to hold back undesired change. Well before the formation of the Williamsburg Holding Corporation or the acquisition of lands by the National Park Service in the Historic Triangle of Yorktown, Jamestown, and Williamsburg in the 1930s, the APVA significantly defined the character of the Old Dominion for the twentieth century and after. It helped inaugurate, moreover, a noteworthy trend in which tradition-minded Americans preserved their history in order to shape their identity, embolden their resolve, and promulgate their heritage. As the first statewide preservation movement in the nation, it also set a focus on cultural preservation that every state in the Union would ultimately adopt. What the APVA did, and why, is significant in the study of how the cultural identity of Americans was defined in modern times.

Throughout the East in the late nineteenth century, diverse contestants strove to shape the nation's culture. In New England and much of the North, millions of immigrants from central and southern Europe flooded the nation's gates. Their very numbers, as well as their staunchly held beliefs, upset old-stock Yankees who worried that their traditions would be swamped by a foreign tidal wave. At the same time, economic dislocations magnified these cultural battles as industrial capitalists swept aside customary practices, and their workers rose up to demand the rewards of the American Revolution. All of this occurred in the midst of a swelling population, burgeoning cities, and what many old-timers perceived as chaos.[4] Northern preservationists, as a result, did not meekly limit their attention to deteriorating buildings and crusty curios but instead worked to defend their culture on numerous fronts.

Similarly, southern preservationists feared for their future. Like no other event in United States history, the Civil War forced the South to question its culture and society. Historians have often focused on the resultant New South of Atlanta publisher Henry Grady and his animus toward the backward ways of the Old. While the South's economy and society were in disarray, however, partisans of the Old South tried to conserve what they could of its antebellum culture. Students of the South have examined the Lost Cause movement and its defense of the Confederacy. An important element within this movement was historic preservation, and it included everything from erecting monuments to laying gravestones. Rarely did the Lost Cause movement enshrine old buildings, simply because those structures still had worthwhile uses for families or governments in an impoverished area. What is noteworthy is that Virginians were the first to preserve a famous Confederate shrine, the White House of the Confederacy in 1890. What is equally important is that one year earlier, the APVA acquired its first colonial landmark, the Powder Horn in Williamsburg. Thereafter, Virginians linked the colonial and Confederate eras and used each as a means to shape their contemporary world.[5]

Those who controlled culture could virtually shape Virginia, the South, and the United States. As is commonly understood, culture is defined by traditions, rituals, language, and symbols that are inherited, invented, or revised to give meaning and form to a people. After the Civil War many Americans grappled with such words as *liberty, democracy,* and *progress,* while seeing a confusing mélange of symbols that ostensibly represented the nation and its people. These included not only the Mount Vernon grave of George Washington and the Richmond home of John Marshall but an immigrant youth saluting the flag and a humble worker bowing before an all-powerful employer. Such symbols and rituals included as well those of alternative cultures, such as the mysticism of the Plains Indians in their Ghost Dances, the merrymaking of Germans at a beer hall, or the parades of the Irish on Saint Patrick's Day. All of these symbols, rituals, and traditions expressed culture, but the question remained, Which ones would primarily shape the ways of America's future? In the cultural battles of the day, it was uncertain just whose ways would become primary, and whose would be pushed aside.[6]

Traditions, symbols, and rituals define a people's identity. As the United States assumed more complex proportions in the nineteenth century, many Americans of wealth and standing found comfort and meaning by preserving and transforming old forms. In fact, powerful elites within Western society in general from 1870 to 1914 not only preserved but invented traditions and "history" to meet their contemporary political and economic needs.[7]

The Colonial Revival movement in American architecture and the decorative arts is a case in point. What it offered its proponents were not only reassuring roots in a mythical past but symbols through which they could express their aspirations for present and future. The movement actually began in the years before the Civil War.

As westward expansion, the industrial revolution, and the market society altered old ways, tradition-minded Americans of the 1850s worried about the days ahead. In the North the Know-Nothings audaciously called themselves the American party and expressed their nativism and traditionalism by capturing George Washington's legacy and the drive to build a monument to his memory in the nation's capital. Similarly, the Mount Vernon Ladies' Association, the first national organization in the historic preservation movement, acquired Washington's home in the late 1850s. It symbolically rebuffed not only those who threatened to break the Union but those Irish immigrants, urban political machines, and northern industrialists who opened Pandora's box and forever changed the nation. The MVLA's metaphorical use of Mount Vernon became a precedent for future preservationists.

In 1876 the nation celebrated the centennial of its birth in Philadelphia and at the same time dramatically showed the land's cultural confusion. At the fair it was evident that the United States paradoxically wanted both the wealth that progress might bring and the surety that history could offer. Competing elites seized Washington's portraits and mantle, as well as those of other colonial figures, in order to sanction their power and agenda. Whether in New England, Virginia, or the "civilized" West, elites commonly used colonial styles and historically defined forms to rebuff dissenters and reassure the worried, while forging ahead into an uncertain future.

Similarly, gentlemen and ladies of wealth and standing preserved or invented traditions, symbols, and rituals in their campaigns to Americanize immigrants and their children. Pledging allegiance to the flag, reciting a Founding Father's speech in the English language, accepting established laws and customs, and learning the history of the United States became means through which old-line Americans could shape the future in the mold of the past. Remarkable disagreements existed, however, within the ranks of America's elite. Most of its members wanted particularly to uphold old habits, including a respect for hierarchy, work, and law. Less often, the elite wanted to protect the past's material culture.

Tradition-minded Americans of all stripes recognized the need for some type of cultural preservation. Threats came from all sides, as old sureties gave way to newer uncertainties. Historic buildings were being demolished, old customs forgotten, and old families lost amidst the hustle and bustle. At the same time the lure of modernity and progress captivated the United States. The Columbian Exposition of 1893 in Chicago, for example, revealed the nation's ceaseless cultural drift. Did the fair's grand Beaux Arts designs of Richard Morris Hunt identify the ground on which America stood? Or the Midway Plaissance and its freak shows depicting bizarre but strangely appealing ways? Or the nondescript, easily forgettable building that the Commonwealth of Virginia erected at the fair?[8] Observers could not ignore the fact that so-called Progress was also accompanied by a devastating depression, the Populist Revolt, and the Spanish–American War.

As a result, scores of preservationists organized in the 1890s and early 1900s to protect their culture. Each movement accented different blends of cultural, historic, and architectural preservation. Many restricted membership through ancestral or family lines. Patriotic groups, such as the Daughters of the American Revolution (1890), saved many historic houses across the country as they tried to define the cultural loyalties and behavior of true-patriotic Americans. The National Society of the Colonial Dames of America (1890) similarly banded together to delineate the proper ancestral lines for true-blooded Americans. Aristocratic ruling classes, whether in ancient Egypt or modern Britain and America, have tried to define history through genealogy and, in so doing, naturally excluded those who did not fit. Increasingly in the late nineteenth century, what counted was having the correct pedigree and, as important, wealth.[9]

Other elites founded societies to protect the historic landscape. Even these historic preservation organizations developed different priorities. The American Scenic and Historic Preservation Society (1895) organized in New York to protect both the natural environment and architecture associated with history-making events in the state. The Society for the Preservation of New England Antiquities (1910) formed in Boston, on the other hand, primarily to save the vestiges of architectural craftsmanship of seventeenth-century Yankees.[10] The APVA preceded both the ASHPS and SPNEA and mixed buildings, blood, and culture in its mission. Weaving together these architectural, ancestral, and cultural threads, it made a concerted effort to define and preserve its memory of old-time Virginia. Amidst the chaos of the late nineteenth century, the APVA preserved symbols of the Old Dominion and suggested that the United States emulate Virginia's conservatism. Like most tradition-minded Americans in the late nineteenth century, its members longed for the security of the old order.[11]

Preservationists in the Old Dominion plunged into the cultural battles of their day and tried to find new meaning for old symbols. Time and again, the APVA claimed that Virginia's ancient buildings, historic sites, and generations-old antiquities had much meaning for the modern age. Preservationists in the APVA, unlike those in SPNEA, did not consider the artistry, landscape, or craftsmanship of an antiquity to hold much import. They instead valued these antiquities as symbols of venerated ancestors, time-honored customs, and the cultural environment of early Virginia. Nurtured in filiopiety, patriarchy, and traditionalism, preservationists religiously believed in their fathers' ways. Refusing to commit Adam's sin, they praised their forebears' morality, strong character, and orderly society. They found little wrong in the Old South and elevated its history and traditions to sacred proportions.

The APVA was motivated by a Gospel of Preservation. Just as a minister mounted his pulpit to read from the past in order to instruct the present, preservationists regularly delivered their gospel, a sermon that used the symbols of the Old Dominion to educate modern Virginians. As in mnemonics where one's memory is improved by a steady use of certain formulas, APVA speakers repeatedly invoked a gospel which warned that certainty and success could be assured only by reordering modern society according to customary lines. Whether the case involved a well-established respect for the First Families of Virginia, the usual promotion of states' rights, or recently invented customs such as middle-class domesticity and a factory-style work ethic, preservationists defined these principles as the canons of Virginia. In a nutshell, their gospel told Virginians that they could only guarantee progress in the present and surety in the future by learning from the past and emulating the ancients.

Tradition-minded Virginians acknowledged such wisdom after the state's social foundations had been severely shaken by successive tremors. Defeat in the Civil War had physically devastated the Old Dominion, dashed its states' rights politics, and hurt its deeply rooted pride. Emancipation turned its social order upside down. Reconstruction unleashed a democratic movement, culminating in the Readjusters and Populists who threatened to change forever what had been America's most aristocratic society. The New South movement further heralded a new breed of aggressive capitalists who sometimes mocked the Old South's civility and decorum. Perhaps no generation of Americans ever witnessed such social calamity as the tradition-minded Virginians of the 1880s. They accordingly sought salvation in their history.

Americans have long been obsessed with the future and studied the past largely to enhance their present standing.[12] However, tradition-minded easterners, whether Cavalier or Yankee, worried that their locale and culture would be eclipsed as the nation expanded to untold dimensions. While nineteenth-century Americans raced to catch the setting sun over the Great Plains, Rocky Mountains, and Pacific Ocean, and while old habits gave way to newer devices, the APVA reminded those who were infected by this western fever and by modern ways that Jamestown was the nation's birthplace and its cultural traditions should be respected. It refuted as well the popular notion that these western pioneers, like Americans in general, were free individuals without roots or commitments.

Many Americans, moreover, regarded their European past as an albatross. Ever since the Revolution had severed the bonds between motherland and colony, many claimed that the United States had embarked on a new course—a "Novus Ordo Seclorum." They claimed, as Alexis de Tocqueville had pictured in *Democracy in America* (1835, 1840), that the New World freed them from history, tradition, and ancestral ties. A virulent Anglophobia also swept the West in the late nineteenth century as Populists fought those British interests who purportedly controlled international finance. Tradition-minded Virginians stood apart from such thinking. They equally prized their history in both the Old and New Worlds. They not only added their weight to the Anglo-Saxonism of the day but built better bridges to their homeland in England. At every opportunity Virginians curried the favor of Britannia. In so doing, historic preservation had much weight in promoting transatlantic amity and countering the West's Anglophobia.[13]

Historic preservation is a very selective process. Society is anything but a pack rat which squirrels away every nut; only a small fraction of "history" is actually preserved. Whether in the APVA, ASHPS, or SPNEA, tradition-minded elites saw America turning away from the course set by their ancestors. They founded private organizations that were chartered and sanctioned by their respective state governments. Those organizations defined just what was meaningful in the past and strove to preserve it.[14] Their past became "our history," but it must be remembered that this "history" served their present needs.[15]

Preservationists in Virginia waged a three-fronted campaign, therefore, to assure the hegemony of their culture. They first worked to win the support of those families of wealth and standing who supported the traditional ordering of society. As teachers, ministers, journalists, legislators, and writers, these men and women of old Virginia carried the gospel to their respective audiences. Second, tradition-minded Virginians used the preserved past to shape a future in which aspiring blacks, restless Populists, and turbulent workers would accept such traditions as deference to their betters, reverence for established law, and a hierarchical ordering of the populace. Preservationists enshrined churches, homes, and government buildings that illustrated their story about an old-time Virginia where life was good, the church was holy, and the home was the glue that held society together. An older Virginia scene provided the cultural props, therefore, to inspire newer Virginians to accept an order and tradition as defined by these elites. Third, Virginians worked to influence the nation. Abandoning the isolation imposed by the defeat of the Confederacy, Virginians preserved a past that proved that the Old Dominion had founded the nation, established representative government, instituted racial order through slavery, and stood for civility and grace. As Virginians tried to reintroduce southern ways into a forcibly reunited nation, all too often, however, they found Massachusetts in their way. They pushed at every opportunity to displace the Pilgrim Fathers, Paul Revere, and Yankees.

What shaped this vision of the past was not only their political needs in the present but the myths and legends wrapped around antebellum Virginia. Preservationists chose buildings and sites that reflected those myths and personified their heroes. Historic architecture symbolized the likes of John Smith, Patrick Henry, and John Marshall. The APVA claimed, moreover, · that the history of the Old Dominion had been so perverted by northern writers that few Virginians knew how sweet and successful antebellum society had been. The APVA worked, therefore, to wrest control of Virginia's history from those hands and reinterpret it in a more favorable light. Such a reading of history, of course, left out the majority of Virginians—toiling men and women of humble stature. It attempted to win through monuments and pamphlets what Lee had lost at Appomattox.

Historic preservation became, moreover, an important means to establish Virginia's own civil religion. As northern patriots worshiped the flag, the Constitution, and heroes of George Washington's generation, Virginians reciprocated; but they qualified the very meaning of the Union and its federal government. The states' rights philosophy had been hurt by the Civil War, but it was reinvigorated by historic preservation. In turn, traditionalism became the creed of Virginia's civil religion, its legendary heroes the saints, and its historic sites the shrines. The APVA admitted that it strove to create "meccas" where moderns could pay homage. Just as zealots in the North defined a 100-percent Americanism, so too did the APVA define the makings of a true Virginian.

In its first half century the APVA protected and enshrined what elite Virginians deemed the symbols of Virginia's greatness. In addition to acquiring twenty-two acres at Jamestown, the APVA purchased such antiquities as the Powder Horn in Williamsburg, Mary Washington's home in Fredericksburg, and the Old Stone House in Richmond. Without expense to its treasury, it also won control over the John Marshall house in Richmond, Jamestown's church ruins, and the site of Williamsburg's Capitol. Through its branch chapters in the state, the APVA acquired properties ranging from a debtor's prison on the Eastern Shore to the ruins of Lexington's Monmouth Church in the Shenandoah Valley, from the Rising Sun Tavern in Fredericksburg to Smith's Fort plantation below the James in Southside. The APVA's sites crisscrossed the Old Dominion.

The APVA's acquisition of buildings depended upon availability, market forces, and expendable revenues. Those sites and events that it memorialized, on the other hand, clearly showed the perspectives of its leadership. A study of these monuments and their interpretation reveals a different sense of "preservation" and constitutes a look at public historiography. As stipulated in the APVA's charter, its gamut of interest ran from 1607 to 1861. Within those two and one-half centuries, preservationists tapped the wellsprings of Virginia traditionalism through bronze tablets, preserved buildings, and public-oriented history. They wanted Virginians to see daily and thus remember their heritage. The APVA's leaders often evoked the sentiments of Father Abram J. Ryan, called "the outstanding poet of the Confederacy," who said, "A land without ruins is a land without memories—a land without memories is a land without history."[16] The APVA kindled those memories also through public ceremonies that combined historical symbols, rituals, and interpretation. Whether it was a pilgrimage to Jamestown, the dedication of a memorial, or a historical pageant, the APVA packaged history in order to appeal to the populace.[17]

In a unique way, the APVA brought men and women together during the blossoming of Virginia's traditionalist renaissance in the 1890s. While gender segregation still defined the membership of historical societies in the United States, historic preservation had been a field in which both men and women intermixed. Women established the APVA, but men climbed aboard the preservationist bandwagon and politicized the cause in their battles against Yankees, freedmen, and insurgents. Meanwhile, women domesticated the movement. They regarded history as a vault of ideas and values that could be used not simply to build their child's character but to reform society as well. Association president Isobel Lamont Stewart Bryan predicted, for example, that annual pilgrimages to Jamestown would "impress upon the minds of our youth the pathetic story of Virginia in her infancy" and thereby teach them the values of work, perseverance, and family.[18] Men and women alike pictured old Virginia, symbolized by its historic buildings and sites, as a land of dutiful leaders who protected liberty, shepherded the populace, and built a prosperous society. As modern Virginians searched for peace and order, preservationists advised them to learn from their preserved past.

Although both genders supported the preservationist crusade, the APVA appeared on paper to be a women's organization. During the late nineteenth and early twentieth centuries, Victorian ideas about separate spheres prevailed in polite society. Women consequently defined their public action largely in the context of the domestic sphere. Virginia's leading ladies contributed the wherewithal for the daily toil of preservation and interpreted their work in the framework of feminine domesticity (see Appendix 1). These women worked as well to empower their gender. In some ways historic preservation would become women's ground; it gave them an important outlet to build women's values in what was all too often a male society. In the male arena of politics, however, they muted or veiled their opinions and carefully used innuendo and historical analogy to assess such issues as political corruption and popular-class activism.

At the same time some of Virginia's most prominent men—often husbands, fathers, or friends of female preservationists—tried to steer the APVA through its advisory board (see Appendix 2). These advisers took a more public role by addressing the problems of society, defining the rationale for historic preservation, and linking it with politics. Preservationists, male and female alike, worked to ensure that traditionalist culture was preserved, established families and leaders were respected, and racial and class order was restored. More important, they hoped that future generations of Virginians would rely upon the lamp of the past to light their way.

Like a careful editor, however, preservationists selectively chose and presented their material. As a college student essayist James Branch Cabell closely observed his landlady Cynthia Beverley Tucker Coleman and her APVA branch in Williamsburg. In his later writings he described not only the attitude of Virginians toward history but the workings of her preservation society. "For in Virginia, I can but repeat," he wrote, "we shape our history with discretion, in the same instant that we decline to stint the higher needs of our patriotism by accepting anything one whit short of the most edifying and pleasing history. When outsiders babble that a great deal of this history did not ever happen, they speak beside the mark. The past is done with; but our beliefs as to the past endure. Upon all imaginable counts, it is far better that these beliefs should be agreeable and inspiring and magnanimous; and that they should so prompt us to live in a manner not unworthy of our forefathers." He stressed that "no history is a matter of record; it is a matter of faith." [19]

The APVA's gospel interwove pleasing myths, romantic legends, and honest-to-goodness history. What is most revealing is the cyclical relationship that existed between traditionalism, historic preservation, and the reinvention of the past. As was so often the case, the first led to the second, the second to the third, and the third reinforced the first. In many ways the APVA invented not simply the now-venerable tradition of preserving the Old Dominion but, more importantly, the memory itself of antebellum Virginia. The association's interpretation of Virginia's history, moreover, served the needs of leading traditionalists by sanctioning conservative leadership, documenting the development of local rule, states' rights, and individualism, and arguing that these traditions represented the foundation stones for the nation's culture. Historic preservation would be used not only to ensure the reemergence of southern ways in a reunited nation but to define Virginia as the Old Dominion.

1

"The Past Was Severed from the Present": Historic Preservation and the Resurgence of Old Virginia

T HE FIRE STORMS of the Civil War torched the lush ground on which Virginia's elite had built its traditional way of life. What was left behind was a wide, burned-out stretch in its historical memory, political power, and cultural vigor. A once-proud people had been humbled, their homes plundered, and their power dispersed in a cataclysmic decade. The succeeding years, like no other time in the history of Virginia, saw an alternative society and culture begin to develop, one marked by political democracy, racial equality, and cultural change. Virginia was much like a burned forest, however. Its rich ashes eventually would yield to the strongest physical growth, and that was the revival of traditionalism. One of its first blossoms was the Association for the Preservation of Virginia Antiquities. In a remarkable manner this preservation movement not only gathered together the scattered remnants of the old order but redefined the past in the light of present necessity. As the preservation movement developed, it simultaneously nurtured the resurgence of political conservatism, the growth of the industrial economy, the development of a new nationalism, and the reconstitution of a leadership class. The work of the APVA was no mere sentimental affair. It instead helped set the future course of Virginia.

The legacy of Civil War, Reconstruction, and Readjusterism deeply scarred the APVA's first generation and shaped its perspectives and public action. The organization's Gospel of Preservation would mirror these perspectives and draw energy from the era's powerful currents, the most important of which were antiradicalism, progressivism, cultural traditionalism, and the civil religion.

Antiradicalism

The experiences of war and Reconstruction were indelibly stamped upon the psyches of the APVA's leaders. The war had killed almost 260,000 Confederates and devastated much of eastern Virginia. APVA historian Mary Newton Stanard acknowledged the tragedy but claimed, without much success, that Appomattox brought "defeat with honor" and "poverty without shame." Lyon Gardiner Tyler, son of President John Tyler by his second marriage and a Williamsburg preservationist who officiated at the founding meeting of the APVA in 1889, poignantly expressed the pain felt by elite Virginians. "The calamity was overwhelming," he wrote. "As a result, the past was severed from the present, the people who survived went about in a stunned condition. After a little, they came to their consciousness, only to face a struggle for self-preservation against reconstruction and negro domination, foisted upon them by their merciless conquerors."[1]

Throughout the South of the 1870s, Confederates felt the aftershocks of the earthquake at Appomattox. The old social order, symbolized by opulent Greek Revival plantation houses and a hierarchy of outbuildings for inferior whites and blacks, lost its grip. While those once-magnificent plantations deteriorated, centrifugal forces dispersed power to newer contestants, including African-Americans. Although the fears of whites always exceeded the actual power of blacks, the years of Reconstruction were marked by a democratic struggle that challenged old southern traditions such as white supremacy, black subordination, agrarian economy, and rule by the betters.[2] Tradition-minded southerners from the Gulf of Mexico to Chesapeake Bay confronted white insurgents, black freedmen, Yankee carpetbaggers, and traitors within their own ranks. The very future of the southern tradition seemed in doubt.

What Tyler called "a struggle for self-preservation" became a battle on many fronts. Preservationists fought for control not only in the political arena but in public history. APVA leaders believed that southern history had to be first purged of the prejudices instilled by those Yankeee conquerors. After the Civil War, observed J. L. M. Curry, an APVA adviser who also served as president of the Southern Historical Association, "the Southern States have shared the fate of all conquered peoples. The Conquerors write their history. Power in the ascendant not only makes laws, but controls public opinion." In his view, what resulted were misrepresentations, distortions, and outright lies about everything from secession to slavery. The APVA assumed the mission, therefore, of revising the historical record.[3]

On every possible occasion, these Virginians told their story about the disastrous consequences of the Emancipation Proclamation. Joseph Bryan, advisory board member and Richmond's most prominent citizen from the 1880s until his death in 1908, called black enfranchisement "the greatest curse that ever befell this country." His friend Curry expressed the prevailing belief among southern traditionalists that the Fifteenth Amendment had been a gross deviation "from the recorded opinions of the Fathers." He warned that "several millions of negroes . . . having behind them centuries of ignorance, thriftlessness, superstition and despotism, cannot be dragged up to civilization and democratic institutions by legislative enactments and the enthusiasm of fanatics." APVA founder Mary Jeffery Galt and countless other preservationists thus urged voter disfranchisement and the renewal of older traditions to assure social order. Although Reconstruction ended in Virginia in 1869, the Old Dominion's traditionalists attributed almost all undesirable change in the late nineteenth century as devolving in some manner from Confederate defeat and Yankee rule.[4]

The Underwood Constitution of 1869, drafted largely by Virginians who wanted to reconstruct the state, became the bogey of their tradition-minded foes. What these conservatives resented was the extension of the franchise to all adult males, most particularly blacks, and they claimed that it led to a period of Africanization. For many years after, conservatives worried that a democratic franchise would permanently undermine their hierarchical social order. Preservationists of old Virginia fought back through politics and culture; they sanctified the old order and sanctioned its restoration by fashioning myths about the woes of Reconstruction and the wonders of the Old South.[5]

After a brief interlude of rule by the Conservative party in the 1870s, Virginia was again rocked by radical efforts to reconstruct its society. Led by former Confederate general William O. Mahone, the Readjusters united small businessmen, mountain whites, workers, and blacks in a political coalition that triumphed in 1879. Pledging a thorough reform of the state, Mahone confronted the Conservatives head on. Although he had been a distinguished soldier during the war, Mahone's background disturbed tradition-minded elites. He was the son of a tavern keeper, a fact which irritated William Wirt Henry, a temperance advocate and hagiographer who conveniently forgot that his grandfather Patrick Henry also had operated a tavern. Mahone had committed other mortal sins when he disdained the customary social graces of the elite, appealed directly to the people for support, and headed a railroad whose interests ran counter to those of Rich-

mond elites such as Bryan. As a result, Curry angrily wrote President Rutherford B. Hayes, his former Harvard classmate, because his Republican party
had aligned with the Readjusters. He warned that Mahone represented
"demagoguism" and "communism" and his victory would reap "incalcul-
able mischief," especially "for the youth, just forming habits of life."[6]

These Conservatives most feared popular-class government. Blending
politics, history, and preservation, as would the APVA a decade later, Curry
fought back and used the centennial of the Yorktown victory (1881) as an
occasion to denounce Mahone's administration. Just as Yorktown represented the triumph of principle over tyranny, Curry identified one of its
lasting "lessons" as the primacy of law over mass democracy. "The spontaneous, irregular, undisciplined clamor of the populace is not the will of the
people," he said, "for their will finds legitimate expression and becomes
authoritative, only when uttered and ascertained in strictest accordance with
pre-ordained forms and methods."[7] He feared, as did many conservatives,
that democracy meant not only rule by the unwashed and unlettered but
the destruction of those allegedly preordained forms.

At the time Virginia also faced a large debt incurred for antebellum
internal improvements. Mahone attempted to readjust the payment sched-
ules on this debt, which was owed mostly to Englishmen and northerners.
Many members of the old Virginia families, some of whom had tied their
economic strings to those foreign purses, denounced these measures as
communism. In their mind any debt readjustment, even when used to improve schools and social services, would be an offense against Virginia's
honor and integrity. The Anti-Readjusters, or Funders, were led by some
of the most prominent men—and soon to be APVA advisers—in the state,
including Thomas Nelson Page, Henry, and Bryan.[8]

Conservatives pulled out all their cards to defeat the radicals. Curry
equated the vox populi of the Readjusters with a "mobocracy" and accused
them of a "saturnalia of misgovernment and ignorance." Control of history
became a weapon in the battles. State Senator Henry, for example, evoked
the spirit of his grandfather. "I trust," he told Virginia legislators, "that some
of the same fire which kindled in his breast when pressed by the heel
of tyranny lingers in mine, and surely no people ever suffered more galling tyranny" than Virginians under Mahone. Henry bristled, moreover,
when the Readjusters characterized his grandfather as a "demagogue." He
retorted that Mahone's government, like the British parliament of the 1760s,
passed tax laws without the consent of Virginia's property holders. Henry

accused the Readjusters of "the baneful principle of taxation without representation."[9]

In subsequent elections, however, Conservatives failed to practice the noble purity that they attributed to their ancestors; in both Richmond and state elections they resorted to ballot-box stuffing and voter intimidation to defeat the Readjusters. Some traditionalists acknowledged their double standard. After their triumph, but not before, they advocated a restoration of old-time traditions, including honest electioneering, to enhance the state's respectability.[10] This resurgence of traditionalism coincided with and defined Virginia's progressive movement.

Williamsburg acted as a fertile seedbed for the historic preservation movement. The Republican-Readjusters won power there, and a contest developed over the meaning of once sacred political symbols. The Fourth of July, once celebrated with glee, lost its meaning for traditionalists. At the same time freedmen created what they hoped would become their own traditions. On New Year's Day they held a parade to flaunt their freedom and praise Abraham Lincoln. Emboldened by postwar radicalism, African-Americans, who comprised about half of the town's population, marched down Duke of Gloucester Street with brightly decorated horses and wagons, thereby constructing a counterculture that explicitly challenged traditionalism. APVA organizer Cynthia Coleman complained, moreover, that even the memorialization of the Confederacy had been fouled by the insurgents. While other southerners commemorated Memorial Day in 1883, some Williamsburgers refused. "The truth is," Coleman wrote her brother, "that many persons think that it would be desecration to dress the graves of our dead heroes" while a Readjuster was in office.[11]

Traditionalists recaptured Virginia's identity from its freedmen and white insurgents. Their resurgence began when conservatives won control of the General Assembly in the election of 1883. Coleman buoyantly watched "the cocks crowing and cannon firing over the great Democratic victory." She knew that had the Readjusters won, "we could not have lived in this part of Virginia, and decent people would have found it hard to live anywhere in the State." Fitzhugh Lee, nephew of the Confederate commander and himself a distinguished general, won the governor's office two years later and hallelujahs rang out from conservative circles. "With Democratic rulers I feel once more as I had a country," Coleman wrote, "and I have never had these feelings since the War." Beverley Munford declared that Reconstruction had finally ended with Lee's inauguration.[12]

Yet insurgents remained strong enough to pose challenges, as in 1886 when the Knights of Labor won the Richmond city elections. The city's conservatives denounced them as radicals unrepresentative of honest Virginia laborers. The Knights, on the other hand, based their struggle against monopoly capital on the democratic rights won in the American Revolution. In 1885 William Mullen, a Richmond labor leader, presented a gavel to Knights' Grand Master Terrence Powderly at the union's general assembly in Richmond. The gavel's construction represented the Knights' own reading of history and appeal to tradition. It was made from three pieces of wood: from the room where Patrick Henry gave his "Give Me Liberty" address, from a tree at Yorktown, and from the ruin of the Confederacy's Libby Prison in Richmond where, as Mullen noted, "patriotic sons of our common country were confined . . . for being engaged in a struggle to liberate a race of people from the galling yoke of slavery." Whereas the Civil War represented America's "second Revolution" and a war against the slave-power conspiracy, Powderly and the Knights of Labor would use the gavel to bring justice to America through a "third revolution"—one to liberate the "slaves of monopoly and oppression." With the Knights in command of Richmond, the city's traditionalist leadership worried that the rise of the popular classes would fundamentally reorder society. As a result, "the best families in the city" organized a local Law and Order League and promoted traditionalism to counter Readjusterism and the Knights of Labor. Bryan realized as well that traditionalism would have to capture the allegiance of the artisans if it was to regain its dominance. He used the pages of his Richmond *Times* in 1889 to urge fellow capitalists to cultivate "closer relations with white workingmen." This would help avert the "communistic feeling that in a greater or lesser degree is hid away in the breast of so many poor men."[13]

Racism and antiradicalism set the framework for the 1889 election. The conservatives surged and swamped Mahone's party. In Williamsburg, Coleman wrote, "Democrats had a beautiful Torch-light procession; and a great many houses were illuminated. . . . We put a light in every front room to show that we were in sympathy with the Democratic victory." Her cousin Joseph Bryan editorialized in his *Times* that 1889 was "the most memorable year in the history of the State after the year that saw the passage of the ordinance of secession."[14]

As a result of Reconstruction, black Virginians exercised significant freedom through the 1880s. Traditionalists worried about the future. Coleman watched her town's African-Americans act in ways she found disrespectful of tradition and property rights. She deplored "the way in which the miserable negroes behave now about everything we hold sacred, or attach any sentiment to." Bryan watched them vote and voiced "a horror of the patent consequences of stirring up the black mass." Mindful of the white-black alliance represented by the Readjusters, Curry baited race fears. He warned that miscegenation would create "an inert, degraded population" and hoped that "every black person could be colonized in Africa." Uncontrolled black masses, Page argued, would threaten white womanhood.[15]

Across the nation late nineteenth-century whites emphasized the inferiority of blacks and the dangers posed by their freedom. The New Orleans (1885) and Atlanta (1895) expositions, for example, included an "Old Plantation" concession that depicted happy banjo-playing blacks on an antebellum estate. According to the exhibit slavery had created contented slaves and racial order. Tradition-minded Virginians in the 1880s yearned for such a past. One civic booster of Richmond demanded that black educators, preachers, and leaders reassert control over their community. "The average negro youth," according to this assessment, "supplies himself with a pistol or a razor, imbibes freely of mean whiskey, and starts out to become a menace to the order-loving citizens of both races. The percentage of this class of negroes grows each year more and more." Genteel traditionalists condemned the widespread terrorism of lynchings, however, and instead worked to return the Old Dominion to the mythical order of its past. When the North abandoned its drive for civil rights in the South by 1890, southerners quickly turned to Jim Crow to restore that order.[16]

Although the Readjusters had been defeated, grass-roots democrats surfaced again with populism in the 1890s. Unlike the radicalism of the 1880s, however, Populists in Virginia were led by agrarian aristocrats. Traditionalists denounced the movement and predicted that it would lead to black rule. Bryan greatly regretted that Colonel Robert Beverley, a descendant of illustrious forebears, would lead what he perceived to be a class-conscious mob. He warned Beverley that Populist theories were "Socialistic & centralizing." Especially dangerous was their disregard for property rights—in particular their proposals for government ownership of the rails and telegraph—which Bryan, a railroad executive, considered "rank tyranny." Likewise, Archer Anderson, chief executive of Tredegar Iron Works and an APVA adviser, called populism a "dangerous and revolutionary experiment."[17]

More than any other Virginian, Bryan led the attack on populism in the Democratic party. Through his Richmond *Times,* and indirectly through the educational mission of the APVA, he promised to use "bell, book and candle to exorcise this flaming spirit of revolution." The publisher's campaign clearly ran counter to popular currents. His *Times* suffered financially and his subscription list "simply disappeared." Bryan lost hundreds of thousands of dollars and gained public enmity. When the Populist-Democratic party standard-bearer, William Jennings Bryan, spoke in Richmond in September 1896, the audience repeatedly yelled catcalls denouncing the publisher. With Henry and other traditionalists, he helped form a Gold Democratic party in 1896. Yet he privately acknowledged that Populists had a valid complaint against the plutocrats. Those corporate barons generally supported the gold cause, but Joseph Bryan denounced their "worship of money." "That thing they call commercialism is really the basis of the attacks of the populists upon plutocrats," he wrote. "That is unquestionably a class of people that think that money is everything and has special rights."[18] Rather than join the Populists, Bryan, like the APVA, appealed to the propertied classes to reform their ways. The Gospel of Preservation translated into conservative elites, not callous plutocrats, exercising a paternalistic hand in society.

Bryan and his fellow traditionalists railed as well against the mass politics of the late nineteenth century. Not only had the Readjusters and Populists appealed to the citizenry against elites, but Richmond's own elections reflected what elite Virginians inaccurately called Tammany-style politics. Munford's old-fashioned notion of elite rule ran aground in his own political campaigns. He came up against powerful men who, he alleged, "personally controlled the voters of certain localities, nationalities, [and] crafts . . . much after the fashion of some tribal chief." The Republican party attracted the votes not only of African-Americans but of Germans, Irish, and Italians. They all resented the mainstays of Virginia traditionalism—the cult of the Lost Cause, Anglo-Saxonism, and economic exploitation by the elite.[19]

The traditionalist resurgence of the late 1880s united established whites by focusing on antebellum culture and sanctioning its preservation. It was a complex phenomenon. Some Virginians evoked past memories to escape the troubling present, while many more used history as a buttress for their drive against postwar democratic change. As an organization the APVA was ostensibly nonpolitical, but its leading spokesmen visibly led the genteel wing of the progressive movement and attacked economic and political democracy. Page and his brother-in-law Philip Alexander Bruce, for example, represented a group of historians, novelists, and artists who glorified the

plantation culture of the Old South and vindicated its ideals. Historic preservationists subsequently preserved sites, shrines, and symbols of the ancien
régime; they fashioned part of what historian Raymond Pulley has called
the "Old Virginia Mystique." Wielding this potent weapon, they first used
the mystique to defeat the Readjusters, then to control the Underwood
electorate, and finally to constrict the franchise and assure the domination
of the Democratic party and its select leadership. Inspired by the colonial
and antebellum past, the shapers of the mystique "struggled to resurrect and
rebuild the Old Virginia system of controls over society and politics" and
thereby turn back the clock on recent change.[20]

Progressivism

Historic preservation ran parallel to progressivism in the Old Dominion. As
the APVA called for the restoration of traditional values and styles of leadership, southern progressives similarly worked to stabilize and protect the local
establishment not simply from northern interests but from challenges by
poor whites and blacks. Progressives, as well as historic preservationists,
yearned for a more orderly and cohesive community that would foster economic progress. Politics would be reformed, social controls applied, and
society purified in order that men be protected from their own weaknesses.
This notion of progressivism, George Tindall has noted, devolved from
postbellum patricians and their "vision of an organic traditional community
with its personal relationships, its class distinctions, [and] its habits of deference to the squirearchy."[21]

   In the Old Dominion traditionalism and progressivism virtually became
one. As Pulley concluded, the progressive impulse was "synonymous" with
the Old Virginia Mystique. Those Virginians who led the resurgence of
traditionalism "were primarily interested in preserving the values of the upper and middle strata of the state, which had been gripped by a feeling of
anxiety and crisis." The APVA's gospel accordingly stressed such essential
political values as honesty, public virtue, and disinterestedness in government. Many tradition-minded Virginians regretted the pervasive corruption
of their own day. "I feel as if our civilization was at stake," Bryan confided
to Beverley; "ordinary political questions are insignificant compared with
elections full of fraud, perjury & bribery." For Virginia progressives, honest
government necessitated not simply a regeneration of the tradition of defer-
ential voting but a constriction of the electorate as well. "I had rather see
the Democrats take shotguns and drive the Negroes from the polls," Bryan

warned, "than see our young men taught to cheat. If they once learn that lesson they will not stop at cheating Negroes."[22]

The APVA sanctioned disinterested leadership by tradition-minded elite. Preservationists interpreted one salient point from the Old Dominion's past—that peace and order hinged upon leadership by public-spirited men of good breeding and property. What was usually unmentioned was that this form of government historically had been a paternalistic oligarchy, where the elite ruled with the support of other propertied elements over the whole of the Old Dominion. Most often, APVA writers and orators praised earlier leaders from the First Families of Virginia. When contrasted with the present day, Charles W. Kent noted in an APVA lecture, such comparisons showed "real grounds for disappointment" because "the standard set by our former statesmen is not always observed by our present day politicians." Bryan attributed this decline to the modern notion of equality. "We all know, and the signers [of the Declaration of Independence] knew it, that all men are not created equal," his newspaper stated. "There are diversities of natural gifts, mental and moral and spiritual and there are certain advantages of birth, according to station and environment, which are 'self-evident.'"[23]

Preservationists suggested that Virginians learn from their colonial history and emulate its leaders. APVA incorporator Sara Rice Pryor thought, for example, that John Smith had turned anarchy into order at Jamestown. "The turbulent, selfish, and ignoble were often in the majority of the Colony," she alleged in terms reminiscent of the denunciations voiced by conservatives against Virginia's recent radicals, "and nothing short of the interposition of Providence could have prevented their being in the ascendant as well. The miracle of its enduring life lies in the fact that a mere handful of men were enabled through superhuman courage and patience, to overcome obstacles, the most tremendous that ever confronted a company of adventurers."[24]

Page similarly read from the history of Yorktown, his ancestral home, to argue the case for elite rule. "It would be difficult to find a fitter illustration of the old colonial Virginia life than that which this little town affords. It was a typical Old Dominion borough," he believed. Although "one or two families owned the place, ruling with a sway despotic in fact," they were "on the main temperate and just, for the lower orders were too dependent and inert to dream of thwarting the 'gentlefolk.'" Unlike the privatism that prompted most of the modern elite to focus on career and homelife, those few Yorktown families regarded government as "their passion and everything relating to it interested them."[25] Pryor and Page expected the elite to take charge and discipline the masses.

The traditionalist campaign culminated when the Constitution of 1902—the hallmark of Virginia progressivism—disfranchised most of the Underwood electorate. Progressives typically argued that such a constriction was needed to save the morality of the state and prevent black domination. Two years after the electoral victory of the Readjusters, Curry had told a Richmond audience in 1881 that "suffrage, so universal, is an appalling peril" because it "remits to ignorance and vice what should be the sacred trust of intelligent and upright patriotism."[26] Bruce, another APVA adviser, predicted that the election laws in the new constitution would "eliminate with equal effectiveness the least intelligent and the least conservative elements among the white and black voters alike. This [would] be of extraordinary advantage to the general moral health and prosperity" of the Old Dominion. That moral health, according to Galt, required deference and humility on the part of the newly disfranchised. "When we have the majority in Congress & take away the right of voting from those who now [vote]," she wrote, "this quality will *have* to be cultivated." Curry reiterated this point continuously. Committed to an elite leadership based on tradition and property, he warned: "There can be . . . no assurance of [the] perpetuation of representative institutions, unless the citizenship is restrained and disciplined and elevated by intelligence and morality"[27]

The advocates of voter restriction were strongest in the tidewater and eastern sections of the state, areas that also had a sizable black population. The Shenandoah and the west, on the other hand, were less enthusiastic and often critical of the new state constitution. What makes this geographical analysis striking was its parallel with the appeal of the APVA. Historic preservation was strongest and most popular in the tidewater and east, and very weak in the west. Like the APVA's gospel, the Constitution of 1902 symbolized the reform of the Old Dominion through the culture of traditionalism. It was, Pulley has concluded, "closely identified with the historic drives so characteristic of and peculiar to Old Virginia—elite rule, rigid administration, and honesty and integrity in public service"[28] Political peace, absent for the preceding forty years, subsequently returned to Virginia.

Although traditionalists overwhelmingly favored black disfranchisement, a few Virginians who were identified with the APVA challenged that cause. Speaking before an APVA assembly in 1901 at the Capitol, University of Virginia professor Charles Kent reminded his audience of the "symbolic significance" of the Capitol and Jefferson's architectural design. "It is the Maison Carrée," he noted, "the building which should ever stand four-square against personal unfaithfulness, public vice or hidden injustice of whatever form, lurking now, for instance, in the publicly uttered threat of disfranchising the best of the colored race because the worst have forfeited their rights, and giving the highest privileges to the worst of the white race because their best have deserved them." [29]

The drive to constrict the suffrage brought most traditionalists together, but their coalition soon splintered. The debates over prohibition, woman's suffrage, and machine government would spark differences within the APVA's ranks. Traditionalists had aligned politically and culturally against popular-class insurgents, but middle-class issues such as temperance and votes for women created dissension within propertied ranks. Despite these differences, traditionalist politicians used the Old Virginia Mystique as a badge of respectability to show their fealty to the ancients. As Virginia politics reverted to "an oligarchic office-holding coterie reminiscent of the courthouse cliques of ante-bellum times," the Democratic establishment identified not only with the romantic history of the state, including the Lost Cause and historic preservation, but with a small minority of its population. [30]

Machine government did not bode well with preservationists when it was thought that the popular classes were the beneficiaries. Some APVA leaders, including President Lora Hotchkiss Ellyson and her husband, were clearly identified, however, with the Democratic "ring" that dominated the Old Dominion's politics after the new constitution. The meaning of historic preservation shifted in such cases from its earlier partisanship against the Readjusters to a call for honestly brokered power among the elite. As the APVA matured, it even developed its own factions; some preservationists lost their political clout, while others gained influence. In 1911 J. Taylor Ellyson was lieutenant governor, an APVA adviser, and spouse of its president. Lucy Parke Chamberlayne Bagby nonetheless confided that she found herself to be "not persona grata" and could not lobby the executive offices effectively for Jamestown funding. [31]

During the progressive era coalitions formed which consisted of professionals, businessmen, and agents for social uplift programs. Dewey Grantham accordingly has called southern progressivism "interest-group politics"; each interest, including historic preservation, competed for the public eye with its own plans for community improvement. All too often, these progressives offered comfortable answers to the most disconcerting issues of the day. Blending philosophies of individualism and environmentalism, progressives generally took their individualist ethic and experimented with social engineering and controls to make it communitywide. The APVA's gospel, for example, posited that the reformation of society depended upon a citizen's allegiance—gained through persuasion, education, or legislation—to older values and principles. Ironically, preservationists also incorporated the aristocratic notions of hereditary and caste rule. Coleman stressed, for example, "the importance of keeping blood pure and feeding the streams from the sources richest in virtue and intellect." Such a patchwork of individualism, environmentalism, and aristocracy might seem contradictory on the face of it, but like the evolving concept of Social Darwinism, it reflected a convenient rationale for conservative politics.[32]

Intrinsic to these calls for social uplift and control was the paternalism of the Old Virginia Mystique. Just as the elite—now a blend of aristocracy and meritocracy—controlled politics, so, too, did it influence education, charity, historical studies, and other institutional means to shape society. Countering the trend of privatism, APVA leaders repeatedly voiced the Gospel of Preservation. As President Belle Bryan phrased it, "In these days of sordid aggrandisement and selfish pleasures, we need to keep steadily in view the pure and lofty ideals of duty and service."[33]

Cultural Traditionalism

Progressivism entailed much more than politics and focused consistently on the relationship of individuals to society. What the APVA taught about character, family, and work had as much importance in shaping Virginia progressivism as legislation passed by the General Assembly. Progressive and preservationist alike feared that society, across the United States, was falling apart as the modern ways of factories and cities displaced those traditions set by farm and town. They worried that the future would be controlled not by their fathers' ways but by those of freedmen, labor radicals, and democrats. As a result, they revolted against pluralism. Lamenting the disorder wrought by the waning of traditionalism and the waxing of mass culture, Coleman believed that a moral crisis pervaded society at the close of the nineteenth century. "In every heart the contest between good and evil is being waged perpetually, it ceases not day nor night," she wrote. "Passion, rage, envy, jealousy, greed for gold, rebellion against God. . . . Who can estimate the effect of these spiritual battles?" She affirmed that the study of

Virginia's history would aid the cause of righteousness in those battles. While she mourned the loss of old-time family and religion, her friend and APVA adviser Edward Virginius Valentine regretted the decline of old customs. "Among the lovers of old Virginia," he said, "there are many who regret not only the disappearance of old interesting landmarks in the shape of houses, but sadder still, the disappearance of more important and revered landmarks, the good, respectable old Virginia customs."[34]

Preservationists mined the past, therefore, to find fitting role models to instruct the present. Whether the hero was John Smith, Patrick Henry, or Robert E. Lee, they praised his strong character, responsible leadership, and moral righteousness. The APVA venerated the heroes of the early republic, for example. They had been patriots who defended their land, scholars who knew art and literature, and gentlemen who lived in grace and cultured refinement. Such republican heroes, moreover, had worked hard, served their community, and showed their manhood. What troubled traditionalists was the fact that these republican heroes had declined in the public's perception by the 1890s. The "cult of Napoleon" arose instead and cast ominous shadows over the virtuous men of traditionalism. That cult enabled uncultured but personable or wealthy men to set society's standards. Like Mahone, they were self-made men, not products of cultured families and guiding traditions. Bryan questioned the materialistic tenor of his day and wondered how a figure such as stock manipulator Jay Gould could have won popular acclaim. "Could the founders of the Republic have foreseen," he asked, "the lowering of public virtue and elevation of the Goddess Success as a divinity to be worshipped?" Coleman derided the "Society *man*" of the Gilded Age who thought "more of the clothing for his person than the culture of his brain, if he has any." She warned her son that "true value" was "to be found in wisdom, knowledge, nature and religion."[35]

Virginia preservationists praised and regenerated those republican heroes. "One of the methods for the 'uplift' of the present generation is the so-called *object lesson*," said Valentine. "The expression was not heard so frequently before the War between the States though genuine 'uplifting object lessons' were more plentiful then than now. Living men and women were pointed to as objects worthy of study." Bryan wanted their biographies in general to serve as "a lamp at the feet" to guide the present.[36] He prized "the best men" of those days for "their simplicity, their piety, their personal courage, and their strong common sense." One who was cast in the mold of individualism, Bryan applauded their self-reliance. They, and not the environment as Darwinists claimed, had shaped events. By the first decades of the twentieth century, however, the national media increasingly pictured patriot-heroes less as individuals known for their character and more as living organization men famous for their results. Tradition-minded Virginians, spearheading progressive reform in the Old Dominion, clearly cherished what they pictured as dutiful leaders who acted principally for community and nation.[37]

Valentine particularly treasured the manners of old-time Virginians. Gentlemen daily showed their "dignity, simplicity, courtesy and naturalness," he said in 1923, and "their demeanor was far different from that of the head waiter manners too often seen in the drawing rooms of today." Just as Oliver Wendell Holmes told Bostonians that it required three generations to make a gentleman, many descendants of the Old South watched in trepidation the rise of arrogant men who put dollars before honor. Williamsburg preservationist Robert Bright, in fact, said it was "hard to define a gentleman in this collapsing age" since there were so many "synthetic gentlemen" and "stuffed shirts" around.[38]

The APVA also wanted the world to recognize Virginia "as the mother of statesmen eminent for learning and honor." John Marshall, for example, contrasted dramatically with aggressive but affluent moderns in the twentieth century. "Maybe it was because intellectual gifts and accomplishments won more respect then," Stanard surmised in 1913, "because modest incomes earned in the learned professions carried more prestige than riches made in business, because men cared more for distinction than for material display. . . . Had the American of Revolutionary times known modern luxuries, from bath tubs to automobiles, perhaps he would not have contented himself with the gentle toil of compounding state papers of thoughts that breathe and words that burn." Such distaste for the trappings of modern capitalism similarly led Page in the 1880s to declare his love for old Yorktown. Steeped in a culture where family, grace, and knowledge of Plato, Locke, and Scott counted, Page idealized Yorktown because "all new ways and things seem to have been held by bay." Valentine did find some reassurance, however, as he glimpsed old ways linger on amidst the modern. "How charming, how humanizing," he mused, "it is to watch the courtly manners of our old time Virginia gentleman who with bland smile bows . . . while conversing with a lady through a telephone."[39]

Preservationists admired other personal characteristics of those heroes of the early republic. Stanard thought that the bombastic orators of her own day should learn from Marshall's manner of speech. His debates, she said, "were colored with no flowers of rhetoric, but were spoken straight to the

judgment, for the single purpose of convincing." Coleman praised George
Wythe's sobriety and common sense. Like many parents of her day, she
worried that society's fast-paced change would compromise her children's
morality and respect for past customs. She accordingly commended Wythe
for throwing off "the dissolute trammels of youth" and becoming "one of
the most brilliant intellects and grandest characters of his age and time. . . .
Examples of such wonderful determination and self-control are not numerous," she admitted, "and are therefore, entitled to reverence and respect."[40]
General John Roller told an APVA audience during the turbulence of the
1890s, moreover, that the German settlers of the Shenandoah had practiced
a laudable trait, "submission to law and order." Rev. W. A. R. Goodwin
even lauded the religious nature of Virginia's early republican leaders. Mud-
dling up the deism held by men of Madison and Jefferson's mettle and forgetting their republican hostility toward the Anglican church, he said that
"these patriots believed in God and were not tainted by the French infidel-
ity of the age."[41] The French Revolution, according to so many preservationists, had unleashed wave after wave of assaults on tradition.

Preservationists worried that the 'cult of Napoleon" would lead Americans along the path of selfish individualism. John Smith had been best
known for his "soldierly qualities," Pryor admitted at a time when Theodore
Roosevelt stressed marital vigor. But Smith was no ambitious Napoleon,
she explained, because he was compassionate, "pitiful to the sick and weak,
tender to children, [and] watchful of the comfort and rights of the unfortunate." He embodied strong leadership, not self-aggrandizement. Goodwin's
similar fears prompted him to call the "will to power" of modern Napoleons
"personality run riot." His Social Gospel sentiments heightened his anxie-
ties, and he worked to rebuild the southern community along traditional
lines. "The permanent enrichment and elevation of human life," he
thought, required an individual "to contribute his ideas to the permanent
inclusiveness and solidarity of the corporate Body." Progressives commonly
used the model of such a corporate body to picture society. As the body-
society analogy was pictured, much was fat, some was muscle, a small part
was brain. Society's elite, of course, represented the intelligence which
would control the muscle and trim the fat, and preservationists wanted that
elite to be mindful of its traditions.[42]

Traditionalists generally pictured communities in the light of rural
towns and a preindustrial past. In an age when cities and machines cast
dark clouds over America's rural ethic, progressive and preservationist alike
romanticized the countryside and preached the virtues of agrarian life. Bry-

an's Richmond *Times* advised, for example, that "there is a moralizing agency . . . in contact with the soil, in making things grow, in having a part in the creation of things necessary to man." His friend Page, notwithstanding his rather luxurious urban ways after his marriage to a rich widow, similarly praised rural living and believed that cities encouraged indulgent and evil habits. Typically, Stanard attributed John Marshall's "unaffected manners . . . to his country breeding."[43]

Although the APVA mostly honored the state's forefathers, female preservationists did find their heroine in Mary Washington. As modern state builders moved the nation's first president from Mount Vernon to Mount Olympus, his mother followed in his footsteps. "The apotheosis was complete," historian Bernard Mayo has said, "when they compared Washington to Christ and his mother to the Virgin Mary." Steeled by the Civil War's privation in Petersburg, Pryor lauded Mary Washington's character and posed it as an alternative to modern Gibson Girls who encouraged material consumption and personal display. Pryor wrote *The Mother of Washington and Her Times* (1903), and it became the source for interpreting the APVA's Mary Washington house in Fredericksburg. Steeped in the tradition of republican motherhood, Pryor told the "sheltered, treasured" women of her own day to remember that "industry, simplicity in living, ungraceful dress and manner, [do not] mar the portrait of a noble woman whose lot was cast in a narrow and thorny path, whose life was necessarily a denied one, and yet who accomplished more for her country than any other woman ever did or ever can do." Implying that modern women should act similarly, Pryor pictured her not only as religious but as "self-denying, diligent, and frugal."[44]

Pryor pointed to Mary Washington's "self-denial" and submission to family responsibilities as a shining example. Her model would counter what Pryor perceived as the selfish materialism and iconoclasm of those modern women who challenged patriarchy. What Pryor failed to mention was typical of her writing of history, however. George Washington had bitterly resented his mother's power and purchased the house in Fredericksburg precisely because he did not want her to live at Mount Vernon. In fact, she never even visited his Potomac River estate. She retaliated by seeking a pension from the Virginia legislature and deliberately humiliating her son. Her self-denial and simplicity partly stemmed from her son's parsimony.[45]

Progressives romanticized the home and praised homelife to no end. The idealized separate sphere of women had emerged with the early nineteenth century's market society and industrial revolution, melded with the tradition of republican motherhood, and pushed women to protect family and homelife. Increasingly this meant either the dirty business of wage-earning work for popular-class women or the taxing stress of social reform outside the home for women of some wealth, but paradoxically it expected them all the while to maintain their social grace. The ideal lingered long in southern society and reinforced woman's placement on a pedestal. So typically, Valentine turned a blind eye to the past's female majority and only remembered the ladies on the plantation who had "always displayed gentleness, refinement and modesty." The APVA broadcast to the world, moreover, that Virginia was known "for women pre-eminent in goodness and all the qualities that should endow them." As in antebellum days, tradition required women to protect home and culture through self-restraint, domesticity, and obliging companionship. They had been the glue that held together their families, but their identity required regeneration. Rev. Dr. Randolph McKim told an APVA audience in 1900 that "love of home" was one of the "strongest pillars upon which the honor and dignity of a government can rest." Such old-time homelife, moreover, was shaped by tradition, and "not driven by the nervous intensity [typical] of modern life."[46]

Such idealization of the home obscured the real dangers that it faced. The era's divorce rate, for example, climbed 35 percent each decade from 1870 to 1920. Like an illusion which distorts one's sight, the ideal of a protected home was endlessly repeated in school primers, romanticized history, and other conduits for traditional culture, but it denied the dramatic changes wrought by modern industrial capitalism. What defined homelife for most was the chaos of the slums, factories, and the New South's competitive world. The idealized home nonetheless became the lens through which past and present would be seen. What preservationists deemed important was the individual and home, not the outside environment. Any real reformation of the larger society would necessitate changes beyond their mental reach.[47]

Although these preservationists descended from family backgrounds with varying degrees of wealth, they commonly pictured family stability from a Victorian middle-class standard. Belle Bryan grew up in an affluent family of Scottish merchants; her husband on a large plantation; Stanard in a relatively modest minister's home. What they had in common was the belief that Virginia's once-sacred homelife was endangered by cultural drift and economic polarization. Amidst the traumatic shifts in economy and society, the widening rift between rich and poor sets the context for this preoccupation with home, culture, and morality. According to an interpreter of the 1890 census, 1 percent of the nation's population controlled more wealth than the remaining 99 percent. Half of America's families lived without property. Pryor conceded that these poor masses resultantly suffered a "heart-break . . . in witnessing the undeserved contrasts and inequalities of life."[48]

The Jeffersonian yeoman and his dream of an equalitarian society evidently had gone with the wind of Gilded Age capitalism. Despite the great extremes of wealth, whether in the seventeenth or nineteenth centuries, many Virginians still dreamed of a classless society rooted in respected traditions. Preservationists pictured Virginia's colonial period, for example, as one when peace and property had been more plentiful. Just as Stanard argued that the real builders of Virginia had been a strong middle class of small gentry and freeholders, so, too, did Goodwin rewrite Williamsburg's history as one without the extremes of plutocrat and proletarian.[49]

These progressives were deeply troubled by the modern disparity of wealth and responded to the crisis by reinforcing and inventing traditions. Preservationists regenerated traditionalism, for instance, with what had once been a foreign practice, the Yankee's Protestant work ethic. The "lazy South" of antebellum aristocrats gave way to the virtue of work. Bryan's Richmond *Times* recommended that boys take up manual training to tame the "vandal" in their nature. In an age of union strikes and industrial development, however, the *Times* wanted employers, and not the union apprentice system, to teach future workers. It advised that "when a boy has been taught in the manual training school the dignity and value of labor he will be disposed to build up rather than to pull down and destroy property." Likewise, Hall told an assembly at Jamestown in 1891 that Virginia needed their labor to develop mines, farms, and factories. "Will you heed her earnest summons?" he asked. "She needs educated muscle. She needs intelligent mechanics. . . . She needs men that have studied the history of her past, and from that study drawn inspiration for the future."[50]

Business-minded traditionalists regarded work as a force to stabilize the masses. Tyler, himself a booster of Williamsburg, admitted in 1917 that poor Virginians "had never known discipline." What they needed was leadership. Coleman in turn praised John Smith as a man "second to none" in an era of great men. She lauded not only his "energy" and "endurance" but his hatred of "sloath." Without him, Jamestown would have failed. Page, on the other hand, found a different hero in Jamestown's early history. In his address at the tercentennial celebration of Virginia's founding, he extolled Sir Thomas Dale, acting governor in the colony's first decade. In a paean to the work ethic and free enterprise, Page set Dale as a role model for modern emulation. Dale "had reclaimed almost miraculously those idle and disordered people, and reduced them to labour and an honest fashion of life." Not only did he institute a regimen of work, he "abolished communism, under which the colony had languished, and gave them their holdings in severalty." Elizabeth Henry Lyons, an APVA leader and daughter of William Wirt Henry, even praised Virginia's first assembly for passing the nation's earliest "anti-tramp ordinance" and "law against idleness."[51]

Preservationists in turn stressed the civilizing function of individual labor. During the progressive era and 1920s, a "cult of success" influenced popular attitudes. If one worked hard, it was said, he could win recognition, mobility, and honor. Values such as frugality, sobriety, perseverance, initiative, and obedience would have to be cultivated, however. Page praised Henry Clay as a self-made man who, unlike Napoleon or Mahone, defended inherited culture. "His beginning was so modest," he said, "that no young man of integrity, ambition, industry and character need ever fear henceforth that however narrow his means, and contracted his sphere, the highest position is not open to him. His life was so strenuous that no young man, however great his parts, can ever dare despise the necessity of earnest and persistent toil." Clay, in fact, had been the first to extol the virtue of self-made men. Whether in the APVA's interpretation of history or its own leadership ranks, this meritocracy mixed well with the aristocratic caste built by the First Families of Virginia and formed the state's modern elite.[52]

Explicitly challenging the ideas of working-class solidarity and socialism, preservationists pictured an old-time Virginia where a man's character counted for everything but required the discipline of tradition and elite rule. Bryan believed staunchly in "diligent & intelligent labor" but admitted that a Darwinian competition marked modern work. "There is no doubt," he wrote, "that in the intense competition now in all professions the weaklings are crushed, and only those who are very strong, or well armed, are able to win in the struggle." Such a belief revealed the long conflict between virtue and commerce. As historian J. G. A. Pocock has noted, men of the early republic would have seen this preoccupation with business and economic competition as "a rebellion against virtue" and a retreat from res publica. James Alston Cabell, in what was a unique view, even praised Patrick Henry for being a business failure and implied that it took some immorality to succeed in those early ventures. Obviously, tradition-minded modern Virginians could not have it both ways: their long-sought economic prosperity required an economic competition that contradicted their prized republican values. Traditionalism would be reinvented, therefore, to provide the intellectual fuel for a more aggressive capitalism.[53]

Such growth depended upon Virginians who pledged allegiance to the Old Dominion. The antebellum dream and Confederate goal of an economically independent South with its distinct society lingered long among these traditionalists. Bryan declared, for example, that "a Virginian is first and foremost a Virginian." Yet, Tyler thought that privatism and profiteering had stricken Virginia after the defeat of the Confederacy. He perceived "a marked decline" in the caliber of public men as they were allured by "Federal offices, Northern capital and personal preferments." They "sold their birthrights for a mess of pottage and deserted the old Southern ideals." As a result, preservationists praised men of Patrick Henry and Henry Clay's mettle. Like classical liberal reformers of the Gilded Age—the progenitors of turn-of-the-century progressives—preservationists held that society's stability depended upon such men. Clay had "obey[ed] the call of Duty," said Page, and devoted his life to public service. Lyons praised her great-grandfather Patrick Henry for coming out of retirement to oppose Jefferson and the democrats. While Jeffersonians were denouncing the partisanship of the Federalist administration and its notorious Alien and Sedition Acts (1798), Washington confidentially asked the elder statesman, despite his declining health, to return to politics in 1799 "in order to save his country from the threatened horrors of anarchy."[54]

These preservationists disdained rule by the populace, whether they were Jeffersonians, Readjusters, or Populists. Preservationists not only exaggerated but scorned mass democracy. At the time, however, progressives commonly voiced platitudes about the virtues of popular government. So typical of the era's linguistic battle over the definition of the American system, Curry was forced to draw a sharp line between freedom and democracy, or the good and the bad. Much like his admiring colleague Samuel Chiles Mitchell, he defined "freedom" as "keeping willingly within the limits traced by law and order and justice." Those progressives expected, of course, that they would be the arbiters of tradition and the solons of society.[55]

White solidarity was essential, moreover, at a time when the youngest generation of African-Americans had been raised during the relative freedom of the Reconstruction period. After many years working to "uplift" and effectively control blacks, Bryan turned pessimistic and spiteful. "I have undergone a sad change in feeling about Negroes," he told his cousin and longtime APVA leader Parke Bagby in 1906. "I cling to the memories of bygone days, but I loathe the realities of today. It is nearly all memory with me. . . . When they come to be judged by the White Standard it goes very hard with them." Professor Mitchell, another APVA adviser, similarly believed that the great mass of blacks were "in a low state of moral development" and too often were "swayed by superstitious feelings more than by a pungent sense of right."[56] What tradition-minded Virginians found, therefore, was the utter necessity of regenerating elite rule, black submission, and Christian paternalism. Under its new constitution, of course, Virginia excluded most of its electorate, and the resultant law and order hinged upon the forced deference of those masses.

Progressivism entailed not only a rebuilding of individual character along traditional lines but active work by society's leaders within the community. APVA preservationists practiced their noblesse oblige and typically worked in diverse areas of volunteer activity. Belle Bryan, for example, founded a kindergarten and worked for the Young Women's Christian Association; her husband Joseph served on commissions to uplift the blacks, reform the penitentiary, and improve education. Mitchell, professor of history at Richmond College, was one of the state's paramount progressives and was active in a gamut of causes from prohibition to public health reform. During his early years he saw firsthand the exploitative labor system of the agricultural Deep South, the terrorism of the Ku Klux Klan, and the human "wreckage caused by the opium traffic." He also witnessed the spiritual promise of Dwight Moody's religious revivals and felt that the South was ready for "social progress" and reform movements by the end of the nineteenth century.[57]

The Old Virginia Mystique imparted the notion of community responsibility and prompted many reform activities. "Not one of us, old or young, is living in the past," APVA president Lora Ellyson explained. "Our sympathies are with the poor and suffering; . . . but I would instill into the minds of the present generation a love of the past and a desire to work for the ideals and objects of the association." While the APVA stressed the duty of the individual—rich or poor—to the community, progressives gainsaid the real need for governmental efforts to abate the ravages of industrial capitalism. These APVA notions were typical for progressives who largely relied on moral suasion and voluntary institutions.[58]

In tandem with these plans for social uplift, progressives wanted to impose vaguely defined controls that would quell the perceived chaos. Many southern progressives thought that the 1890s represented a crossroads of history as they watched the progeny and culture of antebellum society fade away. They often voiced the need for social cohesion through education, culture, and professional administration. Many of them lived in Richmond, a bustling city and APVA headquarters. They experienced firsthand its unsettling economic and social changes and felt a heightened concern for order and collective action.[59] Most important for the tenor of the APVA's gospel was the fact that the organization's most prominent spokesmen and shapers, including Page, Bryan, and Henry, were first-generation émigrés from the countryside. The APVA brought them together, but their laments reflected their changed identity.

The educational revival of the progressive era combined elements of social control and uplift in the Old Dominion. At the time, Virginia public schools lacked compulsory attendance laws and held classes only 119 days per year. Curry, the most prominent educational reformer in the South, repeatedly warned that peace and prosperity depended upon an educational system that "restrained and disciplined" the populace. Mitchell likewise wanted the school to be "the exponent of Americanism" and to teach a philosophy which stressed community and history. Both men held a deep antipathy toward mass democracy in Virginia.[60] Richmond's elite spearheaded the drive to improve public education and prompted what Mitchell called the "right people" to meet at the dilapidated John Marshall house and inaugurate the May Campaign of 1905. Joseph Bryan presided, and Governor Andrew J. Montague, Mary Branch Munford, and a select few added their ideas. Bryan's *Times* became "the organ of popular education" and historic preservation.[61]

This goal of civic education prompted the APVA not only to open its historic shrines to child and adult alike but to offer free public lectures. In Richmond they were held usually in the Hall of the House of Delegates, and the site indicated APVA's semiofficial status. Governor J. Hoge Tyler, for example, introduced and chaired a January 1900 lecture by Randolph McKim on "The History of Homes of Old Virginia."[62] Speaking to audiences of patriotic groups, leading professionals, and public officials, the lecturers included Woodrow Wilson, Tyler, Bruce, Bryan, and Henry. Usually reflecting the studies of well-bred amateurs and chroniclers, the lectures covered diverse topics from Virginia's past heroes to its earlier culture, but all were relevant to modern battles in politics and culture.

Because attendance at its lectures was limited by the state's rudimentary transportation network, the APVA relied on its *Year Book* to preach the gospel to distant members. At the time in the United States, an iconographical revolution was radically altering the publishing industry. Rapidly chang-

ing technology created publications that were mass-produced, heavily illustrated, and geared to more select audiences. Some journals such as *McClure's
Magazine* (1893) tried to stir their audience's emotions and turned to muck-
raking; others such as *Good Housekeeping* (1885) catered to the refined tastes
of middle-class women and encouraged domesticity. Even in historic preservation, the *Bulletin of the Society for the Preservation of New England Antiquities*
(1910) revealed that a wealth of photographic images could be used to promote the agenda of preservationists. From its first days, however, the APVA
failed to take advantage of these new media. Fiscal conservatism, together
with Virginia's limited publishing abilities, created *Year Books* that were re-
petitive in content, little illustrated, and sporadically published. Packed with
dry business detail, the *Year Books* often printed the same few photographs,
repeated the founding documents, and offered limited perspectives on architecture and history. Notwithstanding complaints from the Library of
Congress about the irregularity of the APVA's publications, local Virginians
apparently received the *Year Book* well.[63]

Civil Religion

What further brought antiradicalism, progressivism, and cultural traditionalism together in the late nineteenth and early twentieth centuries was the
APVA's active part in America's civil religion. Throughout the nation
tradition-minded Americans promoted patriotism as an effective means to
foster a respect for history, an appreciation of historic sites, and a reverence
for law and the customary ordering of society. Revealing the political workings of culture, elites defined patriotism in such a way that they could control restless farmers, striking workers, and new immigrants. To be patriotic
meant obedience to law and submission to authority. The question was, of
course, Who defined law, authority, and history? Preservationists in Virginia, drawn from society's upper echelons and hostile to democracy, contributed their energies. Like preservationists elsewhere in the United States,
they selectively enshrined historic spots. "Stimulate your patriotic minds to
renewed effort," Coleman told the APVA. "Love of Country is religion for
it is God given, and the heart that is not moved by it is fit for 'treasons,
stratagems and spoils.'"[64]

As a movement to regenerate traditionalism and its hegemony, the civil
religion tapped history for its symbols. Historic sites and buildings served as
its shrines. Ceremonies conducted at those sites became the rites through
which it was solemnified and popularized. Traditionalists acted, moreover,

as interpreters of the sacred legends and guardians of the shrines. The control of history, the flag, and tradition subsequently enhanced the power of the elite in its battles against contemporary foes. Its civil religion not only became a means to revitalize an embattled culture but took on different shades of meaning as it reflected the perspectives of its adherents.[65] More so than preservationists in SPNEA, who allowed the patriotic societies to carry on such efforts, the APVA zealously devoted itself to the civil religion.

Deeply rooted in the American past, the civil religion offered an interpretation of history and a model of the future that accorded well with the vision of tradition-minded progressives. Like a theological system, it was based on a belief that God had created the United States as his special force, and the Declaration of Independence and Constitution were his guiding documents. Civil religionists affirmed as well the sanctity of the American Revolution, the mission of the United States in the world, the righteousness of constitutional republicanism and laissez-faire economics, and the holiness of patriotism. They believed that Washington, Henry, and Marshall had been divinely inspired, and it was the responsibility of moderns to protect their legacy. Originally concerned with the nation's founding years, the civil religion later took on added dimensions. Northerners added Lincoln to their hagiology, for example, while southerners honored Lee.[66]

Assuming cult proportions, the national civil religion intensified after the Civil War. Its adherents invented traditions to win the loyalty of the populace. Patriots celebrated the first Flag Day in 1877, for example, to commemorate the centennial of the adoption of the Stars and Stripes. Yet the context of the celebration revealed the politics of culture. Not only was the Union going through the throes of a forced reunification, many traditionalists lamented as well that the Philadelphia Centennial Exposition in 1876 had focused too much on machines, money, and modernity.[67] Civil religionists surely believed in progress, but not at the expense of tradition. Like preservationists, they wanted present and future built upon the bedrock of the past. Countless patriotic groups formed in the late nineteenth century and assumed the task of promoting the flag and controlling its use.

At the same time, patriotism was not necessarily the sole domain of conservatives. In the late nineteenth century, striking workers marched in solidarity under Old Glory's banner, freedmen demanded the liberty represented by the flag and Constitution, and immigrants with foreign beliefs and customs flooded the gates under the sheltering arms of the Statue of Liberty. Labor interpreted its own struggle in the context of patriotism, for example, and issued alternative Declarations of Independence against monopoly capital, tapped the rhetoric of the American Revolution, and asked for the freedom which Tom Paine had seen as common sense.[68] The question again bears mention, Who defined tradition, patriotism, and history?

As a result, conservatives worked to define the meaning of America in light of their heritage and economic rights. They invented traditions to order society and turned increasingly to historic preservation and public education to buttress those inventions. In 1888, for example, the *Youth's Companion,* a periodical for schoolchildren, launched a campaign to put a flag over every schoolhouse, a relatively unknown practice at the time. The Junior Order, United American Mechanics—a nativist group which Tyler rightly associated with the Ku Klux Klan—followed suit when it presented an American flag and a Bible to Williamsburg's Nicholson School in 1903. Those who controlled the flag defined patriotism. The *Youth's Companion* instigated a second campaign in 1892 when it asked every schoolchild to recite Francis Bellamy's "Pledge of Allegiance." Those who could not accept such a pledge fell beyond the pale. "He who does not look lovingly on the hallowed memories of his and his country's past," said one Williamsburg preservationist in 1891, "is recreant to his race, his lineage and himself."[69] A battle ensued over the meaning of patriotism and culminated in the victory of the 100-percent Americanism of civil religionists during the 1920s.

Civil religionists spotlighted the material culture associated with the Revolution or Founding Fathers to kindle a love of country. Relics abounded, for example, at the era's expositions. Not only could one see memorabilia associated with the Revolution, but the centennial exposition even blended America's fascination for machinery with history when it included a nine-foot-tall working model of George Washington. At regular intervals Washington rose from the dead, while the toy soldiers who guarded his tomb saluted. The Liberty Bell also traveled to Atlanta for its fair, and its arrival on a school holiday declared expressly for the occasion created a pandemonium during which schoolchildren kissed the bell. The APVA, of course, enshrined its own relics. Whether a candlestick from John Smith's day or a musket from the Revolution, such relics became material props which preservationists used to visualize their interpretation of Virginia's history.[70]

Not only did schools inculcate those ideas and loyalties, but patriotic groups such as the Daughters of the American Revolution and the National Society of the Colonial Dames of America rallied to the cause. The Sons of the American Revolution, for another, spent over half of its national income after 1907 on educational programs, particularly for new immigrants and their children. Staple themes in this teaching included a reverence for the Constitution, the Founding Fathers, private property, and law and order.[71] Preservationists acknowledged that historic sites, such as those in Williamsburg and Jamestown, buttressed that work. "These old land-marks have an exhilirating effect on our youth," said a Williamsburg writer in 1891. "They fan the embers of patriotism, and keep alive a just appreciation of the rights our forefathers bled and fought for. We should have them to remind us of our race's and country's past, and inspire us with a zeal to measure in life up to the full criterion of our ancestor's patriotism, pride and love for their race and country." APVA adviser Samuel Yonge measured the association's efforts and concluded that it had achieved "remarkable results" in its task of engendering "a spirit of true patriotism." The APVA worked shoulder to shoulder with other patriotic groups, moreover. The Daughters of the American Colonists, for example, helped the APVA preserve Jamestown because that project furthered the group's objective "to inculcate and foster the love of America and its institutions by all its residents; [and] to obey its laws and venerate its flag, the emblem of its power and civic righteousness."[72]

Hero worship became an integral part of the civil religion. More meaningful than the ancestor worship typically associated with genealogy, hero worship is rife among tradition-minded Americans who believe that role models are necessary to shape future generations. Virginians looked back to figures such as John Smith, Patrick Henry, and Mary Washington to personify their ideals and aspirations.[73] The APVA's reverence for Washington and Henry prompted its acquisition of their homes as sacred shrines. As George Washington stood at the apex of American patriots, it was little wonder that his mother was canonized as well. Sara Pryor even compared her with the mother of Jesus. "She conducted herself through this life with virtue and prudence worthy of the greatest hero that ever adorned the annals of history," she wrote. "There is no fame in the world more pure that that of the mother of Washington, and no woman since the mother of Christ, has left a better claim to the affectionate reverence of mankind." The life of Henry evoked similar homage. James Alston Cabell urged Virginians to study his portrait, an icon in the civil religion, "as an example of pure and exalted manhood, of devotion to his country, and consecration to duty. The habit of recalling examples will soon produce the habit of imitating them."[74]

History's heroes could best be grasped through their material legacy, and Virginia's first two capitals accordingly captured the attention of preservationists. As civil religionists in the North all too often focused on the Mayflower Compact, Paul Revere, or Philadelphia's Independence Hall, Virginians not only felt eclipsed but wanted their unique brand of patriotism to gain recognition. A reinterpretation of Virginiana would solidify the South's notions of local government, hierarchical society, and elite leadership. The buildings and grounds of the Old Dominion became, as a result, meccas where moderns could pay homage. As in any symbol, however, multiple interpretations could be glimpsed. Old-time Virginians saw one vision of Jamestown as the home of the states' rights principle, Anglo-Saxonism, and elite rule, while modern Yankees embraced it as the first settlement which acknowledged the legitimacy of a racially separate society. Virginians further contended, but with limited northern acceptance, that Jamestown was the foundation stone for America's Protestantism, government, and family life. It was "hallowed by a thousand memories" and, as president Belle Bryan reported, "the Mecca of our hearts and hopes." The nation owed the APVA its thanks, said her successor Lora Ellyson, because it had "recreated this hallowed ground and made it safe for patriotic organizations to build memorials and shrines, which upon becoming our property are faithfully protected and cared for."[75]

Although Jamestown was the APVA's most sacred ground, it enshrined other sites, including the old Capitol in Williamsburg, Mary Washington's home in Fredericksburg, and the Richmond home of John Marshall. As Coleman told preservationists,

> The spot where some great struggle for life and liberty had been made, some powerful resistance to the oppressions of government became a "Mecca of the mind" to this Association. To secure the spot, to place upon it some memorial that he who comes may read of the heroic sacrifice made by the early settlers of the Colony, the strength of mind and will that framed the laws for the wise administration of a new and untried government, the patriotism that . . . [won] freedom from injustice and tyrannous actions—is an object lesson which may well arrest the attention of the most careless and awaken the interest of the most indifferent.[76]

While the APVA praised men of Marshall's stature, it paradoxically enshrined the man who symbolized the greatest challenge which his republic faced, Robert E. Lee. The APVA memorialized Lee's Richmond home and used it as its headquarters. If the homage paid Marshall represented Virginia's legalistic sense of nation, its adulation of Lee symbolized loyalty to

the principle of states' rights. The figure of Lee, however, remained controversial in the 1890s. As Joseph Bryan hinted, "Washington remains the unri-
valed example for the youth of this country. We Virginians have another to
whom with increasing admiration we may point our sons, but his merits
are as yet not understood by a large body of our fellow countrymen. It will
not always be so." James Branch Cabell, iconoclast that he was, admitted
that his own elders spoke of Lee "in the tones which other, less fortunate-
favored nations reserve for divinity." By the early twentieth century, southerners compared Lee with Christ, while northerners did the same for Lincoln. Adulation of Lee ran deep. Richmond preservationist W. Gordon
McCabe, for example, left his schoolroom each day, walked to the Lee
statue regardless of the weather, and saluted the equestrian figure. His son
did the same.[77]

Like the mighty James River, Virginia's historic preservation movement
derived, therefore, from many streams in the late nineteenth century. Antiradicalism, progressivism, cultural traditionalism, and the civil religion all
shaped the APVA in a remarkable way. The Gospel of Preservation called
upon the leaders of society to exercise their duty, take command, and bring
order to the Old Dominion through a mixture of self-improvement, psychic
uplift, and social control. The democratic movement born during Reconstruction was countered by the progressive era's stress on order, stability,
and tradition. The APVA's gospel urged progressives to erase the imprint of
recent radicalism.

2

"Whatever Is Un-Virginian Is Wrong": The Growth of the APVA

T HE BURGEONING of the preservation movement in the late nineteenth century carried traditionalism to a wider audience. Centennial celebrations of the Declaration of Independence and the victory at Yorktown attracted the masses. Tradition-minded Americans realized, however, that only permanent organizations, not short-lived pageants, could protect the visible symbols of the past and convey their brand of patriotism to what was becoming a mass culture. The APVA stood in the vanguard of that cause. As Coleman explained, it preceded the establishment of other women's patriotic, ancestral, and Confederate societies. It was "the first born of that wave of patriotism . . . sweeping over the country" after the Civil War which "has left the soil enriched by awakened memories of the past." But as Curry warned at the celebration in 1881, the Readjusters jeopardized the American experiment by challenging "established authority."[1]

The APVA was founded in 1888 by Mary Jeffery Galt (1844–1922) in this context. A resident of Norfolk who descended from two of Williamsburg's oldest families, Galt was the daughter of William Richard Galt, a well-known Norfolk schoolteacher. Her uncle Alexander Galt had shown considerable genius as a sculptor but died of smallpox while in Confederate ranks as an aide to Jefferson Davis. The burning of Richmond in 1865 destroyed many of his best works. Privately schooled in art, she opened a studio in Norfolk, taught art, and exhibited her sculpture and paintings. Preservation came to her mind in June 1888 when her mother showed her an article in the *Southern Churchman* about the collapse of Powhatan's Chimney, a seventeenth-century ruin in Gloucester County that was attributed (incorrectly) to John Smith's men in 1608. According to her recollection, the elder Galt, with tears in her eyes, lamented that "all our Virginia land-marks are passing away; nothing is being done to save them, before long all will be gone." The following day Mary Galt spoke with Barton Myers, Norfolk's mayor and an influential railroad developer, about organizing a preservation society "something like the Mt. Vernon Association."[2]

In the years immediately preceding the Civil War, Ann Pamela Cun-ningham had formed the Mount Vernon Ladies' Association of the Union. A unmarried invalid from a South Carolina plantation, she devoted her life to the preservation of Washington's home and grave. In 1853 she appealed to the nation as "A Southern Matron" to keep Mount Vernon from becom-ing "the seat of manufacturers and manufactories." Apparently a syndicate had proposed turning the neglected and deteriorated Potomac River estate into a resort with bowling, a race track, and a bar to lure the nation's newly established industrial wealth. "Pilgrims to the shrine of pure patriotism," she wrote in the Charleston *Mercury,* would find Mount Vernon "forgotten, [and] surrounded by blackening smoke and degrading machinery!—where money, only money enters the thought; and gold, only gold, moves the heart or nerves the arm." Like many southerners reared in an agrarian, aris-tocratic tradition, Cunningham pictured the North as a land of dollar wor-shipers and factory builders who conspired to change the nation forever. Aiding Cunningham's cause before the Virginia legislature in 1855, Gover-nor Joseph Johnson praised the MVLA's "female philanthropy." He warned the developers that "dollars become as dust when compared with the inesti-mable patriotism inspired by a visit to the tomb."[3]

The MVLA broke new ground with its acquisition of Mount Vernon. Not only had these tradition-minded women stretched the bounds of their feminine sphere, they had taken public action to challenge the sphere of those commerce-minded men. More importantly, the MVLA's women voiced a Gospel of Preservation when they used Mount Vernon as a symbol in the political battles that preceded Fort Sumter. Contrary to the opinion of one historian that "southern women were scarcely to be seen in the political crisis of the 1850s," the MVLA interpreted Washington's legacy in such a way that it directly influenced the political discussions in Congress. Arguing the case for Unionism, Cunningham claimed that Providence had called upon the nation's women to rescue the "sacred ashes" of Washington during the "darkest days of the Republic" so that his sepulchre "could be made *all-powerful* in regenerating and healing" the Union. Like many south-ern Unionists, she ignored the question of slavery and focused on the bonds that tied the different regions together. She undertook a national crusade that trumpeted Washington's unifying role and labored to draw the whole Congress to Mount Vernon for a grand excursion in April 1860. Instead, much to her dismay, the Democrats held their party convention in Charleston and the nation soon fell apart. Unable to save the Union, she regarded her failure "to overcome the apathy existing over this whole country" as her own Valley Forge.[4]

Cunningham reiterated common fears about the decline of virtue in the nation. She criticized, for example, Irish immigrants who swarmed into the North's large cities. The "degeneracy . . . who crowd our metropolis," she told a southern audience, supported corrupt political machines and a new breed of politician who paled in comparison to the august Washington. These congressmen practiced not the disinterested and enlightened statesmanship of the nation's first president but a vicious "self-aggrandisement" that created the political crisis of the 1850s. "Once our Congressional halls were the resort of wisdom, integrity and patriotism," she said in her appeal "To the Ladies of the South." She regretted, however, that "Washington and his principles and his spirit appear no longer to influence the City which bears his name."[5]

Organizing the MVLA as a national association in 1858, Cunningham enlisted a veritable "Who's Who" of tradition-minded elites in each state. Edward Everett, a retired senator from Massachusetts, lent his voice by delivering an oration on "The Character of Washington" 129 times, usually to packed auditoriums. Descendants of southern signers of the Declaration of Independence symbolically joined hands through the MVLA with northern offspring of Alexander Hamilton and Robert Morris. Abraham Lincoln even gave aid as a member of the Gentlemen's Advisory Committee of Illinois. At the same time, the MVLA won the support of Cunningham's cousin, Senator William Lowndes Yancey of Alabama. Evidently, Mount Vernon could be interpreted in several ways. While Cunningham admired its owner's Unionism, her fire-eating cousin praised Washington as one who had rebelled against oppression.

Holding on to Mount Vernon through the ravages of the Civil War, Cunningham grew ever more weary of the nation's changes during the Gilded Age. In her farewell address to the MVLA in 1874, she asked that it guard Washington's home as a monument to the model American:

> Let no irreverent hand change it; no vandal hands desecrate it with the fingers of progress! Those who go to the Home in which he lived and died, wish to see in what he lived and died! Let one spot in this grand country of ours be saved from change! . . . When the Centennial comes, bringing with it thousands from the ends of the earth, to

whom the Home of Washington will be the *place* of *places* in our country, let them see that, though we slay our forests, remove our dead, pull down our churches, remove from home to home, till the hearthstones seem to have no resting-place in America,—let them see that we do know how to care for the Home of our Hero!

Disconcerted by America's materialism, chaotic social mobility, and reckless individualism, the MVLA enshrined Washington's home as a symbol of traditionalism's prized values. It became a monument in the nation's nascent civil religion.[6]

Inspired by the MVLA's gospel and work, Galt launched the APVA. In October 1888 she traveled to Richmond and sought support for an "Association for the Preservation of Our Colonial Monuments." While some gave encouraging words, others voiced pessimism, including Joseph Bryan who "intimated that it was a wild goose chase." Galt also met Bryan's cousin Cynthia Coleman and wrote her the next week asking her to compile "a list of the outdoor objects of historic interest to be rescued and restored." Rather than haphazardly beginning their work, Galt thought that "nothing can be done until we have a list of the most interesting monuments." She particularly referred to the ruins of Powhatan's Chimney and identified two formidable problems: pilfering by the poor and speculating by opportunists. "I am so much afraid that the colored people will carry off the stones, maybe they have done so. I have also been warned 'whenever our people think any one wants to buy—or that any money may be made on anything, they pile on the price.'"[7]

On 2 November Galt called on Coleman at her Williamsburg home and asked her to join the association. Galt pointed to "the first object to try and save": the old Powder Horn on Market Square. When she added that she would ask a lawyer the next day to make out a charter for the association, Coleman reportedly threw up her hands and said, "Oh no!" Coleman had already tried to buy the Powder Horn, but her offer of $200 was much below the asking price of $600. Galt worked the owner down to $400 for the building, ten feet of land around it, and a front lot to Duke of Gloucester Street. Thinking (incorrectly) that a deal had been reached, she borrowed $50 and sent it as a down payment. Thereupon, Galt left Williamsburg and, like Cunningham and later W. A. R. Goodwin, she went to New York to recruit friends and funds.[8]

In New York, Galt received strong encouragement from Mrs. Roger A. Pryor and Mrs. Burton Harrison, two southern expatriates who championed the Lost Cause in the Yankee lair. Sara Rice Pryor (1830–1912) helped incorporate the APVA and urged Galt to "make it a national association."

Born in Halifax County and thought to have descended from rebel Nathaniel Bacon, she married Roger A. Pryor, who became a fire-eating secessionist editor, United States congressman, and Confederate legislator and general. His war record was anything but illustrious, and a cloud hung over his name from charges of cowardice and incompetence. Perhaps James Branch Cabell had Pryor in mind when he tried to correct Virginians' romantic conception of the Confederacy. "Did your elders discourse," he asked, "as to another illustrious person, who, so they said, had hid in a barn when he ought to have been fighting; and who had been forced, quietly, to get out of Virginia, and to go north, where, in addition to being made a judge, he had become a professional Confederate veteran with a prestige so enormous that it still nurtures his descendants. None envied him these glories; nor did anyone wish to remove his bogus lustre. . . . It was simply that he could not ever come back to Virginia." Economically ruined by the war and lost in Reconstruction-era Virginia, the Pryors had moved to New York City and lived in a modest fashion. As she described it, they went "into the arms of the enemy," but "the enemy was always good to us." Her husband became a Wall Street lawyer and eventually associate justice of the New York Supreme Court.[9] In an act of atonement, the Pryors influenced the nation through the neo-Confederate revival.

Coleman, meanwhile, determined to exert her own leadership by organizing a Virginia preservation movement. Daughter of Nathaniel Beverley Tucker, an eminent law professor at the College of William and Mary, Cynthia Tucker Coleman (1832–1908) had been in her youth Williamsburg's "peerless queen of society." The trauma of war and Reconstruction severely tested her pride in locale and family, two of the deepest taproots of preservationist sentiment. She told herself, without success, that "we must drop the curtain over these dark and stormy days with their humiliation and pain." Forever loyal to old Virginia, she grieved that "our State Rights doctrine was crushed out at Appomattox" and replaced by an alien culture.[10]

Coleman believed that women had an obligation to carry on traditions and improve society. After the death of her young daughter Catharine in 1884, she channeled her grief into historic preservation. The Catharine Memorial Society inaugurated the first phase of Williamsburg's restoration when it focused its work on the much-deteriorated church and graveyard of Bruton Parish, potent symbols of the town's former eminence and present plight. She had earlier expressed interest in forming a "Woman's Historical Association" and subsequently tried to circumvent Galt.[11]

The APVA held its first official meeting on 4 January 1889 in Williamsburg. As Mary Newton (later Mrs. William G. Stanard) described it, "Our little company of earnest women" gathered that day in a "dormer-windowed, colonial home." In Coleman's library "the pictured faces of colonial heroes looked approvingly down from their places on the wall" as the APVA formed "a Committee of Safety." Lawyer James Alston Cabell accompanied them and helped write the charter.[12] Coleman had invited Williamsburg's leading citizens, the College of William and Mary faculty, and Ellen Bernard Lee, the wife of the governor. Lee had never been to the colonial capital but voiced her interest in traditionalism and brought an official sanction to the APVA. She earlier had refused to commit her name to Mary Galt's planned organization, believing, as she told Coleman, "that there was a Northern woman of that name getting up just such an Association" in opposition to Coleman. In fact, Coleman tried to organize the APVA without Galt. Unwilling to attend nighttime events because she was in mourning, Galt had been told by Coleman that the meeting was only a social occasion. Step by step, Galt would be cut out from the APVA's leadership.[13]

Lyon Gardiner Tyler explained the APVA's rationale and objectives at the meeting. Because Victorian social restraints inhibited women from public speaking, Coleman often used him as her "mouth piece" and APVA promoter.[14] President of the recently reopened College of William and Mary, Tyler rarely missed an opportunity to boost Williamsburg. As years went by, the rebirth of the town and its college became intertwined through their efforts.

Realizing that the APVA needed clout in Richmond, both Galt and Coleman wanted to locate the association's administration in the state capital. Both asked Lee to be the society's first president. After the state granted the APVA a charter on 13 February 1889, Lee held its meetings during her one-year tenure at the Governor's Mansion. As Lee pulled together a list of prominent women to lead the APVA, her husband gave his suggestions, as did William Wirt Henry. They linked position to social standing and included as first vice president Mrs. Joseph Anderson, wife of a Confederate general and head of the Tredegar Iron Works; as treasurer Mrs. Joseph Bryan, spouse of the owner of the Richmond *Times* and the city's wealthiest businessman; and as secretary Mrs. James Lyons, daughter of William Wirt Henry and spouse of a leading conservative lawyer. Coleman became second vice president, while Galt was deliberately overlooked. The ladies of the APVA also imitated the MVLA and invited Henry to assist the organization by helping to choose a Gentlemen's Advisory Board (see Appendix 2).

According to Belle Bryan, those advisers held an honored position that

could not "be bought in any way." Composed of overlapping circles of
acquaintances, the APVA's advisory board included the leading lights of
Virginia's cultural traditionalism. These advisers shared membership in the
Virginia Historical Society, Confederate organizations, and professional societies, as well as ties through marriage, business, and residential neighborhoods.[15] These men typified what James Branch Cabell called "the custodians" of culture in the Old Dominion. They were a "coterie of highly
estimable tax-payers in the higher brackets" who shaped the arts, literature,
and even the writing of history, despite the fact that they "happened to
know very little, or else precisely nothing, about that special art which was
their protégé." Indeed, he humorously suggested, they excelled in "the superb and philanthropic romanticizing of Virginia history and in a free-
spirited invention of priorities and relics."[16]

As a frequent adviser, orator, and interpreter of history for the APVA,
Thomas Nelson Page (1853–1922) illustrates the limitations of the advisory
board. Born on a plantation in Hanover County, he was descended from
some of the most prominent families in Virginia. Loyal to that tradition, he
mourned the defeat of the Confederacy and worked throughout his life to
redeem the South's reputation. He turned to writing, and his first volume
of stories, *In Ole Virginia* (1887), launched that crusade. A charter member
of the Southern Historical Association as well, he warned that the new
history of the South must "not be written upon the theories of its author."
He was trained as a lawyer, however, and wrote his histories like the barrister
who knew which evidence to exclude and which argument to enhance.
Further complicating his writing was his mixing of two contradictory styles:
one for romantic novels, the other for history. In the process he became
perhaps the nation's most popular novelist at the turn of the century, but his
historical writing took on the romantic invention characteristic of a novel.[17]

Obsessed by his defense of the South, he elevated legend, lore, and
myth to the point where others, including preservationists in the APVA,
cited them as documented evidence. Fiction all too often became fact.
While many in the United States were advocating a new scientific history,
the literature cited by APVA leaders often resembled that of Page. Journalist
Wilbur Cash thought that he created "a sort of ecstatic, teary-eyed vision
of the Old South as the Happy-Happy Land." One night in the home of
Richmond banker Thomas Branch, for example, Page presented a reading
from his soon-to-be-published *Marse Chan,* a tale of the relations between
antebellum master and slave. The story was "so affecting," Beverley Munford
remembered, "that all present were soon in tears." Branch asked Page to

stop reading, "protesting that the pathos of the recital was more than he could bear with composure!" Page acknowledged his greatest literary debts of gratitude to George W. Bagby, spouse of the APVA's corresponding secretary, and Sir Walter Scott, who thrilled him with accounts of Scotland's Lost Cause.[18] This pervasive romanticism was not confined to the literary efforts of Page, or Pryor and Coleman, but included the sculpture of Edward Valentine and the paintings of William Ludwell Sheppard, both of whom sat on the advisory board.

Surely Lillian Smith had writers of Page's caliber in mind when she dissented from this tradition of "stained-glass writing." During the trying days of the late nineteenth century, they purged their writings of the unfortunate truth about the South: "Rarely did one of them put other than his carefully self-censored thoughts on paper, sifting them through layers of taboos and proprieties and decorums. Little appeared in print that could not be read as an inspirational thought at family prayers."[19] Traditionalists, as a result, carefully edited their historical records and excised anything that could harm or embarrass the reputation of Virginia.

Membership in the APVA, though ostensibly open, actually was limited by a number of devices to a select number. At first it was a joint-stock company, wherein the members purchased $10 shares and thus held personal ownership of the past.[20] The APVA eventually established branches in dozens of Virginia cities, in metropolitan centers such as Chicago and New York, and in states such as Minnesota and Tennessee. Whether through Pryor leading the neo-Confederate revival in Gotham, and attracting a considerable number of members, or through homesick émigrés from the Old Dominion in distant cities, the APVA wanted a national movement.

Ancestral lines were not required for membership, as was the case in the National Society of the Colonial Dames and the Daughters of the American Revolution. The APVA did restrict its ranks, however, to those who were invited by a fellow member and were "in good standing in the community." Evidently, Readjusters, blacks, and radicals would not apply. As one preservationist acknowledged, "Social lines were very closely drawn" in these Virginia communities and acted as an informal block against undesirable applicants. Galt also suggested that the branch directors should be "selected with such discrimination that they will . . . keep out or control any objectionable element that is likely to harm [the] Association." All in all, the APVA opened its ranks to those who accepted traditionalism as the Old Dominion's culture, even to the point where a Jew and a Roman Catholic could serve on the advisory board.[21]

Despite the obvious prominence of the APVA's leadership, historic preservation was slow to catch on at first. Lee admitted that even her husband's name failed to draw supporters. "I do not think many people take much interest in the project," she lamented early in 1889. "I have seen so many people in Richmond about the society and was quite disheartened at the little interest taken." Nine months later Belle Bryan reported the same lack of interest in the antiquarian society. 'I haven't very much in my heart," she admitted, "but I don't find any other who has." Galt heard a similar story when she spoke with one of Richmond's leading businessmen the following year: "Nothing for a *general* association could be a success," he told her. Yet slowly success came. By 1895 the APVA had over four hundred members, by 1902 over a thousand.[22]

Isobel Lamont Stewart Bryan (1847–1910) became the organization's president in 1890 and held the post, albeit sometimes inactively because of illness, until her death in 1910. When Lee had first accepted the presidency of the new organization, her husband thought it was "so important that Mrs. Bryan should be one of the Incorporators and officers of the Association." A lineal descendant of Colonel William Byrd of Westover on her mother's line, Belle Bryan was the daughter of John Stewart, an affluent Richmond merchant of Scottish descent. She embodied the merger of Virginia's first families and its Scottish merchants and thus inherited not only wealth and ancestry but a steadfast loyalty to the Old Dominion. She was nearly fourteen years old when the Civil War broke out and daily saw Confederate soldiers at the hospital that her father established at their Brook Hill home outside Richmond. She affectionately remembered General Robert E. Lee visiting Brook Hill, as well as her father renting the Stewarts' Richmond house on Franklin Street to the Lee family during the war. The Confederate commander, it was said, "made a special pet of her" until his death. She married Joseph Bryan in 1871 and spent the next fifteen years raising her family.[23]

One of the leading ladies of the Lost Cause, Bryan served as president of the Hollywood Memorial Association, a women's organization that cared for Confederate graves at Richmond's Hollywood Cemetery. Throughout the South in the 1870s and 1880s, women such as Bryan launched the historic preservation movement in their local graveyards. In conjunction with the Lost Cause movement, ladies tied past and present in a tight knot to hold their society together. The HMA actually laid much of the groundwork for the APVA's gospel and ideology. In its appeal "To the Women of the South," the HMA strove "to rescue from oblivion" the memory of Confederate greats through "durable monuments" and to attract "the countless throng, who would do homage to such dead." The HMA pointedly tried to shape the future. "Their memory," it predicted, "history will transmit from age to age, propounding without number illustrious examples from which the noblest of every age may catch new inspiration."[24]

Bryan also became the first president of the Confederate Memorial Literary Society. An offshoot of the HMA, it organized to prevent the destruction of the White House of the Confederacy, which was used at the time as Central School and had been the wartime home of Jefferson Davis. After the Richmond School Board recommended the demolition of the 1816–18 building in 1889, Joseph Bryan took to the editorial page of his Richmond *Times* and denounced the plan. "To destroy an object around which so many imposing and inspiring moments cluster," he thought, "is to break one of the very strongest links in the chain of our city's historical continuity, and diminish the interest which those living outside of our limits feel in the city itself. In our opinion, one of the gravest mistakes that a municipal corporation can commit is to allow any of the important historical landmarks . . . to be destroyed or so far altered as to change its original character." Not only did the home of Jefferson Davis attract tourists, it implicitly showed the capital's own preeminence in the state. Joseph Bryan further valued the landmark as a "means of inculcating patriotic or heroic sentiments in the hearts of our people."[25]

Through the 1890s Belle Bryan championed other drives to honor the Confederacy. She planned the Confederate Bazaar of 1893 and raised $30,000, half of the moneys needed for the Soldiers and Sailors monument that would be sculpted by Sheppard and erected in 1894. Five years later she also assumed leadership of another bazaar to help finance the Davis monument, sculpted by Valentine and erected in 1907 in Richmond. Her son John Stewart Bryan, who later published the Richmond *News-Leader* and served on the APVA's advisory board, attributed her efforts to preserve Virginia's past to her religion, her loyalty to the Confederacy, and "the influence of the supreme figure of the war, General Lee, himself." Although Joseph and Belle Bryan brimmed with enthusiasm for Virginia, even they put limits on their time. Their son remembered his childhood: "Rarely, if ever, did any of us get out, and mother never. She would, if compelled to do so, attend evening meetings for the A.P.V.A., or some Confederate Bazaar, but I cannot recall a single occasion when she went out to a dinner or a party. Father was also a stay-at-home. Often he would groan and say: 'I have got to go back to town tonight to attend a Virginia Historical Society meeting and nobody can know how much I dread it.'"[26] Apparently their lives revolved around the feminine sphere of home, the male sphere of business, and their shared duties to Virginia traditionalism.

More than any other Virginian, Joseph Bryan (1845–1908) epitomized that traditionalism. Born on a plantation in Gloucester County, Bryan loyally served the Confederacy, most notably with Mosby's Rangers. Economic ruin followed, and his father lost the two family plantations and over one hundred slaves. Trained as a lawyer, Bryan ultimately blended the traditionalism of the Old South with the economic progress of the New and became Richmond's most successful entrepreneur. He manufactured locomotives, boomed land developments, and published newspapers. Never forgetting his roots, he served as president of the state historical society in 1892–1902 and 1906–8, consistently supported the Lost Cause movement, and was a paternalistic reformer in countless causes.[27]

With Belle Bryan as president, the APVA made its first real bid for community support in January 1890 at a Richmond public meeting. Curry presided, and the rostrum was shared by Page, Henry, Joseph Bryan, Robert Alonzo Brock, and Mayor J. Taylor Ellyson. In the audience sat Richmond's political and cultural elite. Setting the tone of the meeting, Page recounted the sweet flavor of the old civilization and reminded the audience of the utter necessity of reversing the neglect, documenting the past, and preserving the extant symbols of the old order. With his resonating voice he commanded:

> Go to Jamestown, the sacredest spot on this continent, with its crumbling or long crumbled wall, its very ground perishing under the advancing tides of our great river; go to Williamsburg, still redolent of the perfumes wafted from the most romantic society which ever existed in this hemisphere, where the echoes have hardly died away of the daring words which called a nation into being; go to Yorktown, where tyranny was smitten down; go to the old graveyards through the length and breadth of this Commonwealth, where sleep in unmarked graves a race the like of which we shall never see again. What will you find? Desolation and ruin; cowpastures and sheep walks.[28]

Page rebuked Virginians for allowing the North to write national and southern history from its perspective, thereby influencing the image that Virginians held of themselves. Spurring Virginia's rivalry with New England, he claimed with considerable exaggeration that northerners actively preserved their historical landmarks: "Go to Boston and note how every spot with any historical association is hallowed and protected. Bunker Hill, Faneuil Hall, the Old South, the Common, the graves of the heroes and sages of Boston. Do you think that had the North possessed Jamestown and Williamsburg and Yorktown it would have neglected them, and have allowed the elements to wear them away?" He rejoiced that Virginia women had undertaken the holy task of preservation because, he affirmed, "it has been proved that women are more efficient than men" in this work, as shown in the memorialization of Confederate heroes. Ironically, at the close of the program, Captain Frank Cunningham sang "The Sword of Bunker Hill," unconsciously illustrating the South's acceptance of the North's claim to leadership in the Revolution. Only as an encore did he accommodate southern sentiments by singing "Way Down upon the Suwannee River." [29]

Joseph Bryan seconded Page's remarks and regretted that the great deeds of the past had become a "shadowy tradition." With the seventeenth-century church at Jamestown in mind, he mourned that the "most sacred monument" built by these forefathers "has well nigh crumbled into indistinguishable dust." Evoking the rationale for the APVA's Gospel of Preservation, he reminded his audience that "the birthplace of a parent is approached with a sense of reverence and awe. The long-vacated home of some great man is regarded as partaking of his spirit, and is often—but not too often—carefully preserved, that the virtue of its illustrious master may be the more forcibly perpetuated and impressed on the visitor." Believing that no other spot on earth equaled Jamestown in providing heroic inspiration, he compared its ruins with the "broken walls of Jerusalem." "Join us in rebuilding our sacred places," he asked, and lend a hand "in this holy work." [30]

On the following day he wrote an editorial in his *Times* and used biblical verse to spur the cause of preservation. "Every Virginian who regards with reverence the earlier history of his native State," he suggested, "is gratified to know that at last something is being done towards rescuing from oblivion a few, at least, of 'the fragments that remain' to remind us of that ancient and honorable past." The opportunities and work of historic preservation seemed "boundless," and he urged his readers to lend their "most ardent support" to the APVA. [31] The association's public debut in January 1890 thus revealed important strands in the historic preservation movement. Whether Virginians joined the preservation bandwagon out of state pride, reverence for their ancestors, conservative politics, Lost Cause sentiment, or social camaraderie, the fact was that in Virginia, and increasingly throughout the South, traditionalists turned to their history to understand the present.

Perhaps Edward Virginius Valentine (1838–1930) best expressed the deeply held pride, or state chauvinism, with which traditionalists regarded the Old Dominion. Best remembered for his many stone monuments to the heroes of the Confederacy, particularly the marble recumbent figure of Lee in Lexington, Valentine not only served as an APVA adviser and president of the Virginia Historical Society, he gave Galt those rare encouraging words in 1888 when she approached him about forming a preservation society. A raconteur who held no breath in praising the Old Dominion, he picturesquely claimed: "You may rest assured that whatever is un-Virginian is wrong. Envious outsiders would call this narrowmindedness. Narrowmindedness! Bah! Is it narrowmindedness to say that our mother State is the best place to live in?—the best place to die in? Why, Sir, when death stares one of her sons or daughters in the face, how sweet, how comforting at that moment will be the thought that the jump from Virginia to heaven will be a short one." Whether that sense of pride represented what David Potter has called the distinctive folk culture of the South or what Thomas Connelly has pictured as the inbred conceit of Virginians is less important than the evident fact that tradition-minded Virginians felt culturally adrift in the era's turbulent seas.[32] The goals of social unification and order, perennial themes of southern history, would be attained through culture, as defined by traditionalists and symbolized by relics and monuments from the past.

The APVA's crusade closely resembled the revitalization movements within besieged traditional societies. As they faced a troubling present and an uncertain future, preservationists tried to establish their identity through the study of history so as to restore the central components of their old-time culture and apply them to modern life. Such revitalization, of course, entailed a selective adoption and a discriminating application of those traditions. The past was most important for its influence in molding the present and future. As one Jamestown preservationist admitted, "We cherish our *past* for the sake of our *future* so that while preserving the one we are building the other for ages yet to come." Such a focus often included inspirational biographies and hero worship. As Joseph Bryan frankly advised, "I do not see how a better service can be rendered our present generation than by holding up before them constantly renewed exemplars of the former men of dignity, character and learning, who made the old standard of Virginia morality and patriotism so high." In fact, James Alston Cabell suggested that the study of history should ensure that "the virtue of one generation was transfused, by the magic of example, into several."[33]

So typically, Jabez Lamar Monroe Curry (1825–1903) directly revealed the political uses of the past. A Baptist minister, Harvard-trained lawyer, and former United States congressman and diplomat, Curry had served also in the Confederate Congress. As a professor at Richmond College and agent of the Peabody Fund, he actively battled the Readjusters. Together with his wife Mary, an APVA vice president, he promoted and intertwined historical studies, education, and conservative politics to deter future popular-class movements. Speaking in 1881 at a centennial celebration of the battle of Yorktown, he reminded his audience that Washington had won there the freedom that Patrick Henry had demanded earlier at Richmond in his "Give Me Liberty" speech. Curry admitted that those sites symbolized grander values: "Yorktown in itself is nothing; St. John's church-house is nothing; battlefields and birth places are nothing, except as 'historic events, historic deeds, sublimed memories' have invested them with associations that kindle loftier aspirings, and stimulate to grander deeds. . . . We are not concerned simply with the past. Our institutions may be the daughter of the past, . . . but society is 'the mother of the future.'"[34]

Not only did historic preservation serve Curry's goal of political educa-tion, it helped uncertain moderns find surety in genealogical lines. Like many, Coleman prized her ties to the First Families of Virginia and regretted that Alexis de Tocqueville's warning had apparently come to fact, that the American spirit now devalued its historical roots. She often began her ad-dress to preservationists with the quip that "at this day . . . it is deemed arrogant to remember one's ancestors, if indeed one has ancestors." Not all Virginians held such priorities. Even the editor of the *Lower Norfolk County, Virginia, Antiquary* in 1901 accused the ancestor hunters of "vanity" and urged them to "stop wasting their time and fooling away their money in ridiculous searches after noble and royal ancestors."[35]

Traditionalists also hoped to seize the past through the preservation of a family home, burial ground, or ancestral relic. Therein lies the fragile connection between myths and material culture. Throughout recorded his-tory, myths have expressed a people's emotional need and intellectual vision. Whether they involve real events, romanticized history, or invented legends, they validate the canons of society, are manifest in ritual, and are embodied in concrete forms such as artifacts and buildings. Just as the Lares or guardian spirits of ancient Rome protected the material heritage of the past, so, too, did the APVA take pride in its possessions. As Henry pictured it, a preserved heirloom of the Founding Fathers "does indeed bring us face to face with the illustrious dead, and enables us to see, and to touch, as it were, the honored men whose names we have been taught to revere from childhood, the fruits of whose arduous and perilous labors we have inherited, and which it becomes us to transmit to our posterity, wasted by no prodigal hands." The APVA, in fact, made that plea when it invited Virginians to join the association. "These relics of [Virginia's] past history are passing away," preservationists said; "and when they are gone, which will inevitably soon be the case, important links in her history will be broken, never again to be re-united."[36]

No more important link could be found than the family home, and Victorian sentimentalists placed great importance on it. Amidst the modern uncertainty, it symbolized strength and continuity through the years. Its loss was a traumatic and ominous event. As Joseph Bryan explained, its destruction was "something even more than a death in a family for the lives of men are at best limited, while an old house . . . may go on from generation to generation comforting, protecting and encouraging with all its sacred memories and associations the children and the children's children of the founder." After the Civil War many ancestral homes in Virginia wasted away as planters moved to the city—what Cash has called an exodus—and abandoned their mansions to occupancy by poor blacks and whites. A few preservationists later reclaimed their old homesteads after gaining wealth in the city. Bryan, for example, settled his troubled identity by purchasing his boyhood home in 1901. As he worked on the "old home down in Gloucester," he admitted to Colonel John S. Mosby, his old Confederate commander, that he could not "imagine anything more delightful than to get off there away from telegraphs and railroad cars." The return to ancestral homes and the study of genealogy—what Bryan called "pious work"—represented the resurgence of the genteel rural tradition, the romanticism of the old aristocracy, and a popular antimodernism amidst the whirlwind of change.[37]

The growth of the APVA benefited from a parallel historical movement, the cult of the Lost Cause. Both the United Confederate Veterans (1889) and the United Daughters of the Confederacy (1894) shared leadership with the APVA, as in the case of the Bryans, Currys, and Ellysons who gave equally to colonial and Confederate causes. Both movements searched for a system of beliefs that would help create a modern order based on Old South traditions. Their historical interpretations also dovetailed. Whether voiced by Pryor or Page, preservationists pictured a seamless web of events. The regeneration of traditionalism would not simply buoy Virginia's deflated pride but help reorder society by challenging the demands of African-Americans, Readjusters, and the proponents of democratic change. On the national scene, Virginians such as Pryor and Page led the cult of the Lost Cause.[38]

Virginia traditionalists also campaigned to revise the biased content of schoolbooks. These textbooks generally equated the United States with New England. Repeatedly criticizing the South for its supposed lack of religion, enterprise, and morality, school primers taught that democracy was foreign to the aristocratic South. The South's leading families, moreover, were found guilty of immorality, ostentation, and dissipation. In the 1880s southerners fought back on many fronts. Instigated by the United Confederate Veterans, the South gradually began to produce its own textbooks. Until then, southern teachers asked their students to pin together the offensive pages of northern texts. A literary battle ensued between the regions. As southern traditionalists scrutinized their books, so too did northern zealots in the Grand Army of the Republic which acted as the guardian of patriotism, demanded loyal history texts, and agitated for the exclusion of those that were sympathetic to the South.[39] Partisanship saturated the writing of history.

All in all, the APVA's mission was charged by the tenets of its gospel. Determined to reassert the dominance of traditionalism, preservationists used the dim light of history to show the way into an uncertain future. They believed in the tradition of elite rule and called upon Virginia's aristocracy to exercise its duty to the Old Dominion. At the same time, they feared the influence of those generations raised during Reconstruction and Readjusterism and worked to reeducate and discipline this citizenry. Preservationists were convinced that history would prove their cause right. They labored not simply to document the links between the colonial, Confederate, and modern eras but to redefine those earlier eras so that the past became meaningful to the present. Amidst the hustle and bustle of change, such a past could sway present and future generations to believe that only traditionalism would solve their malaise.

3

"Leaning on Virginia as Children Resting on a Mother": The Feminine Hand in Historic Preservation

I F THE APVA's leaders and daily work were any indication, it was largely a woman's organization. In 1894 the Lynchburg *News* stated as well that its ranks were "composed entirely of ladies." But from its first days, the APVA actually recruited both genders as members. Like few other contemporary societies of patriots or preservationists, it bridged what Alexis de Tocqueville had earlier described as separate male and female spheres. To be sure, the APVA still reflected gender divisions within the larger society. Its incorporators, officers, and board were entirely women (see Appendix 1). Befitting the distinct spheres for genders, the advisory board was male. These advisers met separately, performed the public speaking until the 1910s, and influenced the association's rationale. It would be inaccurate, however, to overlook the real power of women in the organization.[1]

Those ladies pictured themselves as "the representative women of Virginia," but their descent from the Byrds, Lees, and other FFVs belied that claim. Their personas and history, most importantly, became identified with those of Virginia as a whole. These preservationists defined their agenda in feminine terms, as the APVA described in its 1889 invitation to potential members. Late nineteenth-century Virginians were like careless children who had strayed, the APVA said, but "still feel themselves a part of that great family, leaning on Virginia as children resting on the bosom of a mother, who, in her faded grandeur, is still dear to their hearts."[2] As shepherds of the Victorian family, women were bound not simply to nurture their children but to be forever loyal.

These elite and middle-class women performed the daily toil in the

APVA. James Alston Cabell, an adviser since 1889, admitted in 1915 that the reason for the APVA's success was that "most of the work is done" by the ladies. Throughout America this volunteerism kept countless private and public institutions afloat, but it was only possible because society expected women to contribute to home-oriented reform. They joined organizations such as the APVA when both their leisure time and domesticity's expectations increased. Initially, however, few gave their time as generously as Galt. Bagby, a widow, confided to her in 1895 that "but for you, Mrs. Bryan & me . . . I think the A.P.V.A. would die in a week." In fact, gender segregation in Virginia, as well as customary practices, kept women as the APVA's stalwarts for years to come. For example, a Richmond convention of businesswomen in 1919 warned ladies that too much club activity impeded their commercial opportunities. Lora Ellyson plaintively asked, "What will become of the A.P.V.A.?"[3]

These women crafted the APVA as an exclusive, socially delineated organization. Galt suggested that each APVA branch be "selected with such discrimination" that "any objectionable element" would be excluded. When the APVA formed a branch in Leesburg, for example, Coleman reported that "though small [it] was very representative and aristocratic." Pryor admitted that "a spirit of exclusiveness" characterized such patriotic and ancestral groups, and the choice of APVA branch directors revealed that pattern. Galt proposed that the APVA include as a charter member "the social leader" of Portsmouth in order to attract more members. She also wanted the APVA to include in its Washington branch the daughter of Senator William Stewart, a rich Nevada miner, because she "was the debutante then most admired in Washington and could do much towards making any effort to raise money on any occasion the fashion." Such exclusivity and social hobnobbing led Joseph Bryan to muse about the "'Blackball habit' among ladies." He described it as "the passion that women have for making a fuss with each other by turning down applicants for places in their societies just for the sake of making a row and raising an excitement; that there really was no malevolence in it, but just a love of using arbitrary power."[4] Bryan's point is only partly on the mark. It was equally evident that such exclusivity defined a community of interests that shaped historic preservation. The wives of the likes of William Mahone and Booker T. Washington need not apply for membership. In a remarkable way the APVA became a defining element in the life of proper Virginia ladies. Over the years it became the most respected of traditionalist groups and one which ensured the cultural cohesion of the dominant class.

Within recent years women's historians have noted that elite and middle-class women in the nineteenth century were strongly influenced by social structures which maintained separate spheres for both genders. While Linda Kerber has focused on the ideology of republican motherhood as a key component, Barbara Welter has described a cult of true womanhood. Both ideological systems protected America's traditions during the upheavals of economic modernization. While women safeguarded the home sphere and increasingly exercised moral authority in society, men triumphed in business and politics. Associated with this domesticity was the feminine responsibility to teach virtue, refinement, and patriotism. Historical studies, as a result, often fell within the feminine sphere. Proper Christian women, it was said, not only read the Bible and inspirational books but studied the history of their family, town, and nation so as to instruct their children.[5] Men still dominated the historical societies and the writing of history, as in Virginia, but they had abdicated a role in preservation by choosing books over buildings.

Early female preservationists cast their work in the domestic context but easily crossed the line into the purported male sphere. In the 1850s, for example, the Mount Vernon Ladies' Association took a pedagogical, nonpartisan stance when it rescued Washington's home, but it stretched domesticity by using Mount Vernon and the *Pater Patriae* as symbols that dramatically refuted modern ways. In so doing, the MVLA condemned the intense sectional strife, the immigrant-based politics of the Northeast, and the industrial factories. This mid-nineteenth-century America, the MVLA noted, compared poorly with the high-minded values of the Founding Fathers and their world.[6]

During the Civil War and the breakdown of existing structures, women in both North and South further extended the reach of their domestic responsibilities. Advocates of woman's suffrage in the Union, for example, subordinated their drive during the hostilities and established soldier's aid societies and contributed to sanitary fairs. In the South the privation and day-to-day struggle seemed to harden the endurance and fortitude of women. No sooner was the conflict over than they created volunteer organizations that cared for the graves of fallen heroes and built monuments in their cemeteries. Throughout the South tradition-minded women rebuilt patriarchy, soothed the wounded psyche of their men, and willingly restored the old order.[7]

The APVA built upon these well-established precedents. Pryor had her eye on the next generation when she claimed that this work reflected the desire of true women "to leave this world better and happier." She wanted women "to borrow from the fires of the heroic past to kindle the fires of the future." Accordingly, she helped found the Daughters of the American Revolution and other elite women's societies that preached their own gospels of preservation. She did recognize America's suspicion of rule by the upper caste, however, and wanted its elite based not simply on birth but "on the republican foundation of merit, character and service done."[8]

Gender lines still divided those groups. Men first formed the Sons of the American Revolution, the United Confederate Veterans, and other male-only associations, and women retorted by establishing the Daughters of the American Revolution and the United Daughters of the Confederacy. Keenly reflecting the Old Dominion's own gender divisions, the APVA at first acted as an appendage of the Virginia Historical Society. Like the APVA, the VHS had been established in the throes of a social crisis—the Nat Turner Rebellion in 1831—but it devoted its interests to manuscripts, not monuments. The APVA's mission, it was said, would be to correct this neglect. When Belle Bryan and her mother donated the Lee house to the VHS in 1892, the two organizations shared separate rooms of the building as their headquarters for the next twenty years. Just as the VHS left historic preservation to the APVA, so too did the APVA decline to develop a library, relying on the VHS to study Virginia through its written records. At first both organizations split their membership along gender lines, but the APVA, more so than its counterpart, quickly accepted both men and women.[9]

As Virginia's men failed in their drives to preserve remnants of the colonial past and memorialize the Confederacy, they handed the task to women. They asked Virginia's female preservationists, like other virtuous women, to teach a reverence for tradition and history. "As a general rule," Episcopal bishop A. M. Randolph told the APVA, "society develops these ideas in the realm of religion and ethics, through the impulse originating in the mind of woman." Randolph, an APVA adviser, admitted, although implicitly, that male-led, progress-minded historical societies had failed to consider preservation. "We have neglected our monuments for two centuries," he said, but "the present generation is witnessing a revival of a sense of duty to ourselves and to our children." Just as contemporary sociologists pictured the stages of an evolving society, Randolph saw the nation entering its mature period and beginning to show a "spirit of reverence for historical monuments and the appreciation of their ethical and spiritual value."[10]

As men struggle to gain wealth and influence in the get-rich-quick

Gilded Age, they sanctified women's work and used it as an anchor to stabilize a society buffeted by waves of change. Southern men such as Page and
Bryan placed women on a romanticized pedestal and idealized them beyond
human proportion. Curry told one Sons of the American Revolution convention in 1896, for example, that late nineteenth-century southern women
were following the traditions of their antebellum mothers. He affirmed that
"no civilization nor country has produced women purer, nobler, more cou-
rageous and patriotic and resourceful and self-sacrificing" than these women
and their descendants. John Lesslie Hall, professor of literature and history
at the College of William and Mary, amused his audience at a Jamestown
pilgrimage in 1895 by picturing these women as both faith healers and flirts.
"In prosperity, though 'uncertain, coy, and hard to please,'" he said, "they
fascinate us with their very coquetry. In adversity, the touch of their minis-
tering hands is a benediction. In war, the Virginia woman suffers with the
fortitude of a Spartan. In peace, she restores the waste places and makes the
desert blossom a rose. Here she is to-day in her work of restoration." Wilbur
Cash has called these sentiments "gyneolatry," but the female caricature
drawn by the likes of Page and Hall should be taken seriously. It not only
prompted many women to try and fit the unreal image on the pedestal but
revealed men's troubled mind about the era's women and society.[11]

Women stretched the domestic sphere to guard home and virtue more
effectively. As industrial capitalism and modern culture changed traditional
society, their tasks became enormously difficult. Southern women subsequently organized diverse clubs during the 1880s and 1890s to create a social
and intellectual setting where they could address the complexities of modernity and domesticity. Some clubs offered escapes from the unsettling times,
but most clubs at the very least enabled women who shared a class and
cultural background to establish psychological bonds, a like-minded perspective, and a plan of action. Many clubs relied on the devoted labors
of unmarried women who found community acceptance of their status
through such activities. The Women's Christian Temperance Union (1874),
for example, promoted the empowerment of women and the extension of
female benevolence to help cure society's maladies. Women would protect
their cultural traditions, promulgate them among the larger society, and thus
reform the nation. Women's work within this context was public but very
conservative in that market capitalism was not challenged. While critics
from Eugene Debs to Elizabeth Cady Stanton demanded substantive re-
forms to save America, conservatives focused on individual character, resisted meaningful federal action, and suggested personal philanthropy and

respect for the traditional ordering of society. At the same time, more and more women did push their domestic concerns into the public discourse. What had been private increasingly became public.[12]

As women emerged from the home sphere and entered the fray in preservation, they occasionally experienced a disquieting anxiety and the symptoms of neurasthenia. It afflicted many traditionalists at the time, from Harvard professor Charles Eliot Norton to SPNEA founder William Sumner Appleton. Neurasthenia, or nervousness as they called it, accompanied society's transition from traditional communities to modern civilization. It was particularly difficult for women, as was the case with both Annie Galt, Mary's sister, and Belle Bryan. As Galt negotiated to buy land in Williamsburg, for example, her nerves became frayed. Only her nervous tonic kept her going. Similarly, Bryan was incapacitated for part of her tenure as APVA president by endless maladies, including neurasthenia.[13] Norton and Appleton eased their minds by an immersion in cultural conservation, while Galt and Bryan found solace in family and church.

Southern churches encouraged women to work for benevolent causes, including temperance, public morality, and preservation, but not suffrage. Believing that a moral crisis threatened America, Coleman lent her energies to these church-sanctioned tasks. As she told her son, the world around them was "full of sinners, the worthless, the profligate and the base," and her action was necessary. Church work for many southern women, whether it was restoring the gravestones of the dead or the sobriety of their community, thus became a stepping-stone from the domestic to the public sphere. Typical was Coleman's formation in 1884 of the Catharine Memorial Society. Composed largely of children, the society not only sewed for money and picked daffodils for the New York market but helped repair Bruton Parish Church and its yard. Just as preservation rekindled old memories, Coleman's society partly reflected a mother's love for her deceased daughter because it would "keep people outside of her own family from forgetting her." In the same vein she helped preserve graveyards in New Kent County. The APVA would follow this pattern as women preserved buildings such as Abingdon Church (1754) in Gloucester County and Yeocomico Church (1706) in Westmoreland County.[14]

Woman's care of cemeteries increasingly merged with the civil religion of the day. Unlike preservationists in SPNEA and the ASHPS, societies dominated by men, the APVA devoted considerable energies to the preservation and maintenance of graveyards. Its care of graves revealed distinct elements in historic preservation: the South's preoccupation with cemeter-

ies, the filiopiety of preservationists, their links with organized Protestantism, and their advocacy of the civil religion. As Cash noted fifty years ago,
southerners generally went the extra mile to honor their dead. After the
Civil War, and despite the region's poverty, they spared no expense in moving thousands of fallen rebels from the North to the South. The Lost Cause
inspired such commemoration, but the APVA focused on those sites that
had associations with colonial and Revolutionary leaders. Speaking for the
APVA on a recruiting tour, Coleman declared, for example, that those
tombs were "all calculated to stir the blood of those who can trace their
ancestry to these Colonial grandees. Their old homes in many instances,
are gone or else crumbling into decay, but their *dust* remains a sacred legacy,
and the epitaphs on their tombs, broken and falling away record their
abounding virtue." The "sacred ashes" of these ancestors, said another preservationist, deserved protection because they had been "illustrious pioneers
in the cause of Progress and Freedom, the fruits of whose labor we enjoy."
The separate spheres of Victorian society, as well as its patriarchy, lingered
long in the APVA. Belle Bryan wanted it not only to protect the ashes of
the grandees but those "of the pioneer settler of the community, the head
of a family, the honored pastor, or the young soldier who gave his life for
his home and country."[15]

The APVA took charge of many graves associated with George Washington. It also helped in the removal of the remains of the wife and daughter
of James Monroe to Richmond in 1903 and the tombstone of Nathaniel
Bacon to Williamsburg in 1920. Sometimes APVA members joined others
to preserve these cemeteries. Pryor, for example, rallied with female patriots
to form the Mary Washington Memorial Association. Like Vestal Virgins
of ancient Rome, they pledged to hold "a perpetual vigil over the tomb
of Mary Washington, thus forming a Guard of Honor of six hundred
women."[16]

Although the domestic ideal charged women with the duty of honoring the dead, the cultural politics of traditionalism also shaped the practice
and reveals where men stepped in. For example, gentlemen preservationists
who served on the boards of the APVA and the VHS considered a proposal
in 1920 to remove the remains of Patrick Henry from Red Hill to St. John's
churchyard in Richmond because a railroad had built its tracks within one-
quarter mile of Red Hill to boost company revenues through tourism. The
advisers thought that the removal would dash such commercialism, create a
burst of patriotism, and prompt a more respectful owner to acquire the
house. Morgan P. Robinson, archivist at the State Library, endorsed the

removal because "the consecrated ground of St. John's will not be inva[d]ed by vandals of either social-climbing, or commercialistic proclivities." A generation earlier Hall similarly feared that "new-comers are selling some of the old monuments to relic hunters." A dyed-in-the-wool Anglophile, he even asked the VHS to help remove "many of the old, uncared-for monuments to some central point. Can we not have a great mausoleum for our most famous colonial dead?" he wondered. "Let us have a veritable Westminster Abbey of Virginia."[17]

Such veneration of the ancients contrasted with the actions of those who had removed the body of John Randolph of Roanoke to Richmond in 1879. The funeral party, including Joseph Bryan, whose father had been adopted by Randolph, let its curiosity get the upper hand, and some of them opened the coffin to inspect his throat to determine why his "power of utterance [was] so superior to other men." Advocacy of the civil religion had little connection, moreover, with a proposal by the APVA's Williamsburg branch in 1920 to remove the tombstone of Lady Skipwith to Bruton Church, "hoping by so doing her ghost, which is said to haunt the [Wythe] house, will thereafter sleep quietly." The willingness of Virginia preservationist to move their ancestors' remains contrasted sharply with professional practices elsewhere. SPNEA's Appleton, always most interested in the material aspects of the past, thought that the only thing of "permanent value" in the cemetery was the gravestone, and definitely not the ashes, or "slime" as he put it. In England a speaker before the Society for the Protection of Ancient Buildings censured an American archaeologist who, in looking for the grave of Pocahontas, destroyed a local graveyard. This "cult" of the dead, he said, was "antiquarianism run mad."[18] Such contrasts reveal the dramatically different notions of historic preservation in the early twentieth century.

The ideal of republican motherhood also encouraged women to learn history and literature for their children's education as well as their own edification. Literary societies offered women the chance for self-development and education, precious commodities in male-dominated society. Women socialized through the APVA and developed emotional bonds and a community of interests that reflected their class and culture. The APVA essentially tried to shape class solidarity through traditionalism. With the growth of cities and middle-class life, more women found the time and energy to join these clubs and spur various causes. Coleman explained in 1885, for example: "We formed a club for literary culture, not for amusement at all but profit. . . . Elevating the tone of society is a high mark at which to aim."

The APVA likewise held literary exercises or historical lectures at its sites to inform its audiences. In distant cities and states, the local APVA branch often became a literary society. The Washington, D.C., branch, for instance, listened to a member read an oration by Patrick Henry and the travel narratives of the marquis de Chastellux. That branch undertook no architectural preservation itself and focused instead on establishing cultural and social solidarity. Private literary clubs sometimes filled a void as Virginia's municipalities failed to provide adequate public libraries. Even by 1918 the Old Dominion still had no regional or county libraries and only twenty-two city libraries.[19]

Women's sense of republican motherhood and domestic duty increasingly led them in the late nineteenth century to exert their influence over culture. Although marked by inherited features of capitalist economy, European ethnocentrism, and Victorian notions of society, science, and progress, this women's culture offered priorities different from those of the male world. Marked by a sense of personalism and its focus on individual bonds and contacts, women's culture was less impersonal, less oriented to the market and its values, and more mindful of the human costs of America's rapid change. Women's culture, whether in the form of children's aid groups, reading clubs, or preservation societies, implicitly countered not only the excessive materialism and individualism of male society but its incorporation of business values, usually cloaked in the garb of professionalism, into what had been the practice of female benevolence.[20]

It must be remembered, however, that the APVA was a gender-mixed society. Had it been a single-sex organization where women's views were unchallenged, its work would be viewed differently. Perhaps James Alston Cabell's sense of chivalry prompted him to credit the APVA's success to its ladies, but the question must be asked, What role did the male advisers play in the APVA? More generally, how separate could male and female be in an organization committed to traditionalism? Perhaps the answer could be glimpsed from three strategic vantage points: acquisitions, interpretations, and daily policy. Within each area, men wielded significant influence in setting the broader meaning of historic preservation, while women used the organization to advance their own interests. Within each area, a complex relationship existed in the distribution of power.

As the APVA acquired diverse sites across the Old Dominion, women exercised considerable authority. They took the first steps in the acquisition of the Williamsburg Powder Horn, the Mary Washington house, the Jamestown church ruin, the Eastville government buildings, and many others. On most occasions female and male preservationists shared the commitment to protect those prominent sites which traditionalism and republican mother-hood held sacred. Only in a rare instance did male advisers actually alter a policy set by the ladies. The preservation of Richmond's Old Stone House was a case in point. Upon the recommendation of the advisory board, fe-male preservationists had declined its purchase in the 1890s; but the advisory board later reversed course and suggested its acquisition, largely because of fiscal considerations. Without any hint of disagreement, the ladies accepted that decision.

At times, men and women did tap into history in different ways. Mod-ern actors in the male world of politics used the APVA's acquisition of the Capitol in Williamsburg, the John Marshall house in Richmond, and the Rising Sun Tavern in Fredericksburg as their own stage props in the sym-bolic battles against Readjusters, Populists, and radicals. Female preserva-tionists used those sites more generally to teach acceptable codes of individ-ual behavior. On the other hand, some acquisitions definitely served feminine interests. Whether it was the Mary Washington house in Freder-icksburg or the many Anglican churches which the APVA helped to pre-serve, women used those sites to affirm their role in family and church. Regardless, inanimate objects were meaningful as symbols only through the use that accompanied their preservation.

In this matter of interpretation, male preservationists set the context for the APVA's action on countless occasions through their oratory, writings, and daily experiences in politics and the economy. What meaning a historic site had for the present was a matter of interpretation, and the gentlemen advisers commonly set this meaning within the politics of conservatism, the culture of traditionalism, or the economics of the New South. When ceremonies and rituals were held, it was Page, Hall, Bryan, and other advis-ers who publicly spoke and defined the site's context. In the pages of the APVA's *Year Book,* the women who generally wrote the text rarely ventured into what would be considered public controversy. They seldom advanced an overt political interpretation of a historical site, one which would directly repudiate the likes of Mahone or Debs, for example, as that would be enter-ing the male sphere of politics. Although Ann Pamela Cunningham had directly challenged corrupt politicians and scheming industrialists in her campaign to save the Union in the late 1850s, APVA women such as Pryor and Coleman were much more circumspect. They only politicized their interpretation of sites indirectly and used historical allegory and innuendo to make a point. Women could safely cite history, a study in the realm of republican motherhood, and suggest it as a precedent for action. Unlike their male advisers' direct statements, these women used nuance to address controversy.

Moreover, up until the writings of Pryor, Stanard, and other female preservationists began to appear, these gentlemen advisers, including Page, Henry, and Tyler, had written the history that set the framework within which a preserved site found meaning. What was considered "historical" all too often pertained to the male worlds of politics and warfare. Even when women such as Pryor wrote history, they usually fell into the same mold, but in a much-romanticized way. Only when they ventured into the newer field of cultural history, as did Alice Morse Earle in *Home Life in Colonial Days* (1898), would women's interest in domestic life and everyday society receive a wider public hearing. Mary Newton Stanard followed that tack herself in her *Colonial Virginia: Its People and Customs* (1917) and *Richmond: Its People and Its Story* (1923). Up until that time, women largely shared their ideas about women's culture with other women at meetings and discussions. Their views were not hidden, but they were heard by relatively few men and seldom printed in the newspaper.

Women did often add their own layer of interpretation to a site. Undaunted by the grimy history of the Powder Horn, Williamsburg women domesticated the arsenal's site by using it for their chapter's afternoon teas and soirees. All the while, these women still promoted the traditional male-oriented history of the building. On a different note, the grizzly history of early Jamestown did not keep Stanard from picturing it as a Garden of Eden where America's first Adam could make an Anglo-Saxon home for his Eve. Whether a musty arsenal or a near-barbaric settlement, a site's importance evidently was open to an interpreter's imagination.[21]

In the realm of day-to-day policy, the APVA usually met in afternoon sessions and showed a definite feminine presence. Women steered the course of the association while most men were at work. Even in those mostly female meetings, however, women were still inhibited by their conservatism, Victorian domesticity, and southern mores. If APVA ladies held a meeting and a man was present, he took the chair and symbolically mastered the discussion. As in the case of those conservative women's benevolent societies which formed alliances with men, these gentlemen commonly asserted their presence through the rhetorical argument that they were more capable of ensuring efficiency, order, and professional discipline. Whether under the guise of patriarch or professional, men tried to assert their control.[22] This is not to suggest that either gender acted independently, how-

ever. What kept them together was the courtesy of gentlemen and the deference of ladies; to have acted otherwise would have been "un-Virginian."

Gender inequality placed other limits on women's work. Although
Coleman was shrewd, articulate, and resourceful, she used Tyler as her
"mouth piece" in tradition-minded Williamsburg as she organized the
APVA. So, too, did Richmond's men articulate the views of female preservationists. Associate president Ellyson, for example, received a scolding from
her husband when she went before the General Assembly in 1903 to appeal
for public funds. She submitted to his wishes and refrained from further
lobbying. Frustrated, she admitted: "He is opposed to my ever again going
before the Committees of or the General Assembly, so I could not ask the
ladies to do what I can not lead in." J. Taylor Ellyson, soon to be elected
lieutenant governor, instead lobbied for the bill. Fifteen years later these
strictures had dramatically loosened. After an APVA adviser drafted a bill to
rebuild the bridge at Jamestown, Lora Ellyson distributed materials to each
legislator, appeared before the General Assembly, and successfully pleaded
for the allocation. Ellyson and her committee reported that they "had enjoyed their experience as lobbyists."[23]

If Ellyson's experience is indicative, female preservationists only slowly
gained liberty of action and even then won limited results in the still-male
world of politics and business. Despite the much-ballyhooed chivalry of
Virginians, those legislators often turned a deaf ear to the pleas of female
preservationists. After Ellyson's bid for more extensive aid for the APVA's
Jamestown project failed, Hall addressed the legislators in 1919 and compared the women of the association with the followers of Jesus who "were
first at the tomb of their Master." He faulted the General Assembly for its
failure to support "the guardians of our shrines and meccas" and wondered:
"Have we left our dear women to stand lone sentinels at the tomb of the
prophets." Fearing that the legislature's parsimony would embarrass the
state, he warned that "thousands of pilgrims" would find "the dear women
of Virginia, standing by the tottering walls of the First Temple of America
begging a pittance from the sneering Diveses of other sections." Shaming
the legislators, he asked: "Must they hold up supplicating hands to ignorant
parvenus for farthings and pennies?" Two votes in the following year
showed the legislature's mind. It made a handsome appropriation to the
APVA, but notwithstanding the Nineteenth Amendment's surety of national ratification, it still rejected woman's suffrage.[24]

The issue of suffrage visibly divided the ranks of Virginia preservationists like no other. A majority of traditionalist women reaffirmed the

virtue of deference, protected the status quo, and refrained from participating in the campaign in any way. Most often, they considered the vote a distraction from the home sphere and a threat to the racial barrier of Jim Crow. Bagby, whose spouse lost his job because of his orthodoxy during Readjusterism, represented those women who remembered the popular classes challenging the leadership of Virginia's traditional elite. Just as she rejected universal male suffrage, so too did she hold that male rule had divine sanction. Giving all women the franchise, she thought, was like a dice game of chance; it would leave to nature the task that God had given man. "What a scheme to substitute for the revelation of God's eternal law," she wrote, "the official declaration of the account of heads!" Just as southern manhood had been undermined by war's defeat, so too did she question the vigor and strength of those modern men who accepted female suffrage. "It is as if men had abdicated their right" to rule society, she thought, "and with melancholy resignation had agreed to give it up, and take temporary peace and good agreement as a substitute." She declared woman's suffrage "eternally wrong."[25]

Women attending the UDC convention in Richmond in 1911 similarly spoke out against woman's suffrage. As one explained in a letter to the Bryan family's newspaper, "No daughter of the Confederacy will be a suffragette. No veteran will permit female Negro suffrage—if it brings on another war. For when the cook comes to the meeting and puts on her bonnet quick, and goes to the polls and votes for Dr. Booker T. Washington as President of the United States, or 'You gets another cook,' . . . the women will be in the saddle with sabre and Pistol galore." Years earlier, the DAR showed similar acrimony. DAR member Susan B. Anthony twice addressed the group's Continental Congress on the suffrage issue, but President M. V. E. Cabell warned one colleague early in its history "to keep our Sisterhood of Daughters free from entangling alliance with bands of women aiming at any of the fads of the day."[26]

A handful of prominent tradition-minded women did join the ranks of the Equal Suffrage League of Virginia. Sally Nelson Robins, an APVA vice president in later years, eagerly supported the cause. Mary Johnston, a life-time APVA member and author of popular historical novels, also joined the drive and made many public addresses on the issue. As one of her novel's heroines put it, "I am writing for plain recognition of an equal humanity." Lila Meade Valentine, a long-standing APVA supporter, militantly led Virginia's suffrage drive. Unable to attend college because of her gender and poor finances, Valentine educated herself, immersed herself in many reform causes, and linked the degradation of women, labor, and children to the capitalist economy. A powder keg among Virginia's elite women, Valentine led both the suffrage drive and Richmond society. An unusual southern belle, she readily questioned the established order but won few allies. Together with her friend Mary Cooke Branch Munford, she tried to politicize Richmond's women. When Munford injected a political topic into the conversations of the Woman's Club, for example, the ladies simply would not hear it and thumped their umbrellas on the floor. In 1911 Valentine and Munford pressed the APVA to endorse the call for women's access to higher education at the University of Virginia. The APVA at first endorsed the drive but later erased this endorsement from its records and refused further action. President Ellyson and the old guard determined that "the matter *was* foreign to the objects of the Association."[27] Actually, she was historically correct. There was not much left to preserve about woman's rights in the Old Dominion. Like a neglected colonial building, they had eroded since the Revolution.

The differences between Parke Bagby and Lila Meade Valentine were as wide and intractable as Big Stone Gap. They were partly generational, partly philosophical, and partly social. The women of Bagby's generation—including Coleman and Bryan—had been hardened by the bitterness of the Civil War, the politics of antiradicalism, and the passion of the Lost Cause. Valentine had narrowly missed the worst of the conflict, and her spouse had little to do with those politics or passions. Both Bagby and Valentine advocated female benevolence but drew the line differently between the purported spheres. At the same time, the women most identified with the APVA and the resurgence of traditionalism were adamantly opposed to the suffrage drive. What further separated women was the fact that some, including Valentine, were more exposed to ideas circulating in northern and English reform circles.

Almost in unison, the APVA's advisory board denounced woman's suffrage. Edward V. Valentine, a relation of Lila's by marriage, represented the reactionaries who rallied successfully to defend traditionalism. "So far the South has seen the offensive disease in its mildest form," he sighed in relief. Instructing one audience, he claimed that "thousands of women of all classes who have any knowledge of their history and ways, look upon them [suffrage advocates] with a feeling of repugnance." Valentine associated the suffrage cause not only with the "most intense South haters" in the North but with Mary Wollstonecraft who had attacked the eighteenth century's traditions. According to Valentine, she "presented the most radical theories of French philosophy on morals and government." Woman's suffrage was un-Virginian, while his friend Page spoke for many men who preferred the pedestal, not politics, for their women. Bryan called the issue superfluous since "the wishes of the women of Virginia . . . were in the main carried out by their husbands, sons & brothers." [28] Tyler, on the other hand, was the most prominent male Virginian affiliated with the APVA to support the suffrage campaign. As early as 1896 he claimed that "the presence of woman is essential to perfection in any field, political, social, or literary." [29]

Lila and Edward Valentine had at least one sentiment in common—a love for high-society entertainments. Like southerners of the antebellum period, the women of the APVA valued their social occasions. APVA historian Mary Newton Stanard even claimed that "sociability and fondness for social pleasure is, as it has ever been, perhaps the leading characteristic of Richmond people." Indeed, these social gatherings brought many women to the APVA's fold. Belle Bryan had a particular flair for these stagings. In addition to the public appeal that inaugurated her presidency in January 1890, she planned an APVA ball to coincide not only with the unveiling of the Lee statue in Richmond but to serve as the inaugural ball of Governor Philip W. McKinney. [30] The timing of the event was no accident: the Democrats had been restored, the Lost Cause movement surged, and the APVA blossomed. All defined Virginia's traditionalism.

The grand ball had been a prized Old South tradition. As the APVA planned its revival in 1890, William Sheppard pledged that it would uphold old standards because its staging was "in the hands of the refined and cultured class of the community." He particularly wanted to assure such quality because an earlier ball with a colonial theme had been so successful that it was "reported in full in the Northern papers & made quite a stir in the *Century.*" The APVA spared no pains to guarantee colonial appearances; it allowed no one on the dance floor unless dressed in costume. The sight of Richmond's elite dressed as Smith, Pocahontas, and Rolfe not only helped re-create history but reaffirmed an identity based on antebellum myth and tradition. "Lookers-on" believed that preservationists "had called the old days and scenes themselves to life again in spirit and in truth," said Newton. "But alas, like all phantoms and illusions of the night, these ghosts of stirring times fled at cock-crowing." [31]

Beverley Munford recalled that the guest book for the APVA's ball in 1891 included "the names of most of the persons at that time composing Richmond society." He described as well a different legacy that the APVA endeavored to project. "To the younger generations of Richmonders these men and women of a day now gone have left the social traditions that deserve to survive, and memories of homes that were once notable in the story of Virginia." Joseph Bryan admitted to Parke Bagby that the APVA "gives life to our Modern Society. It has become the silken thread around which crystalizes the best efforts in our social life."[32] What proved most important about these balls, pageants, and social occasions, however, was the fact that those who attended were those who ruled. Tradition-minded men competed daily on the battlegrounds of politics and commerce, but they came together on the dance floor. The APVA's silken thread ensured a solidarity within Richmond's ruling class.

Thereafter the APVA held periodic balls and galas. These social occasions recruited new members, raised critically needed funds, and established a centripetal point where the APVA shaped the community's identity. As Newton observed, these annual balls were "among the most notable social events in the annals of Richmond." Such events obviously entailed great effort. Bryan watched his wife become exhausted while making preparations for the 1891 ball. After she took to bed that January, he hoped that she would "stay there several days, if for nothing else but to get rest & escape the importunities of the ladies who are wild over the Association Ball."[33]

Feminine historic preservation organizations commonly held such entertainments. Pryor, for example, organized a great ball at White Sulphur Springs to finance the construction of the obelisk over Mary Washington's grave. "Old White," as Virginians called the resort, served as sometime headquarters for APVA preservationists as they escaped the summer's heat. Munford described it as "the social center where gathered the best society of Virginia and the South." The social exclusiveness of "Old White" served not simply as a common ground for ballroom dancing but for elite cultural politics.[34]

The APVA held other social affairs, including afternoon teas, literary excursions to Jamestown, and even a play where "Pompeiian Dancing Girls" entertained. Planning for a "Persian Garden" party at the Governor's Mansion took up so much time at one meeting that Newton moved a resolution (which passed) "that hereafter only the business of [the] association be taken up at regular monthly meetings & that all meetings to arrange for entertainments be called especially for that purpose." As it was, her priorities were not shared by many in the organization. Those social events, after all, defined traditionalism and elite harmony. The APVA also held an annual reception at the John Marshall house after it won custody of the building in

1911. With the improvement of Virginia's transportation facilities, "many out-of-town guests" could now attend these once–only Richmond affairs. The APVA's reception, said one journalist, "is always one of the leading social events of the entire season, and many handsome gowns were worn by the women in attendance."[35]

On 27 January 1923 the APVA held another grand pageant in Richmond. So large it had to be held at Gray's Armory, it depicted the presentation of Pocahontas to the Court of King James I. The pageant filled the auditorium to its capacity and harked back to the grand balls of the 1890s. As the *Times-Dispatch* reported, "Not in many, many years has Virginia society witnessed such a gathering of interesting personages. Never such a literal combination of old and new Virginia." The APVA whetted the appetites of the younger generation when it brought almost a thousand children to the dress rehearsal. The pageant included the presentation of many dances and a grand ball with Virginia's elite in costume. It was said that Virginia Taylor played Pocahontas so convincingly that the chief of the Pamunkey Indians wanted to take her back to his reservation. The elaborate costumes elicited praise from all spectators. The cost of the ball was phenomenal, however, and said much about the priorities of Roaring Twenties Richmond.[36]

The grand APVA balls, fanciful social gatherings, and elite culture of the capital did not appeal to all of its residents. Some women wanted an undistracted focus on Virginia's glaring social and economic problems. Ellen Glasgow, Virginia's leading novelist of the early twentieth century, wrote critically about her hometown of Richmond. There she saw "a shallow and aimless society of happiness-hunters, who lived in perpetual flight from reality, and grasped at any effort-saving illusion of passion or pleasure." Glasgow realized that many of her affluent neighbors shut themselves off from what she perceived to be Virginia's duty to the less fortunate and instead immersed themselves in high society's way. Traditionalists, on the other hand, valued elite solidarity, and the APVA's social events established a comity and unity among Richmond's elite as the city became modern and industrial. The APVA helped to resolve, therefore, the historic divisions within Richmond's elite among the old families, old merchants, and old citizens. Whether one descended from the FFVs, the Scottish (or even Jewish) merchants, or colonial yeomen, the past that the APVA celebrated became Virginia's heritage.[37]

4

"And They Shall Build the Old Wastes": Early Preservation Efforts in Williamsburg

T HE APVA first preached its gospel in Williamsburg. After three generations of desolation and neglect, the second capital of Virginia pitifully
symbolized the abandonment of tradition and the poverty of postbellum
years. When the state moved the capital to Richmond in 1780, the town
lost much of its meaning. As English and colonial customs fell into disre-
pute, residents modernized once dignified structures. The Civil War further
traumatized the residents, as the blood of Johnny Reb and Billy Yank spilled
during the devastating Peninsula campaign.

The war ruined many of the town's noted buildings. In 1862 Federal
troops burned and pillaged the College of William and Mary's main building, an 1832 structure built on the foundations of Sir Christopher Wren's
original design. The early eighteenth-century Governor's Palace had burned
during the Revolution, and its last two outbuildings were destroyed during
the Civil War. What once had been a small barracks and an office, Coleman
lamented, were "torn down brick by brick by Federal soldiers." A similar
fate befell two other brick buildings, the Revolutionary-era James City
County clerk's office and Williamsburg's 1701 jail. Raleigh Tavern, so much
associated with Patrick Henry and the burgesses who challenged King
George, had burned to the ground the year before Lincoln's election. Federal troops occupied the town for three wartime years, forcing able-bodied
men and many women, including Coleman, to flee. They abandoned the
town to its fate. Clapboard buildings became firewood, artifacts war booty,
and vacant homes dwellings for freedmen. What remained went unrepaired
and unpainted. A pall of defeat and gloom pervaded the town for years.[1]

Tradition-minded Williamsburg residents despaired further during the

1870s and 1880s. With poverty ever present, residents stripped historic buildings, youth packed their bags, and even the venerable college closed its bankrupt doors in 1881. While the town fathers desperately sought revenues by selling the green around the Powder Horn, another resident pulled down the adjacent James City Courthouse of 1715. Sensitive about the town's plight, Coleman even resented northern tourists. When she heard that an editor from *Harper's Magazine* was coming to town, she told her son, "I do not like these fat, sleek Yankees to come and spy upon our poverty." Though impoverished and distraught, some residents prided themselves on their past. "These daughters of Williamsburg," said Mary Newton, regarded "their beloved town" as "sacred ground." These legacies became more distant in time and less tangible to their senses, however, with the physical changes in the landscape.[2]

Not only had Williamsburg's buildings deteriorated and its economy collapsed, its social order was overturned. Coleman and fellow traditionalists supported the Democratic party, but the Readjusters carried the town's elections until the resurgence of traditionalism. The African-Americans, who lived in close proximity to the whites, celebrated their freedom, as blacks did elsewhere in the South, by holding a parade on 1 January. Honoring Abraham Lincoln and the Emancipation Proclamation, the celebrants tried to establish a new tradition and identity for the town. Watching Williamsburg so dramatically change, Coleman claimed that blacks showed disrespect, and she deplored the behavior of "the miserable negroes."[3]

The tide shifted slowly during the 1880s. In 1881 the nation marked the centennial of the Yorktown victory. Addressing patriots from near and far, President Rutherford B. Hayes laid the cornerstone for an obelisk that would be finished four years later and tower over the town. Tradition-minded Virginians could hardly ignore the wounds of defeat and the odor of decay that still pervaded the area. The celebration's pyrotechnic displays, grand ball, and military reviews nonetheless drew large audiences. At the same time, the president's former classmate Curry addressed a Richmond audience, denounced the Readjusters, and reiterated his belief that education, conservatism, and patriotism were one and the same. As far as he was concerned, the Readjusters represented the wrong kind of American revolutionaries.[4]

The Yorktown celebration placed the spotlight on the Old Dominion's heritage. For the commemoration, a national association restored the Moore house, the site of the surrender of Lord Cornwallis. The guidebook published for the occasion presented over forty pages of information relating to the history and architecture of Yorktown, Williamsburg, and the James River area. The author, John A. Stevens, editor of the *Magazine of American History,* included sketches of Williamsburg's remaining historic buildings and noted that the town "still retains an air of serene and antique dignity, which rendered it one of the most interesting remains of the colonial period—perhaps unique in its almost entire absence from the innovations of modern civilization." Ironically, the very fact that drew outside attention to Williamsburg was its lack of modernity, the other side of the impoverished coin that troubled so many residents of the town. The simultaneous introduction of the Chesapeake and Ohio Railroad to the peninsula brought both commercial development and tourism. At first the C&O laid its tracks in the middle of the historic town, but it soon moved them to the outskirts. More importantly, the hamlet fell within relatively easy reach of the metropolitan East. The next generation could catch one of eight trains departing daily for points north.[5]

Williamsburg's leading families undertook a restoration that entailed not only architecture but the moral tone and economic strength of the town. The local APVA branch exerted such a strong influence that Coleman's granddaughter compared its influence with that of "the church." "You didn't dare disapprove of it," she recounted. "It was like motherhood, and all that." The town's upper crust solidified around the APVA. The college faculty (or their wives) joined the association, but the school secretary and sexton did not, showing the selectivity of the APVA chapter.[6]

During the first decade Coleman exercised a dominant hand over the branch. A descendant of the famous Tuckers of Williamsburg, she at times cajoled like a southern belle and at other times indomitably wielded influence. Tyler confided to Annie Galt that he "did not know the person lived who could intimidate 'Miss Cynty.'" Carter Glass remembered her as "the peerless queen of society" in her youth. Upon her death, however, Belle Bryan praised her in terms that underscored the concept of true womanhood. As "an earnest Christian, a loyal Virginian, a true patriot, a staunch friend, a worthy daughter of her house, and a fond Mother," Coleman had set the standards of domesticity. "What more can be said—or desired?"[7]

Laying the foundation for later Williamsburg preservation work, Coleman and her Catharine Memorial Society raised funds for the beautification of the interior of Bruton Church and the repair of its much deteriorated graveyard. She simultaneously worked to reform the morality of the parish. Rebelling against its minister, Coleman even threatened to attend the nearby Methodist church unless he left. After his resignation, she remarked that he left behind not "the order of sanctity," but the odor "of whiskey. . . . A Minister of the Gospel drinking, the thought is horrible." Coleman in turn became intoxicated with Virginia's history. In her letters to her son George, for example, she regularly quizzed him on his command of history and expected him to respond correctly in the next week's letter.[8]

Coleman wrote extensively on Virginia history and submitted some essays to northern publishers, but little, if anything, was published. Twenty-six years after Appomattox, she sent her manuscript "Williamsburg during the Occupancy of the Federal Troops" to the *Century Magazine*. Its editor replied that it would "not be wise to print it," because similar articles "have stirred up more feeling than we thought possible at this time." Concluding that it "would do more harm than good," he returned her essay. Coleman did not hide her sentiments, and Confederate general William H. Payne was delighted "to hail one whose feelings seem as untamed and as unreconstructed as my own." Their mutual diehard spirit came out in his lament: "I *know* that we had the meanest enemies to encounter that ever succeeded in defeating a righteous cause, and the saddest thing to me now is that I and mine are tied to those wretched people for ever; that their cause is to be my cause, their country is to be my country, and whither they go, I am obliged to follow."[9]

An eloquent champion of the Gospel of Preservation, Coleman evoked the past to kindle the strength to shape the future. Sounding much like Brooks Adams, she watched America's material wealth and overseas empire grow in the late nineteenth century and warned that "it is a law of nature, that the rising grandeur and opulence of a nation must be balanced by a decay of its heroic virtue." The wealth and power of the North, she believed, accounted for America's flaccid and gilded ways. The colonial-era buildings of Virginia, on the other hand, symbolized a heartier and superior civilization. She admitted that Williamsburg was important for its associations and lessons, not its aesthetics. "The houses themselves possess no special architectural attraction, other than the softened lines or neutral tints of age, not even amounting always to picturesqueness. Many of them are rambling and irregular, none of them more than two stories and a half in height." Paradoxically, she expressed most interest in the Georgian period of increased colonial wealth; she found only one impressive house in town. Within the George Wythe house (1752–54), "there is no attempt at ornamentation, only durable simplicity which amounts to elegance, and which characterizes the generality of its contemporaries." Like many adherents of the simple life, she evidently preferred wealth without pretense, comfort without ostentation, simplicity without privation.[10]

Working hand-in-hand with Coleman during these years was Lyon Gardiner Tyler (1853–1935), the president of the College of William and Mary. Tyler watched the Civil War from his mother's New York home but never lost his loyalty to the Confederacy. Educated at the University of Virginia, he later held a seat in the General Assembly and in 1888 persuaded the state to reopen Williamsburg's college as a normal school. His restoration of the town focused not only on the college and the APVA but on its moral fabric. Like Coleman, he regretted what he called the "stagnant and depressed" tone of society. As he remembered, when the college reopened it "was the day of free drinking," and numerous saloons lined Duke of Gloucester Street. He combated "the ill effects of liquor" through a temperance crusade, and it "cleared immensely the moral atmosphere of the college." The decayed appearance of the town only slowly gave way to change, however. In 1898, one student recalled, "there were cows on the campus. . . . There was no pavement on the streets or sidewalks, and there were a lot of old rundown houses at the entrance to the college."[11]

Tyler also used Virginia's history and the APVA's successes to promote his college and its cultural legacy. He published the *William and Mary College Historical Quarterly,* edited *Tyler's Quarterly,* and wrote a score of books and pamphlets on the Old Dominion. He preached the Gospel of Preservation incessantly to his readers and students. Reviewing the historic events at Jamestown, Williamsburg, and Yorktown, he claimed that "it is impossible that the students can live in the presence of these and other similar associations without being inspired by them." Schooling at the college, he promised, would "quicken the pulse and inspire the heart of the young with all those elevating principles and lofty desires which make ambition virtue." He pictured each human life as a block of marble "waiting for the monumental inscription, and it is the inspiration born of such localities as these that may cut the letters deep." Tyler played up the area's history because each visitor to the Historic Triangle—and there were about 80,000 "strangers" annually by 1905—inevitably saw the spotlight which Tyler placed on the college. Hoping to find better-qualified and more affluent students, he capitalized Virginia history.[12]

Under Coleman and Tyler, the local APVA branch centered its focus on the colonial magazine, the foundations of the Capitol, and Bruton Parish Church, the three principal remnants of Williamsburg's belle epoch. Shortly after the APVA's formation, Richmonders traveled there to see the sights. Beverley Munford led one party in the spring of 1889, and Coleman relished the opportunity to "show off old Williamsburg" and its historic aura. "I tell you, my dear," she told Belle Bryan, "I was in my element and perfectly delighted. . . . It was an ante-bellum day of ladies and gentlemen and made one feel good all over."[13]

The magazine, or Powder Horn, first drew the APVA's attention. An octagonal structure with a conical roof built in 1715, the magazine had curious uses after the Revolution. The city held a market there until the Baptists used it as a meetinghouse. When they built a Doric temple church in 1855 up the street, the Baptists dismantled the wall around the magazine's perimeter and used its bricks for the foundation of their new building. After that, the Powder Horn became a dancing school and again a magazine during the Civil War. Following the Yorktown Centennial, Coleman complained that the building "is now debased to the vile uses of a stable . . . [and] if she had the money would buy it and convert it into a Museum."[14]

The APVA purchased what Newton called "this queer-looking" old building for $400 in 1889. For "a mere pile of bricks and mortar," Coleman admitted, "they were aware that they were giving an extravagant price, for which they would be inexcusable but for the historic associations connected with it." Soon after, a fire of unknown origins "seriously damaged" the vacant building, leaving it in a "precarious condition." Coleman asked Richmond for help because "two of its sides have long ago fallen and two more are bulging in such a way as to make it unsafe to be in their neighborhood." The rest was "liable to fall in at any moment," and the local branch had difficulty getting anyone to work on it.[15]

Richmond preservationists in turn played up the historical associations of the building. Spurring the cause, Bryan wrote an editorial in his *Times* in which he equated the magazine with Fort Sumter: "It was to the colonies in 1775 what Lincoln's proclamation proved to be to the Southern States of America in 1861." Traditionalists remembered that it had been built "to suppress negro insurrection," and it would remind modern Virginians that the Revolutionary, Civil War, and Jim Crow eras were united.[16]

Now "a tottering ruin," the Powder Horn sadly represented "Virginian indifference and ingratitude" toward its past, Bryan told his readers. This neglect had not always been so, as "for many years its fate has engaged the serious attention of those who look with reverence upon everything calculated to preserve the traditions of the State or perpetuate the deeds of her illustrious dead." The building long ago "should have been religiously preserved from decay as a relic of the great struggle through which our ancestors had successfully passed." Reflecting the late nineteenth century's concept of controlled space and natural scenery, he wanted to give "it the dignity of seclusion" by wrapping it in "living green." He urged all Virginians to support "so holy a cause" and announced that the APVA would hold a colonial ball to raise funds.[17]

At first the APVA jerryrigged the building's repair by removing bricks from the ruins of the Governor's Palace and Capitol. As soon as it became feasible, the APVA wanted to use it as a museum for colonial relics, but the local branch immediately ran into difficulties over use and design. Coleman admitted in 1890 that "in trying to preserve the integrity of the building as a Magazine we will hardly have sufficient light for the display of relics." The magazine still stood in great disrepair, but Coleman and her branch turned their attention to a campaign to acquire stained-glass windows to honor Alexander Spotswood and Nathaniel Bacon.[18]

Galt's attempt to purchase the front lot to Duke of Gloucester Street in 1888 had failed. In 1908 she resumed the campaign to raise the purchase price of $3,000. Bryan gave $500, but few others followed. Annie Galt admitted to her sister that the pressure was too intense. "I have had a siege of neuralgia," she wrote. "It all comes from nervousness & loss of sleep. I have been so wild about this front lot that it has about wrecked me."[19]

By this time the APVA kept the Powder Horn museum open seven months a year and paid a salaried caretaker. With nearby Bruton Church, it became the principal tourist attraction in Williamsburg; in 1919 for example, 582 persons visited the building. The local branch also used it for their receptions and attempted to re-create the scene of a family dinner, not a dirty arsenal. They pictured one such reception in what was definitely domestic and feminine tones. "The light of innumerable candles, in rare old silver candlesticks," these Williamsburg women reported, "shed their soft light over a beautiful old mahogany table, black with age, spread with exquisite lace, dainty old colonial china, rare old silver, and quaint little spoons worn thin with use and age, handed down through many generations, and giving an added flavor to the delicious tea."[20]

To the east on the Duke of Gloucester Street once stood an even more prominent Revolutionary-era building, the Capitol where Virginia's burgesses had challenged the rule of the British monarch. After Governor Thomas Jefferson moved the capital to Richmond in 1780, the old Capitol fell to disuse. In 1794 the assembly authorized the demolition of one-half of the building in order to defray the cost of the other half's upkeep. In

1832 the Capitol burned to the ground. Eight years later part of its brick wall was used to build a female academy, but that school, too, was pulled down when the plot was acquired a half century later by the Old Dominion Land Corporation. Williamsburg residents mined the site for bricks and stone, as did the APVA for the walls of the Powder Horn.

Calling the site "holy ground" for its ability to spark patriotism and civic duty, Coleman inaugurated a drive to purchase the Capitol foundations after it "passed into the hands of [those] strangers." Representing northern capital, the ODLC was a subsidiary of the C&O Railroad and speculated on lands along the rail route. It set a $1,000 price on the Capitol lot. On behalf of the APVA, Bagby wrote C&O magnate Collis P. Huntington in 1895 asking him to donate the plot to the APVA. The campaign for the 1896 election was under way; fearing regulation of the railroads and the radicalism of popular-class rule, traditionalists and industrial leaders lined up against Democratic-Populist William Jennings Bryan. M. E. Ingalls, president of the C&O Railroad and a lifetime member of the APVA, warned Virginians that a Democratic victory would require the company to cancel all work projects and slash its work force. The railroad keenly realized the benefit of rewarding its friends and soon donated the one-acre plot to the "worthy cause" that the APVA represented. Conservative-minded leadership, economic boosterism, and a fear of radicalism brought the C&O and APVA together.[21]

The APVA's work at the site of the eighteenth-century Capitol illustrated a major theme within the historic preservation movement of that day. Not only could "preservation" be undertaken through the protection of extant buildings but through the placement of plaques and monuments at sites obliterated by the hand of progress. To be sure, the preservation of an authentic building, a more costly undertaking, adds much more to an aesthetic environment than does the erection of a small monument or tablet. But the placement of a relatively inexpensive plaque also affords the opportunity to educate the public, commemorate an event, and inspire comparable behavior, those being the APVA's specific goals. Antiquaries and historians throughout the nation were regularly, almost endlessly it seemed, marking historic sites. Columbia University professor A. D. F. Hamlin told the American Scenic and Historic Preservation Society in 1902, for example, that the act of marking a site with a plaque "is to open a perennial fountain of inspiration, to establish a silent but effective preacher of virtue." Robin Winks not only has called plaques "a public historiography" but has concluded that "preservationists thus influence the image that the future will have of its past, and by inversion, of the image of what the future will be or ought to be." [22] This point must be underscored within the context of the APVA's gospel. As its leaders worked to reestablish traditionalism after the tumult unleashed by the Civil War, they found it necessary to prove that antebellum society had been noble, peaceful, and efficient. The hegemony of traditionalism in the present and future depended upon its control of the past.

Concerned that if it failed to act, "important links in our history will be broken never to be restored," the APVA constructed a chain of memorials, including one at the site of the Capitol in Williamsburg, to regenerate the past in the public memory. Actually, these preservationists marked sites more often than they preserved extant buildings. As they interpreted their mission, they considered the commemorative tablet as effective as the preservation of the actual object in evoking the memories and inspiration of the past. Accordingly, the APVA established a select, standing landmark committee to "identify and suitably mark" sites, but it had no committee on architectural preservation. At a time when many important buildings faced demolition or alteration, moreover, associate president Ellyson considered their "special work" for 1910 to be "the placing of tablets or other suitable markers." [23]

Preservation of historical knowledge, as well as the vitality of traditionalism, required that these monuments educate the public. Edward Valentine participated in a Virginia Historical Society study "on Marking Historical Spots." He recommended marking a long list of sites, many of which the APVA subsequently enshrined. Valentine suggested "that upon the occasion of the unveiling of each tablet appropriate public exercises be held, to which all the school children shall be especially invited, at which a short historical description of the spot marked be read." [24] As a rule, the APVA followed this advice and publicized its cause.

Not all outsiders understood the APVA's motivation. Sometimes Virginians openly competed with New England in laying historical memorials. Many Virginia traditionalists, for example, thought it was "humiliating" that their cities and squares, unlike those in the North, lacked monuments to their forebears. The APVA's subsequent concentration on the placement of markers, however, led SPNEA's William Sumner Appleton to note critically that Virginians were "somewhat given to tablets and memorials," rather than preserving actual buildings. Similarly, Charles R. Ashbee, an English advocate of the arts-and-crafts movement, traveled to the United States in 1901 and tried to form an American National Trust. Interested in a wide range of social issues relating to work and environment, he expressed his disappointment with the caliber of preservation work in Virginia, specifically the APVA's use of memorials. Criticizing the APVA for overdoing the practice, he thought that tablets on a vacant site produced "barren" results. "It is of little use to those whose aesthetic or historic sense we wish to stimulate," he reported, "and as such is of comparatively little influence as a factor in the education of the democracy." Ashbee and Appleton misunderstood the APVA's work, however. Virginians most concerned themselves with documenting a history that, they believed, had been stripped from their memory. Like a stone over a grave, a tablet on a vacant site could stir the memory and affirm an identity.[25]

Williamsburg became a chess piece in the match between Virginia and New England over the title of colonial founder. Preservationists in the Old Dominion worried that their rival had already outpaced them. Raising funds to build the memorial at the site of Williamsburg's Capitol, Coleman acknowledged, "A recent visit to New England has so impressed me with the zeal, ardour and patriotism of the people of that favoured section, in the preservation of everything calculated to illustrate their history, that I have returned to Virginia filled with a desire to emulate their example." The APVA enshrined many sites during the first preservation of Williamsburg, including the site of Raleigh Tavern, the clerk's office of the Capitol, the debtor's prison, the Peyton Randolph house, the George Wythe house, and the James Blair house.[26]

More importantly, the APVA enshrined the Capitol foundations. William Wirt Henry, the lawyer who handled the acquisition, advanced a rather fanciful interpretation when he claimed that the state had removed the capital to Richmond in 1780 "so that hereafter no degenerate son of illustrious sires might put a blot on their work. . . . The book of history was closed, and its glorious past secured from tarnish." Leading the campaign to consecrate the site, Coleman predicted that "the youth of the land [will] here learn that true greatness is to be found in love of country and in the performance of Duty."[27]

Documenting the leading role that Virginia played in the Revolution, the APVA placed a boulder with a plaque costing $978 on the site where the House of Burgesses had met. The dedication ceremonies on 26 May 1904 included great fanfare and speeches by Tyler, Hall, Bryan, and Goodwin. Page delivered the main oration and visibly impressed the throng. "His address was listened to with rapt attention as he described in words of burning eloquence the scenes which had been enacted on this spot," a local preservationist reported. Closing his address, Page advised the students of the College of William and Mary to remember the tenets of traditionalism, including the obligation of elites to rule. When Tyler unveiled the monument, it was "greeted with enthusiastic cheers and vociferous college yells." According to one observer, the entire day harked back to olden times. "But for the shriek of the locomotive and a few other modern innovations, one might have imagined Williamsburg had retrograded a century or more, to the period in which Thackery [William Makepeace Thackeray] describes it as 'The gay metropolis so attractive in winter to visitors from the little village of Richmond.' "[28]

Virginians used the Capitol and Powder Horn as props in their battle to recapture the legacy of the Revolution from New England. At times it was impossible to separate the personal agenda of preservationists from that of the association, however. Henry, for example, used the Capitol to redeem the standing of his grandfather as he carried on the tradition of William Wirt, the imaginative biographer who beatified Patrick Henry and created, among other myths, the text of the "Give Me Liberty" speech. The APVA adviser brooked few challengers in defending his grandfather. He rejected not only the claim of John Adams that James Otis had instigated the revolt but the view of Thomas Jefferson that Henry was an egotist driven by love of fame and money. When the stamp tax was decreed in 1765, according to William Wirt Henry, Massachusetts "faltered and vacillated," while Patrick Henry condemned the unjust tax. The Virginians, led by Henry, spoke out "as the Divinity that shapes our ends had ordered." The meeting of the burgesses in Williamsburg also passed the May 1765 resolutions that "commenced" the Revolution. The Declaration of Independence, the APVA adviser boasted, "completed the American Revolution, for all that remained was to maintain the position she had reached."[29] Henry's role in the Revolution prompted the APVA years later to acquire Scotchtown, his house in Hanover County.

Popular throughout the years, Henry's protest against taxation without representation had a modern ring in the early twentieth century. His impassioned rhetoric evidently appealed to wealthy conservatives who equally denounced the Readjusters and the national income tax. Two months after the ratification of the Sixteenth Amendment, APVA adviser Archer Anderson again evoked Henry's memory and asked: "What will the professional demagogues care about the oppression of one half per cent of the population when the 99½ per cent to whose votes he bows, are sitting in the galleries and enjoying the torture of the poor ½ per cent in the arena— butchered to make a Roman holiday?"[30]

The APVA also used Williamsburg to reject claims that the Old Dominion had supported the Loyalist side in the Revolution. Many late nineteenth-century schoolbooks taught, for example, that the South had produced an inordinate amount of Tories. Stanard rejoined that "the majority" of Virginians "saw bowing to the will of a king and parliament turned tyrants, as slavery." Preservationists also pictured those Virginians as selfless idealists, not modern-day Communards. Page often said that his ancestor Governor Thomas Nelson from Yorktown had pledged his personal credit to provision the Continental army. The modern romanticist overlooked such nagging eighteenth-century issues as expansionism, markets, and debts and leaped to a generalization that southern leaders "gave up wealth and ease and security . . . and launched undaunted on the sea of revolution." Curry emphasized, moreover, that they had gone to war "in defence of abstractions" and principle. Traditionalists often built a wall between America's noble revolution and the ignoble English and French revolutions.[31]

Through the first decades of the twentieth century, the APVA toyed with the idea of rebuilding the Capitol as a museum. Meanwhile, it capped the foundation with cement, thus deterring scavengers and erosion. The APVA leaders granted Coleman and her branch in 1898 "full liberty . . . to conduct the restoration as they saw fit," but she resigned as branch director in the following year, and the project fell out of her hands. Alpha Chapter of Phi Beta Kappa, at William and Mary, pushed the APVA in 1909 to begin the project. Comparing the Capitol with Boston's Fanueil Hall and Philadelphia's Independence Hall, the chapter appointed a sterling committee, as did APVA, composed of Tyler, Page, Goodwin, Munford, former governor Andrew J. Montague, Congressman William Lamb, and University of Virginia president Edwin A. Alderman. The APVA asked Samuel H. Yonge, its adviser and engineer at Jamestown, to provide an estimate. Some like Munford wanted then and there to write a contract, and Yonge calculated that to reconstruct the Capitol "as it originally stood would cost about $35,000." "This figure," he added, "is a conservative estimate, and covers the furnishing." Deterred by that sum, the APVA voted to leave the project to what it called the "Alpha Beta Kappa Society," which in turn allowed the project to languish. Stuck with its undeveloped ruin, the local branch unsuccessfully petitioned local officials in 1911 to reconstruct the Capitol as a library, museum, and public hall which would "conform as much as possible to the original plan." There the matter stood for two decades.[32]

The Chesapeake and Ohio Railroad donated another historic structure to the APVA at the turn of the century. At a time when Populists clamored for railroad regulation and reformers decried corporate monopolies, Huntington's railroad evidently sought better public relations. By giving the APVA the icehouse behind the ruin of the Palace, the railroad won the praise of preservationists. Coleman romantically conjectured that the icehouse walls could tell "many a strange story if they had tongues." Fellow antiquary Sally Nelson Robins added a humorous note and showed that though the APVA honored the rebels of 1776, it could also appropriate the legacy of royalists. "Some may call this *cold charity*," she quipped, but they would think differently "when they are told that this ice house belonged to Lord Dunmore, and that its precious contents probably filled tempting glasses of mint julips and other like decoctions."[33]

Williamsburg preservationists also helped the community restore Bruton Parish Church, a once majestic cruciform design built in 1715 on Duke of Gloucester Street. The exodus of the state government in 1780 had left the town unable to maintain the church. By 1811 its condition had deteriorated greatly, and later years aggravated that neglect. In 1840 the parish held a church fair to fund a modernization. The nave was partitioned to create a Sunday school room, and the beautification included the removal of the corner pulpit and the flagstone aisles.[34]

Two generations later when the Catharine Memorial Society inaugurated its work, Coleman called the church interior "a miserable piece of botch work." Overall, the changes had been "many and lamentable," she wrote. "Conventional slip-like pews have been substituted for those cozy square closets in which our ancestors were wont to indulge in devotional exercises or slumber, which ever they had a mind to, shut in from the eyes of inquisitive neighbors, as is every man's right under either delicate circumstances." She admitted, however, that in its unaltered outward appearance, Bruton Parish Church still "stands [as] a sign of the past mellowed by the touch of time, holy with associations, a picturesque pile of inanimate brick and mortar, mute but eloquent." In 1895 Tyler spoke before the APVA's annual meeting and urged it not only to undertake a proper restoration of Bruton Parish Church but to repair Lancaster County's Christ Church (1732), one of the nation's masterpieces of colonial ecclesiastic architecture.[35]

As a visible symbol of the past, Bruton Parish Church embodied those elements which made up the APVA's rendering of history—myth, tradition, and documented fact. Pleasing traditions and legends had long been a part of popular history. Charles Washington Coleman, a local antiquary and spouse of the APVA organizer, advised preservationists in 1891, for example, that "all the pretty, picturesque stories" make "history authentic." His anti-intellectualism got the better of him, however, when he claimed that "all generous minds have a horror of what are commonly called 'facts.' They are the brute beasts of the intellectual domain."[36]

Antiquaries and raconteurs of Coleman's ilk enhanced the South's oral tradition by setting their stories into written text. He told the APVA that "the doings of yesterday told about the firesides of to-day as facts will be [the] legends of tomorrow." His spouse gave an example about an old legend that depicted a time in the early eighteenth century when the bell in Bruton Parish Church's belfry was cast in England. According to the APVA's organizer, "an old lady came with a lapful of silver coins, which she threw into the seething metal, that the voice calling to God out of the wilderness of the New World might be clear and sweet." The legend relied on the classic ingredients—a heroine, a noble deed, and a challenge. A problem ensued many years later when a youth climbed into the belfry and discovered that the bell's inscription attributed the casting to a much later date. Coleman admitted that "it was a great blow," but the legend so inspired the present that "the bell in the church tower still speaks with a tongue of silver its call to prayer. Moreover, it is local tradition and none must gainsay it."[37]

Bruton Parish Church and Williamsburg took a fateful turn when William Archer Rutherfoord Goodwin (1869–1939) became rector in 1903. Born in Richmond and the son of a Confederate officer, Goodwin entered the Episcopal priesthood in 1894 and served at St. John's Church in Petersburg. He came to Williamsburg on the condition that Bruton Parish Church would be restored to its colonial appearances. In May 1903 he persuaded the vestry to accept the project, but only slowly did he marshall the necessary resources. In November 1904 he proposed that the APVA undertake the restoration of the colonial governor's pew. The local branch promptly and unanimously voted to postpone work on the magazine and focus on the pew "as a more interesting historical work." Apparently the ladies felt more comfortable with velvet cloth and church work than with mortar and muskets. During the next three years the local branch spent 75 percent of its funds on the pew—over $1,000 on the restoration and $1,000 for an endowment. Again mixing Revolutionary and royalist traditions, the director described the pew with its "beautiful dark mahogany, rich furnishing and crimson velvet canopy, with letters of gold, as in days of yore when occupied by the illustrious men who made our past glorious." She hoped "that coming generations might be inspired by these noble heroes of the past."[38]

Despite the opposition of some parishioners, Goodwin undertook the restoration of the church in 1905. He inaugurated it on 14 May with a sermon by Rev. Beverly Dandridge Tucker. An adviser to the Norfolk branch, Tucker had married Anna Maria Washington, who had been born at Mount Vernon and descended from the president's brother. His address began disastrously. The organ broke down, a thunderstorm darkened the church interior, and a cat-and-dog fight somehow erupted in the basement below. Tucker meanwhile rejoiced that there had been during recent years "a growing reverence for the past . . . and a recognition of the link that binds one generation to another." Like Valentine, Bryan, and fellow traditionalists, Tucker believed that the French Revolution had broken that link in its attempt "to uproot everything which men held sacred, [and] to break with the past. It was a generation which asserted its independence of all that had gone before, which discarded institutions that had been years in erecting, and which aspired to start the work afresh." Tucker urged his generation to accept both tradition and progress.[39]

Goodwin supervised the restoration from 1905 to 1907. His finance committee included Bryan, Page, and neurologist S. Weir Mitchell. Goodwin estimated that the restoration cost $27,000, of which about $14,000 came from Virginians, including $6,000 from Williamsburg. The donors included King Edward VII of Great Britain, Theodore Roosevelt, Andrew Carnegie, and the C&O Railroad. Although Munford thought that architect J. Stewart Barney "did a splendid piece of work," historians have called the restoration inaccurate, but a milestone nonetheless. Bruton Parish Church was reconsecrated during the 1907 tercentennial celebrations. Goodwin accented the history of the church and town when he spoke before an audience which included J. P. Morgan, another donor, and leaders of the APVA. Like other tradition-minded Virginians, Goodwin declared that history could secure their future. As in the days of ancient Israel, "the key that unlocked the years unborn was oftime the memory of the history of the years that had been." Along with the APVA, he worked to wrest Virginia's history from hostile northern interpreters and to fashion a more favorable version.[40]

Goodwin's interpretation of Williamsburg's material culture offers even more insight into the gospel of these preservationists. In 1907 he admitted that he wanted to preserve the "spirit of the past" in Williamsburg. Infatuated with the town's history and entrapped by its myths, he made the case for traditionalism as a counterbalance to modernity. "The spirit of the days of long ago haunts and hallows the ancient city and the homes of its honored dead," he claimed, "a spirit that stirs the memory and fires the imagination; a spirit that will, we trust, illumine the judgment of those who have entered upon this rich inheritance of the past and lead them to guard these ancient landmarks and resist the spirit of ruthless innovation which threatens to rob the city of its unique distinction and its charms." He believed that Williamsburg's buildings, books, and memorials held "priceless value." Setting the policy for the later Rockefeller-funded restoration, he declared that "no cost should be spared to preserve them." Like many of his day, he personified a building such as Bruton Parish Church to represent earlier Virginians. "It must remain to tell its story of the days that are gone to days that may yet be." The church, he believed, was "typical of the strong and simple architectural designs of the colonial period," and it symbolized those "Nation Builders."[41] His focus on historical symbols, as well as his determination to buttress a sagging traditionalism, typified the work of the APVA in this first restoration of the colonial capital.

5

"Our Inspiration and Our Goal": Jamestown as Mecca

THE CENTRAL CONCERN of the APVA throughout these years was the preservation of Jamestown. "From the first moment of our legal existence," Belle Bryan said, "the hopes and plans, labors and responsibilities of the Association might be well summed up in one word, and that word *Jamestown*. This sacred charge has at once been our inspiration and our goal . . . and our constant endeavor is to keep it and its pathetic history before our people."[1] As England's first permanent settlement in the New World, Jamestown was holy ground to Virginians for its associations with the Anglo-Saxon race, Protestant religion, and representative government.

Ever since John Smith's company of adventurers landed there in May 1607, its topography and environment had created endless problems. Its poor soil, brackish water, and malarial swamplands drove the English out. They moved the capital to Williamsburg in 1699, and Jamestown fell into ruins. What had once been a peninsula slowly became an island. Reeded swamps covered most of its fifteen hundred acres. The small two-mile-long island on the James River attracted little notice, except sporadically for its ruins.

Virginians did celebrate Jamestown's bicentennial in 1807. The editor of the *Virginia Apollo,* like the APVA a century later, called this celebration a counterweight to New England's commemoration of Plymouth. Lamenting that the Old Dominion had apparently forgotten its past, he noted that Yankees proudly honored their forefathers. "The sagacity of that intelligent people," he wrote, "would not permit them to omit an occasion calculated to produce such effects upon the minds and principles of their patriotism, and accordingly the era of their debarkation at Plymouth is celebrated by annual festivals." Virginia's fair included thirty-two vessels anchored off the island, and a carnival setting in which the town of Williamsburg and its college figured prominently.[2]

Visitors came to the island through the nineteenth century but found only a graveyard, remnants of a ruined brick church (a portion of its tower and walls), and a brick magazine. As Edward Everett campaigned to preserve Mount Vernon and make it a shrine to the Union in 1859, he described Jamestown's ruined church as the spot "where the first germs of the mighty republic, now almost co-extensive with the continent, were planted in 1607." Those ruins crumbled even more during and after the Civil War.[3]

In 1879 a New Yorker purchased the island at an auction for $9,000, hoping to reclaim its arable land. While the plow turned up the scattered foundations of Virginia's first capital, the magazine was used as a barn. "Rank weeds choke the yard and cover the tombs," said one visitor to the church. "Vines clamber up the walls of the shattered tower, while the passing gusts occasionally toss down the loosened bricks. The tombstones are all badly broken and chipped, and the inscriptions scarcely legible. . . .'Tis sad to see these relics of by-gone Virginia thus crumbling away beneath the wheel of time, and it is irritating to witness the callous indifference to their neglected condition, but 'tis shocking to see their decay hastened by the depredations of that modern vandal, the Relic Hunter."[4]

After the APVA organized but failed to attract many members, Galt tried to spur activity in Norfolk by focusing on the Old Dominion's first capital. Coleman's established power in Williamsburg and ties to Richmond effectively cut Galt off from preservation work in Virginia's second capital. In June 1889 Galt, therefore, asked the central committee in Richmond to give her branch permission "to undertake the care of the ruins at Jamestown," for the Norfolk members "had no object of antiquarian interest in their midst." She admitted privately to Bagby: "Besides if the Jamestown ruins are put under our care officially Mrs. Coleman cannot in any way interfere. You will understand that my work ought to be separate entirely from hers so that she may not again attack me."[5]

After Richmond gave her the near-impossible task, Galt took an engineer to Jamestown to determine the cost of a breakwater. She also inquired from the island's owner an asking price, but it was "so astonish[ing]ly high," Annie Galt reported, "that we felt helpless." Rather than concede defeat, Mary Galt devised an initial strategy whereby the Episcopal church might regain the title to its building. She wrote letters asking help to implement this plan. Acknowledging her own church membership and the fact that her mother, Mary Ware Galt, had "descended from one of the projectors of the Virginia Company," she knew that once the church regained possession, it would "put the ruins in our care."[6]

Concurrent with this plan, Galt worked to buy the entire island for the APVA. She thought that she could buy it for less than $25,000 but knew that only two women on the executive committee—Bryan and Bagby—were "truly interested." As a result, she decided "that everything must be quiet" and that "all money will have to be raised independent[ly] of the Ex[ecutive] Comm[ittee]." She wrote Henry, chairman of the advisory board, and made her case for the acquisition of the island. He replied, however, "that the price asked is extraordinary," and he would not "advise an effort to raise the funds for the purchase." She then spoke before the APVA's annual meeting in January 1890, describing her hopes to raise $5,000 simply to buy the church ruins. She raised the idea of challenging the owner's title and in the ensuing months followed that tack by writing the church's lawyer and historian, as well as the clerk of courts and descendants of early Jamestown families. Both Galts searched for "documents that would prove that the title of the owner of Jamestown to the ruins in *not a good title*." If those documents could not be found, they could still gain a bargaining position by calling on the owners "to prove their title." Preservationists feared all the while that Jamestown might be sold to a speculator who would bring in a colony of foreign farmers and establish a town, as later happened at Norge, about ten miles to the north. The APVA blew hot and cold about purchasing a plot—more than fifty acres for $3,500—offered by the owner.[7]

Galt's strategy came to fruition on 1 March 1892 when the APVA persuaded the General Assembly to convey to it whatever rights the state held on Jamestown Island. Under the assumption that the crown's control of ecclesiastical properties had reverted to the commonwealth, Joseph Bryan and Henry drafted a bill that not only ceded the land but empowered the APVA to exercise "the power to condemn lands" as "an internal improvement company."[8]

At the same time the APVA revised its own charter. In 1889 the founders had drafted an organizational scheme whereby the members purchased stock and collectively owned the properties. In February 1892, expecting to acquire the large tract at Jamestown, Bryan and Wyndham Meredith helped draft a new charter of incorporation which would enable the APVA to hold its land "free of all taxes, either State, County or Municipal." Bryan admitted that the revision was rushed—"We have no time to lose"—and necessary before the association acquired any part of Jamestown. The new charter was quickly approved by the legislature and redefined APVA's role so that it could acquire historic grounds, as well as relics and monuments.[9]

On 30 November 1892 Edward E. Barney, a former Ohio industrialist, purchased Jamestown for $15,000. He denied the right of the state to give the church ruins to the APVA but affirmed his intention to preserve the site and build a seawall. Bryan contacted Barney and began the "strictly business" proceedings of enforcing the General Assembly's legislation. With eminent domain proceedings a distinct probability, Barney donated a 22½ acre plot to the APVA in March 1893. That plot contained not only the church ruins and graveyard but a colonial magazine and a Confederate earthen fort. Galt immediately proposed that her Norfolk branch undertake more extensive work on the site. Thereafter the APVA made Jamestown its principal focus and ordered its branch leaders, specifically Coleman, to affirm the priority of that project.[10]

As it worked to preserve Jamestown, the APVA interpreted the site in terms that partly reflected prevailing historical viewpoints and partly served the politics of traditionalism. The two became inseparable as history was written by gentlemen and gentlewomen in North and South who worried about the dramatic changes in the United States after the Civil War. Historians began to look to the seventeenth century in order to define America in the late nineteenth century. For example, the nation faced an unprecedented foreign immigration beginning in the 1880s, and those newcomers included a great number of Roman Catholics from Slavic and Mediterranean countries. In response, old-time Anglo-Saxon, Protestant Americans wrote history, reclaiming the nation as their own. Similarly, the United States had reunited after a bloody civil war, but North and South alike, led by Massachusetts and Virginia, used history to argue that one side, and not the other, had founded the nation and won its freedom. The implication followed that the founder would have the stronger hand in defining the country.[11]

Not only did issues of region, ethnicity, and religion shape the writing of history; so, too, did matters of class and democracy. Late nineteenth-century battles between elite and popular classes over the distribution of wealth and power permeated the writing of history. The interpretation of Jamestown's development had much to say, therefore, about such questions as, Who would lead the government, shape the economy, and define the future? As tradition-minded Virginians understood their history, Jamestown's past answered those questions to their liking.[12]

Reflecting the shared belief of genteel historians and conservative politicians, Virginia preservationists particularly used Jamestown as a tool to teach traditionalism. Their teachings reiterated the prevailing idea of Manifest Destiny, a staple not only in school primers but in the patriotic oratory of the day. No better sanction could be offered for their perspective than to attribute it to divine providence. Page exclaimed that "God had set His stamp" at colonial Jamestown. The conquest of Spain in North America by Protestant England had been the work of the divine hand, he said, because Catholicism had created "a bigoted and mind-cramping ecclesiasticism" in Spain. As a result, not only had early Virginians acted as God's "instruments to accomplish His mighty work," but the implication followed that the nation should guard its gates against the Catholic menace.[13]

The APVA equally stressed that the United States had been founded by Anglo-Saxons to advance civilization. In the late nineteenth century Populists and workers often voiced a strident Anglophobia, but genteel Americans commonly sounded their admiration for Great Britain. Schoolbooks and popular history tracts likewise glorified Britain, enhancing the prestige of WASP Americans. Infected by Anglo-Saxon racism, historians generally looked askance at the new immigrants and supported the idea of black inferiority. Jamestown acted as a keystone in this American structure of Anglo-Saxonism, as it held "National and Racial, not sectional," significance. "The good Providence of God" allowed Jamestown's settlement in 1607, the association's president declared, and "America was rescued from the grasp of Spain and France, and reserved to become the home of the Anglo Saxon Race."[14] When southern and eastern Europeans flooded America's ports at the height of the New Immigration in 1907, Page claimed in a keynote address at the tercentennial celebration that because of Jamestown "this Country belongs to the English Speaking Race, and the Civilization which it represents." The currents of the James River had eroded much of the island settled by John Smith's band, but he imagined a positive sign whereby the river "has borne that dust to all shores, and thus the work they performed has been borne on the tide of time to leaven and advance all the institutions of mankind." Other Anglo-Saxon shrines had been effaced by time and progress, but Pryor promised that this milestone in the "onward march of the great Anglo-Saxon race . . . will ever be 'remembered.'"[15]

Jamestown became a chess piece in two simultaneous games waged by the Old Dominion's elite, one against gentlemen Yankee historians and the other against earthly popular-class Virginians. In the first case the leaders challenged New Englanders in a genteel contest over the question, which state had priority in the nation? The prize was not simply historical fame but political weight in deliberations on states' rights, centralized federal authority, and restrictions on mass democracy—some of the very same issues over which the Civil War had been fought. In schoolbooks New England was shown as the nation's birthplace. Whether basing this claim on the Mayflower Compact or the Pilgrim Fathers, Yankees had so successfully popularized it, and negated the counterclaim of Virginia, that, according to APVA adviser John Stewart Bryan, "the descendants of the Pilgrim Fathers, by histories and by hymns, had 'Stopped the mouth of Chesapeake Bay with Plymouth Rock.'" Virginians had long preached a "sermon [that] stresses the importance, from the viewpoint of history and truth, of not permitting New England to spread abroad any longer the false doctrine of its priority—without sharp contradiction and convincing proof of its falsity from Virginia." Even when Virginia-born President Woodrow Wilson traveled to England in 1918, the welcoming contingent rehashed the glories of the Pilgrims. In frustration, Ellyson asked, "When will Virginia get on the map in Europe?" [16]

Virginians prized Jamestown as a document that proved the Old Dominion's priority. Tyler told an assembly there in 1895 that "its first log cabin is of more consequence to the Union at large than the proud mansion of the chief executive." The APVA considered Jamestown "our modern Pompeii" and declared in its own version of 100-percent Americanism that "every detail of the life of that colony is of concern to all true Americans." The proof of Anglo-Saxon precedence in Virginia was not necessarily in the Jamestown pudding, however. Ellyson expressed disbelief when she heard that Spanish Jesuits had sailed up the Chesapeake (and into the York River) and established a mission prior to the English. "I was surprised," she told Tyler, "for I had supposed that when the May 13th 1607 Adventurers landed & named the Panunsuler Jamestown, had never known any other settlers." [17] The APVA did not memorialize the Spanish arrival.

APVA speakers often compared Jamestown with New England's first permanent settlement. Repeatedly the APVA exaggerated New Englanders' respect for their landmarks, trying to goad Virginians to do more. "How piously, how reverently, they tread on Plymouth rock!" Hall exclaimed. "To them that rock is literally the corner-stone of New England, and they would fain make it the corner-stone of American civilization." A precious part of Jamestown had washed away, but the island still offered quite a contrast with the "uncertainty and vagueness [that] hang around Plymouth Rock." Questioning that rock's authenticity, he declared that no Pilgrim had ever touched it. [18]

Not only did the APVA resist the claims of New England, but those of the West as well. A few years after the APVA's establishment, historian Frederick Jackson Turner suggested that the American character and liberties stemmed not from the *Susan Constant* and Jamestown, or for that matter from the *Mayflower* and Plymouth, but from the frontier and forest. Virginia traditionalists rejoined that their state had been first in government, education, religion, and other keystones of Americanism. Tyler went his customary extra mile to establish its leadership. "The rightful name of the republic," he pronounced, was not the United States of America but "the historic name (first given by the greatest of English queens and accepted by the Pilgrim Fathers in the 'May Flower' Compact) *Virginia.*"[19]

These Virginians wanted Jamestown recognized as the birthplace of representative government in the United States. Ironically, at the same time in the 1890s and early 1900s, elite Virginians were campaigning to disfranchise a large percentage of the electorate precisely to make the government less representative. Tradition-minded Virginians saw daily the equalitarianism of the Underwood Constitution and opted instead for the aristocracy of medieval Anglo-Saxons to define their notion of representative government. Professor John Lesslie Hall (1856–1928) frequently spoke at Jamestown and linked it with medieval times. Born in Richmond, Hall developed a keen interest in early English history and literature, earned a Ph.D. from the Johns Hopkins University, and taught those fields at the College of William and Mary for thirty years. He evoked medieval England when he compared Jamestown's Great Charter of 1618 and the assembly of 1619 with the Magna Charta at Runnymede. "Patriot, put off thy shoes," he told pilgrims in 1891; "this is holy ground." The Declaration of Independence and Revolutionary War, he claimed, "fade into insignificance" when compared with the provisions passed by the first assembly. Elizabeth Henry Lyons also professed that "the ruins of that old church should become the mecca of all true worshippers of free government."[20]

The APVA publicized the history of this first representative assembly. Virginians took offense when northerners overlooked Jamestown's 1619 assembly. For example, the APVA protested to New York governor John Alden Dix when he unveiled a tablet in 1911 in memory of Father Thomas Dougan, "Father of the First Representative Assembly." As late as 1914, Bruce complained that even Virginians had forgotten Jamestown's importance. "That site exists today," he wrote the Richmond *News-Leader,* "without a single stone to show to the world that we are not so sunk in intellectual barbarism, commercial greed, and patriotic indifference as to have forgotten one of the very greatest events of our past." The APVA then encouraged the Old Dominion to hold a tercentennial celebration of its first assembly in 1919. In what can only be considered a bizarre juxtaposition, while the APVA praised the nation's unceasing commitment to "the cause of civil liberty," the hysteria of the Red Scare led to the mass repression of labor unionists and anarchists in 1919–20. The tercentennial to honor individual freedoms incongruously became the "birthday of law and order" in the United States.[21]

Contrary to Bruce's complaint, the APVA had dedicated a memorial in 1907 to honor the first House of Burgesses. Its tablet, together with an obelisk erected by the United States government, recognized Virginia as the initiator of representative government in the New World. Built by the Norfolk branch, the memorial revealed the limits of its sponsor's work. While old Norfolk fell before a building boom set off by the Jamestown Exposition, its preservationists admitted that "in completing this monument . . . the Branch feels it has reached a climax in its history and a sort of 'Nunc Dimittis' spirit has now settled down upon it."[22]

Preservationists used Jamestown not only to dispute the claims of genteel Yankees but to challenge local insurgents. They made it a "shrine of patriotism" to help reeducate youth raised during the tumult of Reconstruction and Readjusterism and to inspire them through its "lessons of loyalty." Just two years after the defeat of Mahone, Hall spoke before a throng of Jamestown pilgrims and used history to lay claim to the future. He worried about both the return of the Readjusters and the rise of populism in the South. The popular orator evoked the spirits of John Smith, Thomas Dale, and Alexander Spotswood to fight such popular-class movements. He told the youth in his audience that Jamestown offered valuable lessons: "As you stand on the graves of former generations, and listen to the voices of the past; as your spirit holds converse with the spirits that hover around this consecrated place, learn lessons for the coming years. Let us realize that Virginia needs *living* heroes; that she needs earnest and devoted Smiths to save her from drones and laggards, and from treacherous leaders; that she needs Dales to give her strong and well executed laws, and Spotswoods to develop her wonderful resources, so that the desert and solitary place may blossom as the rose." Reminding the audience of its duty to the Old Dominion, he asked for "help to lift the burdens which have so long oppressed her."[23]

Whether for John Smith or Thomas Dale, Jamestown was remembered for those strong, virile leaders who offered inspiration to the future. During an era when Teddy Roosevelt's cult of martial vigor commanded public attention, Yonge praised the strength, perseverance, and fortitude of that colonial elite. In a much-acclaimed study of Jamestown, he conjectured that they did not succumb during the colony's direst days because they were "in the prime of manhood and inured to hardship" by their military experience. Such an interpretation pleased many Virginians who descended from those FFVs, but a more likely reason for their survival, one to which a parallel could be drawn for the Gilded Age, was that they hoarded basic foodstuffs, extracted backbreaking labor from the multitude, and left the poor and weak to die.[24]

Similarly, Pryor praised Smith, Dale, and those who redeemed the colony from the anarchists. The popular author contended, and the implication about the Readjusters could not be missed, that after Dale asserted authority "it was not long before the disturbances and confusion which had been the natural consequences of disaffection and revolt were succeeded by the happy fruits of peaceful industry and order." Before the restoration of order, martial law had disciplined the masses. Yonge's archeological investigation of the graveyard in 1896 revealed the means used to enforce that regimen when he uncovered "several human skeletons" whose remains suggested "a military execution." Yonge pictured Jamestown's plight and claimed that "the sufferings of the colonists . . . have probably never been surpassed or even equalled in measure or degree in any other pioneer colony." [25]

Preservationists stood on common ground when they saw the necessity for strong, elite rule by propertied whites, but they sometimes glimpsed contradictory visions of Jamestown's links to modern progress. Obsessed by Virginia's claim to priority and determined to boost development, Tyler claimed that the freedom, enlightenment, and progress that Americans prized in the modern age all began at Jamestown. He boasted in *Virginia First* (1921), a classic in state chauvinism, that Jamestown was the "Cradle of the Union" for having the first of everything that mattered—"the first church, . . . the first State House, and the first free school." He pushed New England aside, telling Yankees that the South had even pioneered in the nation's business sector because Jamestown had "the first wharf, the first glass factory, the first windmill, [and] the first iron works." Even the staid *Virginia Magazine of History and Biography* declared that Jamestown had begun "a commercial development which would change the appearance of the globe." [26]

Typical of modern-minded Americans, Yonge defined progress as an increase in material goods, scientific knowledge, and individual freedom. Looking back on 1607, the engineer was struck by "the contrast between then and now, in the mode of living, in the knowledge of the sciences and the liberal arts, and in the supersedure of intolerance and blind superstition by freedom of conscience and enlightenment!" This lofty prose ignored the actual scene in fin-de-siècle America. At the time, 1 percent of the nation's population commanded more wealth than the remaining 99 percent. Most Americans lived without property or access to the knowledge he extolled. Whether the case was tested by freedmen, Populists, or suffragists, his prized political freedoms withered on a vine pruned by political bosses, corporate barons, and elite reformers. Like the gold of the Gilded Age, Progress was tawdry, uneven, and tarnished.[27]

Hall glimpsed some of the underside of Progress. Although he regularly called for boosting Virginia's depressed economy, he saw at Jamestown much of what disillusioned moderns found appealing in the preindustrial order. The island's remoteness, natural environment, and spiritual peace particularly appealed to this dyed-in-the-wool Victorian romantic. His blend of historic preservation accordingly revealed a sweet mix of the eighth century's Anglo-Saxon mythology and the nineteenth century's romantic revival. "The very stillness of the spot makes our object-lesson more impressive," he confided to pilgrims in 1895. Had Jamestown, like historic Boston, given way to skyscrapers, sweatshops, and macadam streets, it would have compromised the island's symbolism. "If the songs of birds were drowned in the roar of trade," he thought, "we should find it difficult to *realize the day*." As a contrast with modern, urban America, Jamestown would become "a Mecca of the soul." In a nation making the traumatic shift from farm to city, he thought that it was "good for us to leave the busy haunts of men; . . . to forget the hum of the engine and the whistle of the locomotive, and to repair to this quiet temple of nature and this sacred altar of freedom."[28]

Jamestown's rustic, primitive appearance reinforced the antimodernist feelings of those troubled by the fast pace of recent change. Newton predicted one year after the APVA's acquisition of its ruins that these qualities would be foremost in the minds of preservationists. They would do "everything . . . to preserve the atmosphere of quaintness and calm to which belong so much of beauty and enchantment in contrast to the newness and restlessness of to-day." Held hostage by time, the ruins embalmed Virginia's early history but "were fast yielding to the persistent siege of that most certain of destroyers, Time." To the pilgrims of 1891, Hall further lamented that Time gave Jamestown's "most ancient temple to the moles and the bats" and threw "the dust of your early dead to the winds and waters."[29]

Hall hoped that Jamestown's premodern serenity would stir the heartfelt sentiments of Virginians steeled by privation and obsessed by development. When prosperity returned to Virginia, he hoped that her sons and daughters would write more poetry, sing more verse, and preserve more landmarks. The youth who visited Jamestown's ruins would gain inspiration. "So may some young Virginia [Patrick] Henry catch here his first beatific vision, or some Virginia poet, sitting pensively near the graves of his forefathers, sing the great anthem of our race." As it was, however, the Old Dominion was caught in a pragmatic, almost single-minded race for wealth. The preservation of history, some claimed, obstructed that growth. "The utilitarian spirit of the age may hinder us in our efforts," Hall admitted in 1895. "Many may ask, why not expend this time and money in building railroads? For such, we have no argument. . . . These scoffers are aesthetically dead. They can no more understand our feelings than can the unregenerate man comprehend the things of the spirit."[30]

The romanticism of the late nineteenth century blended with the myths and legends associated with Jamestown, Williamsburg, and old Virginia. Perhaps nowhere was this sentimentalism stronger than in the South; it affected southern notions of home, women, and honor. In the nation as a whole during the Gilded Age, it revealed a pervasive dissatisfaction with not only the traumatic changes wrought by industrial capitalism but the emergence of a new genre of scientific realism. Revealing his skepticism about modernity, Hall told an audience of pilgrims at Jamestown in 1895 to forget their crowded cities, smokestack industries, bank failures, and hurlyburly life. Instead they should imagine the olden time's aura. "The witchery of the day is on us," he said. "We are led captive in the gentle bonds of imagination. . . . Let us drink deep of the pleasures of imagination. Let us revel in the realms of fancy. Let us forget the cares, the burdens, and the ills of life, and spend these hours with the muses." While the North gradually abandoned this literary romanticism as the century ended, the South immersed itself even more in the sentimental and nostalgic.[31]

This sentimentalism permeated the APVA's reading of history. Mary Newton Stanard, for example, considered Jamestown to be the birthplace of the Virginia family and called the island in 1607 "a new Eden." The popular historian thought that the colonists had been looking for "a safe spot to which to bring an English maiden who would transform the cabin or the cottage into a home about which the new Adam and Eve would plant a garden." As popular historians and preservationists so commonly did, she transposed her own modern values, in this case domesticity, into the colonial era. That safe spot, she continued, would be where "the wife could

be left with her babies and housewifery while the husband went forth to till
the fields or to fish and hunt in river and forest for food." In contrast to her
romantic rendition, Jamestown was anything but an Eden. Even Coleman
admitted that incidents of human cannibalism had occurred. Women, as
well as men, faced the toil, starvation, disease, and Indian attacks. These
first maidens in Virginia, moreover, were hardly the "Eves" that the APVA
pictured in its float, "The Coming of the Maids to Jamestown," in a 1922
Richmond pageant. Many of the women had been sold off the boat as
indentured servants to please a man's fancy.[32]

Stanard further contended that the banquet that Jamestown's settlers
held for Chief Powhatan "sealed the first American League of Nations."
Pryor thought that the Jamestowners' choice of a leader in 1607 represented
"the first presidential election in the United States of America." Coleman
took their competition with New England to heart when she declared that
Jamestown in 1623 passed "the first authorized act for the annual observance
of a day of Thanksgiving," and therefore, "this time honored custom had
its origin at Jamestown."[33] Tyler discovered that the celebration first occurred in 1619 at Berkeley Hundred. When Jamestown later celebrated the
350th anniversary of its settlement, an organization called Virginia Thanksgiving Festival, Inc. made the Berkeley Hundred commemoration a regular
affair. Jamestown, to be sure, had other firsts that the APVA chose to ignore,
including the first African slaves brought into the English colonies. Preservationists refused to memorialize the degradation associated with that 1619
event, but a Richmond newspaper crudely admitted that "politics and nig-
gers" had "their beginnings in this country contemporaneously."[34]

The romanticism about Jamestown had a limited effect on those northerners who dominated historical publishing and scholarship. According to
some of their tracts, colonial Virginia sprang from economic adventurers
who cared little about the great gulf between rich and poor. Yankee historians had depicted Virginia's leaders and their descendants, Goodwin said in
a Williamsburg sermon, "as a gay and careless set of wild adventurers whose
minds were set upon material gain, and whose hearts were pleasure bent."
Those histories, Hall further complained to the General Assembly, "represent the settlers of New England as all holy elders looking for a prayer-
meeting, and the colonists of Virginia as fox-hunting squires, ready for a
julep. The phrase, 'Pilgrim Fathers,' with its magic ring, its psychological
fascination, has become standard; while we have tamely accepted for our
fathers the colorless phrase, 'Virginia colonists.' This gives New England a

great advantage," he warned. "'A good name is better than great riches' is true in more senses than one." [35]

Preservationists further argued that the leaders of colonial Virginia and their families had not descended from convicts, felons, and harlots. Elizabeth Lyons heard that women from the Society of Mayflower Descendants thought that "Virginia was settled originally only by jailbirds" and its women "were sent over to them [and sold] for tobacco." Only later did some "good blood" come over, "but [there were] not many who left descendants as they could not stand the climate." Outraged by these claims, Stanard rebutted that "not a single instance of a Virginia family descended from a convict has ever been found by any genealogist." [36]

Apparently the rare iconoclast, Bagby conceded, but only in an unpublished manuscript, that Gloucester County had been inhabited partly by English convicts. These "jailbirds" eventually were "incorporated into the body politic." She joked that "no one has ever met with one of their descendants, but sometimes the suspicion is irresistible that Mrs. A. or Mr. B. is closer akin to 'Captain Jack' [a convict] than to the English gentleman, whose coat of arms they claim and prize so highly." More commonly, genealogists pursued their studies to boost their pride and enhance their power. Hall spoke before an APVA pilgrimage at Jamestown and advised preservationists to "encourage those who are writing the true history of Virginia, and weed out of your libraries those nauseous volumes filled with lying abominations which, under the name of history, are teaching the youth of Virginia that they are sprung from convicts and felons rather than from the flower of the Anglo-Saxon race." [37]

Preservationists did differ on the question, Who established the Old Dominion's greatness: the aristocratic Cavaliers or the lower gentry and middle class? The legend of the Cavalier migration found fewer adherents after the Civil War. Speaking before an APVA assembly, Richard S. Thomas of the advisory board defended that tradition and argued that the nobles, although a minority among the era's immigrants, had established the colony and defeated the Indians. These Cavaliers, much like their later descendants, had been maligned by Yankees who ignored "the earnest, the resolute, the serious, and the daring" side of their characters and instead denounced their supposedly frivolous society and ostentatious living. As a result, it has been "customary to laugh at the number of gentlemen in each boat load and to ask sneeringly, what could they do towards felling the forest and civilizing the wilderness?" [38]

Mainstream historians concurrently questioned the Cavalier legend. John Fiske popularized the view in the 1890s that the middle classes had made both New England and Virginia and were devoted to the economic and political traditions of their fathers. Thomas J. Wertenbaker's *Patrician and Plebeian* (1910) further undermined the Cavalier legend, as did novelist Ellen Glasgow in *The Battleground* (1902). William E. Dodd, a historian of the Old South and editor of Woodrow Wilson's papers, joined the fray in the 1920s. As the Democratic party appealed to the plain folk of the South, Dodd advanced the premise that Jefferson's democracy of small farmers had been subverted by increasingly powerful slaveholding aristocrats.[39]

In this context, some Virginia preservationists took a second look at their history and posited that the lower gentry, small planters, and middle class had been the backbone of society. Bagby corrected the impression that a large number of Cavaliers came to Virginia, for example. She wrote that their "numbers and influence had been magnified and [they] are not to be considered as scarcely an element in the colonization of the Old Dominion." Stanard also rejected the picture of a polarized society and "emphatically asserted" in her *Colonial Virginia* (1917)—a book that the APVA highly recommended—"that neither during the colonial nor the state period was the population of Virginia made up mainly of large land owners and 'poor whites.' The great majority of our people have always been the respectable, independent middle class." Not one to slight his good blood, Page still accented the influence of aristocrats. He admitted that "half-strainers" (middle-class whites) had lived in his native Hanover County, but "they had the vices and virtues of a middle class the world over; they were arrogant to their inferiors, obsequious or rude to their superiors, brave, ignorant, narrow, honest and mean."[40]

Colonial Virginia lacked a structured capitalist economy, however, and the term *middle class* is problematic. Actually these Virginians wanted to picture their ancestors much like themselves. Stanard, a middle-class writer who personalized Virginia's history, saw them in her own likeness; Page, on the other hand, relished his aristocratic status and consequently stressed the high standing of his forebears. The only agreement between Stanard and Page was that they regarded their ancestors as propertied, respectable, and public-minded. The Stanard interpretation superseded that of Page, indicating that the more modern view of America as a middle-class nation was gaining influence in shaping the interpretation of the colonial past.

Preservationists evidently wanted role models on which to build their lives. What resulted was not only hero worship but mythical history. Essayist

James Branch Cabell understood their sentiments and watched how they wrapped their myths around preserved buildings. As a college student in Williamsburg in the late 1890s, he boarded with Coleman and saw the APVA's work firsthand. Years later, he relied on his tongue-in-cheek humor to describe why hero worship prevailed and remained unchallenged:

> To investigate the noble epic of Virginia's settlement in the bleak light of common-sense, or of mere probability, is, not only for the Virginian, but for every correct-thinking American, to repeat the sin of Ham. It is not wise for us to uncover the nakedness of our forefathers. We have no need to know the exact physical truth about them, but we do have an exceedingly strong need of those high ideals which, even if they did not pursue or even hear about any such ideals, they have bequeathed to us through our Virginian version of Virginia's history. To impugn this version is to rob ourselves of our own legacy and, like less long-headed Esaus, to lose our birthright without getting so much as a mess of pottage in exchange.

Every society needs heroes, but after the Old Dominion's trials, traditionalists needed them even more. Models suitable for emulation would hardly be lifelike, however, and the APVA inherited from the planters a defensiveness toward outside critics.[41]

The southern mind, according to historian George Brown Tindall, seemed "unusually susceptible to mythology." Southerners resisted pure abstraction, and the *mentalité* of the South, as a result, included a more complex and powerful mythology than that of other regions. Of course, every nation and people inherit myths and use them as lenses to see the present, but postbellum, tradition-minded southerners apparently relied on myths much more. They used them to unify society and identify its goals and values. Consequently myths made the lives of individuals meaningful, particularly those beset by change. Accepted myths became reality and the test of truth.[42]

Romanticized history, popular myth, and pleasing traditions became important tools to restore the pride and reputation of the Old Dominion. The APVA did not originate this process, but it did create symbolic expressions for these interpretations through its preserved buildings, memorialized sites, and historic shrines. It found a most willing and eager audience as well. The defeat of 1865 and the subsequent upheavals in the South, especially when contrasted with the booming confidence of northern society, led traditionalists to seek a history which would provide comfort and reassurance. Cabell illustrated this while contrasting the methods that Virginians and professional historians used to write history. He said, "How very differently do we shape our history in Virginia, where we accept such facts as we find desirable and dismiss those which are not to our purpose! We have thus enriched the field of American folklore with that stirring epic which is the history of Virginia." Wilbur Cash thus concluded that history became nothing more than "a form of folk-boasting" in the South as a whole. The mythical past became the glue to repair the fractured identity of traditionalists. It functioned much as a religion by sanctioning a moral code, establishing social roots, and unifying experience according to the contours of the myth.[43] The effectiveness of any myth, however, depends upon its popularity. The APVA and fellow traditionalists labored, therefore, to popularize their reading of Virginia's past.

Jamestown served as a powerful symbol for much of that mythology, whether it involved Manifest Destiny, Anglo-Saxonism, the First Families of Virginia, or hero worship. After acquiring its plot in 1893, the APVA held regular pilgrimages there. The rituals which it established became emblematic of the association's work. Patriotic groups had traveled to Jamestown earlier in the nineteenth century, but the APVA revised the practice. During the first pilgrimage to commemorate the founding, held in 1807, Virginians tried but failed to find Jamestown's "oldest stone"—their own Plymouth Rock. Fifteen years later, some two thousand visitors came from as far away as Baltimore. Later Victorians objected, however, to this group's lack of decorum; in 1822 "the scene was enlivened by music and dancing, while it was disgraced by the faro table and wheel of fortune." Another organization, the Jamestown Society of Washington, D.C., was formed in 1854 specifically to commemorate the founding. With a tinge of state chauvinism, Hall regretted, however, that "the society was founded and officered by men not residents of Virginia." Their celebration at Jamestown in 1857—their first and only one—brought former president John Tyler to present an oration. Shortly after the reopening of the College of William and Mary, his son and Hall reinstituted the yearly pilgrimages, at first under the auspices of the college, then jointly with the APVA.[44]

These public ceremonies served to renew traditionalism, to observe Protestantism, and to commemorate the civil religion. The APVA claimed, for example, that its pilgrimages to Jamestown's church, graveyard, and historic grounds "germinate ideas which might otherwise be dormant." Incorporating historical addresses and recitations, costumed characters and pageantry, and the decoration of buildings and sites, these rites fulfilled the APVA's mission of uniting past and present to foster traditionalism. They reproduced the ambiance of a distant era, heightened personal commitments, and renewed a sense of historical continuity. These rituals should not be discounted. In a remarkable way they combined emotion and intellect through the use of symbols and ceremony to shape subsequent experience. In a 1907 ceremony at Jamestown, for example, six hundred Colonial Dames arrived to transfer control of the newly built Memorial Church to the APVA. The Richmond Light Infantry Blues, long epitomizing order and patriotism, headed the procession before a white-robed choir singing the "Jamestown Hymn." Page delivered his customary, and typically florid, address, and the patriotic ceremony closed with another procession through the church and graveyard. "It had a quaint effect as of an Old World pilgrimage," reported the Dames.[45]

The most important ritual held by the APVA was its annual pilgrimage to Jamestown. Held on (or about) 13 May, it celebrated the founding of Virginia. This pilgrimage best illustrated the APVA's sense of traditionalism and civil religion. Hall instigated the regular celebrations in 1895. That year's pilgrimage brought about four thousand people to the island. Seven hundred of "the best people of Richmond" sailed to Jamestown on the steamer *Pocahontas,* while the small town of Williamsburg sent nearly one thousand. Belle Bryan demonstrated the APVA's official sanction by bringing along the wives of past and present governors. Her husband's newspaper set the context for the celebration in an editorial. Rejecting the claims associated with Plymouth Rock, the Richmond *Times* asked readers to preserve the memory of Virginia as the pioneer colony. Bryan urged Virginians to "neither neglect it nor permit it to be supplanted by any pretensions for other States or places." The 13 May program thoroughly accented that theme. The APVA first planted four willow trees, symbols not only of man's vitality but of his rebirth at Jamestown. Preservationists then listened to stirring orations by Hall and Tyler. Belle Bryan assessed the day's events and pledged "annually to visit Jamestown, and thus impress upon the minds of our youth the pathetic story of Virginia in her infancy."[46]

The APVA thereafter did its best to make the pilgrimage its identifying mark and the day a state holiday. By so doing, the association invented a tradition through its monuments, pilgrimages, and commemoration of Virginia Day. Its widespread promotion of Jamestown, colorful pageantry, and reinterpretation of the colonial settlement put Jamestown on the map as the birthplace of the republic. Tens of thousands came yearly to the island to commemorate the Anglo-Saxon's advent in Virginia. Soon 13 May stood higher in the esteem of tradition-minded Virginians than the Fourth of

July. Independence Day had once been "celebrated with great fervor and enthusiasm," Curry admitted, but it fell into "desuetude" with the Civil War. Confederate defeat ushered in new holidays. When blacks celebrated their freedom on 1 January, whites turned to Virginia Day, Confederate Memorial Day, and Lee's birthday, until they had reappropriated the Fourth of July by the 1920s.[47]

With but a few exceptions, the APVA made a pilgrimage to Jamestown each year. William G. Stanard, secretary of the Virginia Historical Society, acted as interpreter and later published a booklet for the pilgrims, *Notes of a Journey on the James Together with a Guide to Old Jamestown.* Accustomed to the bustle of Progress, however, some pilgrims expressed their lament that the island was left barren and undeveloped. "One cannot help but feel an air of sadness about the place, however, so beautiful and significant a spot," said one in 1909, "and yet so deserted of human habitation, with only the ruins, the tombs and monument."[48]

Most pilgrims immersed themselves in the romantic, vicarious thrills of imagining the trials of early Virginians. As pilgrims sailed on modern ships such as the *Brandon, Berkeley,* or *Pocahontas,* they imagined the sights of Indians, caravels, and muskets. "What cared you," one pilgrim remembered, if "the ice-cream always had the same faint strawberry hue, tasted somewhat of salt, and inevitably was eaten in an odor of smoke and engine oil." Before 1895, but not afterwards, visitors even had a chance to inspect closely the ruins of the church tower. Galt had the caretaker "unfasten the wire net from the ground and we would go in on our hands and knees. This was looked on as a joke and they willingly paid [an extra five cents above the dime admission charge] and behaved well."[49]

Generally pilgrims had to be closely watched, however, to prevent their rummaging through the ruins. The stirring ceremonies sometimes served as cover for the souvenir hunter. Most of the APVA's workers, Galt wrote, "get so much interested in what is going on—the sentimental—or in individuals that they do not notice the theiving." Sometimes the stealing shocked her. When pilgrims left the boat after one visit, she heard that "the lower deck looked [the] same as a brick kiln [with] so many bricks laying around."[50]

Later pilgrims included a wide range of professional groups, including the American Bankers Association, the American Tobacco Association, the Garden Club of America, and the Southern Educational Association. Illustrating the ties between the church and the APVA, the General Convention of the Episcopal church traveled to the island in 1898. Over three hundred bishops and clergy met to commemorate the planting of the gospel in British North America. They placed a stone monument on the site, the first of many on the APVA's small plot.[51] Countless thousands also visited the island during these years. Foreign visitors came and heard the APVA's lore, and they took back to their own lands not only the memory of Jim Crow but the mythical story of early Virginia's love of freedom and its legacy of political rights.

Like many antiquaries at historic house museums, the APVA placed little emphasis on a structured interpretation for these visitors. Preservationists believed that the values and lessons associated with their sites would be automatically imparted to the visitors. The APVA published a guidebook for its river pilgrimages but on the whole provided scant written materials to these visitors. It expected the aura of the site, together with the words of an informed custodian, to convey its significance. The APVA also encouraged excursions by children from academic and Sunday schools. Preservationists felt pleased "that interest in this hallowed place is spreading forth into another generation." It was suggested, however, that school groups be chaperoned and "under the espionage" of adults while at Jamestown. They urged schoolchildren to bring a tree for planting on the island as a living monument. Even the Native American students at Hampton Institute came to Jamestown and held a pageant that took them "back to the days that were real," evidently commemorating a different side of the island's history.[52]

Quite a stir was raised in 1902 when a group of New York women proposed an excursion to Jamestown. Pryor, Mary Hatch Willard (founder of New York City's Home Bureau), and a handful of other elite women planned an Old Dominion Pilgrimage and sent out five hundred invitations to a "limited and exclusive" list who would visit the historic grounds from Norfolk to Richmond. At a time when Theodore Roosevelt praised the strenuous life, these Gotham elites hatched their own romanticized version. They planned to "pitch a tent" at Jamestown and "have a luncheon on the spot where Pocahontas was married to John Rolfe." When the proposal reached the APVA, an acrimonious debate erupted in several meetings. "A vehement protest" was lodged against an incursion by these Yankees, but emotions eventually cooled, and the APVA voted to "pour oil on the troubled waters by forgetting the past" and allowing the visit.[53]

Ultimately the APVA invited all groups to Jamestown except African-Americans. Official guidelines mirrored Jim Crow segregation, stating that "negro excursions or picnic parties are not admitted." Black individuals—

presumably servants accompanying white families—apparently paid the regular admission fee, but groups were barred. In spite of the well-known fact that the first Africans came to Virginia by way of Jamestown, the APVA quite early declared that the sacred site was a shrine for white America. J. M. Gandy, president of Virginia Normal and Industrial Institute in Petersburg, a school established by the Readjusters for blacks, had requested permission from the APVA to place a monument on the island to those first black immigrants. After a discussion at a general meeting in 1916, preservationists denied his request and stated that "Jamestown was the first permanent Colony of the English speaking people in this Country . . . and the incident of bringing the negroes by the Dutch ship to Jamestown forms no such part in the life of the Colony as will justify our granting permission to erect a memorial to that event."[54]

The APVA's blind eye toward those first blacks corresponded with the tack taken by popular writers on the Old South who glossed over the subjugation and dehumanization of African-Americans. Moreover, just as Virginia whites overlooked the fact that their fathers' plantations had depended on this forced labor, so, too, did they try to shift the blame for slavery to New England. Page claimed that slavery "was brought upon the South without its fault, and continued to be forced upon her against her protests." Bryan focused narrowly on the trading of slaves, not their subjugation, and found it "a source of great gratification . . . to know that careful investigation has failed to show that any Virginian was ever engaged in the African slave trade."[55] Some Virginians, notably Page and Fitzhugh Lee, even made the claim, based on local Virginia tradition, that the *Mayflower* became a slave trader after taking the Pilgrims to Plymouth. This assertion was pleasing to Virginia's pride, as were most other attacks on New England, but it illustrated the extremes of regional partisanship and the deep denial fostered by patriarchy and racism.[56]

During these Jim Crow years the APVA ironically employed trusted black custodians, who often acted as interpreters, at Jamestown and Williamsburg. Searching for a good custodian in 1902, Galt preferred a white over a black man, but as she told Bagby, "all I ask . . . is *please* be sure that he is a Protestant." These African-American interpreters immersed themselves in the APVA's rendition of the past and revealed the powers of the hegemonic culture. They were much like John F. Fitzgerald—an Irish immigrant and later Boston's mayor and grandfather to a president—who sympathetically interpreted Boston's history as a young tour guide despite his recognition of Yankee bigotry.[57]

While the APVA brought pilgrims to Jamestown, it stabilized the ruins, investigated archaeological sites, and abated river erosion. During the 1890s Galt most influenced this work and relied on the help of Lucy Parke Chamberlayne Bagby (1842–1927). A descendant of Colonel William Byrd, she married George W. Bagby, the very popular novelist and editor of the *Southern Literary Messenger,* in 1863. She called herself "eternally a Confederate" and served the cause as a clerk and hospital worker. In the 1870s her husband became active in the Funders but lost his position at the State Library when the Readjusters came to power. The Bagbys had ten children, and his death in 1883 left her with a large family. She devoted her time to popularizing her husband's writings and promoting women's philanthropic and historical work. Chair of the APVA's Jamestown committee for twenty years, she was outspoken and persistent, and Coleman feared her like no other.[58]

Bagby described Jamestown Island in 1894 as "a picture of desolation," while Galt saw "a wilderness of poor farm land." At first their project appeared so immense and the advice so complex that Galt did not know where to begin. Unsure of her own abilities but believing in the providential hand, she told Bagby, "I have often a feeling that if we go on trying & doing the best we can God will make it all straight some how." In 1896 she met Howard Constable, a New York engineer and architect who occasionally came to Williamsburg to direct the construction of a home for a millionaire patient at the insane asylum. Galt took Constable to Jamestown, but her no-nonsense disposition turned sour when the architect seemed more interested in flirting with her young companion than inspecting the ruins. He became "very quick and high tempered" after Galt endlessly asked questions about the site. His "dictatorial" manner so tired her and compounded her neurasthenia, she told Bagby, "I went to-day and got my tonic for nervous prostration renewed."[59]

Galt quickly endorsed Constable's advice to avoid "making any hurtful change" at Jamestown. She sympathized with his thinking precisely because of her own training in art. Most concerned about the battered seventeenth-century church tower, Galt "confidentially" wrote Bagby that the central committee knew little about either Jamestown or restoration methods. "The real true patriotic ideas—real artistic ideas," she said, were "to alter as little as possible—to avoid all artificial appearance—all striving after affect— to keep attractiveness subordinate to the main features."[60]

Galt asked the central committee in Richmond to allow Constable to strengthen the tower and remove the vines that were destroying it. The committee approved the scheme, but only after William L. Sheppard warned Constable "not to alter [the] appearance of [the] tower" because "irregular outlines must be preserved." Richmonders knew well how towered ruins should look. When Hollywood Cemetery's entrance had been constructed forty years earlier, it was designed in the romantic style to resemble a Gothic ruin, complete with an uneven jagged wall. Constable accordingly strengthened the tower with iron rods, removed the vines from its top, and cemented the exposed top bricks. In the following years Galt wrote that her work resembled the way "they take care of old buildings in Italy—a little here and there—day after day—'to preserve & not make new.'"[61]

Although Constable and Galt wanted the vines removed to protect the brick, Coleman disagreed. Unlike the trained architect, she personified the ruin and wanted to wrap it in sheltering vines. The prophet Micah had said, "They shall sit every man under his vine . . . and none shall make them afraid" (Micah 4:4), and Coleman wanted Jamestown's relics to be so protected and to speak to the present. It was a privilege to plant "clinging vines around the ruins that seem so human like in their despair so stunned with grief." The ruins stood as a metaphor for the days gone by.[62]

Despite Galt's endless labors, she felt cut out of the Richmond power circles. "I have worked faithfully at Jamestown for 6 or 7 years," she wrote Bagby, "and as far as I know in that time all official position that I had has been taken from me." Bagby defended Galt's interests against the Bryan-Coleman faction to the point that her work on the Jamestown committee destroyed her health and got her "nerves all out of gear." She privately told Galt that her "patience is being exhausted" by the endless haggling in the committee. Both particularly resented William Stanard when he came regularly to Jamestown to represent the central comittee. Galt faced the "danger" of his interference and meddling. In 1902 that frustration finally drove her from Virginia.[63]

The feud between Galt and Coleman reveals much about the APVA during these years. At times it seemed personal and petty, but the era's movement was in great part defined by strong personalities. Surely Ann Pamela Cunningham had set the MVLA on her course, as did William Sumner Appleton with SPNEA. Galt and Coleman each claimed to have conceived the association and, like a good mother, tried to shape its development. Coleman defended her turf in Virginia's Historic Triangle, while Galt apparently took more of a professional interest in these matters. The feud also showed a deep-seated rivalry between the Williamsburg and Norfolk branches, as each wanted credit for establishing the movement in Virginia.

Moreover, the feud developed because leading preservationists in Richmond encouraged it, as they knew it could only add to their power. Galt had founded the APVA, but Belle Bryan and others shut her out and aided Coleman's hand. Not only did Bryan have family ties to Coleman, but Richmond assumed influence by right of geography over Williamsburg. The APVA leadership knew as well that the Norfolk branch most opposed a centralized, Richmond-dominated organization. Galt lost out in the game of power politics because Norfolk and Richmond epitomized two different Virginias. Many in the capital thought that Norfolk emulated too little traditionalism and too much of the New South.

Until exhausted by this feud, Galt supervised the archaeological work at the church which had been erected in 1639 and burned reportedly by Nathaniel Bacon in his 1676 rebellion. All that remained of the church was its tower, built after 1647 and formerly three stories high with a belfry, supported at its base by a three-foot-thick brick wall and foundations. Only in 1895 did the APVA restrict public access to the ruins and graveyard. Searching for remnants of the earliest construction, Galt dug with her own hands "quite deep inside of the South wall of the Church and discovered the inner wall composed of large bricks and cobble stones." She concluded that "this must have been the foundation of the Argall Church, built in 1617, or of the earlier one repaired by Lord de la Ware in which our beloved Pocahontas was married." Yonge and John Tyler, Jr., son of Lyon G. Tyler, helped uncover the walls, which rose from six inches to three feet above the foundations, and covered them with cement.[64]

The ancient graveyard held little visible sign of the once-bustling colony. Elizabeth Lyons reported in 1891 that only a few gravestones remained, and without much proof blamed the Yankees: "Many of them were taken away during the late war by Federal soldiers; others have been destroyed by rude hands and broken into pieces by relic hunters." Even the graves had been robbed, Galt added, and "the holes filled in with anything at hand." Yonge investigated as well the "Country House," which the APVA discovered in 1903. Part of a five-block rowhouse, the Country House stood a short distance from the eroding shore. Rebuilding its cellar walls to ground level to prevent further deterioration, he found numerous artifacts there in 1906, including cannonballs, a bottle seal dated 1710, a hasp, and two knives and forks. The APVA used moneys appropriated by the federal government for the tercentennial to build a "Relic House" for their display. Even then, one visitor was fascinated by the "number of interesting relics" but shocked that they were "so poorly protected"; a fire or "an evilly disposed person" could destroy the collection.⁶⁵ The APVA's archaeological work uncovered the older sections of the "New Town," a fifty-acre development begun during the administration of George Yeardley after 1619. The APVA explored the sites of former statehouses, blockhouses, and fort, but not the 1607 stockade.⁶⁶

At a time when Americans were civilizing the wilderness and establishing well-groomed urban parks, Jamestown's rough-and-tumble look embarrassed many in the APVA. Bryan told her following in 1895 that they must not cease until it was "made to blossom as the rose." It is unlikely, however, if Jamestown ever resembled the concept of beauty that these late Victorians admired. Galt, on the other hand, wanted to retain a primitive look for the APVA's plot. Her own work in art led her to accept Constable's conservative standard as "*the* only right school of 'landscape gardening.'" The APVA's site would be quite different from the adjacent farm. "Mr. Barney's land is beautifully laid off and cultivated. It is a *beautifully kept farm*," she wrote. "It has the regular 'florist-seedsman's book' look—but I hope the Good Lord will never let our property have *that look*." Echoing the antimodernism of Hall and Newton, she advised that "dignity and solemnity must cloth[e] the ruins—and there must always be a pathetic and romantic idea . . . and the old place altogether should not look *modernly 'smart.'*" By 1900 she thought that the APVA's plot looked "so lovely and natural" and admitted that she "dread[ed] the stylish look."⁶⁷ She feared, however, that Barney would force the APVA to beautify its site and thereby enhance the salability of his own section of the island.

After Galt left Virginia, later preservationists gradually beautified the island. Forgetting that Jamestown's point in history reflected an era of near barbarism and simple circumstances, the APVA worked "to develop and beautify the entire 22½ acres" before the tercentennial celebration. Like many romantics who mixed the primitive medievalism of early Virginia with the refined standards of the late Georgian, Mary Minor Lightfoot, chair of the Jamestown committee, for example, wanted to plant shrubs and flowers "as are found in old gardens of colonial homes throughout Virginia." She then planted flowers such as roses, violets, cowslips, and lilacs at Jamestown.⁶⁸ As it turned out, the longer the APVA held the island, the more it felt obliged to improve the site. The APVA's own measure of progress required it to develop the once-primitive scene.

Barney also pressed the APVA to embellish its twenty-two acres. Through the 1890s and well into the new century he and his family tried to sell his large section of the island. His donation of land in 1893 actually served that intent. Knowing that the APVA had promoted the construction of a breakwater as early as 1889 and that such an improvement was quite costly, he realized that his cession to the APVA would protect and enhance his interests. His problem was that the APVA's primitive look so contrasted with his well-polished lands. He pressured the APVA to fulfill its role as an internal improvement company. His schemes led Bagby in 1895 to fear that he "will injure us in any way possible." She concluded to Galt that "Mr. Barney is now our enemy." Often speaking "disparagingly of its condition," the Barneys subsequently asked the APVA to return its twenty-two acres once the breakwater was finished and a stone revetment was authorized by Congress. The APVA steadfastly refused, as it had virtually wrapped its own identity and the resurgence of traditionalism around Jamestown.[69]

6

"With Reverence and Due Regard for History": Jamestown in the National Focus

I N 1902 A PLAN to develop Jamestown Island aired in the New York
City newspapers. Edward H. Hall of New York, an APVA member and
secretary of the American Scenic and Historic Preservation Society, wrote
that "speculators are trying to get the island for a trolley terminal and pleasure resort, probably with a view to setting up merry-go-rounds and similar
money-making devices." Reminiscent of the 1850s proposal to convert
Mount Vernon into a hotel and casino, the 1902 plan prompted Hall to call
for "the creation of a National park." Hall praised Edward Barney's widow
Louise but implied that she could not defend the gates against these infidels
for much longer. Indeed, the APVA soon received a request from a promoter who wanted to build an electric railway to Jamestown but needed a
right-of-way through the APVA's land. The APVA nonetheless described
Hall's report as of "such an exaggerated nature" as to warrant explanation.[1]

The origins of Hall's story are indeed mysterious, but Barney's plans
could only have been furthered in the process. In 1903 she pressed a bill
before Congress to authorize the federal government's purchase of the *entire*
island. The APVA opposed such a plan, yet Joseph Bryan thought it might
be necessary. He wrote Barney and concluded that it was in "the interest of
all parties that the government should own and care for the Island, as I do
not believe that the State of Virginia will do it, and I fear the A.P.V.A.
cannot continue indefinitely to do so." Barney tried to win Lyon Tyler to
her side during the tercentennial. Promoting the purchase, she wrote, "If
Congress can be asked to appropriate $50,000 for a picture of 'Pocahontas
saving John Smith,' it certainly ought to be able to give three times as much

for the home of John Smith—a place that is capable of being made into a beautiful Park or could be made a splendid experiment station."[2]

Barney persisted. Another bill was introduced in 1911 to purchase the island as a national park. Written by the ASPHS, it made no provision to protect the APVA's plot. The ASPHS even persuaded Virginia congressman John Lamb to introduce the measure. President Ellyson denounced the plan at the APVA's annual meeting and affirmed its intention to hold on to the site "as a sacred trust for posterity." Another member pictured the matter as a "stand for the rights of Virginians" against federal usurpation. Jamestown obviously was more than the APVA's chief emblem and financial draw; it had become a matter of elite Virginians holding the line against federal intrusion. The APVA's resolve matched Barney's determination to sell the island. By 1916 Barney also won the help of the Daughters of the American Revolution and raised her price to $350,000—a twentyfold increase from the late 1870s.[3]

By the 1930s Barney reportedly wanted a million dollars for Jamestown. Forty-one years after Edward Barney's grant of twenty-two acres to the APVA, the federal government finally acquired over fifteen hundred acres of the island. After a congressional authorization and an allocation by the General Assembly, a suit was filed to condemn Jamestown Island in 1933. A petit jury placed its value at $165,000; the United States government contested, but lost, the claim. That amount was awarded in 1934, and the property vested in the United States government. The federal government paid $85,000, and Virginia added $80,000.[4]

The APVA retained its small patch of the island. Ever since its acquisition in 1893, the association had carried on a long, learn-as-you-go restoration of the ruins. In so doing, the preservationists frequently clashed over the meaning of their work. Galt's preservation ideals seemed quite conservative when juxtaposed with others in the organization who tried to commercialize the venture. The plight of an old magazine was a case in point. The APVA initially claimed that John Smith had built it, but the General Assembly actually had ordered its construction in 1697; it was the last building constructed at Jamestown by the colonial government. Over the years the river edged toward the thirty-two-foot-long magazine with a paved and vaulted ceiling. Although the building was intact and entirely on high ground before the Civil War, the waters ebbed and flowed over its collapsed ruin by the 1890s. In 1893 Louise Barney suggested that the APVA collect its loose bricks, stamp them with its emblem, and sell them as souvenirs at the Chicago World's Fair. Only bureaucratic indecision prevented action. The APVA soon considered a similar scheme, and Belle Bryan wanted the proceeds "used for handsome stationery."[5]

Galt responded to these proposals with undisguised outrage. She was flabbergasted that the APVA would take the magazine's bricks—what she incorrectly called "the ruin of the oldest house in the U.S."—and sell them. She asked Bagby, "What is the Asso[ciation] for?" Instead she suggested salvage archaeology, lifting the magazine to higher ground and carefully reconstructing it. "If our ruins are to be broken up and sold for souvenirs what are we going to preserve?" she asked. Such ignorance left her "bewildered and depressed." Bagby blocked such projects, and APVA leaders slowly came to realize that keeping the bricks was worthwhile. Feeling the economic pinch, Galt suggested other moneymaking ventures. "One of my schemes for raising money," she told Bagby in 1896, "is to have some popcorn planted and then have it popped and sold in bags to tourists—'Corn from Jamestown where it was first grown by the white man.'" Soon after, the APVA sold wood from Jamestown's trees as relics.[6]

Erosion was the most pressing threat to the island, and at its worst point—north of the magazine—over five hundred feet of shoreline had been washed away since 1680. As early as 1889 Galt asked the APVA to seek federal support for a breakwater. After the APVA acquired its portion of the island, she hurriedly excavated some graves as waters approached. Despite his repeated denunciations of special-interest legislation, Bryan and the advisory board began lobbying in 1894 for state and federal aid to protect the island. Page and Mary Thomas Curry appeared before a congressional committee to plead for assistance.[7] Active in a range of historical, social, and benevolent societes, Curry tapped her husband's influence in Congress to attach a late-hour amendment to a harbor and rivers bill. Backed by Massachusetts Republican senator George Frisbee Hoar, the bill authorizing $10,000 for a breakwater became law in 1894. Bryan realized that only the northwest section of the island would be protected, but he knew that "when one appropriation is made it is easier to get another." Completed in June 1895, the breakwater soon broke to pieces. The APVA immediately appealed to the General Assembly for a $10,000 grant, but the bill languished, prompting preservationists to question "the patriotic pride of the legislators." After more lobbying by Curry, Bagby, and Robert Lancaster, Jr., Congress appropriated $15,000 in 1896 and other moneys in later years for a stone revetment.[8]

The construction of the breakwater and revetment created endless headaches for Galt. The federal government brought in not only its army engineers but black workers from South Carolina. She worried that her sacred site looked like a labor camp, not caring to remember that was what Jamestown had been in its early years. She was particularly disturbed by "the unsightly tents of the colored people so *very near* [the ruins]—the scene cannot be very attractive." Bagby in turn worried that these laborers would disturb an upcoming pilgrimage and wanted police on hand "to keep order & ensure protection." In 1902 the state made the APVA's own care-taker the local constable. Galt suggested other means to control these work-ers, including a company store where expenses would be deducted from the workers' $10 monthly salary.[9]

Although Congress had appropriated moneys for the revetment, the War Department expected a conflict with Spain and froze the funds. When war broke out in 1898, "the United States engineers were summoned afar," Bagby sadly reported, "to destroy, not to build up." Leaders of the associa-tion particularly resented this delay, and it colored their attitudes toward the Spanish-American War. Many hereditary and patriotic societies brandished jingoism and welcomed the war and its imperialism. The Sons of the Amer-ican Revolution, for example, advocated spread-eagled expansionism. Its leader, William McDowell, urged his members to abandon the collection of relics and the genealogical quest for ancestors. Instead, he wanted the SAR to promote the expansion of American culture and influence. In con-trast, however, Boston's Bunker Hill Monument Association deplored the abandonment of America's republican traditions.[10]

APVA leaders expressed sentiments decidedly in opposition to the war. Although one popular history pictured Virginians as eager to go to war, Joseph Bryan, Richmond's foremost publisher, noted on the day war was declared that if a referendum was held in the state, "the war party would be snowed under deeper than any avalanche that ever fell from Mont Blanc." Even after victory was won, he claimed that "the war is more unpopular today than it ever has been." Advisory board member and historian Samuel Chiles Mitchell looked back on the war years later. "Big business had pushed President McKinley into war," he regretted, "with the result that the American Republic was changed overnight into an Empire."[11]

Bryan's war opposition, like that of Curry, stemmed from his belief that the reformation of America's own character was a more important task. Fearing the consequences of imperial war, he watched "the departure from our old course with absolute alarm." "I am alarmed lest pride and 'fulness of bread' should lead our country astray from the faith of simplicity and moderation which had been so clearly laid down for us by the founders of the Republic." Unlike Mitchell, Bryan feared that radical forces—Populists, labor unions, and yellow journalists—had initiated the war to undermine traditionalism. In Bryan's mind populism and jingoism were threads of the same radical fabric. They threatened elite rule, Anglo-Saxon supremacy, and states' rights.[12]

Coleman likewise expressed grave doubts about a war that seemed to clash so much with traditionalism. She declared that "it is a law of nature, that the rising grandeur and opulence of a nation must be balanced by a decay of its heroic virtues." While the United States grabbed distant lands in the Pacific and Caribbean, national decay and imperial expansion seemed intertwined. "As governments extend their dominion either by conquest, colonization, or annexation there is an increase of wealth, luxury and power which ends by sapping the true virtue of a people." Noting that "the corruption of the Roman state" began with its own imperialism, she looked back to early Virginia where a "nation that was here born and wrapped in swaddling clothes has now become a giant." That ominous giant cast dark shadows over the traditions she prized.[13]

An unbridled ethnocentrism buttressed the nation's claim of global mission. Long evident in the near-genocidal war against the Indians, as well as in the 1890s conquest of dark-skinned Cubans, Hawaiians, and Filipinos, the ideas of mission and Manifest Destiny all too often cloaked selfish and sordid motives. Driven by Protestant millenialism, national pride, and economic competition, the United States pictured destiny, not dollars, as its impetus. Virginia preservationists heard this reasoning in the heat of the Spanish-American War when the APVA invited Professor Woodrow Wilson of Princeton University to speak in Richmond. On 2 November 1898 the future president spoke, and, according to the Richmond *Dispatch,* considered the global role of the United States. While China was devoured by Europeans and Japanese, the United States grabbed Cuba and the Philippines. Having often praised Anglo-Saxons and pictured the threat of ostensibly inferior races, Wilson apparently preached mission and destiny that night in Richmond. The United States represented "the power of light," he said, while Germany and Russia embodied "the power of darkness." In this imperial competition, he said, "if somebody is to have all the world, let it be us."[14] As the South was swept by populism and racism and its new industries faltered in the devastating panic of 1893, even Bryan had accepted the logic of imperialism. Traditionalism would be redefined to include empire.[15]

During the Spanish-American War preservation work ground to a halt. Hospital work commanded the attention of many women, Jamestown pilgrimages could not be held, and wartime charities drew dollars from potential donors. Galt not only watched erosion increase but saw soldiers on leave come to Jamestown and wreak havoc. She personally went to Hampton's Fortress Monroe and asked the commandant to prohibit his men from visiting the island.[16]

After the war the revetment project slowly advanced. The $15,000 authorized by Congress in 1896 covered only twelve hundred feet of the shoreline. Brigadier General A. MacKenzie of the United States Army's Corps of Engineers wrote Congressman Lamb in 1904 that his office's concern was only "the interests of navigation," not archaeological or historical matters. That obviously put into question earlier promises made to Galt by the revetment contractor to "faithfully . . . preserve all relics which they shall dig up."[17]

Equally worrisome was the charge that the most historic section of the island had long before washed into the river. In his address to Jamestown pilgrims in 1895, Tyler cast doubt upon the antiquity of the APVA's twenty-two-acre plot. Richmond newspapers reported as well that the APVA's church tower "appears to be comparatively a modern structure, and there does not seem to exist any evidence of its great antiquity." Citing the fast rate of erosion, the newswriter felt "safe to conclude that almost, if not quite, all of the site of the ancient 'James Cittie' is now in James river."[18]

Dashed in her hope of finding tangible proof to undercut the Pilgrims, Galt lamented that Tyler had "proved that the ruins and our property at Jamestown, were not any part of the first settlement and are not as old as Plymouth or the Dutch [settlement at New Amsterdam] of 1612." She had warned the APVA leaders about Tyler's remarks, and Belle Bryan, fearing any damage to the APVA's reputation, unsuccessfully asked him to delete those assertions. Bagby tried to soothe Galt. "His historical remarks can't hurt us," she said. "No one will believe him & the town & church yard is ours anyway."[19]

Samuel H. Yonge (1850–1935) took up the defense of Jamestown's priority as a settlement. As the engineer who supervised the revetment project, he rebutted Tyler's claim and declared it "erroneous" to say that "the greater part of the ancient town has been washed away." He told Williamsburg's noted historian to learn how to read those old court documents. "The proof of the error," he said, "is furnished by the old 'James City' patent records, which when properly interpreted, show that but a small portion of the town site has been destroyed." A three-cornered contest ensued between Yonge, Tyler, and the APVA, but their debates hinged on the near-impossible task of finding remnants of three-century-old impermanent buildings.[20]

Having worked as an engineer on river shoals projects, as well as on the Brooklyn Bridge and Niagara Falls Suspension Bridge, Yonge surely had an engineering expertise. What became more important was his newfound interest and unflagging commitment to Jamestown's legacy. Admitting that his politics were "entirely unreconstructed," the Savannah-born youth had entered Washington College in 1866 because its president was Robert E. Lee. Brought to Jamestown in 1900 by the federal government, he became "entranced" by his archaeological explorations of the ruins. He identified one ruin, then at river's edge and partially underwater, as a five-part row house that contained the Country House, Ludwell house, and the Fourth Statehouse and helped preserve what remained. Yonge brought together his findings—library and archaeological research—in four articles for the *Virginia Magazine of History and Biography*. The APVA placed Yonge on its advisory board and republished his articles as *The Site of Old "James Towne," 1607–1698* (1904). His commanding influence further prompted Galt's exit, and he undeservedly has received almost sole credit for Jamestown's archaeological work.[21]

Yonge's work was financed by another $15,000 appropriation from Congress in 1901. Before the Jamestown Tercentennial of 1907, the penurious General Assembly even authorized funds for improvements. By 1918 the federal government alone had spent $50,000 on the erosion project. Moreover, the ultrapatriotic mood of the Red Scare years of 1919–20 prompted Virginia legislators to increase their funding to a select number of history-minded organizations, through which state policy could safely be pursued. When a $10,000 appropriation was granted to the APVA early in 1920, John Stewart Bryan's newspaper editorialized that "patriotism largely is historical and can be prompted by visualizing the great deeds of the past. . . . Surely no money could be better spent![22]

Public attention on Jamestown peaked during the tercentennial in 1907. One of many expositions that followed the nation's centennial in Philadelphia—Grover Cleveland said too many—the Jamestown fair put the national focus on Virginia's colonial heritage. The state's congressional delegation solicited the help of their colleagues but learned with much disappointment that many congressmen had never heard of Jamestown. Flattering the ego of Congress, Virginians noted that the House of Bur-

gesses of 1619 had laid the ground for the nation's own representative assembly. The exposition clearly was a chance for the APVA to boost its own
fortune and standing. In fact, the APVA had sent photographic displays of its
work and an explanatory leaflet to earlier fairs at Charleston and St. Louis.[23]

Determined to take credit, the APVA claimed that its call for a fair in
1900 was the first, but Hall actually had suggested nine years earlier that a
celebration be staged in 1907. Traditionalists saw the tercentennial as an
opportunity to champion Anglo-Saxonism, the cause of Virginia in the nation, and their own custodial care of culture. A debate followed, however,
over the nature of the exposition. The APVA recommended that it contrast
past and present by illustrating "the progress, manners, customs, & c., of the
thirteen original colonies and of the States formed from Virginia." The
General Assembly also resolved to support the commemoration "as much
in the aspect of duty to the past as affording an inspiration to the future."
President Theodore Roosevelt ultimately stole the show, however, and
shifted the focus from Jamestown to jingoism. In 1903 he called for "an
international naval, marine, and military celebration."[24]

The lucrative issue of the exposition's site was decided in 1902. The
port cities of Norfolk and Portsmouth had jointly proposed a naval and
marine fair to boost their New South commercialism. Too far up the James
River to accommodate maritime projects, Richmond only slowly joined
the fray, while the APVA's women refrained from active lobbying because
of Victorian strictures and their own inexperience. In the battle between
Richmond and Norfolk, one capital-city editor slyly suggested that the
APVA should decide the issue because "they are perhaps the only persons
concerned in the proposed celebration of 1907 who have purely unselfish
and patriotic motives and have no axes to grind"; he did not note in print
that the association was controlled by Richmond. When the Hampton
Roads site won out, Joseph Bryan protested, "You shall not yoke imperial
Virginia to Norfolk's commissary wagon!" In the end, yoke them they did
as Norfolk's exposition portrayed the progress of the New South, rather
than the traditionalism so prized by Richmond.[25]

The APVA had limited influence on the Norfolk fair. Congress appropriated $50,000 for a Jamestown Commission, one of whose members was
J. Taylor Ellyson, lieutenant governor of Virginia and spouse of the APVA's
vice president. He also served as governor of the History Building at the
Sewell's Point site. Showing Roosevelt's intent to advertise America's naval
strength, Congress appropriated additional moneys, including $125,000 for

entertainment of foreign military representatives and $10,000 for exhibiting the "scene" of the battle between the *Monitor* and the *Merrimac* so as "to illustrate the progress of naval construction."[26]

This militarism dismayed many Americans. Celebrations of war accounted for one-half of the fair's attractions and included races by submarine warships, displays of war curios, and pyrotechnic reproduction of battles. Americans as diverse as social worker Jane Addams and James Cardinal Gibbons of Baltimore regretted the blatant militarism. Monster dreadnoughts from the world's naval powers anchored off Hampton Roads. Galt feared that Jamestown would suffer from adverse publicity because these military features were "exciting among the people and fostering a spirit of militaryism." She suspected that criticism of the fair mostly emanated from Yankees and Catholics. Not only did northern papers "not whoop it up," but "some people north and northwest seem to feel that the Civil War is still going on." Worse yet, she thought that there were secret "orders by 'holy church' to freeze out the Expo[sition]."[27]

Tradition-minded Virginians sensed more controversy. While the APVA scrimped along, Congress appropriated $100,000 for a Negro Building, but the Virginia legislature refused to give any support to such a project. In line with Jim Crow, exposition officials separated African-American materials at the fair from those of whites. Giles B. Jackson, onetime personal slave of Robert E. Lee and one who subscribed to Booker T. Washington's accommodationist strategy, led the Negro Building venture. His exhibit drew 750,000 people and included one sculpture of Africans landing at Jamestown.[28]

Traditionalists also expressed displeasure at the obvious profit-seeking of Norfolk's New South boosters. Edwin Alderman, president of the University of Virginia, described to an audience at the exposition how "an ancient, forceful and unique civilization, bred into the bone of the people, is going down before the strenuous influences of invention and modernism." Those New South ways could not provide adequate hotels, food, and facilities for the fair's visitors, however. One frustrated member of the Ohio delegation quipped, "If John Smith had founded that exposition when he landed, he would have been mad at Pocahontas for saving his life."[29]

Most of the buildings were unfinished when the fair opened on 26 April. They presented a confusing array of colonial themes that bore little relation to Jamestown. While Pennsylvania modeled its building on Independence Hall and Ohio copied Adena, a Chillicothe estate designed by Benjamin Latrobe, Virginia built an elaborate Georgian Revival home with

a monumental two-story pedimented portico. So much for colonial simplicity, as boosters readily forgot Jamestown's primitive conditions and focused on more comfortable later days. Seventeen of these grand buildings
were ultimately purchased by the federal government in 1917 for its naval
base, and now "Admiral's Row" serves as officers' housing.[30]

The APVA's part in the Jamestown Exposition proved quite different
from the unvarnished militarism and profit-seeking of Norfolk boosters.
Even in the amount of congressional appropriations, it was apparent that
Jamestown received a low billing. The APVA did use its little plot to the
hilt. Congress softened its loss of limelight by appropriating $50,000 for the
erection of a memorial obelisk. Yet preservationists had mixed minds about
the monument after hearing that it would have to be placed on their land,
not Barney's. The APVA begrudgingly donated an acre and a quarter of
what Sally Nelson Robins called "this sacred soil" with the proviso that the
land could never be alienated.[31]

What the APVA and Jamestown most needed was not another monument but a pier to handle the thousands of visitors who were expected to
come up the river from the Norfolk fair. In 1906 the APVA asked Congress
for help. Congressman William A. Jones of Virginia chastised the ladies for
"not pressing your claims upon the attention of Congress earlier and more
vigorously." He maneuvered to allocate moneys for a wharf on the APVA's
property, and in turn the association suspended entrance fees to Jamestown
for the tercentennial year. Since its identity and revenues depended so much
on Jamestown, Belle Bryan suggested that the APVA hold twice-monthly
pilgrimages there in 1907. "If we do not occupy the grounds," she warned,
"some one else will, and reap the harvest which we throw away. Our only
hope, therefore, is to make something from our excursions."[32]

The association planned a gala pilgrimage on 13 May to celebrate the
1607 landing. It persuaded Governor Claude A. Swanson to declare a state
holiday and to suggest that 13 May be celebrated ever thereafter "by all
Virginians all over the world." On behalf of the APVA, Page invited British
ambassador James Bryce to be the principal speaker that day. In his much-
publicized book *The American Commonwealth,* Bryce had focused on the
deterioration of political leadership and spoke the APVA's mind when he
blamed that decline on the spoils system, black franchise, and mass democracy. He longed for a return to the older traditions of elite rule and social
deference. Like-minded Joseph Bryan served as master of ceremonies for
the day's speeches by Governor Swanson, Lieutenant Governor Ellyson,
and Bryce.[33]

Never had Jamestown seen such a fete as on that Virginia Day. Ships of every sort anchored off the island, including specially constructed replicas of the vessels that brought Smith and company to Virginia, the *Susan Constant,* the *Godspeed,* and the *Discovery.* The crowd, estimated as high as eight thousand, was described as "orderly" and "reverent," yet the orators still had the task of simply being heard. B. C. Moomaw, poet of the ceremony, declined lunch on the boat to Jamestown, saying, "Thank you, no. An empty drum makes the most noise." The APVA first invited Theodore Roosevelt to present the day's address, but he declined. Roosevelt did take the time that year, however, to lay a cornerstone for the Pilgrim Memorial Tower in Provincetown, Massachusetts, which President Taft dedicated three years later. What brought Roosevelt to the exposition was not Jamestown but opening-day festivities on 26 April and an imposing naval spectacle. Roosevelt sailed down the Chesapeake in his yacht, the *Mayflower.* In his opening address he praised America's long list of immigrants and pioneers and attacked both plutocrat and mob. He paid scant attention to Jamestown and never once mentioned John Smith, Christopher Newport, or Pocahontas.[34]

On the following day the president took "a purely private excursion" up the James to visit the historic plantations at Brandon, Shirley, and Westover, as well as the Jamestown ruins. Roosevelt insisted that the trip was "entirely informal," warning that if any ceremony was expected, he would not make the scheduled stops. At least he chose not to sail his yacht *Mayflower,* but the *Sylph* instead. Roosevelt returned to the exposition, but not Jamestown, on 10 June for Georgia Day. That state had cleverly chosen as its building a replica of Bulloch Hall, the house of Roosevelt's grandfather at Rosewell, Georgia. The president called it "an act of gracious courtesy and consideration" when Georgia chose "the house in which my mother passed her youth and where she was married to my father." The APVA had hoped that he would speak on the Fourth of July at Jamestown, but the president stayed at Sagamore Hill and watched a fireworks display.[35]

Jamestown's historic ruins nonetheless received "a very large percentage of the exposition visitors." Knowing that the island would be in the limelight, the APVA embellished its landscape and voted in 1903 to "welcome the assistance of any organization or individual in the erection of buildings or historic memorials." This could have invited disaster by destroying Jamestown's value as an archaeological site. But the 1903 resolution was totally in keeping with the APVA's memorialization of history. The next year the National Society of the Colonial Dames of America proposed spending $6,000 to erect a memorial at Jamestown. The APVA advised the society that "the most desirable and interesting work" it could accomplish would be the erection of a brick building over the ruins of the ancient church. Yonge and W. G. Stanard proposed that "the walls of this friendly building, as well as its windows, will also afford opportunities to place suitable cenotaphs to and portraits of early colonial worthies."[36]

These plans ran counter to those of Bruton Parish rector Goodwin. He addressed the APVA's annual meeting in 1905 and asked preservationists to raise a memorial to the colony's first Anglican minister "on the spot where stood the ancient church." The APVA declined, principally because it had already relinquished the area to the Colonial Dames. Goodwin then suggested consecrating the Dames' structure as an Episcopal church. The APVA accepted that idea in May 1906, and the building became a gallery and a chapel. The APVA hoped that the memorial would "be an influence drawing all Christian Churches together, especially those who took part in the Colonial history of our Commonwealth, and they shall be welcomed to hold their own religious services from time to time therein." It was consecrated in 1908, and the Episcopalians, Baptists, and Presbyterians symbolically united against all foes.[37]

Whether in mind or matter, traditionalism and Protestantism often shared common ground in the late nineteenth and early twentieth centuries. It was no wonder, therefore, that Jamestown became a mecca for Protestant America. Upon the petition of Joseph and Belle Bryan and Bishop A. M. Randolph—forces that could hardly be resisted—the APVA donated a different tract of land to the Episcopal church so that it could mark "the spot . . . where it was born on this Continent." Disregarding the sixteenth-century French and Spanish colonists, Randolph declared that "Christian worship of the true God found its first expression on the continent of North America" in Virginia. Because Jamestown had the first Protestant service, marriage, and Indian conversion, the APVA regarded the Memorial Church as a Protestant mecca.[38] The Episcopal Church prized the site as proof of its own priority and, as some hoped, an inspiration to many a church congregation fixated by materialism.

Yonge initially designed the brick memorial so as to, in Belle Bryan's words, "practically reproduce the old church." Believing that nearby St. Luke's Church in Isle of Wight County was "almost contemporary" and of a "similar character," the APVA chose it as the model. Yonge described their common points as the squat tower and chancel door. He wanted the new structure to adjoin, not attach to, the ancient tower, which would not be changed. He deemed it "inadvisable and impracticable to place the new building on the decrepit brick foundations of the former church." The Memorial Church required, therefore, greater dimensions, additional buttresses, and large mullioned windows "suitable for receiving memorials to colonial worthies." All in all, the structure would "be suggestive of strength and solidarity, and bear an air of quaintness."[39]

Controversy ensued over the APVA's choice of the Isle of Wight County prototype. Local legend attributed the construction of St. Luke's to 1632, but some Virginians, including Tyler, thought it improbable that a primitive colony could have erected such an edifice. Scholars still disagree over the date. Jamestown's brick tower is dated by some as 1699—an addition to the church of 1639. Whatever the mixture of dates, the reconstruction was speculative.[40]

Even more controversial was the decision to build anything on the ruins. The APVA had approved the Colonial Dames proposal at a small meeting, and some members later protested. The association called a general meeting in 1906 to discuss the question of consecrating the memorial building, and some had their first opportunity to voice objection against reconstruction. Conway Whittle Sams of Norfolk wanted the APVA as a whole, not its narrow leadership, to vote on the project. Because the tower was "the only surviving remnant of the original settlement," he argued that it "should not be tampered with" and asked the APVA to rescind the concession. A lively discussion erupted, but before the protest could sufficiently develop, J. Taylor Ellyson, acting as chair, ruled the motion out of order. Immediately "members uttering emphatic 'noes' made themselves heard throughout both rooms."[41]

The controversy spilled over into the newspapers. Letters to the editor protested the reconstruction. One argued that the Dames were "about to commit a fatal and egregious error." Believing that the tower and foundations would be ruined by such a reconstruction, the writer thought that the rebuilding, intended to impress "our foreign visitors next year," instead "will subject us to ridicule." It would be "a calamity rather than a blessing," and would compound the "fatal mistake" already made at Jamestown when Barney decided on her own to remove the old tombstones from their original locations. Criticism did not abate even after the dedication. Mary Minor Lightfoot, chair of the Jamestown committee, admitted to Yonge that she heard these complaints from "outsiders." Rather than reply, he urged "silent contempt [as] the best treatment it deserves."[42]

Although Yonge made the first sketches, the architect for the Memorial Church ironically was a Bostonian, Edward M. Wheelwright. Like St.

Luke's, the building reflected a Gothic styling, a favorite of American anti-modernists who admired its medieval associations. Harvard professor Barrett Wendell, a student of seventeenth-century Puritanism, praised the styling. His wife Edith oversaw the Dames' project, which "rebuilt and restored to its pristine condition the ruined church of Jamestown." The "rough brick" of its original design, he said, "attempted to preserve the then still prevalent forms of perpendicular Gothic, and the stubborn material combined with imperfect artistic skill to produce a singularly vital and picturesque effect." The newer materials of the Memorial Church had been stripped from two colonial homes that were demolished for their salt-glazed brick, making the effort a case of robbing Peter to pay Paul. The APVA rejoiced when the Colonial Dames deeded the building to them. On behalf of the Dames, General Francis Henry Appleton presented it to Joseph Bryan and the APVA on 11 May 1907.[43]

A decade later John Stewart Bryan wrote admiringly of the reconstruction. Arguing that the APVA deserved a state appropriation, he stretched the definition of restoration and embellished the APVA's work. "It is difficult to say whether the A.P.V.A. deserves more credit for what it has done in the restoration of the church or for what it has not done," he wrote. "For 'restoration' in the accepted sense often is as great a crime against history as neglect: There is always the temptation to 'restore' what one thinks *might* have been or *should* have been, rather than to restore only what one knows existed. In the church at Jamestown, with a taste that would seem positively providential if it were not innate in such an organization, the A.P.V.A. has labored with reverence and due regard for history."[44]

That reverence prompted the APVA to use every available spot at Jamestown, whether rough ground or pointed window, to place memorials to such heroes as Smith, Pocahontas, and Bacon. Stressing the importance of the individual, preservationists reiterated their belief in the personal strength of heroes. They claimed that these Virginians had not been motivated by economic gain or self-interest, as was implied by Marxian- and Beardian-influenced historians, but by altruism and idealism. As Curry explained: "I do not belong to that school of determinists which makes of individual and collective life mere mechanism or bland fatality. Human history is the evolution, largely and mainly, of moral causes, of virtues and vices of men, of ideas and volitions, of conscience and reason." The APVA resolved in 1897 "to preserve the memory of the men who have made the history of Virginia a lesson to ourselves and to the future."[45]

The APVA laid memorials to those heroes who illustrated its contention

that a strong individual, despite a hostile environment and foes, could perse-
vere and prevail. If any one character symbolized that hero and the APVA's
own resolve to vindicate Jamestown's reputation, it was the controversial
John Smith. The Washington branch placed a tablet honoring Smith in the
Memorial Church for the tercentennial; it also issued a commemorative
plate called the Persimmon, or John Smith, Plate. The APVA also constructed a larger-than-life statue of Smith on the island because, Belle Bryan
told the association, "he 'discovered' Jamestown, almost as much as Columbus did America, and saved more than once the infant colony from destruction, swift and entire. We owe it to ourselves, and to him, that he shall be
there!" With much fanfare in 1909, the association unveiled the statue that
Bryan donated as a memorial to her deceased husband. The ceremony, typical of the APVA's public affairs, drew "many of the most prominent persons" of Richmond. Allmond Blow, the day's orator and chairman of the
APVA's John Smith Monument committee, called Smith "the foundation
stone of our Anglo-Saxon lineage, the father of the Cavalier and the sponsor
or promoter of the Puritan Colony in America." The future of America,
Blow declared, had hung on Smith's shoulders; had he failed, Catholic
France would have dominated these shores.[46]

The fate of Smith's reputation hinged on the ability of these traditionalists to rebut contemporary critics. Blow castigated those writers who had
depicted Smith "as the dramatic hero of a dime novel incident." A more
serious wound to his fame had been inflicted by prominent New England
writers, including Charles Deane and Henry Adams, who accused him of
deceit, vanity, and incompetence. Deane, a Boston merchant and antiquary,
had questioned the truthfulness of Smith's story about his rescue by Pocahontas and noted that the story did not appear in print until fifteen years
after the alleged event. Many years later James Branch Cabell agreed with
Deane, pointing out that a variation of the legend and its basic ingredients—ruthless foe, brave captive hero, and rescue by a young woman—
appears in the mythology of every known land. He concluded that Smith
"either invented or else borrowed the entire affair," but he admitted that the
story, despite its apparent fiction, had become part of "the official history of
Virginia." Blow, on the other hand, expressed the APVA's lament that "history has distorted and belittled" Smith. "In truth," he said, "Smith himself
attached so little importance to this episode that he did not refer to it at
all in his first history of the Jamestown settlement, though he later made
mention of it."[47]

William Wirt Henry, a historian in the hierophant tradition who chaired the advisory board, assumed the duty, as he called it, of rescuing "the fair name of Capt. Smith, from the imminent peril which threatens it."[48] As one writer described Henry's defense of Smith, "After the war, when there was little left but wreck and ruin to our Southland, he appeared as the fearless and successful defender of the honor of Virginia in numerous cases of aspersion cast upon her by the whole school of New England critics." Henry took Adams to task. "If his side be triumphant," he said, "then indeed we must blot out from the pages of Virginia's history this most beautiful instance of female devotion, doubly interesting because it was the act of a savage girl."[49]

Pryor likewise ennobled Smith for his role at Jamestown. She repeated the oldtime schoolbook's depiction: he had disciplined the effeminate and anarchic, instilled the work ethic into the idle, and saved the colony through his craft in command. Speaking at Jamestown in 1926, Yonge pictured him as the "single thread" on which Virginia's future had hung. Even the APVA's guidebook to Jamestown praised Smith for recognizing the need to escape the disease-ridden site and occupy higher ground. Yet "the stupid colonists" had refused. So went the dichotomy between wise leaders and ignorant masses that the modern elite stressed.[50]

The bronze and stone memorials to Jamestown's greats also included tributes to the Indians Pocahontas and Chanco. In the nineteenth century the nation perpetrated near-genocidal policies against Native Americans on the western frontier but pictured some colonial-era Indians as noble savages and even placed an Indian on the penny. Pocahontas also had become a folk hero in American romanticism. In the 1830s Congress had commissioned John G. Chapman to paint the *Baptism of Pocahontas at Jamestown* for the United States Capitol's rotunda. The APVA honored her life with a number of shrines. It preserved near Petersburg "Pocahontas's Basin," a stone formation where, according to legend, the Indian had bathed. Preservationists also placed tablets honoring Smith and Pocahontas in Jamestown's church. The APVA claimed that these were "the first monuments to either one of them in America." Most imposing was an eighteen-foot statue erected at Jamestown by the APVA and the Pocahontas Memorial Association, an ancestral group of privileged white women who traced their descent from the Pocahontas-Rolfe marriage. When the statue was unveiled in 1922 with pomp and ceremony, Page and Tyler spoke for the APVA.[51]

The dedication ceremonies included nine descendants of the Indian woman and one "full blooded Indian of the Rappahannock tribe in native dress." These Indians used the Pocahontas revival to advance their tribal causes. Recently organized in a Rappahannock Indian Citizen Corporation, they asked the APVA to help them gain tribal recognition and the right to vote. Assisted by James Mooney of the Smithsonian Institution, the Indians wielded the APVA's endorsement in their petition drive. The Rappahannocks courteously replied to the preservationists that "they were pleased at the great work that you are doing."[52] The Indians demonstrated that the door of history could swing both ways.

In contrast to the modern Rappahannock tribe's search for its ancient identity, the APVA lauded Pocahontas for abandoning her culture for that of the English. The daughter of Chief Powhatan had converted to Christianity, married John Rolfe, and moved to England. She became "the only 'Royal Princess of America'" and "the ancestress of many distinguished Virginia families." Pryor and John Randolph of Roanoke both claimed her as an ancestor. Coleman suggested as well that she had been God's instrument for the triumph of Anglo-Saxonism: "Was it an accident that gave to this gentle savage the Christian attribute of heavenly charity? Was it not rather the divine preparation for the preservation of a Colony destined at this time to be planted and nourished into growth. The time had come when this fair western world was to be redeemed from the dominion of the savage to yield its wealth of soil and climate to that race which should dominate the world."[53]

Countless Anglo-Americans contended that Native Americans had been earmarked by God to hold the land temporarily until the Europeans arrived. They would not recognize the Indians as landowners. "They had been stationary, so far as progress in the arts is concerned, from aboriginal times," Conway Sams reasoned. Because they left no buildings or discernible changes in the land, ethnocentric, material-minded Americans dismissed them. Indians did not alter the environment, build a permanent legacy, or conquer nature, as did the Europeans. These were the marks by which their successors measured progress.[54]

Preservationists memorialized Pocahontas, most importantly, because her example underscored Anglo-Saxon America's own proud belief in its cultural superiority. Pryor believed that these Indians "had not a single virtue or single trait of true nobility." In a description more revealing of Victorian domesticity, Western progress, and cultural imperialism than about the daughter of Powhatan, she said: "Pocahontas is to be honoured all the more inasmuch as she conquered every instinct in her savage nature, becoming reverent, gentle, pitiful, and patient; and correcting every blemish in her 'manners barbarous,' learning to 'live civilly,' and behaving in all situations, with discreet gravity. Like the lovely pond lily, the root was in slime and darkness; but at the first touch of the sun the golden heart was revealed of a perfect flower."[55]

Virginia's admiration of Pocahontas carried over to her father. According to Edward Valentine, one of the legends "which all Virginians know" was "that King Powhatan had such a hard foot that when angry at Smith's escape he made an impression of it in the rock which can now be seen at historic Powhatan." In subsequent years that stone took on various stories itself; some called it Powhatan's gravestone, others his "seat." The APVA received the rock as a gift in 1922 and immediately suggested that it be placed on a pedestal with a bronze tablet at Chimborazo Park in Richmond. Believing that it was his gravestone, preservationists asked the Smithsonian Institution to decipher its markings. Despite the archaeologist's description of it as an Indian trail marker, not a gravestone, the stone still sits in the park as Powhatan's burial marker.[56]

Preservationists also paid tribute to Chanco, the Christian Indian boy who informed his English master of Opechancanough's plan to attack Jamestown and "saved the colony from extermination at the massacre of 1622." According to Smith, thousands were saved "by this converted Infidel." In 1908 preservationists laid a "chaste and simple" limestone tablet to his memory in the Jamestown church, and in 1929 the APVA dedicated a boulder and plaque on the green of Surry County Courthouse.[57] Another APVA branch memorialized Debedeavon, the "laughing King of Accomacke" whose warning also averted a massacre in 1622. Smith called him "the comliest, most proper, civil Salvage we incountered." The tablet was unveiled in 1938 in Northampton County, and the APVA admitted that Debedeavon "even betrayed his own race to save" the English. When the critical moment came in history, Chanco, Pocahontas, and Debedeavon had all proved their loyalty to the English invaders. Because in this case Anglo-Saxons wrote and preserved the history, they became heroes, not quislings. After the 1622 attack, Coleman said, the attitude of Englishmen "towards the Indian was one of hostility and repugnance, mingled with dread and a hopelessness of conversion." The bloodbath that followed, historian Richard Slotkin has suggested, became the means to regenerate the white man's power and identity. The conquest of the Indians and the destruction of their environment—what Slotkin has called "the structuring metaphor of the American experience"—would define America for centuries to come.[58]

So many memorials occupied the APVA's small parcel at Jamestown that some observers, including Cabell, questioned their rationale. "There is not at Jamestown any settlement, nor for many decades has the forlorn island been inhabited except by mosquitoes and a caretaker," he charged. "Jamestown is a mere mob of monuments and memorial tablets. The more charitable might admire Jamestown as a cemetery pleasingly deficient in corpses; but most certainly no one could call it a settlement." Only this FFV skeptic could describe the island as being "burdened with a collection of serio-comic sculpture."[59]

Oblivious to those sentiments, the APVA also lauded the role that Virginia had played in overland expansion. Ever since the Jamestown settlers had moved up the peninsula or across the James to Southside, the Old Dominion had spearheaded the creation of the continental empire. "The Southern spirit bore the ensign of the Anglo-Saxon across the mountains, seized the West, and created the American continent," Page boasted. "Had the New England influences, which were opposed to the Annexation policy dominated," Tyler conjectured, "the United States to-day, if it existed at all, would be confined to a narrow *slip* along the Atlantic shore."[60]

As it commemorated this expansionism, the APVA marked distinct stages in the process that began at Jamestown. The Bloody Run Spring monument near Richmond celebrated the ouster of the Algonquian Indians and the battle in 1656 that, the APVA noted, was the "last successful stand of Indians" against Virginians. The next generation of preservationists marked the site where in 1676 Bacon defeated the Occaneechee Indians. The monument left unexplained the story behind the battle. Those peaceful natives had earlier aided the English, but Bacon's quest for land and racist hatred prompted his action. In a surprise attack, he plundered and destroyed their village.[61]

In the APVA's estimation of westward expansion, Bacon's illustrious rebellion of 1676 had foretold Virginia's future. In the process, of course, Bacon had burned Jamestown's church, leaving the ruin that the APVA acquired over two centuries later. Coleman imagined that the ashes of the smoldering church had made an incense that roused Virginians to act in defense of traditionalism. She spearheaded a drive, which culminated in 1901, to place a stained-glass window in Williamsburg's Powder Horn to honor "the gallant rebel." At the same time the APVA also placed a window there honoring Governor Alexander Spotswood. Both tributes were largely financed by their descendants as acts of filiopietism. Mary Newton, chair of the landmark committee, endorsed the Bacon memorial because he was "the first Virginian to enjoy the distinction of being dubbed with the title of 'rebel'—since made so dear to Southern hearts." As Bacon's major biographer at the time, she interpreted the rebellion in Virginia as "the most portentous, the most dramatic, [and] the most picturesque event of its seventeenth century history." Her opinion reflected a century-long effort by Virginia to revise the historical record. Through the eighteenth and into the nineteenth centuries, Bacon had been remembered, even by John Marshall, as a troublemaker and subversive. His stature as a hero, in turn, stemmed from the Old South's increasing distrust of centralized government, as well as Virginia's search for a hero and tradition apart from the Pilgrims. Stanard and the APVA followed that tack, as did Thomas J. Wertenbaker in *Torchbearer of Revolution* (1940), which compared him to Nathan Hale.[62]

Like many contemporary historians, the APVA's orators and writers called Bacon's Rebellion a foreshadowing of the American Revolution. Page, for example, equated Bacon's actions with those of Washington in 1776; they both fought for the "inalienable right of British subjects to have self-government." Both rebellions were justified, as was that of 1861 if the implication followed, because they were "based on the people's rights against the government supported by a privileged class." Bacon was a gifted leader who "arose, as one sent from Heaven," Coleman wrote, and he won a "popularity among all classes" as he fought for liberty and "a bitter vengence wreaked upon the Indian foe." Although in "many ways a Lost Cause," Stanard observed, his rebellion succeeded because it provided "comparative safety from the Red Peril for Eastern Virginia."[63]

More definitive accounts, however, have exploded the myth of Bacon as a democratic reformer. The APVA's interpretation actually reflected complex reasoning. Preservationists embellished Bacon's reputation in order to enhance Virginia's claim as the seedbed of the Revolution. By firmly placing his revolt within that context, they buttressed the legitimacy of the Confederacy's rebellion. More implicitly, the APVA underscored two other conceptions. Just as Bacon had worried about an internal enemy and united his followers against the Indian, so, too, did modern elite Virginians unite society against integrationists and radicals. Preservationists also stressed the notion that the American style of revolution was democratic and noble. The "Red Peril" that America faced when Page spoke and Stanard wrote was not the Indians, but socialist revolution. It was a curious fact that groups such as the APVA and the DAR sanctified the American Revolution yet cringed at the sound of European-style revolt.[64]

To assure peace after Bacon's Rebellion, King Charles II sent presents and insignia of authority to the Indians of eastern Virginia. The queen of

the Pamunkey Indians, whose husband Tottopottomoy had died at Bloody
Run fighting for the English, received a red velvet cap with an inscribed
silver frontlet. The badge apparently stayed in Indian hands until after the
Civil War. The new owner—how he obtained it is uncertain—offered it
to the APVA in 1890 for $800, a sum which the association refused to spend.
After the Smithsonian Institution refused its purchase, the APVA then
agreed to buy it in 1896. This first "relic" acquired by the APVA partly
symbolized the English conquest, but Newton also said that "the heirlooms
I have bought are my heirlooms." The preservation of material culture entailed as well an ownership that affirmed authority and status.[65]

Just as this silver frontlet represented a custodial care of culture, so, too,
did the acquisition of Jamestown. The APVA deserves credit for protecting
the island from the elements, but its leaders dramatically differed over the
meaning of preservation. While Galt wanted to retain its primitive features
and preserve its artifacts, many saw Jamestown, symbolized by its ruined
church, as a re-creation of the memories and inspiration associated with
the colonial ventures. The APVA considered the moral, spiritual, and social
symbols of early Virginia history as the most important aspects of its work.
It therefore implemented its Gospel of Preservation by reconstructing the
church, beautifying the site, and sanctifying the surrounds. The APVA's
historic preservation may have been romantic and unscientific, but it succeeded in making Jamestown a mecca for Anglo-Saxon, Protestant, and
traditionalist leadership not only in the Old Dominion but in the United
States.

Isobel Lamont Stewart Bryan.
(Courtesy of the Virginia
Historical Society)

Joseph Bryan.
(Courtesy of the Virginia
Historical Society)

Thomas Nelson Page.
(Courtesy of the Virginia
Historical Society)

Cynthia Beverley Tucker Coleman.
(Courtesy of the Colonial
Williamsburg Foundation)

Duke of Gloucester Street, Williamsburg, c.1890.
(Courtesy of the Colonial Williamsburg Foundation)

The Powder Horn, with the old Williamsburg Hospital at right.
(Courtesy of the Colonial Williamsburg Foundation)

The foundations of the Capitol and the APVA monument, Williamsburg.
(Courtesy of the Colonial Williamsburg Foundation)

William Archer Rutherfoord Goodwin and family.
(Courtesy of the Colonial Williamsburg Foundation)

Bruton Parish Church, Williamsburg.
(Courtesy of the Colonial Williamsburg Foundation)

Prerestoration Jamestown Church Tower. (Courtesy of the
Association for the Preservation of Virginia Antiquities)

Pilgrimage at Jamestown, 1895, including the principal orators, John Lesslie Hall *(seated at center)* and Lyon Gardiner Tyler *(seated at center right)*. (Courtesy of the Valentine Museum, Richmond, Virginia)

Group of pilgrims at Jamestown. Included are Lucy Parke Chamberlayne Bagby *(seated at center)*, William Glover Stanard *(second row, second from left)*, Mary Jeffery Galt *(second row, sixth from left, with umbrella)*, and Edward Virginius Valentine *(standing, eighth from left)*. (Courtesy of the Virginia Historical Society)

Jamestown Memorial Church. (Courtesy of
the Colonial Williamsburg Foundation)

Columbia, at an APVA fund-raiser in 1896.
(From *Souvenir of the Kirmess* [Richmond, 1896])

"Getting the Lowdown on Hard Times." Cartoon by Fred O. Seibel.
(Courtesy of the Richmond *Times-Dispatch*)

"Jamestown Day!" 1927 cartoon by Fred O. Seibel.
(Courtesy of the Richmond *Times-Dispatch*)

John Marshall house, Richmond. (Courtesy of the Virginia Historical Society)

Old Stone House, Richmond. (Courtesy of the Virginia Historical Society)

Mary Washington house, Fredericksburg. (Courtesy of the Association for the Preservation of Virginia Antiquities)

"The Coming of the Maids at Jamestown," an APVA representation in a Richmond pageant in 1922. (Courtesy of the Association for the Preservation of Virginia Antiquities)

Dedication of Robert Hunt memorial in 1922. (Courtesy of the Association for the Preservation of Virginia Antiquities)

Pocahontas at the Court of King James, the APVA's grand ball of 1923. (Courtesy of the Association for the Preservation of Virginia Antiquities)

The White Glove Brigade of the APVA, c.1930s. (Courtesy of the Association for the Preservation of Virginia Antiquities)

"How Jamestown Was Saved for Posterity." Cartoon [1938] by Fred O. Seibel. (Courtesy of the Richmond *Times-Dispatch*)

7

"Keeping Alive a Proper Veneration for the Past": Patchwork Memories of the Old Dominion

THE APVA ORGANIZED its work through local branches. More often than not, the Richmond headquarters tried to direct these locals, as it did when Coleman toured the state, formed chapters, and presented her paper "Objects of Historical Interest Needing Preservation in the State of Virginia." As these branches developed, they occasionally contested Richmond's authority over their work and funds. Conway Whittle Sams and the Norfolk chapter led this challenge, especially after the controversial decision by Richmond's central committee to rebuild Jamestown's church. Some annual meetings in Richmond ended with "animated" arguments over centralization. As a result, the APVA worked on diverse projects, but each held importance for its memories and object lessons.[1]

Many Virginians held a deeply felt localism which, as in antebellum days, defined community and religion as the cornerstones of life. As a result, they restricted their preservation work to the care of their colonial-era churches. During the past century countless colonial churches had been abandoned, vandalized, or seriously damaged. In the Civil War, for example, St. George's Church (1738) in Pungoteague was used as a stable by Federal troops who ripped out its woodwork and destroyed its walls. In the 1880s the church was repaired as a rectangle, not as the original cruciform. Another church, Lower Southwark Church (1751) in Surry County, fell to disuse after the Revolution, was burned by freedmen in 1868, and is in picturesque ruins today.[2]

When the APVA acted to save such churches, it served largely as an adjunct of the vestries. The Smithfield branch in Isle of Wight County, for instance, treated St. Luke's Church "as its special object of work and care."

After many years of neglect, its roof had fallen in June 1887, jeopardizing America's only original Gothic church. Part of an exposed wall bore a brick with a date that appeared to be 1632. The *3* was rubbed, however, and it easily could have been an *8*. Parishioners held great pride in what they thought was the oldest brick building of English origin in North America. The Southside APVA members who heard Tyler question the 1632 date in his oration at Jamestown in 1895 were shocked. "As loth as I am to dispute the claims of the Smithfield church," he cautioned, "I am too well acquainted with the backwardness of architecture in the colony to believe without the most positive evidence, that an outlying settlement, barely a few years old, surrounded by Indians, could vie with the Capitol in producing a brick structure."[3] "Old Brick Church" was partially restored during 1891–94 with the help of the APVA. Some locals nonetheless resigned from the association when asked to help fund the preservation of Jamestown, only twenty-five miles away, because "they feel it is incumbent upon them to extend all the help they can give to . . . our own Colonial Church." Such parochialism proved to be a double-edged sword; it attracted local interest to an antiquity but failed to diffuse support to the larger commonwealth.[4]

The APVA also assisted the preservation of one of Virginia's finest examples of colonial architecture, Christ Church in Lancaster County, built by Colonel Robert Carter of Corotoman in 1732 in a Greek cruciform pattern. Upon the urging of Tyler, the APVA donated $500 in 1897 for a new slate roof and other repairs "on condition that no alteration should be made to the original plan of the church." The APVA assisted other projects, as in 1910 when its amateur archaeologists in Hampton discovered the cobblestone and brick foundations of an early building thought to have been the first church at Kecoughtan, built in 1624. The local APVA branch raised money through a card party and enclosed the foundations with a fence. To the south in Princess Anne County the APVA assisted the restoration of Old Donation Church (1736) in Lynnhaven Parish. Abandoned in 1850, the building was gutted by a forest fire in 1882. By the turn of the century trees were growing between the ruined walls. Local residents acted through the APVA and restored the building in 1916. At the same time the APVA received a request from King William County citizens. Cattail Church (1748) had long been abandoned by the Episcopalians and was used by African-Americans. After the roof fell in, they, too, deserted it. The APVA was asked to "arrest its decay and destruction before it is too late," but racial barriers apparently deterred action.[5]

Forest fires, freedmen, and Billy Yank may have harmed these colonial churches, but first fault lay with those Virginians who abandoned them because of Anglican disestablishment, economic modernization, or cultural tastes. A case in point occurred early in Lexington. Old Monmouth Church, built in 1788–89, had been abandoned by a congregation that moved to a more comfortable neighborhood and built a newer church in 1843. The APVA encouraged its local branch, formed after a recruiting tour by Coleman, to take care of these ruins. Although the APVA largely drew its inspiration from tidewater culture—Anglo-Saxon ancestry and Episcopalian religion—its interest in Lexington revealed that it also appealed to the "stern liberty-loving Scotch-Irish Presbyterian stock" who built Old Monmouth Church. John Fiske and other historians had already endorsed the heterogeneity of common European cultures, and the APVA largely accepted this limited diversity in Virginia's history.[6]

Architectural conservation evidently took second billing as the APVA used such buildings as backdrops for its focus on cultural traditionalism. Some preservationists spotlighted their own non-Anglo-Saxon ancestors. Henry praised his Scotch-Irish ancestors. "They were foremost in opposing tyranny in every form," he said, and "their constant warfare with the Indians made them a race of warriors." These qualities were admired by late Victorians, but the same rugged individualism and animosity toward the Indians, when combined with the Presbyterians' "strict" religious unbringing, also fostered what Richard Slotkin has called the "metaphysics of Indian Hating." The APVA also nurtured the Protestant work ethic, Victorian home-life, and ethnic assimilation. In a lecture to preservationists, General John Roller lauded his Germanic forebears for "their wonderful thrift and energy," their skill as workers, and their devout family lives. They had "so intermingled with the others in marriage" that their descendants made up one-third of modern white Virginians. Many lived in the Shenandoah Valley, as did the Scotch-Irish, and they counterbalanced the Anglo-Saxonism of tidewater.[7]

Preservation on the Eastern Shore showed the difficulties inherent in organization and finance for remote rural communities. In 1913 the Northampton County board of supervisors ordered the demolition of the old colonial government buildings at Eastville because a new, though nondescript, courthouse had been built in 1899. In what was a clear question of which historical legacy required protection, the supervisors wanted to demolish the old courthouse (1739) to make way for a new monument to the Confederacy. Mary Macon Aylett Fitzhugh, active in both the UDC and the DAR, appeared before the supervisors with a petition of three hundred names "begging that the old Jail, Debtor's Prison, and old Clerk's office, be allowed to remain in the original beautiful Colonial Group." After a hearing the supervisors decided to demolish the jail but to give preservationists not only an early clerk's office and debtor's prison (c.1814) but the courthouse, too, if it was moved from the site within thirty days.[8]

William Bullitt Fitzhugh, owner of a prosperous farm and a newspaper publisher in Eastville, joined his wife's campaign. In an editorial on "Ancient Landmarks Preserved," he publicized the drive, chided the advocates of demolition, but glossed over the context of the supervisors' decision. Northampton County's economy and society had gone through a painful transition in the past two generations. In 1880 sharecropping and tenant farming dominated its agriculture; African-Americans comprised a majority of the population; and through the 1880s county residents voted the Readjuster ticket. Foreclosures, crop-lien enforcements, and economic failure, he suggested, were symbolized by the old courthouse. "More lives have been ruined and more homes wrecked by that building than in any in the county." Moreover, said critics of Virginia's property laws, the debtor's prison was "a relic of barbarism." Traditionalists, on the other hand, considered the courthouse a symbol of the obligations of credit; the buildings represented their forefathers' "struggle for law and order." Preservationists in the Jim Crow days noted that "the Clerk's Office has the measuring rod built in it where slaves were measured before being sold." Accordingly, the buildings symbolized recently challenged traditions of white rule, the obligations of debtors, and reverence for law.[9]

Fitzhugh noted the general premises of the APVA's Gospel of Preservation: "Monuments of earlier times, like those on Eastville's court green, keep alive a proper veneration for the past, a veneration inseparable from and inspiring of patriotism. The spirit that would see 'old Eastville made a new Eastville' is abroad in the land in a larger way. The American people are urged to abandon old creeds and old philosophies, so that abruptly they may follow new gods." Like many preservationists, his gospel showed striking partisanship as he attacked Roosevelt's Progressive party, which demanded that government serve the needs of the majority, not the wealthy. The former president used his bully pulpit to propose that the federal government reverse decisions of conservative state courts holding back reform. He had clearly recognized that the minority which made and supervised the legal system did not serve the needs of the nation's majority. Fitzhugh's editorial called on Virginians to protect their traditions. "Even the Federal Constitution, the bedrock of well-ordered, just and free government, is assailed more bitterly than ever before," he warned. "The independence of the judiciary is to be undermined if a certain political party ultimately prevails." With Virginia's tradition of states' rights in jeopardy, Fitzhugh believed that Eastville's colonial block rekindled its memory and defense.[10]

Although the supervisors had ordered the removal of the courthouse, preservationists fought to save it in situ. Fitzhugh "bitterly opposed . . . *even* thinking of moving it, from its sacred spot built by our fore-fathers." The former member of the House of Delegates pulled out his political IOUs and persuaded Tyler to speak in Northampton County. Despite his rousing speech, the building had to be moved in 1914. The APVA's local director borrowed the money, and the costs ultimately exceeded $1,500. Before the arrangements were completed, the boss of Eastville's "political ring" threatened to "have it pulled down at night," and she discovered as well that someone was "trying to bribe the Contractor to tear the building down, or shake it to pieces, as he moved it, offering him $500." She even hired a watchman to guard it at night. In 1915 Ellyson praised Fitzhugh for "courageously carrying on" her work. Fitzhugh took sole credt; she had called seven or eight meetings but was left waiting "in that *cold* Clerk's office for 5 hours, hoping that, at least, *one member* would come."[11]

The branch's corresponding secretary, Kate Savage, tried to win friends but admitted that local "people are not interested in these old buildings." She wrote a broadside that played up the typical themes, including the fact that "strangers" came to Eastville to see the buildings and their colonial-era records. "Were these buildings in some Northern county," she suggested, "they would be cared for and preserved as priceless relics of the past. Can we, as an enlightened and intelligent people do less?" In 1917 another supporter contrasted the ideals of traditionalism with the profit motive of business. The historic buildings represented an "investment" in older values. "It means more than commercialism can understand; it means reverence for the Virginia that made America great."[12]

Eastville's APVA branch fell apart during these years, illustrating the failings of decentralization. Who supports whom in such structures of power? Richmond asked for its dues, but the Eastern Shore could not pay them. Encumbered by the courthouse debt and set back by the war, locals thought that the central organization should "take care of its Branches as a mother does its children." If it does not, Savage thought, "I cannot see what use it would be to its branches." Eastville discovered that Richmond did not take care of its branches. Left to their own devices, these preservationists, as was the case elsewhere, made do with what little they had. Forced to close their colonial block during World War I, Savage asked, "Why should we send our dues to the A.P.V.A. for them to store away for the purposes of keeping up other places if they cannot take care of this one?" Knowing that the APVA used a collector for delinquent membership fees, she hoped that it would not "do such an undignified thing as to try and force payment."[13]

An open rebellion further erupted in the ranks of preservationists. Savage charged that the branch director "has but one idea, and that is to get her money" for the courthouse removal back. She alleged that Fitzhugh alienated many and "has no following, even in her D.A.R., her pet." While the UDC had sixty members, the APVA languished, and Savage predicted that "this Branch is a dead one unless another Directress is put at the head of it." Backbiting became intense as Savage formed an alternative APVA branch and tried to get control over the colonial block. Fitzhugh sent caustic letters to Ellyson that shocked her "like a bolt from a clear skye." Appalled by such "a cruel, Personal attack," Ellyson tried to distance herself from the fracas. Fitzhugh retaliated, locking the colonial block shut and declaring that Savage "knows no more about the buildings . . . than some one in Africa." She refused to relinquish either her keys or position and claimed more experience in preservation than the APVA.[14]

Savage predicted success for the new branch director, Nell Nottingham, who was "practically the leader of society" in Eastville. "As she is not married," Savage added, "she has plenty of time." Savage also found the new supervisors on the county board "more broad minded" and attentive to the ladies' concerns. She did not attribute this attentiveness to the newly granted woman's suffrage, for she "never cared for" the right to vote and thought that such clamor would not "make the men listen to us." All the while, other community groups were challenging the APVA's ownership of the historic buildings. Richmond received petitions from the Woman's Club, the DAR, and the UDC asking that it return the Eastville colonial block to the supervisors. The APVA gave Fitzhugh an ultimatum: she had six months to raise the money, finish the restoration work, and open the buildings, or Richmond would take control.[15]

In 1923 the supervisors revoked the APVA's hold on the courthouse. Ellyson expressed relief that it had "no claim on the old wreck of a building & Mrs. Fitzhugh is deprived & relieved of the responsibility of finishing the work of restoring it." She then learned that the board of supervisors had transferred the grant to the new branch, but Ellyson rejected the move, asserting that either the general association controlled the courthouse or it would revert to the county. Evidently Richmond thought it unwise to have local politicians interferring with its control over the branches. To this day, the APVA maintains, but does not own, the three buildings.[16]

To the north, Accomac County preservationists organized a branch in 1910 to save an old one-story, vine-covered debtor's prison. Built in 1782 as a jailer's residence and converted to a prison in 1824, the Accomac building once stood adjacent to a jail, but that was demolished in 1901. The supervisors, who in the late 1890s had also destroyed a charming colonial-era courthouse, transferred the use of the building to the APVA in 1911 as long as it did not become a "public eyesore." Accomac preservationists, much like a library-support society, proposed using the building as a "public reading room . . . and thus to put the old building to some real practical use." Today the APVA maintains it as a local museum. As in Eastville, the APVA became the caretakers for colonial-era buildings which the taxpayers no longer wanted but for which they still held title.[17]

An earlier colonial-era site had long interested Galt, and she proposed in 1894 that the APVA restore Powhatan's Chimney in Gloucester County. The collapse of the structure had caused her six years earlier to form the association, yet in the interim almost no mention was made of it. Sally Nelson Robins spoke to preservationists in 1894 and "clearly proved that the Chimney had been built for Powhatan by Captain John Smith and was therefore the oldest piece of brick work in Virginia." The APVA resolved, therefore, to "make strenuous efforts" to acquire the ruin. The owner refused, however, to sell the structure without the entire farm, and the APVA declined that offer.[18]

Finally in 1912 APVA received the chimney and resolved to rebuild it, but only in the 1930s did the local branch devise a sketch for the reconstruction based on a view in Bishop William Meade's *Old Churches, Ministers, and Families of Virginia* (1857). The APVA rebuilt Powhatan's Chimney in 1934–38, and preservationists made pilgrimages to the site. Years later, however, a research study commissioned by the APVA concluded that the chimney could not be attributed to either Smith or Powhatan. The legend rested on misreadings of documents and maps and the speculations of Charles Campbell and Philip Alexander Bruce. The researchers diplomatically did not blame "the devoted ladies" who "believed what they had been taught to believe."[19]

The Cape Henry Lighthouse, a commanding structure built during the Washington administration, attracted the APVA's attention in 1894. What drew its interest was not the tapered octagonal design and sandstone materials, or the fact that it was the nation's first lighthouse and a symbol of federal power in a local community. The APVA in fact only wanted the ground on which the lighthouse stood—where the waters of the Atlantic and Chesapeake meet. English colonists had landed there in 1607, held a service of thanksgiving, and reembarked for an inland settlement. After a new tower was erected in 1881, the old lighthouse had been "utterly abandoned." Belle Bryan told the United States district engineer in 1894 that it would "answer our intentions perfectly" for a sturdy structure on which to place a memorial. She reported to the association that "the United States will give the Lighthouse to the A.P.V.A.," but the matter was not settled.[20]

The entire Cape Henry area, excluding the lands owned by the federal government, was earmarked for development by the Cape Henry Park and Land Company. William W. Old served as the company's secretary and treasurer and as an adviser to the Norfolk branch of the APVA. The development of land and historical memory were not considered incompatible in Norfolk. At the same time the APVA claimed the site, other locals, such as Henry Sargeant of the Norfolk Public Library, urged the state government to take control. All the while, wind and wave took their toll on the weakened structure. In the mid-1920s the Norfolk branch asked Congress to appropriate $5,000 to repair the damage. Instead, the cost-conscious government gave the lighthouse to the APVA in 1930. Despite the hopes of preservationists to establish a museum there, within a decade they admitted that "vandals and trespassers are giving us much trouble," while sentries at Fort Story kept out prospective tourists.[21]

The APVA came within an arm's reach of acquiring York Hall, the stately mansion of Thomas Nelson in Yorktown. An old spinster descendant, Miss Kate Nelson, tried in 1889 to sell it to the federal government. That having failed, Coleman appealed to her to sell it to the APVA, rather than to Chicagoans who came to Yorktown and also tried to buy the Custom House and Moore house for their Columbian Exposition. Coleman called them "a thorn in my side" as they carried on "negotiations of a vileful character" to purchase sites that "excit[ed] the breasts of patriotic Virginians."[22]

Pressed by Robert Alonzo Brock, the APVA urged the United States government to purchase the Moore house and the adjacent battlefield in order to keep them out of the hands of these Chicagoans. W. W. Henry, recent president of the American Historical Association and current president of the Virginia Historical Society, wrote Senator Leland Stanford, chairman of the Committee on Public Buildings, and asked him to support enabling legislation then before his committee. Echoing the APVA's gospel, Henry thought that the government should protect the site "so that each succeeding generation may be brought face to face with the great events of our revolutionary period." But the committee declined to act.[23]

Page, also a descendant of Yorktown's Nelsons, wanted the APVA to own his ancestral home and suggested that it offer Kate Nelson a yearly stipend in return for her deed. Writing Bagby in 1894, he calculated that Nelson was "60 years of age and in feeble health . . . [and] the annuity plan would not be a bad one for the Society." Although Nelson was interested, negotiations faltered while each quibbled over the terms of the annuity. Mollie Lightfoot, frustrated by Nelson's recalcitrance, called her a "goosey goosey old lady." The APVA left the matter to its advisory board, but no solution was found. Finally, shortly before his death in 1908, Bryan purchased the house for $3,000. It was restored by later owners and, like the Moore house, became part of the Colonial National Historical Park.[24]

Antebellum houses fell so frequently that only unusual circumstances were noted. In 1908 a story appeared in the newspapers which claimed that "Montville, the colonial home of Patrick Henry, one of the most historic places in Virginia, is to be burned to the ground by its owners, the great-grandchildren of the famous Virginian, because the place has become over-run with bats." As the correspondent described the scene, "bats by the thousand hang about the grand parlors and spacious bedrooms of the colossal mansion. Attempts to exterminate them by poison and with clubs have failed. . . . They hang in long strings from the furniture, from the ceiling, from the walls, and they are in such numbers that they form curtains before the windows, darkening the house during the day." This bizarre story, about a house associated with Patrick Henry, made the full run in New York City papers, surely prompting laughter and lament.[25]

Though based in Richmond, the APVA surprisingly admitted a decade after its founding that "not a dollar has been spent" in the capital because it "believed there were objects elsewhere of higher historical importance." The city had lost much of its identity. In 1906 novelist Henry James traveled through the South and devoted a chapter of *The American Scene* to Richmond. Confessing that he "attached some mystic virtue to the very name of Virginia," he searched for the town's character but found "on the face of the scene, no discernible consciousness, registered or unregistered, of anything." He judged that "Richmond, in a word, looked to me simply blank and void." He pictured the city as "a figure somehow blighted or stricken, discomfortably, impossibly seated in an invalid chair," whose eyes only revealed "deprecation" and "defiance." Richmond had "no references" to its past and suffered from "intellectual bankruptcy."[26]

Indeed, a remarkable number of Richmond's historic or stately buildings were demolished after the APVA's creation. Mary Wingfield Scott, a preservationist who formed a chapter of the APVA in Richmond in the 1930s to correct that failing, chronicled those demolitions in her *Old Richmond Neighborhoods*. Swan's Tavern, a 1780s inn that once sheltered the likes of Thomas Jefferson and Edgar Allan Poe, was demolished in 1904. A year earlier the Marshall-Winston-Andrews house, a Georgian brick edifice built before 1792, was pulled down. Richmond also lost its Henrico County Courthouse (1825), a small but charming Greek Revival structure, and Richmond City Hall (1816), designed by Robert Mills. The loss of this unique architectural inheritance undercut Richmond's feeling of distinction.[27]

APVA historian Mary Mann Page Newton Stanard (1865–1929) regretted these changes in Richmond's landscape. Daughter of an Episcopal bishop of modest means, she illustrated the tacit partnership that had developed between the APVA and the VHS when in 1900 she married William Glover Stanard, secretary of the historical society, editor of its *Virginia Magazine of History and Biography,* and APVA adviser. She continued to write, blending sentiment and history as she popularized the Old Dominion's material culture. A reader praised her *Richmond: Its People and Its Story* (1923), for example, because she had "so humanized history, so interlaced & interwoven it with the present that Richmond now seems to me like a beautiful being—a young tender loving maiden, or splendid, noble youth whom I have known since I stood beside its cradle."[28]

As a modern successor to the mythmakers, Stanard increasingly appreciated the value of material culture and the personalism of social history. In her most important work, *Colonial Virginia* (1917), she aspired to picture the lives of "everyday men and women" who were lost when books only concentrated on great events. She also wanted to portray Washington and his peers in more realistic terms. "No matter how ingeniously the string is pulled," she wrote, the people recorded in these past accounts "seem more like puppets than people—to be made of bronze or marble rather than flesh and blood." She instead wanted to present a "round, unvarnished tale" about old Virginia. She focused mostly on the elite, but she included small planters in that group and presented everyone in human, though not unvarnished, terms. The APVA unanimously commended her book, while University of Virginia professor Fiske Kimball praised her "valuable and reliable discussion" of Virginia's early buildings. Her writing was part of the slow shift from sentimentalism to realism.[29]

Stanard showed her blend of folklore and fakelore in 1911 when preservationists joined with the General Assembly to mark the Richmond site of the Virginia Convention of 1775. At a time when Americans increasingly felt apart from the marbleized men who founded the nation, she tried to make the convention's cast of characters more relevant by humorously depicting the human figures behind the plaque's embossed names. Although the convention had conducted the serious business of challenging the king's authority, the delegates still had time to laugh and joke. To her, this showed that Washington, Henry, Jefferson, and their fellows were but "grown up boys." She tried to separate her portrait from the impersonal caricature drawn by earlier hagiographers; she thought that "there was no bronze in their make up," though "marble was sleeping in the soil of Italy" waiting to recognize their accomplishments.[30]

Stanard also incorporated a sympathetic understanding of Virginia's historic landscape in her works. As Richmond industrialized and took on the appearance of other New South cities, she regretted that field glasses no longer allowed a panoramic view of the city from its hillsides. Only the memory of old-time residents would allow them to see "through smoke screens of busy factories" and "view-obstructing buildings." Richmond still had its "dusty old streets" and "dilapidated houses," but the many demolitions made one's memory the best guide. With it, "old paving stones tell stories, old trees gossip, old streets become picture books, [and] old houses store-houses of strange lore." In the Old Market district, however, "the ghost of old Richmond" walked. There sojourners could see "an original fanlight—grimy, but graceful—above some battered door, or a finely patterned iron balcony still clinging to a sagging wall."[31]

What partly accounted for those changes was the development of new transportation and neighborhoods as "Richmond grew and grew and grew." Having built the nation's first commercially successful electric trolley line in 1888, Richmond had its first Ford car in 1907. Both "scattered Richmond's families through what would have been hitherto considered distant country localities." One of the most prosperous residential development schemes was the grand Monument Avenue, along which now stand numerous Confederate memorials. Joseph Bryan invested in many of these schemes and even served as the treasurer of the West End Land Improvement Company. Richmond built newer, more fashionable residences on the periphery, while its antebellum interior and historical identity deteriorated.[32]

Only the proposed demolition of the John Marshall house in 1906 stirred the city's complacency. The culprit in this case was a repeat offender, the Richmond School Board. Pressed by the May Campaign of 1905 to provide better schools, the board proposed construction of a new high school on the Marshall house site. Years earlier the board had proposed demolition of Central School, at one time the White House of the Confederacy, and prompted Belle Bryan to form the Confederate Memorial Literary Society in 1890. In 1911 the board did demolish the grand Greek Revival mansion (1801) of Elizabeth Van Lew, the noted Union spy during the Civil War, in order to build a new school. No protest was heard, however, because the Van Lew mansion symbolized infamy, not honor. Even so, Mary Wingfield Scott concluded that "a beautiful building with the loveliest site and setting in Richmond was sacrificed to blindness and prejudice."[33]

Marshall's house, according to Belle Bryan in 1906, "appeals in a degree hardly less strong than the home of Mary Washington." Rejecting either its demolition or removal, she told her members that "anywhere except in Virginia this house with its memories and its traditions would be guarded with jealous care (for its age if nothing else), and if it is altered or destroyed we will be justly censure."[34] For years, however, the stately two-story dwelling (1788–91) with broad pedimented gables had been the victim of curio hunters who stole any removable piece.

Together with the Virginia Bar Association, patriotic groups, and Richmond civic leaders, the APVA formed an alliance that packed a school board meeting in 1910 and asked the board to convey the house to the APVA. Investment banker John P. Branch gave a "very strong talk" in behalf of the city's business interests. APVA adviser Eppa Hunton, Jr., son of a Confederate general and United States senator, represented the state's lawyers. A former president of the school board, Lieutenant Governor Ellyson, likewise demanded preservation. The board tried to compromise. Pledging to keep the building, it offered the APVA a "choice room" in it "dedicated to the memory of Chief Justice Marshall."[35]

The APVA pressed the city council to overrule the school board. Over the board's protests, the council transferred custodianship of the Marshall house to the APVA in 1911. One Richmond chronicler saw this act, along with the city's segregation ordinance, as the two most important measures taken by the city government in 1911. Both acts entailed the restoration of antebellum culture, and the preservation of the Marshall house symbolically "links the present with the past and points the mind of the youth to the great achievements of the days gone by, inciting them to noble action." [36]

Led by Hunton, the lawyers of the Old Dominion spearheaded the campaign to repair and endow the Marshall house. The participation of the legal profession reflected, in part, its deep reverence for Marshall and the Constitution, but it also bespoke a determination to regain prestige and a reputation for public service. During the Gilded Age the profession's eminence had been tarnished by lawyers who had shown more loyalty to corporate capitalism than to any abstract principle of justice. The legal profession's fealty to Marshall, as symbolized by its part in the preservation of his home, testified to its wish for a better image. [37]

A growing reverence for the Constitution—partly a defense against the democratic radicalism of Populists and workers—also helped Virginia preservationists in their drive. For example, John Fiske, who was popular in Virginia and a member of the APVA, regarded as an axiom of civilized government the ability of the Constitution to hold in check the excesses of democratically elected legislatures. With the Readjuster period branded in his memory, Curry had noted the perilous tendency of "popular assemblages . . . to violate written constitutions [and] usurp authority." Curry maintained, moreover, that many Americans erroneously believed that the United States was first and foremost a democracy. "That the people, in the aggregate, or that a majority of the male adult inhabitants, have the right, natural or conventional, to make or execute laws as they please, when and where they please, irrespective of law or the constituted authorities, is," he claimed, "the insane dream of anarchists, pure mobocracy." [38] The sanctification of Marshall, some hoped, would restrain the public through traditional ways.

Focusing on Marshall and Virginia's founders, preservationists linked this building to the civil religion. Increasingly during the era, tradition-minded progressives held the Constitution and flag with reverence. Congress passed the first legislation in 1917 penalizing the desecration or improper display of the flag, while the National Security League waged a publicity campaign to celebrate the Constitution's birthday in 1919. These acts of homage become transparently political when the era's events are brought into focus. Not only did such groups as the Industrial Workers of the World unsuccessfully struggle to win their political rights through a free-speech campaign, but the Russian Revolution spawned a Red Scare that debilitated the Bill of Rights. Conservatives used the Constitution as a brake against any radicalism.

The APVA played its part through the Marshall house. The jurist's noted biographer, Senator Albert J. Beveridge, helped the APVA recruit money for its endowment. He called the house "a shrine of American constitutionalism"; its preservation was a "well nigh sacred" duty. Beveridge dreaded the influence of both immigrant and Bolshevik in the near future. He called the Constitution a "Rock of Ages" that would steady American society. It was only appropriate, therefore, that Americans should "worship" the Constitution. The APVA interpreted the Marshall house to honor not only the hero within but the Constitution he defended. As a result, one visitor in 1917 wrote in the guest book that he was "proud to worship at the shrine of the greatest Chief Justice."[39]

When the city council transferred custody of the Marshall house to the APVA, it expected that the building would be suitably repaired and furnished. The council voiced the notion that underlay the preservation of material culture: a person can be understood through his property. "Thousands of admirers of John Marshall," it predicted, would relish "the privilege of looking upon those things which either belonged to him personally or were the property of any members of his family." The APVA eventually furnished the Green Room with Marshall's furniture, while other rooms held period furnishings. Female preservationists evidently wanted their heroes to illustrate desirable traits because they also placed in the house "an exquisite love letter from John Marshall to his wife, Mary Ambler."[40]

Despite the building's improved standing, the neighborhood posed further difficulties. The APVA took extraordinary measures to defend the home of America's freedom-loving jurist. The "depredations of bad neighborhood boys" prompted the APVA to erect a barbed-wire fence around the house. Whether the children of Jackson Ward, the segregated black district, merely perpetrated youthful vandalism or were implicitly protesting against the elite's power and gentrification, the APVA's memorial to a man who wanted to recolonize the slaves in Liberia clearly diverged from the hopes of nearby African-Americans.[41]

Consistent with its Gospel of Preservation, the APVA prized the Marshall house not for its stately architecture but for the life and principles of the jurist. Stanard noted that "the house is characteristic of its creator—sturdy and square and dignified; impressive in its simple outlines and ample proportions, well-bred in its sufficient but chaste ornament." She thought

Marshall was worthy of emulation for his love of rural ways, his frugality, and his devotion to family life. He was a preeminent Virginian, and she claimed, "If there had been an Association for the Preservation of Virginia Antiquities in his time, I have not a doubt he would have been on its advisory board."[42]

At a time when Jefferson's legacy and home were deteriorating, the APVA spotlighted his cousin and arch-rival, placing Marshall alongside Washington at the apex of Virginia's hagiology. When the APVA dedicated the Marshall shrine in 1913, Stanard tried to depict him as a human being, not a pedestaled statue. Yet her praise bordered on sanctification. According to the APVA's interpreter, he represented the state's public-spirited elite. He was neither ostentatious nor arrogant, and she lauded him "for carrying the virtue of simplicity to an extreme that made it a fault, and thus saving a sufficiently perfect picture from the monotony of over-perfection." One observer appreciated the fact that Stanard "generously spiced [her account] with the most fascinating personal bits about the life of the great man." He became "a real flesh and blood human being and not the bronze figure of a demigod set up high out of our lives and entirely out of touch."[43]

A poem written by Rosewell Page in 1910 put to verse many of the values which endeared the house to traditionalists. Addressing his lines "To the People of Richmond," he exclaimed:

It teaches lessons hard to learn
Of virtue, love and high emprise,
Of honest living, how to earn
What's best beneath the skies.

Repair it if it needs repair—
For what is money in the scale,
Compared with all the treasure there,
Within its sacred pile!

"Mount Vernon," "Stratford," types of Rome—
Still tell of patriot's high renown—
In God's name, spare the Marshall home—
It adds lustre to the town![44]

As a shrine to conservatism and constitutionalism, the Marshall house attracted pilgrims from near and far. The APVA also moved its headquarters to the house and wrapped its identity around those themes. In 1912, for example, the APVA drew over five hundred guests to its annual tea there and, more significantly, opened the house that year to the Conference of Governors that convened in Richmond. "Many of the most distinguished guests visited the building," Ellyson reported, "and expressed themselves in terms of highest praise for the preservation of this home, so rich in historic memories."[45]

The APVA also opened the Marshall house to other groups, but "only to proper people" for meetings and functions. The Junior Order, United American Mechanics, for example, rented the shrine for its annual board meeting in 1920. Strident in its opposition to Catholics and new immigrants, it promoted an Anglo-Saxon, xenophobic traditionalism that was increasingly popular in the twenties. Apparently in the minority within the ranks of preservationists, Tyler questioned its propriety. In 1928 he denounced both the Ku Klux Klan and the Junior Order, United American Mechanics, and claimed that they were "totally averse, in their conduct and objects, to the principles of Old Virginia." He regretted that "many young Virginians have joined these societies, . . . in total ignorance of what Virginia stands for."[46]

The APVA added Richmond's "Old Stone House," quite different in character, to its fold in 1912. Located in the Shockoe Valley, it had deteriorated before the Civil War, along with "Butchertown," a foul-smelling neighborhood packed with slaughterhouses, tanneries, and soap factories. By the 1890s preservationists looked askance at the enigmatic house. *Harper's Weekly* commissioned Julian Ralph and artist Federick Remington to visit Richmond in 1894, and their sentiments confirmed many doubts. For sale at the time, the Old Stone House contained a museum which struck them as "sentimental rubbish." The guide called one cupboard "Washington's wine-closet' and a room in the story-and-a-half structure "Washington's and Lafayette's sleeping *de*partment." As tourists, they wandered "in a delicious maze of uncertainty, wonder, and speculation" but concluded that "nothing about it or in it seems to have any certain historical value." The fanciful interpretation reflected earlier practices when museums pitched their educational message through showcases of unusual, bizarre, but very appealing curiosities.[47]

The APVA considered purchasing the Old Stone House in 1895. The realtor did not want to sell it "to any northern parties" and offered it to the APVA at what he called a reduced price. Henry warned preservationists that "the only historical value of the house was its age," even though "he doubted if it was really as was claimed the oldest house in Richmond." Like a magnet, however, the house had attracted numerous legends over the years. Valentine spun a yarn "which all Virginians know . . . that Sir Walter Raleigh spent a night in the old stone house on Main Street—arose, took a julep, then a breakfast of sora, Linhaven Bay oysters, and beaten biscuits." Other raconteurs claimed that the house had been Washington's headquarters during the Revolution. Such legends, William Stanard told the APVA, "had long since been exploded." Considering the $6,000 asking price too high anyway, preservationists voted that they did not want it "at any price."[48]

The building subsequently deteriorated "to a dirty and unkempt tenement with a junk-heap for a backyard." Along the rail lines, Shockoe Valley shifted even more to industrial and business purposes, and the owner of the house decided either to sell or to demolish the wreck. His asking price for the house fell to $2,860. At a meeting of the advisory board in 1911, Granville Valentine, brother of the sculptor, offered to purchase the building; preservationists could "repay him at their convenience." The advisers resolved that the Old Stone House had "such historic and architectural value as to deserve preservation." Two days later, the APVA accepted their recommendations because it was "unquestionably the oldest house now standing in Richmond" and it was once "a quarter house of William Byrd." In 1920, however, it even questioned the authenticity of the Byrd connection and faced the quandary of what to call the building.[49]

After its acquisition, the APVA lacked funds for real repairs, and the structure languished. A vendor of curios rented the building, persistently calling it Washington's Headquarters. The APVA then rented it to Archer G. Jones who transformed the building into a shrine to Edgar Allan Poe. The *Southern Literary Messenger* building, where Poe briefly worked as editor, had recently been demolished, and Jones wanted to use its materials in his building. With the APVA's approval, he repaired the house, built a fountain in the rear of the lot, and "completely transformed" the site. As the APVA announced in 1922, "we see it now as it probably appeared in an early colonial period, with charming little garden containing English ivy [from the grave of Poe's mother], old fashioned flowers, and playing fountain." Incongruously, the colonial building became a "repository for Poe relics." The house seems to have served mostly as the "Gateway to an Enchanted Garden" where Jones built a shrine to Poe from the bricks of the *Messenger* building.[50] Although the restoration was farfetched and the building's landscape bore little resemblance to its original primitive surroundings, the Old Stone House had been saved from the wrecking ball.

In approving the establishment of a Poe shrine, Virginia traditionalists

redressed some of the wrongs of their fathers and grandfathers. As James
Branch Cabell noted, the poet had felt only scorn in his adopted home. The
"leading tobacconists and commission merchants" who dominated Richmond's culture had deplored his idiosyncratic behavior. "Here, surely,"
Cabell thought, "is conduct upon the part of Richmond which calls for
reprehension." He could also have reproached Barrett Wendell who condemned the author's bohemian life in 1893 and described his work as "fan-
tastic and meretricious throughout."[51]

A subsequent proposal to erect a monument in Richmond to honor
the poet was killed when, Page remembered, "a violent opposition was
voiced by one of the daily papers." All the while, however, southerners
heard the northern charge that they lacked a literary tradition. In reply,
Virginians pointed to Richmond's *Southern Literary Messenger* (1834–64), and
particularly George W. Bagby, its editor during the Civil War. Yet Poe also
had edited the journal, in 1836. In 1907 the APVA placed the first Richmond memorial to Poe not at the *Messenger* site but at the Allan house.[52]
The site said more about the standards of Victorian culture than Poe's artistry. There, a century earlier, the Boston-born orphan had been taken in
by John Allan, a merchant who later turned on him because of his unwillingness to practice proper Victorian behavior.

In 1909 the University of Virginia celebrated the centennial of the birth
of its former student. The spotlight on Poe prompted a concession from
Wendell that his prominence was deserved. Only then did traditionalist
Richmond co-opt his legacy. Poe's fame was acknowledged, but begrudgingly, said Cabell. At the opening of the shrine in 1922, Valentine presented
an address which revealed that Richmond still questioned the poet's character. He used humor to express his own hesitancy, explaining that "the best
authority on Poe" was an African-American descended from Poe's coach-
man who had said: "I gwine tell you xactly what I knows' bout him, and
dat for sartain. Dat boy wuz ur monstruss bad boy, but he had ur extry head
on him." What prodded the APVA to act was the fact that literary circles in
the nation had finally recognized Poe's genius, schizophrenic or not. Virginia now had a shrine to a great American poet.[53]

During the Jamestown Tercentennial in 1907, the Fredericksburg
branch asked Richmond to appropriate $1,000 to acquire what it erron-
eously called "the only pre-revolutionary house in the town." The Rising
Sun Tavern, a story-and-a-half frame building erected about 1760 by
Charles Washington, the youngest brother of George, became a monument
to the town's Revolutionary heritage. It was in a "most dilapidated condi-

tion," but its associations could not be surpassed. As Jamestown took the limelight, preservationists in Fredericksburg claimed that "there is not in the State of Virginia to-day a building of greater historical value than the Rising Sun Tavern." As Washington, Mason, and the Lees "gathered to determine the course of events," the local director reported, they invested the building with their courage, sagacity, and leadership.[54]

Preservationists prized these memories and legends. According to their gospel, these buildings symbolized the sacred trust inherent in historic preservation. Although they were assembled as a patchwork of memories, the APVA established a network of shrines which educated the public and tried to win their loyalty. Voicing their allegiance to old Virginia, preservationists documented their notions of old-time community, republican values, and forceful but wise leadership. As they asked their contemporaries to study and learn from the ancients, the past became a prescription to remedy an uncertain future.

8

"To Capitalize Some of Its Historic Assets": New South Development and Virginia's Paradox

T HE GAMUT OF THE APVA's interest ended in 1861, the year when the antebellum clock stopped. Preservationists promised not simply to protect vestiges of the Old South but to correct the derogatory image of the South in the nation. After the Civil War opinions about secession, slavery, and the South remained polarized in the nation, as the South stood in ruins and social disarray. Tradition-minded southerners asked, At what cost to our society do we rejoin the Yankee states? Southerners of Henry Grady's stripe, although willing to ennoble the Old South, called for the creation of a New South of industry, modern farming, national Unionism, and racial reconciliation. Progress was measured in those terms. At the same time, the myth of the Old South slowly spread. Its proponents popularized the notion that grace and civility had characterized antebellum society, while racial peace was enforced by a subordination of African-Americans. They reified the myth partly through the symbols and traditions embodied in the APVA's work.

From a later vantage point, it would seem that preservationists were in a difficult position. They had their hearts in the Old South but often their pocketbooks in the New. They looked to the Old to foster social peace, but only the New could bring the prosperity that would guarantee that peace. Their traditions stemmed from the Old, but their future was in Progress, shaped not simply by Yankee capitalists but ostensibly by Providence. As a result of these prevailing forces, preservationists painted a historical picture in which strong continuities existed between the Old and New Souths. Like a sweeping landscape portrait of the Hudson River school, plantation and factory could blend together in a harmonious whole. Preservationists swore fealty to their traditions but pledged allegiance, on their own terms, to a New South characterized by Henry Grady's measures. They hoped to attract to the APVA's cause all Virginians of wealth, ancestry, and power and thus to regenerate traditionalism in the present.

The APVA leadership from the 1880s to the 1930s reveals the continuities between these two generations of men and women. While the first had been hardened by the Civil War, dire poverty, and radical challenges, the second experienced the resurgence of traditionalism, the progressive era, and a new sense of nationalism. The first generation—such as J. L. M. Curry, Joseph and Belle Bryan, and Cynthia Coleman—were usually diehard Confederates and thoroughly loyal to the Old South. The second generation—such as Samuel C. Mitchell and John Stewart Bryan—still pledged loyalty to the past but publicly represented New South progress. Through both generations, tradition-minded women held the APVA's reins and acted more conservatively as they protected virtue and culture. Strong continuities existed, therefore, between these generations. As Wilbur Cash has noted, "So far from representing a deliberate break with the past, the turn to Progress clearly flowed straight out of that past and constituted in a real sense an emanation from the will to maintain the South in its essential integrity."[1]

The two generations of APVA advisory board leadership are best illustrated by Joseph Bryan (1845–1908) and his son John Stewart Bryan (1871–1944). The elder Bryan considered himself "one of the 'régime ancien.'" A millionaire who won wealth through marriage and business, he saw a decline in the South stemming from its race for wealth and its apparent loss of community. Lamenting that the planter had been pushed aside, he urged Virginians to "emulate their distinct civic, military and domestic virtues." "The older I get," he wrote, "the more I admire the old civilization that made patriots and heroes out of the white people, and civilized human beings out of the cannibals of Africa." Stewart Bryan succeeded his father as Richmond's leading publisher and paternalistic reformer and likewise admired the Old South's order and virtues. Yet he epitomized "in a striking way," said one reporter, "the successful transition between the old South and new."[2]

Differences existed between the two Bryans, mostly concerning the Lost Cause and secession. Planning for another Confederate reunion in 1900, Joseph admitted: "I am a hotter Confederate now than I have been in fifteen years. It is a case of streams wearing their channels deeper." His views, he conceded, were "exceedingly narrow," but he could "never get from under the dark cloud which Yankee selfishness and misconstruction of our constitutional rights brought upon us." His eldest son saw countless Confederates visit the family home, Laburnum, but in his maturity lost his father's fascination for the War Between the States. Stewart's son in turn remembered the senior members of the Westmoreland Club endlessly reminiscing about the war "to the boredom of the younger members, including Father and my uncles." Joseph Bryan acknowledged that the next generation would "lose much of this intensity" but knew it shared his conviction that moderns should emulate the ancients.[3]

Similarly, a contrast could be seen between two noted southern educators who advised the APVA. After the war J. L. M. Curry endlessly promoted states' rights, national unification, modern economy, and historical studies, all through an improvement in the school system. As he battled the Readjusters, Curry told an assembly celebrating the Yorktown Centennial that education, conservatism, and patriotism were one and the same. "No proper measure," he said, "should be left unused for awakening in the minds and hearts of the young a fervent love of country, and a firm determination by every personal and civic virtue, to make perpetual what our forefathers began."[4]

In the next generation Samuel Chiles Mitchell (1864–1948) admired Curry but backtracked on states' rights and the Confederate cult. Reared in Mississippi, he had seen the "feudalism" of the plantation system and the Ku Klux Klan run "rampant." He studied at the University of Virginia, where he met Stewart Bryan, and earned a Ph.D. in 1899 at the University of Chicago for a thesis on Virginia's early government. He, like Curry, taught at Richmond College. But he concluded that the Old South's classically oriented education had diverted "the eyes from ugly conditions at the front door or backyard." The modern study of history, politics, and economics would offer instead "the lights to the path of change."[5]

Taking a "pragmatic" approach, he used historical studies to "help in the rebuilding of the South." As he put it, "born in the deep South, amid the strife of sectionalism and sectarianism, I yearned instinctively for an ungagged mind. Tradition weighed upon me as the chief trammel of my destiny." Curry's trust was Mitchell's trammel, and the past offered different insights for these two generations. Mitchell nonetheless admitted to Curry in 1902, a year before his death: "You have entered very largely into my life as an ideal. . . . For all the strength that you impart to us younger men I am profoundly grateful. You help us more than you know."[6]

The New South movement spanned these generations and promoted national reunification, improved race relations, and industrial development.

A principal tenet of its philosophy was national reconciliation and the re-emergence of southern influence in the nation. The APVA played its part by stressing the colonial bonds and shared heritage of Virginia and New England. William Wirt Henry, chairman of the advisory board, spoke out for Unionism in 1893: "It remains for us now to cast out the spirit of sectionalism, that bitter fountain of our woes, and henceforth to unite to realize the sentiment of the poet—'One flag, one land, one heart, one hand, one nation evermore!'" The APVA, likewise, was described as possessing "a membership which knows no North, no South, no East, no West, but inviting all who venerate the early history of this country." The leading light of history was, of course, Virginia. Many preservationists still deeply resented the North. Dyed-in-the-wool Confederate Belle Bryan called New York, for example, "the land of the ungodly." One time when her ship embarked from the port of New York for Europe, she refused to look back upon that modern Gomorrah.[7] The association's public posture, however, supported national Union and intersectional harmony.

The APVA's leaders thought that Virginia had suffered unduly for its unique concept of nation. Mitchell complained that its "political isolation and impotence" were "no longer endurable." He declared that "the South has to-day reverted to its primal National spirit." Tyler, on the other hand, believed that after the Civil War, as before, "the laws of the federal government . . . have favored the North and injured the South." Preservationists worked to reverse that imbalance by propagating southern ways in the nation. Page took this tack, and his romanticized histories were so popular and moving that Thomas Wentworth Higginson, an abolitionist and commander of a black regiment during the war, read *Marse Chan* and wept over the death of a slave owner![8]

The debate on nationalism centered on two antagonistic definitions of the national bond—one legalistic, the other organic. The southern view was the legalistic theory of nationalism, whereby the states had created the Union through a social contract. Curry advocated this states' rights approach and claimed that it "contain[ed] the only principles or policy truly conservative of the Constitution." The South had been true to the Union, he said, and "the real enemies, the true disunionists, have been those who . . . have perverted the name and true functions of the government."[9]

Curry's stance in behalf of states' rights, however, represented a viewpoint that was waning at a time when the organic theory was waxing. Increasingly popular during the progressive era, organic theorists advanced the "revolt against formalism" by challenging classical liberalism's notion of government. According to these organic theorists, the nation was a homogeneous, unified land, and not a mere contractual relationship between states. Unlike southern traditionalists who wanted the state to represent the individual in the nation, organic theorists claimed that the nation protected the individual and his moral freedom, as it would eventually through the Fourteenth Amendment. Rebutting the states' rights position, organic theorists also held that the nation had created the states from colonies.[10] The APVA, on the other hand, enshrined those sites where Virginia had made its own contract, such as at Jamestown in 1619 and Williamsburg in 1776. While Page, Curry, and others sincerely pledged loyalty to the Union, it was to a nation based on this contract and with the expectation that the federal government would acknowledge the South's right to control its own internal affairs.

On many occasions the APVA observed Virginia's establishment of a contractual government. Preservationists placed a memorial at the site of the Richmond Academy where the state's convention had met in 1788 to ratify the United States Constitution. Mary Stanard noted that it was "the most momentous assemblage every convened in Richmond." Indicative of New South Unionism, she regarded it as more important than the Richmond conventions that had challenged King George in 1774–76 or Abraham Lincoln in 1861. Most preservationists still wanted the federal government to recognize Virginia's rights as a state. Henry lauded his grandfather for recognizing "that the powers granted to the Federal Government were too great, and that the result would be the absorption of the rights of the States, even to the freeing of our slaves." Had Virginia's right to control its own destiny not been recognized in 1788, Joseph Bryan contended, it "would never have acceded to that constitution but would have remained a sovereign, independent state until the crack of doom."[11]

Virginia's acceptance of nationalism required, moreover, that Americans recognize the uniqueness of the South. Hall urged southerners, for example, to cast off the shadow thrown by New England over their homeland. For too long they had been ignored, dismissed, or ridiculed. Speaking before the General Assembly in 1919, he urged it to "take immediate steps to fill the press, [and] the libraries of the country with propaganda literature." His colleague Tyler wrote *Propaganda in History* (1920) and specifically suggested the use of an advertising campaign to undercut Plymouth's claim to precedence, challenge the Puritans' reputation as defenders of religious freedom, reject the picture of Massachusetts as the home of democracy, and demolish the image of Lincoln as a saint.[12]

Tyler then wrote *Virginia First* (1921), a polemic brimful of claims about Virginia's precedence in Progress and Freedom. Writing in the hope that the booklet would be adopted by the schools and read by the general public, Tyler hammered away at the point that the Old Dominion had inaugurated the institutions and industries most prized by Americans. His implication, of course, was not only that the Old South had been very progressive, but that it defined what was worthwhile in the nation. Orators, editors, and ministers of culture in Virginia repeatedly cited his claims, but the pamphlet failed to offset New England's influence in the curriculum. When northern schools ignored it, he blamed Albert B. Hart, Harvard historian and author of the schoolbook *New American History* (1917), for giving it "the cold shoulder." Writing Ellyson, Tyler praised the APVA's "loyalty to Virginia and the South" but complained: "We have much to endure through our association with people who really constitute a distant nation. In one respect this wholesale snubbing of Jamestown may be a good thing. It may arouse our own people to a sense of the questionable accuracy of anything a Northern writer says. . . . This impudent defiance of the truth ought to arouse them, if nothing else."[13]

Page complained that world opinion about the South was even worse. He cited the assertion by the *Encyclopaedia Britannica* that the modern-day South was "an ignorant, illiterate, cruel, semi-barbarous section of the American people, sunk in brutality and vice." The reference work pictured antebellum southerners as a " 'race of slavedrivers' who 'contributed nothing to the advancement of mankind' and who started a bloody war to protect their slave property." It seemed impossible for southerners to reclaim the nation as their own. The pride of Anglo-Saxon Virginians was further deflated when traveling to their English motherland, Philip Alexander Bruce recounted in 1914. Englishmen had been taught "that the history of the United States is really the history of the North." Friendly Britons, moreover, would give Virginians " 'Pilgrim Father souvenir spoons,' 'Uncle Tom's Cabin,' or the last apotheosizing 'Life of Abraham Lincoln.' "[14]

Bruce's 1914 European trip made him realize how little Virginia had done to popularize its heritage and shape world opinion. As a result, he campaigned to form "an association of men in Virginia whose single purpose shall be to spread abroad a more correct conception of the achievements of Virginians in Colonial and national history." Composed of professors and scholars, it would "bring a strong influence to bear upon the whole community." At times it would overlap with the mission of the APVA, in that both would stir public action. Yet he even thought that the APVA did too little. Where were the monuments to Winfield Scott, Matthew Fontaine Maury, Cyrus McCormick, and Edgar Allan Poe, he asked? Bruce pointedly told the APVA that this scholarly project was not in its province.[15]

The growth of nationalism in the South paralleled the elevation of the Lost Cause to a sacral system. The two were not inconsistent, for southerners worshiped at the altar of the Confederacy precisely to redefine the bond between the states. As throngs of Virginians rallied to the defense of the Confederacy and Old South, northerners fumed that resistance, not repentance, flowed from Dixie. What simultaneously occurred in the North and West was the sanctification of Abraham Lincoln. Both North and South resorted to mythmaking and partisanship. As James Branch Cabell explained, "In both instances, loyalty required of each myth's makers that more or less should be left out, and that an appreciable deal should be recolored, for the good of mankind at large." Some mythmakers, like Tyler, built one while tearing down the other. He minced no words in challenging the reputation of the Great Emancipator and even claimed that the antebellum slave had been "a better Christian than Abraham Lincoln, who was a free thinker, if not an atheist."[16]

The ideology of the Lost Cause, the philosophy of states' rights, and the interpretations of the APVA usually dovetailed, prompting the APVA to work in tandem with those causes. The magnitude of Confederate celebrations often dwarfed those of the APVA, however, and revealed that Virginians, particularly the older generation, held the Confederacy more dear. Archer Anderson called the unveiling of Richmond's Lee statue in 1890 a "once in a lifetime" event. He told Senator John Daniel, "In every face of the 100,000 . . . there was written a personal participation in the public commemoration," and he shared the crowd's "deep, unanimous and spontaneous feeling."[17]

Lost Cause sentiment had subsided very little by 1907. Amidst the fanfare of the Jamestown Tercentennial, the APVA commemorated the Old Dominion's founding. What was more indicative of Virginia's priorities, and those of the entire South, was the fact that attendance at and publicity given to the APVA's own Jamestown shrine was overwhelmed by another event. In June, Richmond's neo-Confederates unveiled the Jefferson Davis monument. The parade, regalia, and speeches drew a throng of two hundred thousand Confederates. The women of the United Daughters of the Confederacy won not only the hearts but the wallets of the capital. That same year they also unveiled a monument to J. E. B. Stuart.[18] No APVA tribute to an earlier era drew such a crowd or evoked such intensity. It stood in the shadow of the Confederacy but braced the Lost Cause movement by anchoring it in the colonial and Revolutionary eras.

Although the APVA's bylaws stipulated a cutoff date of 1861 for its historical concern, the association still paid tribute to the Stars and Bars. As a Confederate revival captured Richmond in the 1890s and after, preservationists labored to redeem the reputation of the Confederacy. It was a Herculean task. Northern newspapers condemned not only Richmond's bronze monuments but its Confederate reunions. In 1908 the United Daughters of the Confederacy tried both to mollify northerners and to influence would-be teachers when it sponsored an essay contest at Teacher's College, Columbia University, on the topic "Robert E. Lee: A Present Estimate." Although the judges included prominent southern educators, the panel angered these neo-Confederate women when it awarded the prize to a Minnesota woman. She asserted that Lee had been "a traitor in that he sacrificed all to aid the enemies of his country." The prospective teacher also observed that "the [Old] South was intellectually dead; most of its people were densely ignorant." [19]

The APVA did its part to vindicate Lee. It marked the Lee house in Richmond, "one of the landmarks of the Confederacy," which, Kate Mason Rowland reported, was "revered by us all as the home, during the existence of the Southern Confederacy, of its great military chieftain, General Robert E. Lee." After 1893 the house at 707 East Franklin Street served as the headquarters of both the VHS and the APVA.[20] Lora Ellyson, apparently forgetting the Unionism of General George Washington, acknowledged that "it would be strange, if whilst transacting our business within the walls of a building once the home of our greatest general, we had not drawn some inspiration for our work." In fact, the APVA drew a significant share of its philosophy and raison d'être from Lee's Lost Cause. It similarly supported the preservation of Stratford Hall, Lee's birthplace. Because Lee's home Arlington had been confiscated by the Union and turned into a cemetery by vindictive Yankees, Stratford Hall commanded "the greatest reverence and interest of any house save Mount Vernon." [21]

Preservationists likewise mourned the death of Mary Custis Lee in 1918. The passing of the last child of Robert E. Lee meant, according to a nostalgic Stanard, "nevermore shall we touch flesh that was his flesh—nevermore look into the face of one to whom he gave being—who having lived with him in the close tender relation of child and father was cherished and revered as his living memorial." She had been "an ever enthusiastic and helpful friend" of the association and bequeathed the not insignificant sum of $3,000 to the society. Her passing meant that Virginia's human link with the Old South had been broken, and future generations no longer had such a living memorial. In recompense, the APVA perpetuated history's inspiration through antiquities and verse.[22]

Many southerners embraced a newer less hostile Lost Cause movement in the late 1880s which abandoned militant defiance toward the North. But Virginia served as center stage for those who refused to forget. They dominated Richmond by the 1890s and influenced the APVA's reading of past and present. Many APVA leaders, including Page, Curry, Pryor, and the Bryans, stood at the forefront of Virginia's Lost Cause movement. Its principal ingredients resembled the tenets promulgated by the APVA: white rule, local government, strict constructionism, traditionalist leadership, and a conservative philosophy. The changes in national Unionism, industrial capitalism, and urban society affected the meaning of the Lost Cause, but as traditionalists reviewed the past, they believed that they had been long struggling against misgovernment, northern domination, and centralized rule. Therefore, the APVA's reading of history not only salved the wounds of war and reinflated a damaged pride, it substantiated the claims of Confederates that their goals had been noble, sound, and historic.[23]

Many preservationists traced the roots of the Lost Cause to Bacon's Rebellion in 1676. The APVA chose not to repeat John Marshall's depiction of Bacon as a disheveled troublemaker but instead called him a patriot. As Page explained, Bacon and Washington both had fought to win "the inalienable right of British subjects to have self-government." He had inspired Patrick Henry, whose home was acquired by the APVA in 1958. By the late nineteenth century Henry symbolized states' rights and the Lost Cause. The Civil War culminated the struggle, and as Valentine claimed, "if the principles for which these [Confederate] patriots fought were wrong then the landing at Jamestown was a misfortune—Nathaniel Bacon was a rebel indeed—Patrick Henry spoke his eloquence in vain—Jefferson was a dreamer and our august Washington was a tremendous failure."[24]

The APVA similarly linked the history of Jamestown, Williamsburg, and Yorktown with the Civil War. Describing a Confederate fort at Jamestown as a "relic of the 'Lost Cause,'" preservationists told pilgrims that it was "most fitting that an era which was so momentous to Virginia and to the whole country, should have such a memorial at the birthplace of the nation." The APVA's branch in Yorktown compiled the roll of York County's Confederate Company F and placed a marker on the town's golf course to warn errant players against taking divots in the sacred turf of the Confederate cemetery.[25]

Not all APVA leaders blindly loved the Lost Cause, however. Page and Henry, for instance, were old-time Whigs. They loyally defended Virginia, and that included the Lost Cause, but they pointed out that modern problems were even more pressing. Even Coleman, whom one Confederate general called "unreconstructed" in her sympathies, regretted the "love of the Lost Cause" because it competed with the APVA. The preservation of Jamestown also became a thorny problem because the island had both colonial and Confederate ruins. Galt faced the question of which flag should fly over the fort. "As to flags," she wrote, "that is a delicate matter. I have not the love & reverence for the Confederacy that many persons have & the important part of the matter is that they know it. So anything like floating our beloved U.S. flag above the Confed[erate] fort might make some few persons have heart arches." She advised flying the American flag, but not above the Confederate fort. Bagby suggested instead that the APVA place its own pennant in this "most conspicuous" site. She thought that "our own flag" was "more suitable than the State & National flags" because Jamestown's history flowed in "own veins."[26] These elite prized their history but differed in their first loyalties.

Whether in Richmond, Atlanta, or Louisville, the Lost Cause movement took on a localized meaning. Its advocacy surely did not mean any categorical rejection of the New South, and in turn few southerners dared to challenge it openly. Walter Hines Page, for one, called it one of the "ghosts" that haunted the South.[27] New South proponents commonly found it to their advantage to honor Confederate heroes and their cause. They accepted much of the Old South heritage but did reject slavery, secession, and the antibourgeois Cavalier ethic. In the case of tradition-minded Virginians, however, that rejection was certainly qualified. Time and again, preservationists reinterpreted such contentious issues as slavery and secession to vindicate the South.

Despite the passage of the Reconstruction amendments to the Constitution, slavery was anything but dead as white southerners experimented with new ways to restore antebellum controls over blacks. By the 1890s Jim Crow, debt peonage, and outright terrorism would succeed; in the interim traditionalists used culture and history to stymie the Constitution, reinterpret the Old South, and bridge the two eras. One of the most popular and outspoken of these writers was Thomas Nelson Page. Heir to a long literary tradition concerning the plantation, he claimed that the Old South had offered "the purest, sweetest life ever lived" and its "domestic virtues . . . filled the homes of the South with purity and peace." In his romantic stories he commonly used the past as a foil to attack the present. Unlike the 1880s and 1890s when political corruption was abundant, he claimed that "the personal integrity" of antebellum leaders "was never doubted." His rendition was more fantasy than fact, but his invention became the APVA's documentation.[28]

Not only did southerners redeem the honor of the Old South, they reminded northerners of their outright complicity in its peculiar institution. Virginia traditionalists often asserted, for example, that New England opposed the abolition of the slave trade at the Constitutional Convention.[29] They acknowledged that it was best that slavery had been abolished, but Goodwin, Bruce, and Page claimed that slavery had saved the blacks. "In my judgment," Page said, "the system of African slavery was . . . the greatest blessing that has ever happened to the negro race." Couching his ethnocentrism in a history directed by Providence, he explained that slavery was a blessing for "it gave them the only civilization that the race has had the world over. It has given them Christianity."[30]

Even a reader such as William Dean Howells admitted that Page's sketches of antebellum society were very appealing. It required historian W. E. B. Du Bois, the first African-American to receive a doctorate from Harvard University, to challenge Page's fantasy. Du Bois wrote in the *Dial* that "southern slavery fostered barbarism, was itself barbaric in thousands of instances and was on the whole a system of labor so blighting to white and black that probably the only thing that saved Mr. Page's genius to the world was the Emancipation Proclamation,—the very deed that allows the present reviewer the pleasure of criticizing Mr. Page's book instead of hoeing his cotton." Giles B. Jackson, the former handservant of Lee who organized the Negro Exhibit at the 1907 exposition, observed as well that slaves had been 'indispensable" and their work "made Virginia bloom and blossom like a rose."[31]

Rebutting such criticisms, Tyler cleverly linked the antebellum plantation to America's mission of civilizing ostensibly inferior peoples in Asia after the Spanish-American War. "There was no criminal violation of the principle of democracy, or of self-government, in taking naked, savage, dirty and superstitious negroes and making them work," he said in his *Virginia Principles* (1928), "any more than there is today a violation of the rights of the Filippinos in controlling their government and making laws for them.

If the latter is defensible, so is the former."[32] Whether the focus was on "little brown brothers" in Samoa or Southampton County, Anglo-Saxonism imparted a cultural duty to help remake the world.

Traditionalists maintained, moreover, that slaves had been treated most kindly. Master and slave had often shared an intimate personal bond on the plantation. Joseph Bryan, for example, fondly remembered his parents' black mammy and house servants. Indeed, the paternalism of the Old South had explicitly defined the role of each race and permitted such affection. This master-servant bond, in fact, was a major foundation for the special civilization of the Old South. As long as whites felt secure, intimacy could prevail. With emancipation and a generation of blacks raised in freer conditions, however, white Virginians of the 1890s became uncertain about their social peace.[33] The resurgence of traditionalism and its political triumph in the Constitution of 1902 restored the old order, but without the intimacy of yore.

As it blended Old and New Souths, the APVA tried to regenerate the tradition of elite rule. Preservationists attacked the era's privatism and called for enlightened citizens to fulfill their duty to the commonwealth and lift its poverty and ignorance. "Young man, Virginia needs your devoted service," Hall told a Jamestown audience in 1891. "She points to her bottomless mines and to her hills of iron. She shows you rivers teeming with plenty, and lands waiting for the furrow. She points you to schools half-taught, and to children crying for the bread of knowledge. Will you obey her call? . . . She needs intelligent and thoughtful citizens everywhere to raise the level of public intelligence and to give dignity to her citizenship. She needs men that have studied the history of her past, and have from that study drawn inspiration for the future." Knowing that poverty corroded traditionalism, Joseph Bryan likewise thought that the progress of the New South was a godsend. "It is a great blessing to our young men," he wrote in 1902, "that we have some occupation for them than the driving of mules and negroes which was about all that was left to most of our Virginia boys before the new period of industry." Even the APVA's historian thought that "the smoke of engines and the glare of furnaces" of that Richmond industry added "picturesqueness to the scene."[34]

While Virginians focused on cultural preservation, their economy fell into the hands of outsiders. In the frenzy of industrial change, however, traditionalists rarely glimpsed the purse strings attached to northern investments and most gladly accepted development. Few regretted, however, that progress and profits resulted from cheap resources and exploited labor, that community services and education lagged far behind, and that middle- and upper-class boosterism only slowly helped the needy.[35]

Bridging Old and New Souths, preservationists used history to justify the turn toward Progress. The APVA claimed that the colonial, Revolutionary, Confederate, and modern eras were linked in a chain, but preservationists sometimes disagreed over the mettle of the smiths and the metal of those links. In a New South of economic ambition and physical change, some APVA speakers confessed that Jamestown also had been founded by those who pursued wealth and material gain. "Virginia was the Klondike of that period," Randolph McKim told an APVA audience. Page conceded in the 1890s that "the Southern colonies . . . were from the first the product simply of a desire for adventure, for conquest, and for wealth."[36]

Perhaps the New South's ambition had turned to an unvarnished materialism by the time the Jamestown Exposition met in 1907, as Edwin Alderman had complained, because Page took the podium at the celebration and revised his earlier assertion. "It has been charged by those ignorant of the facts or incapable of comprehending them," he now claimed, "that Virginia was planted only for gain." He refuted northern claims that the South lacked religious roots and professed that "no Puritans were ever more zealous than those Church of England colonists of Virginia." The Jamestown settlers, he trumpeted, were "faithful Soldiers of Christ, who came to establish a "great Protestant State." APVA leaders later suggested it was the wealth of the land that had diverted some settlers along a different path.[37]

Many tradition-minded Virginians feared that the New South's materialism and modernism had wrought a similar decline. Richmond's Ellen Glasgow devoted several novels to eastern Virginia and pictured wealthy southerners as decadent, artificial, and devoid of traditions. Preservationists, particularly those in professions set off from the business world, consequently used history as a means to correct the present. Implicitly criticizing the self-serving individuals of her own day, Pryor praised the colonists who had "put their hands to the plough and never looked back, who devoted their lives, with no hope of reward, to carrying on the work assigned them; . . . they sowed; but others reaped the rich harvest." Henry also praised earlier Virginians who worked their farms and chose not "to engage in arduous or speculative enterprises in pursuit of wealth." Evoking the myth that the frontier instilled respect for individual freedom, he said that they kindled such traits as "courage and self-reliance." The King James Bible further taught them that "every man was responsible for his conduct to his maker," and thus God, man, and society were linked in a moral economy.[38]

This line of argument revealed a troubling paradox. While Henry criticized speculative enterprises, many of his cohorts in the VHS and the APVA tried to boom Virginia's economy. Preservationists constantly accented the power of the individual to improve his standing. The hostile environment of the late nineteenth century, on the other hand, cast dark shadows over their concept of individualism. The get-rich-quick mentality of the Gilded Age prompted many elites to focus on their private world, not the chaotic environment of industrial capitalism. Many in the lower classes, meanwhile, felt trapped in wage slavery and peonage and rebelled against the economic system and its cultural traditions.[39]

Preservationists hoped that a moral reformation of the individual could ameliorate these foreboding trends. They popularized their vision of the Old South, while New South leaders were lured by prosperity and higher standards of living. First-generation leaders of the APVA countered this drift with even higher praise for the frugality, hard work, and republican virtues of the ancients, including the Confederates. The next generation of leaders, however, preached the gospel more dispassionately because they lacked the bitter memories of their predecessors. Historic preservation during the first generation of Virginia's progressivism had been defined partly in negative terms, as the likes of Bryan and Curry combated radical democrats. By progressivism's second generation, however, Virginia was safely in the hands of conservatives who single-mindedly pursued Progress. Its leaders still voiced the Gospel of Preservation's tenet that moderns should emulate the ancients, but this group valued traditionalism more for its sanction of their authority than for any call for republican simplicity and moderation.

Like the champions of the New South creed, the APVA rewrote history to create precedents for the sudden flurry of factory building. Virginia's rivalry with New England also propelled preservationists to act. They spotlighted, for example, the early strides that Virginia had made in the iron industry. For years the APVA worked to mark the site where an iron furnace had been built in 1619 at Falling Creek in Chesterfield County. Three years later, the mill fell victim to an Indian attack. Three centuries later, Wallace Nutting, a Yankee antiquary, advertised his Saugus, Massachusetts, ironworks with its extant ironmaster's house of 1636 as the first in North America. The APVA made "very strenuous efforts" to persuade the owner of the Falling Creek site to approve the placement of its memorial. Preservationists manufactured a marker but stored it away until permission was granted. To everyone's surprise, the APVA found the marker forty years later in a basement and only then placed it on the site.[40]

The APVA pictured the Falling Creek foundry as the seed for Virginia industry, but manufacturing had been stifled not by the Indian but by the tobacco plant. Hoping to wean southerners from their lasting attachment to this monolithic agriculture, New South advocates searched for examples of industrialism in the colonial South, leaving unmentioned the fact that those earlier enterprises, like their modern successors, relied on exploitative labor practices and thus sparked workers' protest. Three years after the Homestead Steel strike of 1892, Tyler evoked that comparison in unmistakable terms at a Jamestown pilgrimage by quoting the jaundiced opinion of George Sandys, the wealthy treasurer of the Jamestown colony known for his exploitation of labor. Referring to the skilled Italian workers at Falling Creek, Sandys had bluntly declared, "A more damned crew hell never vomited." Like modern workers at Homestead, their near slavery created resentment and acts of industrial vandalism; one worker "broke the furnace with his crowbar" in order "to promote their return to England."[41]

Colonial Virginia had problems with "immigrant" labor, difficulties that resulted from the bondage of those workers. The APVA marked sites such as Jamestown and Falling Creek as symbols of the Old Dominion's priority in industry, however, not as precedents for Virginia's subjugation of its work force. Even as a symbol of the state's leadership in the iron industry, the commemoration was deceptive. Falling Creek did precede Saugus, but its architectural legacy had vanished, while Saugus retained seventeenth-century buildings. Mercantilistic restraints and the dominance of agriculture thereafter hindered Virginia's iron industry. Two centuries passed before the founding of Richmond's Tredegar Iron Works in 1836.

The APVA boosted Virginia's commerce, but it deplored those in the New South who lusted for progress. Traditionalists, particularly those in a learned profession and with a classical education, attacked not only the North's Gilded Age barons but Virginia's new business class that emerged in the 1870s and 1880s. They repeated those condemnations over the next half century. In 1873 Archer Anderson bemoaned "the decline of private and public virtue heralded by an insidious growth of wealth and luxury." His friend Page similarly lamented in 1892 that "there has been a decadence in the spirit of our people within the last few years . . . I think that there is a less strong feeling of the sanctity of both public and private obligations— a less firm devotion to principles as principles than there used to be. I think that this corner-lot principle—this wild booming of towns, and hastening to be rich is a thing which is destroying the true spirit of our race." Prominent APVA leaders, nonetheless, speculated heavily in development ventures and corner-lot booms. What they deplored was the decline of traditions such as honor and public service. Tyler took it for granted that the New South had declined from the Old in terms of "moral force and vigor." Southerners fell to "toadyism" and "sold their birthrights for a mess of pottage and deserted the old Southern ideals." Whereas "the Old South aspired to furnish men for the ages, the New South cares more to rival the North in producing millionaires." [42]

James Alston Cabell promoted traditionalism as a check against that greed. "In this age of money-making, when the lust of wealth is threatening the ruin of the country," he said in 1907, "it is well that the people should be reminded by the examples of men who have gone before, that they owe something to their motherland. A childlike attachment to the native soil has in all ages been the strongest and simplest basis of patriotism." Groups such as the APVA and the Colonial Dames stressed this patriotism, and Pryor claimed that they acted as "a firm, though silent, protest against that aristocracy which considers itself best because it is highest on the tax list and bank list." Their work refuted "plutocracy, arrogance, and that important assumption of place notable in this country in those who have no foundation for pride beneath the surface of the earth, and no aspiration above it." Some historians, most notably Richard Hofstadter, have interpreted these sentiments within the context of a status revolution, whereby old elites acted as they did because they resented their loss of power. It is misleading, however, simply to see such resentment on a personal basis. Instead, a cultural battle was being waged over the meaning of past and present America. [43]

Notwithstanding their laments about selfishness, greed, and materialism, preservationists recognized that only prosperity could guarantee social peace in the Old Dominion. In this sense, the APVA was little different from New South boosters in Atlanta and Charleston who promoted a local history that served as a convenient backdrop for their social and economic agendas. Those boosters abandoned their heritage except when it became a handy prop to subordinate blacks, to affirm their leadership, or to chart the path toward Progress. In 1920 an Atlanta pageant included, for example, a scene where the Ku Klux Klan chased the carpetbaggers and their black followers out of town. Only then, it was understood, could Progress follow. [44]

Much more than in Atlanta or New Orleans, Richmond's elite affirmed its loyalty to the antebellum past. Paradoxically, it also demolished many of the landmarks associated with that heritage. As in old Charleston or New Orleans, tradition-minded elites failed to appreciate their architectural environment before much of it was altered, discarded, or destroyed. Whether in the Battery section of Charleston or Vieux Carré in New Orleans, old neighborhoods faced new threats in the form of automobile traffic, relic hunters, and modern fashion. Well before Richmond, New Orleans and Charleston turned to their municipal governments to protect this inheritance.[45]

APVA leaders actually feared that preservation could deter progress. At the Capitol in 1901 Charles Kent warned the APVA, in an address it reprinted, that preservation should not block progress. "A feeling too long existing among us," he said, was the idea "that our past was our most valuable possession, while our present represented our degree of decadence and our future our want of hope." As a commercial and industrial center, Richmond wanted to enhance its growth by tapping all available resources, including its history. APVA adviser Wyndham Meredith spoke in 1906 at a Chamber of Commerce banquet and underscored their "grand plan . . . to advertise Richmond to the world."[46]

In early twentieth-century America town boosters commonly staged pageants to affirm their city's historical identity and social order. The APVA, for example, joined with the Richmond Advertisers Club to develop a pageant to trace the city's history. The APVA mixed its own blend of town and organizational boosterism when it predicted that the pageant would "rival and even transcend the famous Mardi Gras, of New Orleans, thus attracting to the city thousands of people from all parts of the country." In 1922 preservationists helped rewrite history with a float that most attractively depicted "The Coming of the Maids" to Jamestown in 1619. The float did not mention that Jamestown's maids had been indentured servants sold expressly to enhance the dull lives of male settlers. Instead the APVA set up a souvenir booth where it accented more proper behavior by selling "copies of John Rolfe's letter to Sir Thomas Dale asking for the hand of Pocahontas"![47] Romantic love and maiden ladies most assuredly contrasted with androgynous Jazz Age flappers.

Even in the late 1920s, the APVA still defined historic preservation as woman's work. While business was supreme during the twenties, its boosters apparently put the APVA on the defensive despite the fact that it had done little to stand in the way of Progress. Ellyson rebutted a claim that the APVA had retarded economic development. "If our men of affairs will look after the commercial developments," she promised in 1927, "we will see that the past is not forgotten, without neglecting the pressing present."[48] But her proposal failed to address the disparity of power between the genders and their spheres and showed that Virginia's mind was still divided over preservation.

Businessmen did realize the economic importance of Virginia's history. Despite his lament that "commercialism seems to tinge everything," the editor of the Richmond *Times-Dispatch* suggested that the promotion of tourism was "a sound investment." "To put it quite bluntly," he said, "it would be commercially wise and in no sense improper for Virginia to capitalize some of its historic assets." Regretting that "outsiders"—including John D. Rockefeller, Jr.—planned to rebuild Wakefield, the birthplace of George Washington, the newspaper suggested that Virginia "should take the lead" in tapping its resources. Not all Virginians bowed before the reconstruction panacea, however. James Branch Cabell humorously called the reconstructed Wakefield the "supreme gem" in Virginia's "bright treasury of paste jewels." Most Virginians regarded any criticism of this shrine as "criminal folly and mere moon-struck sedition," but he considered it typical of their attempt to reconstruct history in a favorable but distorted light.[49]

Tourism, historic preservation, and economic development became one under Governor Harry Byrd. The origins of this mix go back to 1910 when the APVA placed a tablet in Charlottesville to honor Jack Jouett's ride in 1781. Virginia preservationists obviously wanted to deflate the reputation of Paul Revere, recently strengthened by William Sumner Appleton's successful drive to preserve Revere's Boston home. As the APVA "rescued from forgetfullness" Jouett's historic deed, it declared that he had "surpassed Paul Revere in the number of miles he rode and the exact time in which he accomplished his mission . . . to warn the Legislature of the approach of Tarleton and his raiders." The memorial yielded fruit in 1925 when William E. Carson, Byrd's manager in the gubernatorial campaign, took note. He suggested, as had the APVA earlier, that the state erect markers to inform both native and tourist along the highways that Byrd had pledged to improve.[50]

After Byrd's victory the General Assembly created in 1926 the Conservation and Economic Development Commission and authorized expenditures to mark appropriate sites. Byrd appointed Carson director of the commission and empowered Hamilton J. Eckenrode, the Virginia state historian, to launch the program. Eckenrode sought the advice of historians and APVA friends Lyon Tyler and Douglas Southall Freeman. By 1934 some twelve hundred markers were placed, and another four hundred planned. These markers usually related to military history. According to Marshall Fishwick, they were "closely related to state psychology" because they revealed what Virginians "wish to preserve out of a partly-documented, partly-imagined past." As a result, "Virginia's highways are an open-air classroom which tourists attend, whether they like it or not."[51]

Promoters of tourism also suggested in 1924 that the APVA sponsor "regular peninsula pilgrimages from Richmond eastward to the old shrines" at Williamsburg, Jamestown, and Yorktown. The annual flow of visitors there was reportedly "not the tithe [of] those who would come with the greatest satisfaction if only they knew the delights that awaited them." Besides the Historic Triangle, the APVA led visitors to the ancestral homes of the FFVs on the James River. Many excursions visited Brandon, an eighteenth-century estate that was the home of the Harrison family until 1926. As late as the 1890s, said Charles Washington Coleman, "many traces of the war" lingered at Brandon and served as reminders of Yankee infamy. The estate was particularly prized because it was "one of the few old estates left untouched by the wealth of the North, and it stands today, isolated, aloof, proud and beautiful."[52] Passenger service on the James River waned as car traffic grew, however, and APVA pilgrimages became more difficult.

The APVA promoted Jamestown, but it refused for a long time to open the site on Sunday. "Were the property open," it predicted, "it would mean nothing but a succession of automobile parties through the country, breaking the Sabbath's calm." Preservationists opened the gates first by allowing Sunday church services, then visits by history-minded pilgrims, and finally tourists. All the while, the APVA tried to protect the dignity of its shrine. William Ordway Partridge, sculptor of the Pocahontas statue on the APVA's grounds, praised the association in 1922 because it "managed to keep out the modern tripper, who throws banana skins and paper bags on the grass, so that there is still preserved for us a sanctity and a sense of repose." By 1941 eighty thousand visitors annually came to Jamestown.[53]

Bad roads often held back this tourist flow. In 1900 most roads were potholed and dusty. Horse-drawn carriages dominated these pathways, and the first automobiles could not safely traverse the backroads. Jamestown received only 1,024 registered visitors in 1919, largely because the unsafe wharf and impassable roads halted tourism. Further complicating the matter was the shortage of guidebooks. The APVA heard of one misinformed visitor who took three days to meander the fifty miles from Richmond to Jamestown. As a result, it wanted to place information cards at the hotels and to improve the state roadways. Virginia roads were so bad in the early 1920s that the American Automobile Association warned motorists to stay away. In 1910 the APVA also maneuvered to have the United States government build some of the roads that the commonwealth refused to finance. It "vigorously" endorsed the "proposed construction of a military road from Yorktown to Jamestown," and a generation later the federal government did build the Colonial Parkway to connect its holdings at Yorktown and Jamestown. The APVA also pressed in 1922 for a "capital to coast" highway, soon to become U.S. Route 60. If road building was a mark of progressive governments, Virginia all too often left potholed roads and shaky bridges for its tourists.[54]

The construction of roads, protection of shrines, and image building of boosters ultimately shaped tourism as one of Virginia's largest industries, but such development also exposed the paradox of the APVA's gospel. If Virginians wanted New South progress, how could they protect the ambiance of the Old South that drew their hearts and tourists' wallets? Historic neighborhoods in Richmond became more unsightly as material tastes changed, and Richmonders abandoned them in droves for modern environs. Occupancy by poor whites or blacks, demolition by developers, or escalating deterioration followed. In 1889, the year of both the APVA's charter and the drive to save the White House of the Confederacy, land boomer and preservationist Joseph Bryan warned Richmond, "If we proceed at the rate at which we are now going, it will not be very long before we will discover that though Richmond is an historical city, it is a city without historical monuments." Noting the "practical" side of preservation, he recounted a conversation between a northern correspondent and "one of our colored hackmen." The black carriageman said: "What are we drivers going to tell der Northern visitors when dey come down here? No Libby Prison and no Jeff. Davis Mansion? Oh no, dat will never do. Why de Davis House has put hundred of dollars in our pockets."[55] For years, however, white businessman failed to heed Bryan's warning.

APVA historian Mary Newton Stanard illustrated the divided mind of preservationists. A "bird-man" flying overhead in an airplane, she said, would see Richmond's "squalid spots," many of which were historically or architecturally significant. Embarrassed, she urged him, however, to "look quickly away to quiet, green parks" where he would hear the "shouting of progress and the laughter of prosperity." Visual memories were still "scattered throughout," but preservationists all too often turned their backs on those that were dilapidated. The more appealing Colonial Revival architecture of newer homes, on the other hand, attracted the eye because they usually included "a fanlight, a brass knocker, or white columns" to recall olden times. Yet these dwellings lacked "the sense of permanency and peace given by long association." Richmond could trace its history through monuments, place-names, and books, but the old homes that remained were fewer in number. As fine antebellum mansions were razed, she noted almost helplessly that "the modern Juggernaut, Business, is riding relentlessly up homelike Grace and Franklin Streets." She praised the fact that Richmond had a "personality and atmosphere peculiarly its own" but worried that change might erase it.[56]

The APVA reluctantly acknowledged that Richmond's highest priority was economic development. Because preservation was still a part of the feminine sphere, women deferred to men and the needs of business. Ellyson admitted to her members in 1916 that "trade and commerce demand building sites, no matter what becomes of structures in which history was made." In order "to save the remnant that has been spared," the APVA would "try to create a reverent and sentimental attitude for the historic." Even APVA leaders, however, committed such crimes. Sallie Munford Talbot had served on the APVA's directory board, but her husband Charles demolished an early Richmond landmark, the Charles Ellis home, to construct a more modern edifice.[57]

All through the South, cities failed to adopt a preservationist agenda. In Virginia, the case of Norfolk was obvious. Through much of this time, the APVA's definition of history and its focus on Virginia's two colonial capitals left branches elsewhere groping to establish their own identity. Increasingly dormant after the Jamestown Tercentennial, the Norfolk branch only noticed in 1912 what was thought to be the nation's oldest brick house. It asked Richmond for authority to mark the Adam Thoroughgood house in Princess Anne County. The plaque, establishing the edifice's construction in 1636–40, contrasted strangely with the ruined, unrestored building. Apparently the branch could only afford a tablet.[58]

As the APVA searched for funds, it made strange alliances. The ruins of Jamestown, for example, had only been preserved because of the island's remoteness and lack of access. Preservationist Mollie Lightfoot claimed in 1907, however, that the APVA and the C&O Railroad were "certainly working along very much the same lines in promoting the interests of Jamestown." As the APVA worked to increase tourism, it also "develop[ed] the country through which the C&O passes." Even more troubling was the APVA's willingness to sell advertising space in its programs to land developers. At the same time Hall was praising the island's wilderness, a Richmond real estate company placed a large advertisement in an APVA program for the sale of Barney's acreage at Jamestown and even included a picture of the

APVA's church ruin, implying that it was part of the tract. Ironically, Yonge could state in 1923 that "Jamestown is fortunately situated remote from the activities of our progressive age."[59] As much as the APVA's own work, Virginia's tardy development kept Jamestown protected.

Virginia's second capital, Williamsburg, became another focal point where history and development clashed. After many decades of neglect, the quaint town still held much charm. In a book which promoted Progress, Bruce fancifully described its past to boom its present: "There the ghosts of the most aristocratic society that ever flourished on our continent still flit about, carrying with them the bright colors of the old colonial costumes, the elegance of powdered hair and silver shoe-buckles, and the charm of polished manners not unworthy of [the Court of] St. James itself. To pass down the long [Duke of Gloucester] street is to be lost in dreams of a past that vies in interest with the one suggested by the streets of some old English town, which counts its age by the centuries." What had once been "the miniature copy" of the English court, Charles Coleman told the APVA with chagrin, however, had stagnated. The town's largest employer, a state hospital, set its tone, and "Williamsburg, in the minds of many, has come to mean a lunatic asylum." Tourists more easily heard the shrieks and groans of the patients than they imagined the stirring oratory of Patrick Henry.[60]

As boosters spurred development, Bruce saw no conflict of interest between past and present. The old capital possessed "those two traits which the conservative yet enterprising instincts of the English stock of people have always cherished: namely, a just regard for the sentimental claims of the past, and, at the same time, a clear recognition of the superior claims of the present." Those traits warranted development of the town, as was clearly stated in *Facts about Williamsburg and Vicinity,* published by the local Business Men's Association in the 1890s. BMA president John B. C. Spencer, whose wife was an APVA incorporator, owned the Colonial Inn, an enterprise sure to benefit from any increase in tourism and business. Tyler, one of the BMA's founders, promoted Williamsburg partly to boost his college's reputation, partly to boom the economy. He knew, for example, that the APVA brought Uncle Sam's dollars to Jamestown to check erosion and facilitate navigation. He suggested that Yonge open Archer's Hope River (College Creek), as "its commercial advantages are of equal value with its historic value." Fortunately, his ploy failed, and the pristine lands off College Creek remain a prime archaeological site.[61]

The land boom, economic development, and present-mindedness worried some in the APVA. Galt focused on one culprit in 1895, the Old Dominion Land Company, a subsidiary of the C&O Railroad. "I am afraid," she told Bagby, "this boom around here will ruin the old town—the move to build—making the houses come so close together." She further complained when the town council leased lots on Market Square close to the Powder Horn so that "the best view of it is lost." Coleman feared that boosters like the Spencers were also trying to take over her APVA branch. In 1901 she thought as well that the local development-minded politicians were divorced from Williamsburg's lineage; they were not the "City-Fathers" but "stepfathers" because they so little understood "the true interests of the town." Their plans to build on both sides of Market Square would "destroy the integrity and individuality of the historic old place." Coleman found it frustrating "to live in a place where one must ever be in a fire of contention about one thing or another." [62]

The land boom continued to the point where developers tried to rent the Powder Horn for office space. In 1917 they offered to purchase the dimly lit building for $25,000. By then Williamsburg's main street had radically changed. A Baptist church of Greek temple design, galvanized iron garages, and cheap amusement halls were strangely juxtaposed with the early eighteenth-century magazine. Across from the college entrance stood a dilapidated home that typified old Williamsburg. Owned by an African-American family, it had pigs in the pen and chickens in the yard. Such contrasts set a true picture of the town—Old and New South, rural and city, black and white side by side.[63] Such contrasts showed Virginia's paradox. Wishing to escape poverty, it wanted progress. This development, however, increasingly erased the visible links with the old order. Traditionalists capitalized on the Old Dominion's historic assets largely to assure their own standing and create a stable society, but they found, paradoxically, the necessity of reconstructing the ambiance, if not the actuality, of that which had fallen to the juggernaut of Progress.

All in all, these preservationists accommodated Old and New Souths in order to save their traditions of elite rule, social order, and individualism. As many conceded, there was much about the New South that they found ugly, mindless, and distasteful. In response, they used history, preserved in story and stone, to temper the pace of the New and tie it to the Old. Preserved architecture and memorialized landscapes would be used to educate contemporary Virginians about the errant ways and their intended destiny. What held back historic preservation in New South Virginia was not simply the fact that women were its custodians and men allowed them little actual power in the marketplace, but that it was always secondary to the original goals of the APVA—to restore traditionalism to its dominant role in society. Conservative government, economic development, and cultural politics always came before the actual business of saving endangered buildings or landscapes. Despite those failings, the APVA's recognition of tourism allowed the rescue of some of Virginia's architectural inheritance. By capitalizing on tourism, enough of that material culture was either held in respect or, more likely, in abeyance, for another generation to preserve.

9

"Upholding the Standards of Liberty": The Politics of Anglo-Saxonism and Washingtoniana

I N A REGION sharply divided by class and race, the APVA sanctioned rule by those who descended from Anglo-Saxon worthies and upheld the traditions of elite rule, social hierarchy, and political conservatism. The APVA's preservation of desolate Jamestown, together with its creation of meccas in forgotten towns like Williamsburg, buttressed those perspectives and regenerated those traditions. At the same time, the new state constitution enforced the peace in Virginia. But soon modern Anglo-Saxons fell to bickering not only over woman's suffrage but over the outbreak of war in Europe in 1914. APVA leaders shared no common ground regarding the outbreak of the Great War. Did their traditionalism require them to defend Great Britain, the homeland of Anglo-Saxons? Or should they continue the tradition of neutrality, first declared by George Washington, and avoid European wars? As in their battles against Readjusters, freedmen, and labor unionists, preservationists used tangible sites, familiar symbols, and historical traditions to argue the question. The politics of preservation ultimately would decide the issues of war and peace, as well as the return to normalcy in the years after.

With the war's outbreak, some of the most elite Virginians challenged the belligerents. Thomas Nelson Page condemned the conflict and concluded that civilization had failed. Long active in the campaign to enact legislation that would outlaw war—the hallmark of progressivism in international law—he blamed the bloodshed on the "brazen cupidity" of arms manufacturers and militarists who wrapped themselves in their nation's flag. Lyon Tyler used the legacy of Pocahontas to speak for peace. Three months after the guns of August blasted, he dedicated a tablet to the Indian at Jamestown. He praised her as "a champion of peace" who recognized that all nations should "dwell on this earth in amity and peace forever."[1]

John Stewart Bryan expressed the prowar sentiments that would ultimately prevail. He declared in January 1915 that America was committed to Britain through "Our World War." Bryan participated in the League to Enforce Peace, a group of Anglophiles who held their convening session symbolically at Philadelphia's Independence Hall in 1915. They thereafter called upon the Western democracies to intervene across the globe and control world events. The United States did enter the war in 1917, and Secretary of War Newton D. Baker asked his longtime friend to use his newspaper experience to improve the troops' morale. As a result, Bryan developed a YMCA publication, *Trench and Camp,* to motivate the soldiers.[2]

Even before the outbreak of hostilities, preservationists lined up in England's column. Most noticeably, Philip Alexander Bruce and Barton H. Myers supported Britain's cause. While in London in 1914, Bruce urged Virginia preservationists to strengthen the bond between England and America by placing a prominent memorial at Blackwall, the site from which the John Smith expedition had sailed in 1606. Myers, a preservationist who served as British vice-consul in Norfolk, already had appeared before the APVA's board to suggest that the tense period before the outbreak of war was "the psychological moment for a fitting memorial at Blackwall."[3]

Bruce stressed the uplifting mission of England in the world in both 1606 and 1914. As Europe drifted into war, the Anglophile historian interpreted Smith's expedition as "England's first step towards the erection of her greatest succession of colonies, which has enabled her morning drumbeat to follow the daily circuit of the sun without a break in the roll. It was a step that has been of a vast beneficence to all mankind." He predicted that the Blackwall tablet would symbolically unite Britain's progeny in the moment of the mother country's need. Most cleverly, he set his appeal in the context of Virginia's rivalry with New England, noting that Yankees had already placed a memorial to the Pilgrim Fathers at Southampton and persuaded Ambassador Walter Hines Page, a North Carolinian by birth, to unveil it in 1913. Yankees had also erected tablets to John Harvard and John Endicott. The plantation-born author claimed that Virginia had been "too supine even to follow the pious example set by her sister state." He urged "our wonderfully energetic and intelligent Virginia women" in the APVA to take action.[4]

Problems arose immediately with his proposal. When the APVA's cost-conscious president proposed building a simple memorial, Bruce objected.

Such a minuscule monument would send the wrong message to England's foes, for it would "belittle" Smith, Jamestown, and Anglo-Saxonism. Just as the Washington Monument towered over the nation's capital, showing the power of traditionalism in a changing United States, he wanted a grand Elizabethan figure of bronze atop a granite pedestal—"a conspicuous object to the myriads voyaging on the Thames" that "would soon become one of the most famous landmarks of the kingdom." [5] The APVA seriously considered his proposal, but the logistics proved impossible. It tabled the motion, and Bruce quit the APVA in protest.

America remained neutral from 1914 to 1917 and President Wilson downplayed the nation's strong ties to England, but the APVA broadcast its Anglo-Saxonism and Virginia's lasting debt to the British Isles. Preservationists ceremoniously showed their support through war work in behalf of England and France. Together with the Daughters of the American Revolution and other patriotic groups, Mrs. James Lyons, an APVA incorporator and later vice president, presented a cannon to the city of Winchester, Virginia, in 1915. It commemorated the Englishmen who responded to Washington's plea for weapons to defend the American colonies during the Seven Years' War. Knowing that Virginia's memories of the Civil War were still keen, she couched her appeal in the traditions of duty, self-sacrifice, and patriotism. Elizabeth Henry Lyons told her audience, "These men [of the eighteenth century] had those to whom they were dear—mothers, wives, sweethearts—by whom war was hated, as it is by us, and yet they willingly laid down their lives in defense of that which every nation and every man is lawful guardian—their rights and their honor." The cannon's symbolism was evident; now American merchants were reciprocating the deed by carrying arms to Britain. She rejected neutrality, moreover, and reminded her audience that it was "a Christian duty to go to war" and the American aim was "peace with honor." [6]

Three weeks before Congress declared war, the APVA joined the bandwagon. Just twelve days earlier, the British government had released the text of the Zimmermann note, a message of dubious authenticity that described a secret alliance between Germany and Mexico. At the same time, the Senate debated but killed Wilson's request to arm American merchant ships, reasoning that America had not been directly threatened by the European conflict. Wilson nonetheless stretched existing law to achieve his goal. The APVA unfurled its Anglo-Saxon banner on 13 March 1917 and endorsed his "effort to protect American rights against unlawful invasion and guarding our nation against hostile attack." It rejected George Washington's warning to avoid European conflicts and instead lauded Wilson's "upholding the standards of liberty as designed by our forefathers of this republic." At least one director objected, however, because she thought that the APVA had exceeded its charter by endorsing the war.[7]

Preparedness and preservation easily mixed. The APVA encouraged its women to join the war effort, as they had during the 1898 war, through such organizations as the Red Cross and the Woman's Committee of the Council of National Defense. A month after America entered the war, advisory board member Henry St. George Tucker spoke before a New York assembly numbering close to one thousand which had gathered to celebrate Jamestown's anniversary. After they sang the "Marseillaise," the "Battle Hymn of the Republic," and the "Star Spangled Banner," he invoked Manifest Destiny, described the war as "the greatest event in history since the Coming of Christ," and predicted American victory because "God himself was aligned with the side of democracy."[8]

The APVA's Norfolk branch visibly tied preservation and politics in October 1917. Commemorating Lafayette's visit in 1824, it placed a tablet that showed more interventionist foreign policy than historical coincidence. The affair was organized by Barton Myers—former mayor, incumbent British vice-consul, and longtime APVA adviser. As a military and commercial center, the city's heart, or pocketbook to be more exact, went out to the British. A local newspaper urged its readers to attend the ceremony and packed its front pages with news of the Liberty Loans and French army campaigns. Past and present, monument and war became one. It began with a parade, including a detachment of sailors, a choir of servicemen, and a bevy of schoolchildren, all headed by the navy band. Speaking before the city's elite, Myers focused on Lafayette's assistance during the Revolution and outlined "the great service this country is at the present time rendering France in the war that is being waged against Germany to make the world safe for democracy."[9]

Nearby, Williamsburg offered a more revealing picture of America's wartime divisions. On 26 March 1917 a mass meeting at the old Courthouse, across the street from the Powder Horn, unanimously passed a resolution offered by Tyler which pledged support to the Wilson administration. The local paper reported that "a wave of enthusiasm swept the crowd like magic." In his pamphlet *The South and Germany* (1917), Tyler called it "a just and righteous war" but still resented attempts by northerners to equate Hohenzollern Germany with the Confederacy. He claimed that those Yankees were hypocrites because the United States fought in 1917 for the same rights that it denied Confederates. He asked southerners to compare the conflict with their own history. The German bombing of Rheims was a case in point. The destruction of France's medieval capital stirred preservationists such as Appleton, but Tyler claimed that "Rheims and its ancient Cathedral have suffered less from the shells of the Germans than beautiful Columbia and Savannah from the torch and wanton destruction of the Federal soldiers." [10]

The faces of Williamsburg's women, moreover, revealed a different picture of the war. "We've surely known what war means here," one woman said to a visiting writer shortly before the United States entered the war in 1917. "Its scars are with us to this day. And are we to have our dear ones taken from us again?" Her face showed not the exuberance of elite women such as Elizabeth Henry Lyons but "that look of indefinite sadness that is found so often in the faces of Southern women" who remembered the bloodbath and privation of the Civil War. Mary Custis Lee most poignantly reflected that sadness. Abhorring the cataclysmic destruction in Europe, she called herself "a peace-at-any-price woman." She particularly lamented the wartime psychosis and its "ceaseless" dehumanization of the enemy. [11]

The war ended in late 1918, and leading preservationists again linked past and present. While the Versailles Peace Conference debated such contentious issues as Wilson's proposal for a League of Nations, Lora Ellyson spoke to the APVA and happily reported that Edith Bolling Wilson, the wife of the president, had descended from Princess Pocahontas. "A historian has said that "Pocahontas stood for truth as well as peace,'" she said. "It is to insure to the world a lasting peace that President Wilson is now conferring with the leaders of the countries" recently at war. She expressed great relief that "the old year with its horrors and terrible sorrows, its problems and perplexities is passed. That the war is over and that a lasting peace seems assured gives us unspeakable joy." [12]

Page, who had swallowed his pacifism to serve as United States ambassador to Italy, defended Wilson's diplomacy, citing Virginia's history for relevant illustrations. While the Senate debated the treaty, and before defeating it, he spoke at the tercentennial observance of Jamestown's first legislative assembly. Page used bugaboos most familiar to Virginians. The Germans had been as duplicitous as the Indians who attacked Jamestown in 1622, he said. Their militarism, moreover, devolved from a European autocracy that Americans had overthrown in 1776. Rejecting the "acrid criticism" leveled against the president, he claimed that Wilson had "saved the world . . . much as George Washington saved the cause of liberty." He called the

League of Nations "the one ark of safety of the world" and warned that America's refusal to join would lead to international chaos, America's own militarism, and a second world war. Before another audience, he advocated trade expansion. In the vein of Wilsonian internationalists who joined culture and capitalism, he defined such commerce as "one of the main vehicles for the spread of Civilization, [and] one of the chief promoters of the spirit of Liberty and of Human Progress throughout the world." Tyler went so far as to claim that a restoration of the national Union in accordance with the dreams of the Founding Fathers would require "joining the League of Nations in banishing armies and navies and war." [13]

John Stewart Bryan had attended the Versailles Conference in 1919 and served on the executive committee of the League to Enforce Peace, along with such dignitaries as labor leader Samuel Gompers and publisher William Allen White. Although he supported Wilson's league in 1919, he really wanted Anglo-American control of Europe and the world. "One cannot control this mixed bunch on the Continent by anything less than a good big club," he told his son in 1919. The club "must be swung by England and ourselves combined" until "the rest of the world has learned how to play the game by rules." [14] Bryan's internationalism reveals a sea change in two generations of preservationists. Joseph Bryan earlier had defended a stay-at-home foreign policy and the protection of the Monroe Doctrine's tradition. Now his son saw America's fate tied to European and world affairs.

Stewart Bryan's sentiments undergird a tenet voiced repeatedly by APVA leaders that Anglo-American unity could ensure world peace. Isolationism was categorically rejected through artifact and ritual. The APVA opened its arms to the Sulgrave Institute in 1920, for example. This English organization took its name from Washington's ancestral home and promoted Anglo-American amity as a means to strengthen a war-weakened Britain. Its members traveled to America to celebrate the Pilgrim Tercentennial, and also scheduled stops in New York and Virginia. Their arrival in New York City prompted demonstrations by Sinn Fein, the Irish independence movement, but Virginians created no such clamor when they came to honor Jamestown's first representative assembly. The oratory at the celebration revealed as much Anglo-American politics as commemoration of 1619. Bryan and Hall represented the APVA and greeted the visitors.

As the civil religion merged with the politics of an Anglo-American alliance, Hall told his distinguished audience that the two nations "will ever be found acting in concert in the matter of preserving the peace of the world and of upholding those principles for which both stand." Bryan similarly linked Anglo-Saxonism, Wilsonian internationalism, and the white man's burden. He called the Anglo-Saxons the "exemplars of political . . . and religious liberty" who undertook "the great task of making wide the paths for the feet of mankind and making straight the way for the progress of the work of God." The ceremony that day fully revealed those themes. According to one account, a solemn band of Virginians, New Englanders, and Britons "entered reverently the little church on Jamestown Island for the most remarkable and awe inspiring service in all its long history." Those pilgrims came not "as separate people to worship at this shrine. They came as representatives of one race, whose pioneers have carried the torch of liberty and the ideal of free government to every corner of the earth." This rite may have confirmed the primacy of Anglo-Saxons and the Jamestown settlement, but it also revealed an unvarnished ethnocentrism.[15]

During the 1920s the APVA continued to enshrine points along the route taken by John Smith in 1606–7. Commemorating each step of those voyagers, it ultimately marked the launching at Blackwall, the landing at Cape Henry, the settling of Jamestown, and the exploring near Richmond. These sacred sites became part of the myth of a heroic quest, perhaps the most romantic notion of mythology worldwide, as in Vergil's *Aeneid* or Homer's *Odyssey*. The Virginians were trying to keep up with the Yankees. The Pilgrim monument at Plymouth, begun in 1859 but only dedicated in 1889, also pictured a stirring mythology by depicting the Pilgrims leaving Holland, signing the Mayflower Compact, landing in the New World, and signing a treaty with the Indians. Virginians upped the ante and described Blackwall as the site where "the Odyssey of the Anglo-Saxon" began.[16]

The APVA discovered that the English port "was so commercialized and changed" that authorities did not even want a monument, out of the fear that it would inhibit development. Anglo-American stalwarts won out, however, and the APVA dedicated the tablet with pomp and ceremony in 1928. The United States Navy provided an honor guard, and Bryan represented the APVA. Picturing Blackwall as a "world beacon," he noted that Anglo-Saxon voyagers had carried their rule to distant lands and won "undreamed of wealth and power."[17]

Besides making the much-expected jabs at the Pilgrims, Bryan told the audience of two hundred that his hometown, Richmond, was "more English than London." He referred to the racial mix in Richmond by declaring that "the only people they had there" who were not English "had come there by a 'special and pressing invitation,'" drawing the crowd's laughter.

Lady Astor, a Virginian by birth and the first woman to serve in the British Parliament, followed Bryan's speech with an appeal for Anglo-American unity. A third speaker who paid tribute to the APVA, Lord Charnwood, ironically had written a laudatory biography of Abraham Lincoln, the bête noire of Virginians such as Lyon Tyler. The monument was unveiled to the tune of "Dixie," but the ceremony closed more appropriately with the "Star Spangled Banner" and "God Save the Queen." The APVA had long sought public recognition of Virginia in Britain and gained some success as local papers covered the ceremony. An unhappy slip occurred, however, when a London paper reported that the tablet honored the "105 adventurers who followed the Mayflower to America in 1606."[18] Nevertheless, the monument symbolically tied the Old Dominion to its native shore.

Every American seemed to know that the *Mayflower* had brought the Pilgrims to Plymouth, but very few Virginians knew the names of the ships that came to Jamestown in 1607. Page even admitted to an acquaintance that when first asked their names, he drew a blank. Much investigation followed, but it brought mixed results. The APVA considered the question at a 1921 meeting, and all agreed that the *Godspeed* (or *Goodspeed*) and the *Discovery* had been the two smaller ships. Preservationists found "much diversity of opinion," however, about the third vessel and could not decide whether it had been the *Sarah Constant* or *Susan Constant*. The APVA decided to use the former because "usage and time has made hallowed" the name of *Sarah Constant*. It proved in the end to be the incorrect choice.[19]

With the sanction of church and state, the APVA earlier had marked other points along the 1606–7 journey. In 1896 it placed a bronze tablet at Cape Henry while Belle Bryan, Bishop Alfred M. Randolph, and Charles Washington Coleman officiated. In 1907 the APVA unveiled a monument to honor the explorations of captains Christopher Newport and John Smith at the site of Richmond. Lieutenant Governor Ellyson presided at the dedication of a pyramid of boulders with a bronze cross. Preservationists had hoped to place it at the site of Belvidere, the plantation of William Byrd I, but with chagrin discovered that the state penitentiary occupied those sacred grounds. They chose instead Gamble's Hill, a site which served to confirm not only the wisdom of the settlers but the righteousness of industrial progress. Overlooking Richmond's industries, the panorama included "the smoke of engines and glare of furnaces." As Mary Newton explained, "the prophetic eye of Colonel Byrd" had foreseen "the natural advantages of the situation for a centre of commerce."[20]

Whether pilgrims honored Smith at Jamestown or Washington's ancestors at Sulgrave, these commemorations reflected the pervasive hero worship practiced by tradition-minded Americans. The case of George Washington brings this most into perspective. The legacy of the *Pater Patriae* received much attention in the late nineteenth century as the elite coped with the changing ethnicity, class structure, and ways of life in America. He became a symbol of 100-percent Americanism. Virginia preservationists reverently marked sites associated with his life. While the Mount Vernon Ladies' Association dutifully kept a shrine at his home, the APVA looked for ground where his feet had touched. These places included his headquarters in Winchester during the Seven Years' War, the Alexandria site where he delivered his last public address, and the home of his mother, Mary Ball Washington, in Fredericksburg.[21]

The APVA inherited and transmitted a Weemsian image of Washington as America's highest hero and purest saint. Parson Mason L. Weems had first published his biography in 1800, and by 1850 fifty-nine editions had been issued. Enhancing Washington's legend to the point of downright falsification—the cherry tree legend, appearing first in the fifth edition, is a case in point—Weems helped establish a cult that awed the nation. Later biographers, such as Unitarian minister Jared Sparks, freely added to the corpus of Washingtoniana. Virginia preservationists carried on this tradition and marked it in bronze and stone. The APVA, moreover, wanted nothing to do with anything that could detract from his legacy. It had a chance in 1896, for example, to buy a copy of the 4 January 1800 edition of an Ulster County, New York, journal that reported his death and funeral. Knowing that numerous Democratic-Republican editors rejoiced, not wept, upon hearing of Washington's death, Stanard described the account, sight unseen, as "spurious" and rejected any purchase.[22]

Washington's legend had been so sanitized by the turn of the century that schoolchildren were losing interest. Some writers, including Stanard, tried to put life into his memory but fell to the assaults of the debunking biographers of the 1920s, such as William E. Woodward, who tried to remove America's heroes from their pedestals. The latter approach obviously ran counter to the APVA's efforts to create models for emulation. Emma Read Ball, an MVLA regent and APVA vice president who was married to a great-nephew of Washington, for example, had spent many years documenting Washington's descent from illustrious English nobility. Yet the opening sentence of Woodward's first chapter read: "George Washington came from a family that must be called undistinguished, unless a persistent mediocrity, enduring many generations, is in itself a distinction." Instead of a Washington cast by hagiographers as a saint, Woodward portrayed him as "the average man dignified and raised to the nth power" and "a thoroughly undemocratic" American.[23]

The APVA illustrated its commitment to hagiography in the question raised in 1923 whether Houdon's sculpture of Washington should remain on its high pedestal in the Virginia Capitol. Jonce McGurk, a Smithsonian Institution consultant, appeared before an APVA meeting to describe Houdon's attempt to portray "a living, breathing human." McGurk asked the APVA to help restore that lifelike character by aiding the depedestalizing drive, but it declined and referred the question to the state art commission. The sense of traditionalist Richmond, however, had been provoked. A popular editorialist wrote an open letter to the APVA. Lamenting the decline of traditionalism and the ascent of "flappers and cake eaters," he acknowledged, "I revere the memory of George Washington above that of any other man Virginia has produced, except Lee, and I cannot stand the thought of his looking squarely in the eye a lot of people in the public life of Virginia today." The Virginia Art Commission, headed by Fiske Kimball, reviewed the issue but dodged the controversy. Just as President Coolidge dismissed the debunkers with the quip, "Well, I see the [Washington] Monument is still there," so, too, did Washington remain standing tall on his Richmond pedestal.[24]

The APVA honored Washington's mother even more. From its first days the APVA worked in Fredericksburg to preserve what it called the sacred shrines of the Revolutionary era. Before the APVA's interest, little had been done to preserve the town's heritage. Although Mary Ball Washington had died in the year of her son's inauguration as the nation's first president, her grave went unmarked by any memorial. In 1833 Congress finally decided to build a fifty-foot obelisk, but its cornerstone was laid only in 1893. Meanwhile, Pryor helped organize a Mary Washington Memorial Association. President Grover Cleveland dedicated the memorial in 1894, and Senator John Daniel defined her life largely in the context of the era's domestic sphere. Praising "the homely virtues of her sex," he pictured her as an "unassuming wife and mother whose Kingdom was her family, whose world was her home." Following his speech, the APVA held a reception for these distinguished visitors.[25]

Just a few years earlier, public demand for Mary Washington memorabilia had dramatically increased. This interest could be attributed not simply to the founding of patriotic organizations, the centennial celebration in 1889 of her son's inauguration, and the blossoming of the Colonial Revival

movement, but more importantly to the never-ending trauma associated
with industrialism, urbanism, and modernism. What was juxtaposed with
the Colonial Revival's reverence for custom was the reckless leap into the
uncertainty, and supposed inevitability, of Progress made by the nation's
leaders in the 1890s. Paradoxically, as the elite bowed before tradition, it
directed two of the most unsettling movements in American history, the
industrial revolution and the corporate reconstruction of society. It used the
figures of Washington and the nation's founders to sanction this unsettling
change. During the era, those reassuring portraits were used by any and all
Americans to wrap their cause in the garb of patriotism. Tradition-minded
women sought particularly to protect the domestic sphere amidst the
change.[26]

Female patriotic groups vied as standard-bearer for Mary Washington.
In 1889 George Washington Ball, a distant descendant of Mary Ball Washington, asked the APVA "not to interfere with the Daughters of the Revolution in the purchase and preservation of the tomb of Mary Washington."
The APVA deferred. Six weeks before, Ball had also written the APVA and
asked it not to interfere with the now obscure Virginia Relics Association.
He warned that it would "be most unfortunate" for the APVA "to obstruct
the action of an organization so much more extensive, and capable of doing
much more for a cause that concerns both State and Nation!"[27]

Fredericksburg held Mary Washington's last home, a simple wood-
framed cottage from the 1770s. George Washington Ball claimed in 1889 to
have the DAR's support for his "idea of converting her old Home . . . into
a great Asylum for orphans," but the idea had not panned out. A year later
a Chicago syndicate initiated what Newton called "unholy negotiations" to
purchase it for removal to the Columbian Exposition. There it would have
been used to illustrate the great material advances of civilization and to add
a touch of history to the lure of Progress. The only APVA member in
Fredericksburg, Frances Tucker Carmichael, a sister of Joseph Bryan, wrote
Belle Bryan that it would be a "pity" to lose a site that defined the town's
history and drew so "many tourists." She told Bryan that the house was only
worth about $2,000, but the owner asked for $4,000. He was willing to sell
it to the Chicagoans but offered Virginians the first bid.[28]

Bryan immediately put his money down on a one-year option so that
the APVA's friends could "'aggregate their influence,' . . . in order to acquire this precious relic." The APVA thereafter bought the house for $4,000
with Bryan advancing half the sum at no interest and a mortgage covering
the remainder. He asked his Fredericksburg friends to help out because the

APVA had just acquired the Williamsburg magazine, and "all such articles seem now at fancy prices." The APVA apparently realized that "it would have been a great loss to have the venerated old house removed to Chicago"—another victory for Yankee arrogance and wealth. The APVA later held a colonial ball in Richmond to boost its fortunes, but the acquisition failed to draw recruits to the local branch. By 1893 that chapter had only a dozen members.[29]

The APVA rented out the building's apartments as it considered the logistics of creating a Mary Washington museum. By 1899 the local branch decided "to restore the two rooms in the original part" of the house as Mary Ball Washington knew them. Preservationists evidently differed as to the definition of restoration. Five years earlier Newton reported incorrectly that the house had been made to look "as it did when 'Lady Washington' lived and died in it." By 1904 the museum received 430 visitors; by 1909, 651. The APVA's interpretation of the museum largely reflected Pryor's much-loved book *The Mother of Washington and Her Times,* in which, like Senator Daniel, she lauded Mary Washington's "self-denying, diligent, and frugal" ways. At a time when George Washington was deified, it was only natural that his mother would be equated with the mother of Jesus. Whether preservationists advocated feminine domesticity, the simple life, or the civil religion, she stood as a potent symbol of earlier ways.[30]

Angered by an advertisement that her grave would be "sold at Public Auction," Sara Pryor had helped lead a "Mary Washington Renaissance" in 1893 through both the Mary Washington Memorial Association and the APVA. She attributed such a humiliation to the "disparaging traditions" that described Washington as stern, repelling, and hot-tempered. Pryor rejoined that "the mother of Washington was in no sense a commonplace woman. Still less was she hard, uncultured, undignified, unrefined." Amending the unflattering record, she pictured Mary Washington as possessing "a noble heart, high courage, and sound understanding."[31]

More generally, Pryor lamented that the sphere of domesticity had shrouded woman's deserved recognition. While feminists were demanding equal rights, she protested only that biographers and historians had stinted countless women such as Mary Washington. "It is the noble, unselfish woman who must shine, if shine at all, by the light reflected from her son," she wrote. "Her life, for the most part, was hidden by the obscurity of domestic duties." Meanwhile, "her son is developed for glory, and the world is his arena." Pryor questioned the historical tradition that focused on men's activity in politics and war, protested that such a narrow focus was unfair, and said, "Women have some rights after all." Historians usually "tucked away somewhere, a short perfunctory phrase of courtesy," but neglected women's real contributions.[32]

The APVA developed an active museum at Mary Washington's home and reinterpreted her life. In 1917 Ellyson dedicated a tablet there, delivered an address—an indication that even conservative women could hold the public stage—and helped recast her image. A century earlier Mary Ball Washington had been called repelling, hard, and uncultured, but the APVA's president instead pictured her as "comely" and "a woman of strong will, religious and stern, but kind. She taught her son the principles of truth and honor from which he never swerved, and she was accustomed to say, 'George has been a good boy, and he will certainly do his duty.'"[33]

As a mecca for traditionalist women, the Mary Washington house drew more visitors in 1919 than Jamestown and twice as many as the Rising Sun Tavern. By then it had been superficially repaired and furnished, but the branch wanted a thorough restoration. Beginning in 1929, a full-fledged restoration included the demolition of two small rooms behind the parlor because they were of nineteenth-century vintage. Architect Philip N. Stern and consultant Charles Over Cornelius, associate curator of the Early American Wing at the Metropolitan Museum, also removed the original flooring and trued the windows, baseboards and foundation. Cornelius repeatedly stressed aesthetics, not historical accuracy, and he wanted that quality to stand out at the APVA's shrine. The local director, Mary Byrd Russell, reported to Ellyson that "in the older part of the house—the bedroom and the dining room—there is little to be done—except what might be called *repairs* or *essential* changes."[34]

Ellyson, as well as Appleton, heard a very different story from other sources. Emily Fleming—president of the Kenmore Association, a forty-year APVA member, and former branch director—complained that "the changes have been drastic." The contractor replaced the original flooring with salvaged materials from Baltimore's Camden Street Railroad Station. Every room "has been doctored," except one. Even in the kitchen, the symbol of women's domesticity, the contractors built "a brick oven, which was not there, and will move the crane, which was . . . probably there in Mrs. Washington's time." Fleming most worried about the contractor's prediction that "the place will look like new when he gets through with it." She thought that "is exactly what we do not want" and warned Ellyson that there was no home "more sacred" than this one which was "being desecrated." She asked Ellyson to "keep the matter quiet, for any controversy would do harm," but she wanted the "work stopped."[35]

Appleton heard similar complaints. Revealing the gulf which separated SPNEA and the Metropolitan Museum, and the real diversity in preservation philosophy, he regretted that "the work is in the hands of an architect who had no appreciation of the importance of preserving 'the aspect of antiquity.'" The architect compromised the house's patriotic associations, as well as the intimate bond between Mary Washington's persona and material legacy, by scrapping "the very floors over which Washington . . . and his mother had walked." When the architect trued the foundation, floors, and doors, moreover, he took out "all the picturesque irregularities caused by the passage of time." As a result, the house was "now no longer as attractive as it was from the antiquarian point of view."[36]

Branch director Russell defended her actions by citing the definition of *restoration* in *Webster's Dictionary* as "to bring back to the *original* condition." Oblivious to the professional debate over the meaning of preservation, restoration, and reconstruction, Russell evidently allowed her own feelings, Cornelius's sense of aesthetics, and *Webster's Dictionary* to set the agenda. Not only was the advice from the Metropolitan Museum errant because it reflected a curatorial, not a preservationist, viewpoint, but her architect saw a chance to remake the building. Russell retorted that "it is hard to believe that the 'atmosphere' of the place is gone because it is carefully put back to its 'original condition.'" She rejected all charges of desecration and claimed (perhaps rightly) that the trueing of the slope was necessary "to carry the strain of the thousands of tourists who walk through it every year." She thought that Ellyson had succumbed to an "impulsive and excitable" woman in asking that the work on George Washington's room and his mother's kitchen be stopped.[37]

After the restoration was complete, Mary Washington's home received thousands of pilgrims. The intense and well-orchestrated hoopla of the bicentennial celebration of George Washington's birth in 1932 cast a spotlight on his mother's house. By this time George Washington Ball had also donated an adjoining house to the APVA. It became the custodian's residence and allowed the entire Washington house to be used as a museum. In 1932 the depressed national economy bottomed out, and most Americans reluctantly were living in austerity. While George Washington's somber, if not graven, image stood out on the nation's new twenty-five-cent coin, his mother appropriately became an influential symbol of the simple but patriotic life.

"An intensely interesting event" occurred at the house on New Year's Day, 1932, when NBC radio used the house to broadcast to the United States and foreign nations. As the APVA reported, Mary Washington's "old clock chimed out for the whole world the hour of noon" from the room in which she said farewell to her son George and died.[38] At the time, the clock also tolled for the multitudes who still held hope for Washington's republic.

Another Fredericksburg property associated with George Washington was Kenmore. Once the home of Colonel Fielding Lewis and his wife Betty, Washington's sister, Kenmore was a stately two-story brick edifice of 1750. Badly damaged during the Civil War when it served as a military headquarters and hospital, Kenmore became a boy's academy years later. In 1922 the owner decided to demolish the house and its once beautiful gardens and subdivide the estate into town lots. Fredericksburg's women, including past APVA leaders, formed the Kenmore Association to purchase and restore the house. Ellyson wrote Appleton and asked his help. Appleton agreed that the $30,000 price was "very high" but concluded that antiquities "were worth no more than the ground going with the house." He persuaded patriotic groups in Massachusetts to contribute to the drive and told Edith Wendell of the National Society of the Colonial Dames that Kenmore's "artistic merits"—particularly its highly ornamented stucco ceilings—and its "historical connection" warranted preservation. Kenmore stands today as one of the city's finest dwellings.[39]

As Fredericksburg preservationists enshrined the Washington legacy, those in Norfolk still carried on the preparedness campaign and favored a narrower, military-minded historic preservation. Although architectural jewels like the early seventeenth-century Adam Thoroughgood house still failed to find favor with the APVA, Barton Myers and the local branch organized a drive in 1923 to preserve old Fort Norfolk. Constructed in 1809 after the *Chesapeake* affair, it originally served as a coastal defense work. It was vacated by the military in 1880, and in 1923 the government proposed converting it to a storage facility. The APVA instead urged preservation, predicting that the fort would "inspire the succeeding generations with sentiments of patriotism." The association asked Congress to declare the site " a permanent National historical monument," and at least six Virginia congressmen concurred. President Coolidge refused, however, and the Army Corps of Engineers took over the fort.[40]

After World War I the APVA increasingly used its influence, but not its purse, to help other groups rescue historic sites. In 1923 Fiske Kimball asked the APVA to support a campaign to save the Matthew Jones house at Fort

Eustis. He hoped that Coolidge would issue an executive order on the basis of the National Monuments Act of 1906, as he did in the following year for such sites as Castillo de San Marcos in Florida and the Statue of Liberty in New York City. The APVA pressed the secretary of war, who acknowledged the "extreme age" of the early eighteenth-century structure. The secretary ordered local authorities to "mark the building and care for it," but it was not declared a national monument. To this day, the T-shaped, two-story pre-Georgian building is boarded up like a mummy for permanent preservation. Remotely placed, barren in surroundings, and out of the public eye, the Jones house waits for a more sympathetic era.[41]

Kimball's proposal, like that of Myers regarding Fort Norfolk, invoked the National Monuments Act—also called the Antiquities Act or Lacey Act—which President Theodore Roosevelt signed into law in 1906. Prompted by the Archaeological Institute of America and the Smithsonian Institution's Bureau of American Ethnology, the act was the first major step by the federal government to protect the nation's heritage. Befitting its major sponsors, it originally targeted the archaeological antiquities and natural wilds of the West that were then being raped by vandals and pilferers. The Antiquities Act authorized the president to proclaim and set aside as national monuments government-owned lands that held historic sites, archaeological ruins, built structures, and natural wilds. Roosevelt promptly used the act to establish the Mesa Verde National Park, a Colorado site containing spectacular Indian cliff dwellings and a mesa-top pit houses and pueblos. Many diverse historical sites would subsequently be added to the list.[42]

Through these interwar years the APVA lent its voice to numerous preservation campaigns. In 1923 it protested the decision of Washington and Lee University to build an addition to its Lee Chapel. Preservationists "emphatically opposed . . . any change whatsoever" because the chapel was "one of Virginia's priceless antiquities." What attracted the interest of the APVA was not the building's age—it was only constructed in 1867, six years after the time limit expressed in the APVA's charter—but the fact that it held the crypt of Robert E. Lee and Valentine's famous recumbent statue. Preservationists also opposed the demolition of Ampthill, a Chesterfield County estate built before 1732. The ancestral home of APVA adviser Hunsdon Cary, Ampthill stood on land desired by Du Pont de Nemours and Company for a rayon factory. Not disposed to oppose New South progress and demand in situ preservation, the APVA sanctioned the removal, and Cary moved the brick house to Richmond in 1929–30.[43]

Since its early days the APVA spent considerable time as well trying to protect the integrity of Capitol Square. In 1892 the state inaugurated planning for a library on the square. Joseph Bryan heard that the "old Bell house," dating from 1824, would be demolished. Recognizing its "historic value," he started a preservation drive. A new building so near the Capitol, moreover, would cause "serious injury to the whole ground." What he proposed, and what eventually followed, was the library's construction on the southeastern side of the square. Fourteen years later the Bell Tower again faced demolition. The ladies of the APVA's central committee proposed "a mass meeting to oppose the destruction of the 'Bell Tower' if the Va. His. Soc. thought it would be wise."[44] Evidently the committee deferred to those gentlemen not only because they advised the APVA but because the protest might have been deemed too political for southern ladies.

The most drastic change to Capitol Square came in 1903–6 when the state added symmetrically placed wings to Jefferson's Capitol. As an organization, the APVA surprisingly said nothing about such a controversial move. Most likely, preservationists feared alienating politicians who were then considering an appropriation for the APVA's Jamestown work. Such criticism could also have been construed as disloyal and unladylike. At the same time, some APVA advisers did denounce the addition. After the state claimed that the building's outward appearance would not be changed, Archer Anderson retorted to Governor Andrew J. Montague, "This is like saying half an inch added to a man's nose would not affect his looks." Since Jefferson had exactly reproduced the Maison Carrèe, "any deviation, even the slightest, from these proportions, would probably be a fatal mistake, and destroy the only beauty the building has, that of perfect classic outline." In later years the APVA protested, albeit unsuccessfully, against other changes —another office building on the grounds and the removal of brick sidewalks. As a result, the APVA proposed a bill to the General Assembly that would place Capitol Square in the hands of a new preservation body. It was hoped that the state art commission would better protect historic sites by removing such decisions from the politicians, but matters never worked that easily. When the commission rejected plans to restore the Wren Building at the College of William and Mary, for example, Governor Byrd offered to fire any member who opposed the plans of the Williamsburg Holding Corporation.[45]

At the same time the APVA declined any meaningful assistance to the campaign to save Monticello, the home of Thomas Jefferson. As was often the case, Virginians left this ambitious project to wealthy northerners. The APVA's blind eye toward Jefferson resulted not simply from its tidewater bias but from the short shrift that he received in most schoolbooks, which faulted his admiration for the French Revolution and his partisan opposition to Washington. Many traditionalists worried that Jefferson's legacy was too volatile. Readjusters, Populists, and working-class radicals evoked his name and his democratic republic. As a result, Henry praised his grandfather not simply because of filiopietism but because Patrick Henry had opposed the Sage of Monticello. Both Henrys red-baited Jefferson. Henry said, for example, that his grandfather saw in 1798–99 "the lurid flame of Red Republicanism looming up in France and casting its sparks even across the Atlantic, threatening to kindle along the American coast the destructive fires which devastated Europe."[46] Both Henrys contrasted Jefferson with the conservatism of Washington's Revolution and Virginia's traditionalism.

Page, whose forebears were close to Jefferson, called him "the boldest reformer in America" who "struck at Privilege with all his might, no matter how highly placed or strongly entrenched it was." Because he "believed in the People—not only in the rights of the People, but in the People themselves," said Page, the "Apostle of Liberty" was "still assailed implacably by the forces of reaction and of servility." Historian William E. Dodd, journalist Claude Bowers, and novelist Ellen Glasgow resurrected the common folk as heroes and helped redeem Jefferson's reputation. The leaders of the Old Dominion subsequently pictured him not as a proponent of civil liberties and radicalism but as a defender of local rule and states' rights. Once Jefferson's legacy had been deradicalized, the Democratic party could absorb the dissident agrarians who had fired the Populist revolt. Before that, his controversial legacy, together with the APVA's eastern orientation, prompted preservationists to disregard Virginia's most radical hero. He finally entered the nation's pantheon in 1943 when President Franklin D. Roosevelt dedicated the Jefferson Memorial in Washington, D.C. While the nation combated fascism in Europe and Asia, the United States used Jefferson to symbolize the Four Freedoms, rights which incidentally the nation still denied to a sizable segment of its population.[47]

During the 1920s southern progressives combined Jefferson's legacy and the New South economy in such a way that traditionalism found a new meaning. Old symbols were used to advance new traditions, whether invented, revised, or restored ones. Whereas the progressive movement had contained many strains in its earlier years, it became increasingly conservative in the heat of World War I and the normalcy that followed. In the 1920s progressives in the Old Dominion focused largely on the protection of moral standards, the promotion of traditional culture, and the marketing of history. The APVA had become very fashionable, quite influential, and one of the state's chosen instruments in historical work. In 1922 the legislature empowered the APVA, together with other select patriotic groups such as the Colonial Dames, DAR, and UDC, to place markers across the state. However, Virginia's frugal legislature gave these patriotic groups no public funding but instead allowed them to solicit private funds with governmental sanction.[48]

Tradition-minded Virginians endlessly praised the APVA. John Stewart Bryan's Richmond *Times-Dispatch* editorialized in 1925 that "but for the efforts and activities of the A.P.V.A., much of Virginia's history would be hidden in textbooks, many of her monuments and shrines would have crumbled and gone unmarked, and false history would be spread abroad in ever-increasing volume." It particularly lauded the APVA's "labor of patriotism" in challenging the "legend of the 'Pilgrim Fathers.'" The APVA had been so successful that even Britain's House of Lords yielded to Lady Astor's request and corrected the inscription on a painting which erroneously called Plymouth the first permanent English settlement in the New World. Noting the rescue of shrines such as Mount Vernon and the John Marshall house, the Richmond *News-Leader,* also owned by Bryan, suggested in 1929 that "comparatively little remains to be done in saving the places that have given Virginia her greatest fame."[49]

Such a narrow perspective on historic preservation distressed lifetime APVA member Appleton. In 1923 the founder of SPNEA wrote Kimball, author of *The Domestic Architecture of the American Colonies and the Early Republic* (1922) and chairman of the American Institute of Architects' Committee on Preservation of Historic Monuments. Hoping that the University of Virginia professor had some clout with the APVA, he criticized Virginia's regrettable "neglect" of its ancient graveyards and courthouses. He enclosed a list of courthouses which had been recently demolished or threatened and asked Kimball's help. Appleton failed to realize, however, that Fiske's piedmont and the APVA's tidewater were miles apart both geographically and philosophically. As the APVA preserved Virginia's history, little west of Richmond mattered.[50]

Appleton then wrote Ellyson. Obviously thinking that the APVA was not up to the task, he asked her organization to support the creation of a Virginia commission which would survey the courthouses and seek funds for their preservation from the legislature. Virginia's courthouses were national gems, he declared; revealing his limited sense of aesthetics, he added that "courthouses elsewhere aren't worth worrying about. Certainly they don't amount to anything in Massachusetts [and] not, so far as I know, in the rest of New England." Kimball told him that he was asking too much. "You just aren't talking in Virginia terms when you say 'appropriate money.' They just ain't no money!" he exclaimed. He suggested that "the only chance" for these projects "could be some private individual in the North."[51]

Ellyson told SPNEA's leader that in 1922 the General Assembly had created a commission, which included the APVA, to mark sites and place suitable monuments. She noted Appleton's ambitious ideas but cautioned, "If we are slow, just lay it to the climate—which for some months of the years reduces the energy of most of us." Appleton attributed the inattention to more than the weather. As far as he could sense from the APVA's *Year Book,* he thought that "the Virginia Society is putting most of its time into memorial markers." He asked Kimball: "Can't we stir it up to do some active preservation work on the concrete object itself rather than to mark the spot where it stood?" He had proposed such a commission under the direction of Kimball and other preservation-minded architects precisely to get the APVA moving.[52]

As Appleton inferred, the APVA did place a high priority on the public education that markers provided. SPNEA, on the other hand, cared little for such memorials. Shaped mostly by male antiquaries, it represented a different brand of preservation and regarded antiquities as historical documents that required professional care. The APVA, on the other hand, still reflected women's interest in protecting symbols that could inspire and mold future generations. Ellyson also told him that the narrow-minded modernism of many Virginians inhibited real preservation work. These Virginians did not appreciate old buildings, she said; they "considered [them] unsightly & in the way of modern purpose." The Old Dominion still had not "recovered from the shock of the devastation of the War between the States, particularly in the rural districts."[53]

Twenty years earlier, Joseph Bryan's newspaper, the Richmond *Times,* revealed that lack of appreciation in an editorial on "Virginia's Court-Houses." Congratulating Wythe County for its decision to demolish its courthouse and build a new one, the *Times* argued: "The county courthouses in Virginia, generally speaking, are by no means creditable. They are ugly and unsightly without and within, and often they are about as dirty as tobacco chewers and men with muddy boots can make them. There are no conveniences and no comforts, and nothing about these 'temples of justice' that is impressive or dignified." Reflecting the bigger-is-better syndrome, the *Times* claimed that the architectural environment shaped personal behavior. "A man necessarily feels more reverential when he goes into a magnificent cathedral than when he worships in a small 20x40 church with plain walls and rude seats, and a little unpainted pulpit. The same is true to a certain extent of the 'temple of justice.' The court-house represents the majesty and dignity of the law." At that time, Populists were trying to redefine the Democratic party, and radicals were challenging the elite bias of Virginia's legal system and economy. Bryan's paper predicted that a "handsome" courthouse, "kept in prime condition," would "make the law more impressive, and to make the law more impressive is to make men respect it more highly and reverence and obey it." [54]

Appleton correctly appraised Virginia's historic courthouses as architectural gems. But he failed to consider the attempt by Virginia's elite to escape poverty through New South economic expansion, as well as its search for powerful symbols that showed the majesty of the established system. It was in this context that William Wirt Henry addressed the American Historical Association late in 1891 as its president. In the calm before the storm set off by the People's party, he noted that "no State in the Union has hitherto enjoyed more complete internal quiet than this Commonwealth." He attributed the social peace to "the practical operation of our county courts" and warned that "these courts must be preserved." [55] What interested Henry and Bryan was not the actual courthouse but the majesty of the elite-defined system. In fact, across the nation in the late nineteenth and early twentieth centuries, cities and counties erected magnificent town halls and courthouses as part of their claim to imperial power and economic influence in their region. Although Virginia's new constitution restored social peace, the state's elite still sought those powerful symbols of conservatism for years to come. Whether the case was Wythe County's courthouse or Washington's home, traditionalism required symbols that showed the power of elite, Anglo-Saxon Virginians.

10

"A Spirit That Fires the Imagination": The Historic Triangle and Beyond

D URING THE 1920s and 1930s the APVA kept its main focus on the Historic Triangle: Jamestown, Williamsburg, and Yorktown. What would become the most commercially successful region for the Old Dominion's tourist industry in the late twentieth century was still very quiet, provincial, and thoroughly Virginian in the 1920s. Despite the fact that it was the APVA's top priority and increasingly in the national focus, Jamestown became more difficult to reach because the road-causeway-bridge passage was often impassable. With steamship service irregular at best and the state's roads at their worst, the APVA's income dried up and its treasury emptied. In keeping with one tenet of Virginia progressivism, Governor Henry C. Stuart, an APVA adviser, promoted the "better roads movement" and declared 5 May 1917 as Road Day. The APVA at first hoped that local farmers would voluntarily repair its access roads, but soon preservationists approached the legislature, couching their requests in the context of Virginia's rivalry with Massachusetts. "The condition of our roads is a reflection of our state, and Jamestown has received nothing from the state," APVA resolved (with considerable exaggeration), "while New England . . . and other states have helped to perpetuate their history by giving of their funds."[1]

The roads deteriorated so badly that the American Automobile Association urged members in 1921 to avoid Virginia all together. Four years later, a Pan-American diplomatic delegation canceled its plans to visit Jamestown because the muddy roads were about unsafe as those in the backwaters of Panama. In frustration Ellyson told Richmonders, "The people are getting mightily stirred about it and strangers are wondering."[2] The APVA's complaints added tinder to the hot debate between those Virginians who advocated a pay-as-you-go solution to financing road improvements and those who wanted a bond program to borrow the money. The APVA dodged that question and simply asked for better roads.

Besides asking for moneys to build a new bridge to Jamestown and better roads, preservationists campaigned for funds to erect a new steel pier to replace the deteriorated wooden wharf. Unable to hold its river pilgrimages, and hence deprived of much of its income, the APVA appealed to the legislature in 1920, and amidst the hyperpatriotism of the Red Scare, the assembly allotted $10,000 for work at Jamestown. The APVA apparently used these funds for other purposes, because the pier remained unfixed. On 19 October 1921 the APVA took its message directly to President Warren G. Harding when he made a pilgrimage to Jamestown. Upon seeing the APVA's work, he brimmed with delight, laid some wreaths, but kept his pocketbook shut. Seven years later, the APVA's lobbying finally brought results when Congress and the Virginia legislature each appropriated $15,000 for a steel pier.[3]

During these years Jamestown became a mecca for not only patriotic Anglo-Saxons but Protestants. Through monuments, ritual, and rhetoric, the APVA turned Jamestown into a religious shrine. It commemorated at a ceremony in 1915, for example, the first Anglican communion service. The site symbolically (but conjecturally) stood at the intersection of the "old triangular fort built by the early settlers and a stout rampart reared during the War Between the States—both enduring evidence of a free and fearless race." Bruton Parish rector Edmund Ruffin Jones presented a sermon which pleased traditionalists when he questioned "the fads and fancies of the day, the 'new thought,' [and] the 'new ideas.'" Six years later the same commemoration drew almost one thousand pilgrims, and distributing communion took ninety minutes. When the APVA voted to open its Jamestown grounds on Sunday, it decided that these services would be alternately conducted by Episcopal, Presbyterian, Baptist, and Methodist ministers.[4]

Preservationists also honored the memory of Robert Hunt, the first Anglican minister at Jamestown. Coleman first suggested that a stained-glass memorial window honoring him be placed in Bruton Parish Church. "An appropriate design," she wrote, "would be the figure of John the Baptist in the wilderness." Only slowly was the money raised, but by that time the vestry of the restored church opposed any stained glass in a colonial-era building. In June 1922 the APVA, the Colonial Dames, and the Episcopal church dedicated a memorial to Hunt at Jamestown, an open-air altar constructed of marble with a bronze bas-relief atop a base of antique brick. The design for the bas-relief depicted not a missionary carrying the gospel to the Indians, which he was not, but Hunt administering communion to the English settlers who, incidentally, had received it too infrequently to please the ideals of modern traditionalists. Although the Episcopal church objected to the shrine's placement in a "desolate waste of the swamp," Ellyson tactfully called it a "hallowed spot, whose very remoteness gives it a quiet and holy repose." The shrine itself was a Pyrrhic victory which illustrated the looseness of the term *preservation*. Although the memory of Hunt's work had been preserved, the shrine was "constructed of brick from a majestic old ruin of colonial days, about four miles inland from Jamestown. The building was the *mill* of the colony and was destroyed in the Indian Massacre of 1622."[5]

The Old Dominion's traditionalists used Hunt as a means to recast a proper picture of the clergy in past and present. APVA adviser William W. Old of Norfolk professed that Hunt acted in a manly fashion to civilize early Jamestown. The early "company was overweighted with high-spirited young gentlemen, impatient of any control," he claimed. Other than Smith, Hunt "was the only spirit able to control that turbulent company." Although a carrier of the gospel, he won the colonists' respect because "in the rough, elemental struggle for existence, he played the man." Echoing Teddy Roosevelt's praise for the strenuous life, many of the elite in the early twentieth century feared that their peers had become weak, timid, and even effeminate in the midst of demanding times. At a memorial service at Jamestown, Goodwin emphasized that Hunt's Anglican church had served as "a strong regulative and constructive force in the Virginia Colony."[6] The Episcopal church made Hunt a symbol of a stalwart leader and a model for modern, and often flaccid, congregations.

The APVA used history, moreover, to preach its own sense of morality. While preserving and marking churches and graveyards, overwhelmingly those of the Episcopalian religion, its leaders lauded the religious character and tolerance of their ancestors. Virginia's rivalry with Yankees again came to the fore when Tyler claimed that "the persecuting spirit . . . was never so severe or relentless [there] as in New England." Puritans were always an easy target, but too little was said about modern persecutors. Through much of the United States reactionary Protestants, whether in the American Protective Association or Ku Klux Klan, hounded such modern foes as Catholics and Jews, while more moderate Protestants provided the spiritual fuel driving the engine of progressivism.[7]

Preservationists also tried to rehabilitate the image of earlier ministers. It was customary "to speak of the clergy of Colonial Virginia with ridicule and scorn," Goodwin complained. Even tradition-minded Virginians did so. Joseph Bryan told an Episcopal assembly in Massachusetts in 1897, for example, that Virginia ministers had "often pursued a course of conduct most unworthy of their calling." Bagby described "many" of the same clergy as "little better than professional gamblers." Yet the tenor of late Victorians and the APVA's gospel required more suitable role models from the colonial ministry.[8]

As a result, the APVA reinterpreted and honored Virginia's colonial clergy through bronze and stone tablets, as it did Robert Hunt, but its historical portrait reflected the moralisms of preservationists. A case in point occurred in nearby Hampton in 1907. The Kecoughtan branch placed a memorial window costing $250 in St. John's Church to honor its colonial clergy. Lyon Tyler and Rev. C. Braxton Bryan, Joseph Bryan's brother, compiled a list of the parish's twenty-one ministers. The local preservationists set one name off on the tablet, however, and righteously explained to the association: "The Rev. Jeremiah Taylor's name is enclosed in brackets, indicating that though historically entitled to be included in the record, morally it has no right to this tribute since the records show that he was indicted by the grand jury for drunkenness and conduct unbecoming a minister of the gospel."[9] The APVA valued the past for its lessons in the present and ostracized Taylor, though no mention was made whether he was convicted of those offenses.

Rumors abounded that the APVA would lose its sacred site at Jamestown if the federal government created a park. The legislation considered by Congress shortly after the Jamestown Tercentennial, drafted by the ASHPS, repeated the APVA's gospel by arguing that "knowledge of the history and respect for the traditions of a Nation by its citizens conduce to love of country, civic pride, and loyalty to established institutions." Congress even fell to racial platitudes and voiced "a justifiable pride in the annals of our race." Congress was asked to purchase the island as the "Jamestown National Park," but no mention was made of the APVA's tract. The bill, which did not pass, provided that any archaeological work would be overseen by a reputable museum such as the Smithsonian Institution.[10]

In the late 1920s momentum built in behalf of federal acquisition not simply of Jamestown but Yorktown and part of Williamsburg. An act finally passed in 1930 requiring the government to acquire lands by gift, purchase, or condemnation. Congressman Louis C. Cramton's bill originally pertained to the entire island of Jamestown, but Ellyson and William E. Carson, chairman of the Virginia Commission on Conservation and Development, persuaded Cramton to amend his bill to protect the APVA's small patch of land. Without this change, Ellyson told her membership, "we would now be 'folding our tents, like the Arab, and silently stealing away.'"[11] In 1934, after the condemnation action and dispute over the cost were settled, the United States government took possession of 1,500 acres on the island. The APVA's 22½-acre plot was completely surrounded by government-owned land. Through the Great Depression, Jamestown served as an official symbol of America and its austere beginnings. In 1936 President and Mrs. Roosevelt and Secretary of the Interior Harold Ickes visited the island to see the newly created Colonial National Historical Park. In the following year over 50,000 paying visitors contributed their two bits to the APVA's coffers, though 150,000 visited Williamsburg. In 1939 and 1940 the APVA's pilgrimage included a one-hour broadcast over Richmond radio station WRVA.[12]

For some time the APVA had actively supported federal plans to acquire Yorktown's battlefield for a national park. Over the years Yorktown had deteriorated and fallen prey to outside investors. Chicago businessmen tried unsuccessfully to buy historic sites for their Columbian Exposition of 1893, including the Moore house, where Cornwallis had surrendered in 1781, and the Custom House of 1706. The efforts of Brock and Henry to get Senator Stanford's committee to back acquisition by the federal government failed. When speculator A. O. Manck purchased the Moore house, he offered in 1896 "to cede the house and several acres" to the APVA. He wanted to build a golf course on the site and asked that the APVA lend its name, and presumably its wealthy members, to his promotion, but the APVA declined. Bills reappeared in Congress, and the APVA again declined Manck's offer to sell the house in 1902.[13]

During World War I the federal government moved into the Yorktown area on a large scale, acquiring approximately eighteen square miles of land in 1918 for its Navy Mine Depot. Although it demolished Bellfield, an eighteenth-century clapboard house of two stories, it left standing Kiskiack, an eighteenth-century brick home, and the foundations of Ringfield. All the while, the APVA's branch in Yorktown continued to lay plaques. Not only was its work an inferior means of preservation, it took on trivial proportions. At a time when preservationists such as Kimball and Appleton worried that commercial development could ruin Yorktown, the APVA's branch declared that its principal work in 1921 would be "obtaining . . . data concerning the exact spot of the surrender of Cornwallis, the appro-

priate marking of the spot, and [the] care of same." Appleton understandably
believed that the APVA was misallocating its resources, but missed Virginians' attempt to highlight the historical events of 1781. John P. McGuire, a
Richmond schoolmaster and preservationist, had spoken before the APVA
on the Yorktown campaign years before. The nation had not recognized
that battle as the victory that had won the Revolution, he said, and the
APVA assumed the mission of marking the site.[14]

As commercial and military developers invaded the peninsula and en-
croached upon sleepy Yorktown, the APVA supported another movement
to spur federal acquisition of the battlefield. In 1916 Congress created the
National Park Service within the Department of Interior and empowered it
to maintain the nation's parklands. As the years went by, national authorities
increasingly challenged local interests, as in Yorktown. In 1921, for example,
Congress finally authorized acquisition of the battle site, but the Yorktown
branch worried, not rejoiced, upon hearing the news. Over the years locals
had built on the lands around the hamlet, and they feared that ambitious
federal authorities might force them to move. The APVA "opposed . . .
taking over" the town and "dispossessing the inhabitants," as did the DAR
which expressed those sentiments in testimony before Congress.[15]

Two major problems faced the proposed Yorktown Military Park as it
emerged from its planning stage. Appleton saw one immediately when he
acquired the blueprints. He wrote Kimball in 1924 and noted that the government only proposed including "the attacking and defending lines," making "a national park of a very queer shape." He also voiced his deeply held
belief in localism and states' rights. Six years before, he had successfully
sponsored a constitutional amendment in Massachusetts which empowered
the state to acquire such lands through eminent domain. He thought "it
would be extremely bad policy" for Virginia to cede this land and power to
the federal government.[16]

More seriously, speculators had acquired Manck's land and constructed
a modern golf course. The Yorktown Country Club established its high
status when it included as its founders and honorary life members Calvin
Coolidge, William Howard Taft, John J. Pershing, Andrew J. Montague,
and Gifford Pinchot. Claiming that it had won the approval of the DAR
and the APVA, the country club proposed to use golf and membership fees
"to restore and perpetuate the historic battlefield." Opening its roster to the
progeny of those heroes, the club enabled golfers, as "the descendants of
our Revolutionary patriots," to use "the very ground made sacred by the
heroic deeds of their ancestors." They would presumably imagine the 1781

battle as they used their mashie on the eighth hole, what was called "the spirit of '76," or took a divot out of the thirteenth hole, "Pocahontas," or quietly cursed the sand trap on the first hole, named, of course, "George Washington." As a par 69 course totaling a mere 6,086 yards, however, it could not match the rigors of a real 1781 skirmish.[17]

The club offered a therapeutic escape to its history-minded and dollar-endowed members. Within the manor house, it promised, "the interior furnishings and decorations will faithfully follow Colonial designs, and every object will revive memories of the Patriotic Period of 1776." The club manager did not mention how the casino, Turkish baths, and swimming pool would rekindle such memories but predicted that "every comfort and convenience for rest and recuperation" would be provided. As inspiration and recreation, the club's board of directors rationalized their project: "It is the modern spirit to design for the use of the Living the monuments erected to the Past." The battleground would become "a delightful playground dedicated to the present and future generations." The club intended to meet the needs of wealthy Americans who sought vicarious experiences and historical roots.[18]

The club invited Appleton, a descendant of those Revolutionary heroes, to join in 1924. Declining the offer in his gentlemanly manner, he warned that the construction of a golf course would "interfere with the preservation of the earth works." The club's goals in providing recreation and preservation, he thought, entailed "antagonistic" purposes. He further regretted that the club would alter Yorktown's "old country road" into a "concrete surfaced main street." Such developments would rob "the town of much of its old-fashioned picturesqueness," and he concluded that "the less changes in the way of concrete roads and country clubs come into Yorktown the better it would be for the place."[19] The playground was in the APVA's backyard, but it issued no similar warning.

Three years earlier the APVA's Yorktown branch revealed its priorities when it promoted a drive to declare 19 October a national holiday to commemorate the battle of Yorktown. Claiming that the battle was more important for the United States and world than the Fourth of July and its Declaration of Independence, the APVA sought the support of the Virginia congressional delegation. Senator Claude Swanson resisted, however, because he thought that the battle "took place so long ago" as to be beyond mental reach. Congressman S. O. Bland told the APVA that the nation was already "surfeited with holidays." In an era when the business of America was business, Bland thought that an observance of Yorktown's victory actually required "greater rather than lessened [work] activities." All too often, he told the APVA, most citizens thought little of patriotic events and instead "regard the holiday largely as a day on which to have a frolic."[20] The work ethic and discipline of society were more important principles for these 1920s politicians than commemorating the country's birth.

Despite its unwillingness to declare a holiday, the federal government did create Colonial National Historical Park through the passage of the Cramton bill in 1930. Federal lands included most of Jamestown, the battlefield at Yorktown, and a parkway connecting the two through Williamsburg. John D. Rockefeller, Jr., who had purchased the Moore house in 1928, presented it soon afterwards to the government for inclusion in the park. The sesquicentennial celebration of the battle in 1931 became an elaborate three-day affair, and its proceeds were used to finance the restoration of the Moore house three years later. Even under federal ownership, at the end of the decade a patriot could, for the price of one dollar, still pay homage to the ancients with a round of golf.[21]

As the ownership of Jamestown Island and Yorktown's battlefield devolved to the federal government, a battle ensued in Williamsburg between such local and outside interests. The APVA's branch experienced great activity in the 1920s, but what once acted as the seedbed of the APVA in 1889 almost lay on its deathbed by the early 1930s when the Rockefeller-financed restoration took over the town. Through the 1920s, however, Tyler and Goodwin actively promoted preservation, mostly through the APVA. While in Rochester, New York, from 1908 to 1923, Goodwin preached the Social Gospel in a community marked by ethnic, class, and cultural divisions. He returned to Williamsburg as a fund-raiser for and professor of religion at the College of William and Mary and then resumed his rectorship at Bruton Parish. In these conservative surroundings he translated the Social Gospel's longings for peace and justice through the town's material culture.

Goodwin amplified his profound discontent with modernity in his book *The Church Enchained* (1916). Caught in a volatile class-based strife that distressed so many progressives, Goodwin condemned those capitalists who were guilty of "conducting sweat shops, . . . prostituting childhood to industrial accomplishments," and "oppressing the hirelings in his wages." At a time when the Socialist party and radical unions drew millions of supporters, Goodwin refused, however, to accept the call of socialists "to confiscate property" and to redistribute the wealth that the robber barons had extracted from America's workers. He likewise refused to heed the call of anarchists "to destroy it." Goodwin thought that America was torn apart by these class conflicts and lacked consensus because it was "heterogeneous and hyphenated." [22]

As he watched driving, ruthless entrepreneurs define America's values and culture, Goodwin worried that "civilization has grown materialistic, and greedy, and full of lust and ambition, and has become dominated by the will to power." The "intoxication of high living" perverted the affluent, and their materialism impeded "the spirit of brotherhood." Like so many progressives of old lineage and limited property, he felt caught in the middle, watching helplessly as the nation drifted into industrial warfare. Goodwin concluded that "America is imperiled by the immorality which grows out of fatigue, and from the weariness of pursuit after false gods." With his inbred Virginia traditionalism coming to the fore, he later called for a return to older traditions, a renaissance of older morality, and the building of "a higher national unity." [23]

Hoping to save individualism, private property, and trusted traditions, Goodwin resurrected his grand plan for a colonial-style restoration of the entire town. His Social Gospel sentiments surely could have pictured Williamsburg's past and present in a different light than that glimpsed by southern conservatives. What became apparent in this tradition-minded, southern town, however, was that Goodwin chose not to reiterate those laments about capitalism and its robber barons which he had voiced in *The Church Enchained*. Whether his voice was tempered by his roles as college fundraiser, shepherd to a conservative congregation, and courtier to northern millionaires was not so important as the fact that in Williamsburg, progressivism was Virginia style. As it turned out, Goodwin had written *The Church Enchained* to assert the power of religious spirituality as a counter to materialism and disorder; he wanted his restoration of Williamsburg similarly to show the power of cultural traditionalism.

Goodwin rejected the slow, piecemeal approach of the APVA. He ambitiously wanted instead a restored town and a colonial-era environment, not simply individual and isolated buildings. Such thinking was increasingly popular, whether voiced by progressives who stressed environmentalism or by those who were familiar with European folk village museums such as Skansen near Stockholm. Reiterating the Gospel of Preservation, he claimed that Williamsburg held "a spirit that stirs the memory and fires the imagination"; it would "illumine the judgment" of those it touched to preserve the past "and resist the spirit of ruthless innovation." [24]

Those ripples of modernity had hit Williamsburg in the past decade.

The first automobile traveled its streets in 1912, and a hard-surfaced road followed from Richmond to Newport News. More portentous was the outbreak of World War I. The federal government acquired over 12,000 acres in the Yorktown area for the Navy Mine Depot, while E. I. du Pont de Nemours and Company built a munitions factory on the eastern outskirts of Williamsburg. Employing ten thousand workers, the Du Pont factory brought rapid development to the main street of Williamsburg—restaurants, filling stations, and cheap amusement halls—all of which shocked Goodwin upon his return.[25]

A northern writer visited Williamsburg in early 1917, a time when the lunatic asylum was still its largest employer, and wrote about the town before a whirlwind forever changed it. Describing the old houses on Duke of Gloucester Street, she claimed, probably in honest ignorance, that "almost everyone of them [was] an exquisite example of the best period of the eighteenth century's conception of home architecture." Such homes gave "the town its character," as they were "untouched, perfectly preserved, [and] lived in to-day as throughout the long years." She concluded that Williamsburg was "a stronghold of the past, a sort of enchanted ground, lovely and quiet as a dream."[26]

For some tradition-minded residents, that dream became a nightmare. The land speculation and economic boom brought on by World War I turned the town's quietude into a roar. During these years the APVA branch tried in its small way to preserve the town's legacy, but without much help from Richmond or available funds, it fell dramatically short. After the Courthouse of 1770 (across from the Powder Horn) burned in 1911, Ellyson did call for its restoration. She mistakenly told the town fathers to follow "the plan of the original architect, Sir Christopher Wren"; it seems that most of the town residents incorrectly attributed the building to Wren. The building was repaired with town funds.[27]

The APVA protested against, but failed to stop, the construction of a high school on the Palace Green for the city's white children. The local branch asked Richmond in March 1919 to lobby the state and local authorities against the proposal and even asked the College of William and Mary to donate some of its property for an alternate site. The APVA wanted the school to be "modelled after the Governor's Palace" but not constructed on his green. Preservationists wrote Williamsburg's school board to remind it of the green's association with America's rise to greatness. "We ask you," said the APVA, "would the children ever learn, even through the most vivid imagination, what exquisite beauty, what historic value their school house has destroyed? Never." They reiterated their gospel: "But let it [the green] remain, and every child will enjoy its beauty, and will take a history to it to study what Williamsburg has been in the past, and will remain to inspire students, artists, literati, who will come to the Green, and proclaim, 'And here, with Jamestown Island, began these United States in the name of the Almighty Redeemer.'" If a new school was built on the green, they predicted, "every loyal Virginian will bow the head with humiliation."[28]

While the APVA, patriotic societies, and the college faculty protested such a desecration, a public meeting on the proposal illustrated the town's deep divisions. On one side were those who primarily wanted to boom the economy and protect the social order of the past; on the other side were those who pursued the same goals but also wanted to preserve the actual vestiges of the past. Speaking for the town's boosters, the editor of the *Virginia Gazette* admitted that the battle symbolized a profound split within the ranks of tradition-minded Virginians. "It is the spirit we are fighting, a false sentimentality that is far more dangerous than erecting upon the common a public school building," he wrote in 1919. Castigating the preservationists, he added: "It is the spirit of intolerance and narrowness that this fight has engendered that the *Gazette* would hold to scorn." In retrospect, it is remarkable how similarly the two sides thought on the questions of progress and tradition. The *Gazette* nonetheless belittled those who put any constraint on development. Preservationists lost the battle, and the school opened in 1921, built in front of the Palace ruins on the green. It would be soon demolished for the Rockefeller-financed reconstruction of the Palace.[29]

Preservationists equally resented the disregard of many in the town for its past. Even the revered statue of Lord Botetourt at the college faced what seemed to be never-ending vandalism. During the Red Scare, Harvard jokesters painted Plymouth Rock red; in the heyday of Jim Crow, Lord Botetourt's statue was blackfaced. Such statues continue to be targets. Surry County's Confederate statue on its courthouse square, for example, has been a victim of pranksters since its erection in 1909. It has been blackfaced, and everything from Halloween pumpkins to lingerie has been placed on its head. Even today many Surry County traditionalists still regard the statue as a tribute to the Confederacy's high purposes. That feeling was more intense during the 1920s when their grandparents took any attack on their heritage as an act of barbarism, not mischief.[30]

Unfortunately for the APVA, it fell delinquent in the care of its own Williamsburg properties. In 1916 Ellyson received a request from the Educational and Civic Association of Williamsburg to use the Powder Horn as a library. She considered the idea "feasible" and asked only that the library undertake the much-needed repair of the building. The proposal fell through, and the APVA soon resolved to use the Powder Horn only as a museum, but the building deteriorated. Locals made do with what little they had; in 1922, for example, they used convict labor to repair the structure.[31]

As soon as Goodwin returned to town, he gradually exerted his voice over others in Williamsburg's APVA. College librarian Earl Gregg Swem, who was directing the branch, soon resigned as the two developed a philosophical clash. Goodwin complained about the "unsightly" appearance of the magazine and feared further encroachments on its square. The APVA authorized him to ask the city to convey one lot to the APVA, while Goodwin himself signed options on three other lots to prevent their development. He instigated a campaign, broadcast through the Richmond *News Leader,* to raise the necessary purchase funds. Soon that paper published an editorial, most likely written by John Stewart Bryan, called "Save the 'Powder Horn.'" Comparing the magazine in 1925 with Powhatan's Chimney in 1888, the *News Leader* reported that the "roof is so full of holes that a class in astronomy might be taught within the building." With cracked walls and open roof, the structure could soon collapse, and "Virginia would be disgraced."[32]

Ellyson saw a picture of the APVA's building accompanied by the caption: "The *News Leader* today got behind a movement to raise funds for the *purchase* & repair of this ancient structure, which is mixed up with the early history of this nation." She was "shocked" and "indignant," not at the writer's poor writing, but by the fact that the building's plight and the APVA's inattention had been advertised to the state. She wrote Cynthia Coleman's daughter that she had known nothing of the building's condition and its need for repairs and additional land. Elizabeth Beverley Coleman's reply revealed the intense localism that still impeded statewide preservation work. "We find a great lack of interest here because the property is not owned locally," she complained, and "we really have no control of it."[33] Although the magazine was repaired, the episode illustrated the limitations of the APVA's moralistic gospel and decentralized organization. If a structure was purchased primarily for its memories and symbolism, the obligation to maintain the site, or to restore it professionally, became a secondary concern.

Goodwin offered numerous suggestions to recast the image of Williamsburg in the likeness of the old. In 1924 he warned the local branch that the colonial capital faced the present "danger of losing many of the old houses through their changing ownership and lack of care." He proposed not only preservation but new house construction in compatible Colonial Revival stylings. He suggested that "a series of house plans, conforming to the best of the Colonial Houses be made available and that public opinion be enlisted in an attempt to reproduce the type." Within a year the APVA made available such house plans, paradoxically from a Boston architectural firm.[34]

Goodwin's plans became more ambitious. In late 1924 he formed the Colonial Holding Corporation "to purchase, hold, and beautify such colonial property in Williamsburg as could be secured." He was joined by Richmond publisher John Stewart Bryan, Williamsburg attorney (and son of the college professor) Channing Hall, and William and Mary law professor Oscar Shewmake. Goodwin told the APVA that influential newspapers such as the Baltimore *Sun* had promised their support. Actually the *Sun*'s editorial line was anything but supportive. It noted his attempts to lure the money of northern philanthropists to underwrite the CHC. The *Sun* warned of "the spectacle of the Old Dominion huckstering off her ancient capital to an outsider, in order to get a flivver imitation of departed glory." Such a sight, it cautioned, would "bring a flush of shame to the pale cheeks of her mighty shades."[35]

As a college fundraiser Goodwin cast his net wide, hoping to catch a philanthropist. After he failed to lure J. P. Morgan, Jr., he appealed to flivver king Henry Ford. His request was, however, less than tactful. "Unfortunately," said Goodwin to Henry's son Edsel, "you and your father are at present the chief contributors to the destruction of this city." Pointing to the by-products of the "capital to coast" road that the APVA had promoted, he attributed to Ford's cars the gas stations and garages that were "fast spoiling the whole appearance of the old streets and the old city." In a terse reply Edsel Ford said he was not interested in Goodwin's proposal.[36]

In February 1924 Goodwin cast another line when he spoke before a New York dinner about the college's projected Phi Beta Kappa Memorial Hall. He invited John D. Rockefeller, Jr., to the meeting and personally asked him to visit Williamsburg. Two years lapsed before Rockefeller's first visit, but then another one followed in November 1926. In the meantime, Goodwin placed other irons in the fire. In May 1926 he persuaded the Marshall Foundation, a subsidiary of his church, and the Colonial Dames to give him moneys to purchase the George Wythe house, a dignified two-story brick dwelling dating to the 1750s, as the parish rectory. This move paled in significance to Rockefeller's secret authorization in November 1926 to finance a preliminary survey of the entire colonial town. Within a week Goodwin bought the Ludwell-Paradise house, a two-story brick building of the 1730s, on Duke of Gloucester Street. Another Rockefeller visit in May 1927 led him to agree to restore the "whole area" secretly. Rockefeller told Goodwin to pretend that the funds came from the college's endowment, and his role remained covert until June 1928.[37]

Goodwin never explicitly rebuffed the APVA, but he realized that his ambitious dreams required the verve, talent, and money which only Rockefeller could provide. In case after case, he picked up where the APVA left off. The old Blair house on Duke of Gloucester Street had been threatened in 1917, for example, but Ellyson found it "not feasible" to purchase. The college used it for a while as a sorority house and then sold it. When Goodwin heard that it was to be torn down to provide land for a garage, he purchased it.[38]

A more telling case was the site of the colonial Capitol. Acquiring it in 1897, the APVA had proposed but failed to accomplish the reconstruction of the Capitol as a library, museum, and public hall. In 1924 the APVA again heard proposals to use it as a memorial to the veterans of World War I. Goodwin even thought that the Episcopal Diocese might "purchase the lot and restore the building in cement and steel for use as a preparatory school for boys." After his secret deal with Rockefeller in 1926, Goodwin received architectural plans by the following May for the Capitol's reconstruction. At the same time he bought important town sites but kept his funding secret. His wife, Mary Mordecai Goodwin, became director of the APVA branch that April. If its mission was to guard possession of the Capitol site, it asked the fox to watch the chicken coop.[39]

Apparently Goodwin's plan hinged on his ability to acquire the foundations of the Capitol, the centerpiece of Williamsburg's colonial history. In November he met with the advisory board and proposed that the APVA "give him an option for five years on the foundations of the House of Burgesses. . . . If he succeeds in obtaining the necessary funds during the period of five years, then the property is to be conveyed, for a nominal consideration, to him or his associates, for eventual conveyance to the College of William and Mary; if he does not succeed, the option will expire." The advisers, whose numbers included Bryan of the moribund Colonial Holding Corporation, seem to have believed the Rockefeller-inspired pretense that the college would be the beneficiary. Goodwin told no one about the codicil that he added to his will, stipulating that in the event of his death these properties would revert not to the college or church but to Rockefeller's personal secretary. He told the local branch only that he planned to rent the Capitol lot for ninety-nine years "to those wishing to restore it." The APVA gave its "cordial approval" to the idea. A most persuasive speaker, Goodwin praised the APVA for its work. "Those devoted ladies of Virginia," he said, "bent like priestesses over the dying embers of ancient flames and breathed upon them [and] made them glow again."[40]

Goodwin revealed his plan, but not his funder, to the APVA in May 1928, and Ellyson told her members that he had already acquired "a large part" of Williamsburg. If the APVA would relinquish the grounds, Goodwin and his unnamed associates would "reproduce the Old Capitol on its original site." Goodwin's private corporation agreed to submit its plans to Ellyson and at least five of the following people: VHS secretary William Stanard, state librarian H. L. McIlwaine, Earl G. Swem, historian Douglas S. Freeman, John Stewart Bryan, Williamsburg leader George P. Coleman, historian Robert A. Lancaster, Jr., state archivist Morgan P. Robinson, and Samuel H. Yonge. All were trusted and active supporters of the APVA. Bryan took to his *News-Leader* to endorse the project, but with some qualification: "No age can ever quite recapture the spirit of another. . . . For its part the *News-Leader* is confident that the restoration will not be carried too far—that its purpose will be to retain rather than to rebuild. When attempts are made to reconstruct the more famous buildings of the town, the unescapable limitations will be recognized and historical charlatanry will be avoided." Ellyson asked the APVA members to ratify the agreement through mailed proxies; it stipulated further that the APVA's memorial boulder would be retained, a bronze tablet would be placed in the building recounting the APVA's role, and the building would include an APVA room.[41]

After an affirmative vote, Goodwin let the cat out of the bag. In a June 1928 public meeting he revealed to the town just who had provided the funds. Most Williamsburgers felt flushed with pride, economic longing, or awe. A handful of critics did voice their opposition, however. One commented that Rockefeller had bought the town. In the school auditorium Major S. D. Freeman condemned the plan and asked his neighbors: "If you give up your land it will no longer be your city. Will you feel the same pride in it that you now feel as you walk across the Greens or down the broad streets? Have you all been hypnotized by five million dollars dangled before your eyes? . . . We will reap dollars but will we own our own town? Will you not be in the position of a butterfly pinned in a glass cabinet, or like a

mummy unearthed in the tomb of Tutankhamen?" Evidently others feared
another speculative boom that would burst, as it did in adjacent Penniman
after Du Pont closed its plant. Williamsburg's mayor opposed the plan, but
was promptly voted out of office. Goodwin took any occasion to sell his
ideas to the town. He used his pulpit to the extent that parishioners complained. One lady walked out in protest every Sunday when he began his
sermon. His Gospel of Preservation evidently had intermixed with the gospel of Christ.[42]

Remembering the Williamsburg of his college days, Cabell interpreted
the takeover in the context of Virginia's continued failure to protect its
cultural heritage. He whimsically called Colonial Williamsburg, Inc., the
successor to the Williamsburg Holding Corporation, "that bric-a-brac but
instructive subsidiary of the Standard Oil Company of New Jersey." As it
redid the town, he thought that Virginia had accepted businessmen's control
of culture for too long. What followed that business control was the demolition of much of the town. Over 700 buildings fell to the wreckers or mov-
ers, a process that delighted some youth, including Vernon Geddy, Jr., who
later became Rockefeller's attorney and the town's mayor. Only 88 structures, many of them small outbuildings, remained from the eighteenth and
early nineteenth centuries for restoration. Eventually 350 buildings would
be rebuilt from the ground up. The reconstruction, in turn, primarily represented Rockefeller's elegant but far-fetched conception of a colonial backdrop. It drew 31,000 visitors in 1934, over 90,000 by 1936, and almost 1.3
million paid admissions in 1976.[43]

The APVA heaped praise on the Williamsburg Holding Corporation's
early work on the Capitol, Palace, and Wren Building. As chairman of the
APVA's capitol committee, Swem voiced "its gratification at the thorough
and discerning" work. He reported in 1934 that "the old capitol building as
it now stands represents all that modern research, science and art can avail
in the rebuilding of an ancient structure." The three public buildings, "now
all standing in their original simplicity and beauty, will perpetuate the glory
of old Williamsburg," as well as "remind every American of the discerning
appreciation of historical sentiment which has inspired the generous donor."
Yonge dissented, not in his gratitude for Rockefeller's munificence but
about the accuracy of details of the reconstruction, such as the placement
of the Capitol's cupola and the location of its main entrance.[44]

During the next decade some Williamsburgers resented what they
called the "second Yankee invasion" of the town. A strong sense of Virginia
courtesy confined these criticisms to the back parlor, and they did not ap-

pear in a newspaper. Swem, for example, complained privately to friends in the 1940s about the purse strings of Rockefeller's largess. He deplored the liberal political views of these northerners and their increasingly dominant role in the local study of history. Yet Swem himself relied on Rockefeller's philanthropy for his magisterial *Virginia Historical Index*. Another resident, Robert Bright, sadly watched the Old South wane. In his *Memories of Williamsburg,* Bright, who had spoken for the APVA on occasion, remembered the town of his youth as "a delightful place." With the changes of the 1930s, "it has all gone with the wind." He cited Cicero, "O tempora! O mores!" [45]

In the moment of Williamsburg's renaissance, however, the gratitude of traditionalists swelled. As Samuel Mitchell voiced the gospel, he lauded "the spiritual change" brought on by "the turning-back in architecture to the authentic colonial designs." Noting the metaphorical use of material culture, he admitted: "There are many languages in which history tells its story. The written word is only one. Architecture etches even more deeply its record. The revival of the colonial type invites a return to the simplicity, genuineness and youthful impulses of the nation." [46] Such colonial simplicity could be deceptive. As Goodwin directed the restoration, his romantic notions of colonial values and his whitewashing of social problems in the colonial era became apparent. Although Williamsburg's architecture had been exquisitely restored, the values of traditionalism premised those decisions and designs.

As an organization, the APVA swallowed a bitter pill with Rockefeller's corporate takeover. Almost simultaneously, northern interests took charge of Monticello and Wakefield and the federal government acquired much of Jamestown and Yorktown. Local control of historic preservation seemed like Powhatan's Chimney—a relic of a lost past. After the APVA relinquished control of the Capitol site to what proved to be northern preservationists, it resolved never again to "dispose of or turn over to individuals or organizations any of the property held by it, or even to consider such propositions, as long as it is able, as at present, to maintain its holdings." [47] Ellyson's policy partly reflected the determination of Virginians to interpret Virginiana. It also revealed the APVA's keen sense of a personal ownership of the past. The APVA obviously differed from SPNEA, as well as from preservationists in Charleston, South Carolina, who would develop revolving funds to preserve sites, protect them through restrictive covenants, and then sell them. Only in the 1970s did the APVA accept the sale of properties protected by legal covenants.

Although the APVA had relinquished the Capitol's grounds, it soon gained a noteworthy historic site from the Rockefeller organization. Tyler persuaded Williamsburg's town fathers in 1924 to give the APVA an option on the 1701 jail, and interestingly, the city deeded the building to the APVA in 1929—a year after Rockefeller's role had been revealed. Perhaps Williamsburg hoped to retain some local hold on preservation, but the city stipulated that the APVA would lose the building if a proper restoration did not follow within two years. During these years the local branch nearly died; there were no meetings in 1931 and only one in 1932. Unable to raise the necessary funds, the APVA defaulted on the deal and traded the jail and two acres of land, together with the Palace icehouse, for Smith's Fort plantation across the James River.[48]

This Surry County building first drew the APVA's interest in 1911 when Ellyson incorrectly described it as "the oldest brick house in Virginia." What first attracted the APVA was not the simple dignity of a small plantation house, but its proximity to Jamestown. William Stanard investigated the origins of what was called Smith's Fort—an earthwork fortification behind the house that was built about 1609 on the river's edge to protect Jamestown from a possible Spanish attack. The APVA hypothesized that Smith's Fort "would have been the salvation of Anglo-Saxon civilization in America had the Spaniard attacked, as he did against the French in South Carolina." Tradition had attributed the story-and-a-half brick plantation house on the site to John Rolfe. The Williamsburg Holding Corporation purchased it in 1928 for $9,000 and transferred it in 1933 to the APVA, which soon decided to establish a house museum to honor Thomas Rolfe, the son of Pocahontas. To trim their expenses, preservationists deeded a long strip of land to the commonwealth so that public funds could be used to connect the house to the highway. Like other branches, the Surry County branch used the free labor provided by the Civil Works Administration to ready the site.[49]

After it restored and opened the "Rolfe Property House" in 1935, the APVA faced some rather embarrassing questions about Rolfe's exact association with the house. Cabell humorously described the fray that erupted after some antiquaries investigated the house's lineage and proved that it had no connection to the son of Pocahontas. "Though such iniquity may be difficult of belief," he said, "yet by-and-by did wicked persons, a coterie of mere fiends in the drab form of antiquaries, make public their undesired proofs—which, for that matter, are still suffered to remain impiously upon open record at Surry County Court House—that this revered residence was, instead, built and occupied by one Mr. Thomas Warren, a burgess for Surry County; and that the 'Rolfe Property House' was never at any season owned by Thomas Rolfe, nor by any other member of the Rolfe family." According to Cabell, traditionalists rejected "such babbling," retreated to their comfortable myths, and claimed that "persons who betray to public knowledge any such inconvenient facts are not loyal Virginians." As a result, those who paid their twenty-five cents to visit the property and pay homage to Pocahontas still heard an interpretation oriented to the Rolfe family.[50]

What followed in the 1930s for the APVA depended partly on the interest or whim of local branches. The Smithfield branch purchased the old Isle of Wight County courthouse in 1938. The T-shaped building with an arcaded front, dating to the mid-eighteenth century, was slated to be demolished by the federal government for a new post office. Once possessed of "unusual architectural beauty," it over the years had acquired "ugly alterations and defaced stucco." Admonished by SPNEA's Appleton in 1923 for its failure to preserve courthouses, the APVA now owned a superior example. At the same time, preservationists acquired an old tobacco warehouse in Urbanna, dating from 1766, in order to prevent its removal from the state. In Rockbridge County, the APVA received a wooden covered bridge, known as Jordan's Bridge, built in 1870. When the state erected a new structure, it discarded the old one for a dollar. The small local branch attracted few recruits to its cause, however. It did little work on the bridge, which was soon torn down. The local APVA instead spent considerable time trying to find the "grave of Mary Greenlee, the first white woman to make a home in Rockbridge County."[51] Caught between an interest in dilapidated antiquities and racial mythology, these ladies chose the more traditional pursuit.

The APVA's conservatism showed most in Richmond, where privately owned antiquities fell at an alarming rate in the 1920s. In 1927 the Cunningham-Archer house, designed by Robert Mills and built in 1815–16, fell. The Alexander McRae house, built in 1805 and one of the city's most architecturally significant structures, was demolished two years later. Many properties became run-down tenements that housed poor African-Americans, as was the case with the Patrick Gibbon house, and they were destroyed.[52] The losses eventually forced the APVA to act and brought Mary Wingfield Scott (1895–1983) to the fore. The best of the APVA's third generation, Scott began as an antiquary who studied the old houses of Richmond, but she became frustrated by the unwillingness of APVA directors to preserve much of this heritage. Apparently the APVA's officers regarded themselves primarily as overseers for the local branches. Scott, in turn, formed her own chapter in Richmond in 1935. The William Byrd branch has since been one of the most active in the state. What provoked her interest was the rapid deterioration of the Adam Craig house. A two-story frame building from the mid-1780s on East Grace Street, about two blocks from the Old Stone House, the Craig house was the birthplace of Jane Stanard, the "Helen" of Poe's verse.

Supervising the project, Scott grappled with Richmond's most pressing problems. Situated in the industrial Shockoe Valley, the Craig house had been purchased in 1912 by the Methodist Mission Association. As it proselytized among the poor, the mission removed the trees and garden and created what Scott called "a sort of Salvation Army shelter for drunks and other down-and-outs." The neighborhood, composed of "many charming early nineteenth-century houses," was populated by "a low class of Negroes or by Polish and Russian Jews." The house deteriorated further after the mission closed. Scott's branch bought the dilapidated building, which was "open to the breezes, as devoid of locks as it was of paint. When we first started to clean it, a hoe, not a broom, had to be used." She used Works Progress Administration laborers to repair it.[53]

Scott began with "beautiful visions of buying and preserving dozens of old houses" but soon sensed her illusion. The reasons for her setbacks were typical: difficulties raising money, a surfeit of local museums, and the unwillingness of a good tenant to live in an old house. Publicizing Richmond's antiquities, her branch tried to attract interest. In 1941 she published *Houses of Old Richmond,* while her branch issued postcards "to put historic Richmond on the map," undertook a historic inventory (by 1943 almost five hundred buildings were in its files), and sponsored exhibits on Richmond's old neighborhoods.[54]

With World War II and the cessation of most new construction, she found that the greatest hazard to historic structures was unwise repair, not demolition. Two groups particularly needed instruction on this point—African-Americans, most of whom rented old houses, and "the few large owners of slum real estate." Those few blacks who owned old houses tried to improve their surroundings and tended "to make elaborate and unsuitable alterations" in their historic homes. The slumlords, on the other hand, would "charge as much rent as the traffic will bear and resign themselves to letting unreliable and destructive tenants pull the house to pieces." Slumlords took a "fatalistic" attitude, halted maintenance, and generally showed no interest in historic preservation.[55]

Because slumlords took a mercenary, exploitative stance toward their properties, Scott thought that African-Americans would be "more accessible" to preservation education. In a major break from her predecessors, she appealed to a group that preservationists had earlier opposed. Scott and her branch turned the Craig house into the Negro Art Center and grappled with the social realities of urban preservation. Saving the historic landscape, she said, was anything but "a stuffy museum job unrelated to the bitter world we live in." She urged preservationists to "realize the close connection between mankind's dwellings of yesterday and his life today." Her Gospel of Preservation included more than a moralistic reaffirmation of traditionalism; it recognized the nexus between poverty, private property, and preservation.[56]

The William Byrd branch acquired numerous buildings in the 1930s and 1940s. These included the Pulliam house, an 1856 town house known for its superb cast-iron ornamentation; the Ann Carrington house, a bow-fronted Federal-style dwelling on Church Hill; and the Ellen Glasgow house, the well-preserved Greek Revival home of the author. The APVA showed flexibility in the use of each building. No longer tied to the notion that a historic house must be a museum, it leased the houses to sympathetic organizations.[57]

From the Powder Horn museum in 1889 to the Negro Art Center in the late 1930s, the APVA clearly expanded its focus. Yet any assessment of its work during these years reveals some problematic findings and striking contradictions. The task of preservationists, according to the APVA's constitution, was "to acquire, restore and preserve the ancient historic grounds, buildings, monuments and tombs in the Commonwealth of Virginia." These ambitious aims, however, were beyond reach because historic preservation, whether in 1889 or 1929, was considered primarily to be a pedagogic and moralistic act emanating from women's sphere. The gentlemen of Virginia, moreover, rarely moved to empower women outside of this restricted sphere. They took every available opportunity, however, to use historic preservation and the restored symbols of the past in their modern political battles. They refused as well to commit the necessary capital and energy to preservation.

Later students of the movement have muddled matters even more by using one organization's standard to measure the work of another. It has been asked if the APVA developed a modern, scientific methodology that valued an artifact for its original materials, appearances, and aesthetics. Or did the APVA dwell in romanticism to escape worldly concerns and spend its energies on social teas and slapdash restorations? Neither question adequately addresses the meaning of Virginia's historic preservation in the APVA's first half century.

SPNEA's Appleton insisted on a scientific regimen and a businesslike method in his preservation work. In 1928 he admitted that he knew "nothing" about "the accuracy or excellence of the work" of the APVA. He nonetheless complained that it spent "most of its time" on plaques and markers, and he wanted Kimball to get the APVA involved in "some active preservation work" instead. Appleton's standards, and his suggestions along those lines, were never well received in Richmond. Throughout the APVA's first half century, there was an animosity toward New England that shaped its brand of preservation. Although the APVA called SPNEA its "sister-society," siblinglike jealousy often flared. Ellyson took pride in the fact that the APVA's defense of Virginia's role as first settlement and leader of the Revolution had forced New Englanders to alter their claims. "By a quiet insistence on certain priorities," she said, "we have established a real, and I trust, lasting friendship" with SPNEA. Appleton and SPNEA's other leaders, however, had never made such claims. While Virginians labored to correct what they thought erroneous in the historical record, SPNEA acquired building after building. Appleton preached what he called "a gospel of further acquisitions." The APVA's president admitted that SPNEA had "gone far beyond us in attainments—having five times the number of sites in their possession and five times the amount of dues collected." [58] Those differences illustrated the contrasting means that each organization used to fulfill its gospel. While the APVA preached traditionalism, SPNEA acquired real estate.

The APVA reeled, moreover, when its work was slighted. Leicester B. Holland, chairman of the Committee on Preservation of Historic Buildings of the American Institute of Architects, credited SPNEA "with priority in the work of preservation of historic spots." Virginians thought that it was bad enough for Plymouth to steal Jamestown's priority, but now SPNEA stole the APVA's! Holland admitted that he unintentionally had slighted the APVA but compounded his error when he claimed that SPNEA deserved credit because "the New Englanders have done more actual preservation." What counted was "work done," he told Ellyson, implying that the APVA had served more of "a social function" in Virginia. [59]

As an organizer of the Historic American Buildings Survey, Holland had a philosophy of preservation which actually bridged those of the APVA and SPNEA. Through HABS, Holland called for a scientific inventory and restoration of America's antiquities, but his ideological goals were easily seen. In the depth of the Great Depression, he regarded historic buildings as symbols for the character traits that were necessary to rebuild America's society and economy. According to Holland, who also served as chief of the Fine Arts Division at the Library of Congress, the buildings surveyed by HABS "will express the sturdiness and the heroic spirit of the hardy early pioneers who had such great confidence in themselves and in the land which they loved, toiled for and peopled, and in which they laid the enduring foundations of the greater America of today." The APVA, too, played up these themes. In the midst of the depression, it brought over ten thousand visitors to the Marshal house during a four-year span. Marshall's simple upbringing, traditional values, and respect for order became the APVA's staple themes during the crisis of capitalism.[60]

Appleton, Holland, and architecturally minded preservationists thus misunderstood the APVA. Although the APVA, SPNEA, and even HABS used the preserved past to influence the present, these preservation movements fundamentally differed in their background, purposes, and methods. When evaluated by modern and scientific methods, many of which were pioneered by SPNEA, the APVA fell short. Its use of the past was more symbolic than factual, its methods more ad hoc than planned, its restoration procedures more romantic than scientific, and its abilities more limited than broad. Historical exactitude was not necessary if preservationists were most interested in protecting symbols for traditionalism. What appeared to be real was as good as what was real. The context of the APVA's work should be set, therefore, within the cultural politics of traditionalism.

Epilogue: The Hegemony of Traditionalism

S EVENTY YEARS after its establishment, historian Marshall Fishwick ac-
claimed the APVA's high standing. He felt certain it was "the most
venerated" of all historical and patriotic organizations in the Old Dominion.
Virginians held the APVA in such high esteem because it had declared its
loyalty above all else to traditionalism. Like a plantation house that grew
room by room over the years, Virginia's traditionalism had evolved from
English society in the seventeenth century. It reflected the soil and sentiment
of the Chesapeake and piedmont area and largely developed according to
the perspectives and experiences of the tidewater and eastern elite. The
bedrock for its foundations were beliefs in local rule, states' rights, and the
customary racial and hierarchical social order. Traditionalists further prized
such personal characteristics as honor, duty, and Protestant morality.
Tradition-minded families, and that included all of good breeding, were
rooted in their locale, close-knit, and patriarchal. These Virginians practiced
filiopietism and protected their fathers' customs like a prized inheritance.
Traditionalism joined the ways of the past and future in a seamless web.[1]

Traditionalism became a hegemonic force in the Old Dominion. The
preservation of homes once occupied by the likes of Marshall and Lee, as
well as the sanctification of Jamestown and Williamsburg, not only represented the primacy of Anglo-Saxons and the First Families of Virginia but
gave traditionalism a chance to regain ascendancy in the Old Dominion.
Civil War, Reconstruction, and the popular democracy of Readjusters and
Populists had so severely shaken the elite that alternative cultures rose
through the cracks of the old order. While radicals appealed to the Jeffersonian tradition, others in industrial towns cast their lot with the labor
movement. The freedom of African-Americans perhaps most signified the
collapse of antebellum ways. As a result, Virginia's elite slowly reconstituted
their ranks and reformulated their culture.

Throughout the settled East, tradition-minded Americans similarly
faced new threats to their power. Whether those threats came from the
Irish who supported Tammany Hall and Saint Patrick or the Wobblies who
demanded free speech and sang to Joe Hill, the United States experienced

an upheaval in the late nineteenth and early twentieth centuries. As in the APVA, tradition-minded Americans tried both to ensure their leadership in politics and the economy and to protect what they could from their past. Traditionalism assumed different shades of meaning, depending on the local threats, the individual interpreters, and the historical times.

As in the APVA's merging of Old and New Souths, what is most revealing was that throughout the nation economic development always preceded historic preservation. As capitalism was transformed by industry and the corporation, and as society reflected those changes, the elite who descended from the FFVs, the Pilgrim Fathers, or any other such group pressed to assure their economic standing and then, and only then, their cultural roots. As a result, traditionalism increasingly reflected the new economy. It mirrored what the gentlemen of property and standing needed in their daily lives to catch up or stay ahead. Just as history would be revised, traditions invented, or myths made, so, too, would "modern" traditionalism selectively take from the past to serve the present.

Virginia traditionalism, as a result, was anything but static. Even within the ranks of the elite, it lent itself to individual perspectives. What it ultimately boiled down to, however, was a code of personal behavior, structured class relations, loyalty to the Old Dominion, and a vaguely defined belief in progress through the established order. As a hegemonic culture, it depended upon public acceptance of such principles as white supremacy, social hierarchy, obedience to law, and elite government. Traditionalism was promulgated through diverse institutions and media. Preachers gave sermons, journalists wrote editorials, teachers presented lectures, and employers offered advice on the merits of upholding traditions. Preservationists provided them all with tangible symbols and meaningful interpretations of that order.

A system is not hegemonic, however, if its precepts are not accepted by the leaders and internalized by the populace. From its first days the APVA largely spoke for tidewater and eastern Virginia, where after the Civil War not only disaffected whites but most importantly a sizable black population challenged the control and ways of the elite. There the APVA most exerted its influence by reinstituting a historical identity and purpose for the elite, which in turn exercised control over the land. Throughout the South, in fact, established whites faced similar dissension and challenges. Those southern states which lacked Virginia's well-developed tradition of elite rule and social deference, such as Alabama and Mississippi, turned earlier and more conspicuously to physical intimidation, racial violence, and legal statute to restore order. The Old Dominion, on the other hand, more convincingly used traditionalism as a means to restore the past order. To be sure, the Constitution of 1902, as well as the lynchings and repression, accompanied that resurgence of traditionalism, but Virginia did not experience real social warfare, as in North Carolina during the 1890s.

Whether through statute, intimidation, personal resignation, or cultural acceptance, the Virginia populace apparently did accept elite control. Schoolbooks inculcated traditional values. Protestantism encouraged submission to the divinely ordained order. African-American leaders in the Old Dominion recognized the sheer practicality of accommodation. The new constitution disfranchised the masses and ensured elite dominance. All the while, an emerging mass media and consumer culture stressed hard work, patriotism, and material accumulation, not political confrontation or popular-class solidarity. Only dissident whites in western Virginia or their advocates in chairs of history in the East, such as Thomas Jefferson Wertenbaker, were able to challenge tidewater through a revitalized, but still weak, Jeffersonian tradition.

Wielding potent symbols of Virginia's dominant tradition, preservationists strove to make the past meaningful for present purposes. In a never-ending drumbeat, the APVA used podium, press, and pulpit to sound the necessity of Virginia's allegiance to respected customs and order. This was its Gospel of Preservation. Just as Victorian mothers focused on their children's proper education, the APVA's women looked to the next generation and asked if it would accept traditionalism. "Our annual pilgrimage to the shrine of patriotism" at Jamestown, said Belle Bryan to her members in 1903, "appeals in an especial way to the young, and educates them in lessons of loyalty. Thus we may hope to find them prepared and eager for the work when we must confide this solemn trust into their hands." That work obviously was more than the preservation of old buildings; it was more than fealty to the ancients. It was an acceptance of traditional values, capitalist economics, and conservative politics in the modern day. With the "younger generation" especially in mind, the APVA told its members in 1938 how a half century before, "a few noble women . . . took up the task of saving what was left to Virginia of her glorious past." Success depended on the next generation: "Tell them to catch the vision and follow the gleam."[2]

A hegemonic culture slowly changes to meet the needs of those who wield power.[3] Virginians such as Joseph Bryan and Cynthia Coleman adopted not only the Yankee's Protestant work ethic but the Victorian era's conception of family and woman's role. When preservationists studied Nathaniel Bacon and Mary Washington, they repackaged and popularized myths and legends that served their needs. They also invented traditions, such as visiting a historic shrine, making a pilgrimage to Jamestown, and celebrating Virginia Day, to impart a legitimacy to the views that Page, Hall, and Stewart Bryan propounded. They erected monument after monument to underscore those interpretations. They consciously molded traditionalism to reflect their contemporary world.

Their present needs formed the principal criteria in deciding what was worthy of preservation and memorialization. What prompted the preservation of a building or site was its symbolic relationship to the Lost Cause, conservative government, Anglo-Saxonism, Protestant individualism, or Virginia's priority in the nation. These themes represented two interrelated goals: the perpetuation of traditionalism in Virginia and the extension of Virginia culture and influence in the South and nation. Through these years Virginians repeatedly were on the defensive, acting not only against Pilgrim Fathers and condescending Yankees but against southerners who held different notions of the Lost Cause, New South, and antebellum tradition. The APVA keenly realized that its goals could only be accomplished if the history of Virginia offered inspiration, excitation, and models for emulation. The preserved shrines of the APVA, however, only served part of that purpose. While academic and popular historians revised the interpretation of Virginia and southern history, the APVA buttressed the process by erecting tablets and monuments to stir the memories of the Virginia populace.

Increasingly, Virginia's elite, as shown by the ranks of the APVA, included more than FFVs; it held men and women of professional and business standing who, though not to the manor born in the Old Dominion, adopted the manners of traditionalism. The APVA's most difficult obstacle in the actual conservation of material culture was convincing this elite that Virginia's antiquities symbolized what was important about the Old Dominion. Many traditionalists were willing to let the buildings fall and to restrict their traditions to social discourse, formal education, or political conservatism. Yet in the long run Virginia traditionalists accepted the APVA's premise that buildings associated with Virginia's history should be preserved. Those buildings reified values necessary for social stability. They held memories about home, family, and life that gave personal meaning to preservationists. Most importantly, they testified to the permanence of the Old Dominion as it entered an uncertain future. The APVA pointedly described its mission in those terms: "We cherish our *past* for the sake of our *future* so that while preserving the one we are building the other for ages yet to come."[4]

What was equally important about the APVA's first half century of historic preservation was its interpretation of historical antiquities. It primarily used history to inspire and teach the present. As a result, its historical accounts were often narrow and moralistic. Like a school primer, history became a morality tale; biography became a hagiography. Anything damaging to their ancestors, families, traditions, or commonwealth was carefully excised from the preserved past. What preservationists said and did evidently reflected their class, culture, and times.

Not surprisingly, the APVA largely overlooked the history and perspective of the majority of past Virginians. Absent from its historical rendition were those Virginians who actually built the economy and landscape—African-Americans, poor workers, yeomen farmers, and popular-class women. Its tidewater origins and eastern Virginia outlook resulted as well in its slighting of much of the piedmont, Shenandoah Valley, and the mountains. The documentation cited by these preservationists, moreover, often rested upon romantic traditions and legends which, from a later perspective, appear farfetched. Almost inevitably, the racism and ethnocentrism of tradition-minded Virginians permeated the APVA's understanding of past and present. The association's reading of history was probably no worse, however, than that of the Grand Army of the Republic, the United Daughters of the Confederacy, and other ancestral or patriotic groups which battled against perceived enemies. Those struggles between elite and democrat, conservative and radical, and white and black from 1860 to 1902 shaped the very meaning of historic preservation in the Old Dominion.[5] The APVA's historic preservation cannot be understood, therefore, from a modern interest in aesthetics, architecture, and professionalism.

Virginia preservationists also challenged New England's control over the interpretation of American history. The Old Dominion, they claimed, had been robbed of its deserved fame by the descendants of the Pilgrims. In their rivalry with Yankees, Virginians sometimes stretched their claims to the extreme. Other times, they were on the mark. Preservationists did prove that John Smith, Jamestown, and Williamsburg had been slighted by northern writers. As the association worked for national Union and reconciliation, moreover, it did so on the precondition that the nation recognize Virginia's prior civilization. In the process the Old South's subordination of blacks, as well as its notions of states' rights and local rule, received historical sanction. Many preservationists shrewdly realized that this national recognition went hand-in-hand with an acceptance of the propriety, validity, and effectiveness of the Old South civilization. The past became a prologue to the present.

These leaders strove as well to restore mythical qualities in the actual present. As in the Old South when gentlemen supposedly had devoted their lives to the improvement of government and community, preservationists stressed the need for disinterested elite rulers and deplored the purported selfishness of democratic leaders. When privatism and the pursuit of individual success detracted from modern public life, the APVA called for new Smiths and Henrys to step forward and bring order and progress to Virginia. Similarly, as a centralized federal government assumed more power, preservationists trumpeted the success of Virginia's earlier localistic rule. In the battle of cultures, preservationists redoubled their efforts to restore the vitality of traditionalism in the Old Dominion. While some of the association's leaders undoubtedly were antiquaries intoxicated by the past, most preservationists not only loved Virginia's past glories but realized that the preservation of the past offered the key to the future. The APVA's gospel reassuringly offered what these Virginians knew best—conservative politics and a customary ordering of society based upon elite rule, social hierarchy, personal honor, and local government.

Virginia's preservationists, of course, did not always live up to their high standards. Despite their praise for the simple life, they lived in relative luxury compared with the majority of Virginians. While calling for disinterested rulers, they crafted and supported a system that disproportionately gave them, and not the popular classes, the benefits. Their calls for individual action and noblesse oblige to remedy the day's pressing social ills, however laudable, denied the pressing need for governmental action. While they called for historic preservation, they boosted a New South that like a juggernaut rode roughshod over a fragile past. What is most important to remember about the APVA's early work, therefore, is that traditionalism came first on its agenda, and the Old Dominion's traditionalism historically had been a system which first and foremost served the needs of the state's elite.

The APVA's first half century also set Virginia on a course where the promotion of history became the multimillion-dollar business of tourism. What would modern Virginia be without its historic buildings, landmarks, and sites? Unlike any other organization, the APVA got the preservation ball rolling in the Old Dominion. By focusing on a handful of sites in Williamsburg, for example, the association nurtured a historical sentiment that partly offset the increasingly fast pace of modernization. Had Williamsburg's corner-lot boomers demolished the Powder Horn, built on the foundations of the Capitol, or further modernized Bruton Church, perhaps Rockefeller would have missed the glimmer of Williamsburg's past and turned a deaf ear to Goodwin's pleas. Yet the APVA had a very limited agenda. The Williamsburg Holding Corporation picked up where the APVA had ceased to function. Its financial resources dwarfed those of the APVA, and its developing professionalism outpaced the rather amateurish ways of the APVA. But, the narrow focus of the WHC on the colonial period, together with a half century of interpretation stressing patriotism, elite culture, and the invisibility of the masses, shows much continuity with the APVA's earlier ventures.[6] Its very motto, "That the future may learn from the past," stresses its educational mission, but the question is still pertinent, Whose past will be studied?

The APVA also laid the groundwork for preservation work by the National Park Service at Jamestown. What would have happened to the fragile island had the APVA not acted? Perhaps the ebb and the flow of the James would have totally engulfed the lowlands, the winds toppled the deteriorated church tower, or the farmer's plow further destroyed the archaeological treasure chest. Again, the financial resources of the federal government, together with its professionally trained archaeologists, carried the conservation of Jamestown to another stage of study. If the Park Service practiced restraint, the state took a different tack when it created a commission to build Jamestown Festival Park in 1957 and celebrate the 350th anniversary of Virginia's founding. While it boosted tourism and reiterated Virginia's leading role in the nation, the park melodramatically played up the role of the settlers and included speculative reconstructions of the walled fort, the wattle-and-daub buildings, and the three ships that brought them in 1607. What was built in 1957 for the millions of tourists made the APVA's romanticized reconstruction of Jamestown's church in 1907 seem modest.

As the APVA preserved buildings or marked historic sites through its two dozen active branches, it set a precedent for action by the state government. The commonwealth subsequently erected markers and memorials through its Conservation and Economic Development Commission (est. 1926) and encouraged the preservation of historic sites through its Virginia Historic Landmarks Commission (est. 1966). In many ways tradition-minded Virginians accepted the APVA's gospel. They acknowledged that a preserved historic landscape did create the state's distinctive ambiance and symbolize its ancient traditions. Even more, historic preservation was usually left to the private sector. The state's elite increasingly found its own ancestral homes or historic dwellings worth preserving. Its members found reassurance and comfort living in a home shaped by time's hand.

Before World War II the state and federal governments and the Williamsburg Holding Corporation differed from the APVA in their larger-scale operations, their bigger bank accounts, and the increased professionalism of their staffs. Each in its own way still promoted a brand of cultural politics while emphasizing its organizational structure, scientific regimen, and purported educational goals. Like a corporate takeover, they gradually made preservation into a business. They took much of the passion, emotion, and tension out of the preservation movement and removed it from a personal context. In some ways the National Park Service and Williamsburg Holding Corporation practiced a type of progressivism that emanated from northern corporations—large in scale, impersonal, bureaucratic, scientific, and male. The APVA, on the other hand, held on to Virginia's conservative progressivism—local in orientation, personal, idiosyncratic, eclectic, and mindful of historical patterns, including women's role in preservation.

Whether in 1889 or 1939, the APVA more directly illustrated local forces at work. It was more easily seen just who was preserving what and why. That is the reason why the APVA's pilgrimages to Jamestown, or even its historical pageants, drew the local crowds that they did. That is why the APVA was the most venerated of historical and patriotic organizations in Virginia. All the while, women held the formal reins in the APVA. Although their domestic morality, limited economic power, and deference to patriarchy kept preservation on the track laid in 1889, they still held considerable authority and prestige as the guardians of traditional culture. Ironically, they were eclipsed by men when the professionalism of the National Park Service and Williamsburg Holding Corporation demanded new methods for the preservation movement. Those methods would be oriented to the male world of architecture and archaeology. Just as Rockefeller's restoration company represented a loss of local control over Virginia's second capital, so, too, did the influence of its architects signify a loss of power for Virginia's women. Women had pioneered the preservation movement in the mid-nineteenth century, but they would be marginalized as norms established in the progressive era gained popularity.[7]

What Virginians started in 1889, however, inspired other tradition-minded Americans to take action. Its very existence served as a precedent for preservation activity on a larger scale than that of the Mount Vernon Ladies' Association. Most noticeably, Appleton learned from the APVA's work when he formed SPNEA in 1910. His brand of preservation was different, but he, too, campaigned to make traditionalism a real force in the New England of immigrant politics, congested cities, and rapid modernization. Preservationists in the South as well picked up the banner, in such cities as Charleston and New Orleans, when they formed private associations that similarly accommodated the old and the new in their towns. Such an accommodation characterizes preservation work in the United States and is dramatically different from England's Society for the Protection of Ancient Buildings. Founded by John Ruskin and William Morris, SPAB fought industrialism and tenaciously protected antiquities. The APVA and SPAB represented two diametrically opposed poles in the world of Anglo-American historic preservation.

Clearly Virginia preservationists could have done more during the late nineteenth and early twentieth centuries to preserve the buildings and grounds of the Old Dominion. But the gentlemen of Virginia had resolutely given priority to establishing businesses, fending off democrats, and restoring order. Like Americans in general, the glitter of modernity caught their eye more than a dimly lit history. The past was most important for its use in the present. Yet, historic preservation did take hold in the Old Dominion, whether as a means to buttress traditionalism, to seek personal therapy, or to honor one's ancestors. While protecting Jamestown's church ruin or Williamsburg's Powder Horn, the APVA defined those tasks as fitting for patriotic Virginians. While preserving the Old Dominion, the APVA not only invented the tradition of historic preservation but established the memory and identity of Virginia.

Appendixes
Notes
Bibliography
Index

Appendix 1

Prominent Women in the APVA: A Selected List of Leaders Serving for Five Years or More

Bagby, Lucy Parke Chamberlayne: corresponding secretary (1896), honorary vice president (1898–1927), chair of Jamestown committee.

Ball, Emma Mason Read: vice president (1896–1919).

Barney, Louise J.: director (1898), honorary vice president (1899–1937).

Bryan, Isobel Lamont Stewart: incorporator, treasurer (1889), president (1890–1910).

Coleman, Cynthia Beverley Tucker: incorporator, vice president (1889–1908), historian (1898–1900), honorary vice president (1908).

Curry, Mary Thomas: vice president (1896–98), honorary vice president (1898–1901).

Ellyson, Lora Hotchkiss: vice president (1896–1908), associate president (1908–10), president (1910–35).

Galt, Mary Jeffery: incorporator, vice president (1896–98), honorary vice president (1898–1922).

Lee, Ellen Bernard: incorporator, president (1889–90), vice president (1896–98), honorary vice president (1898–1933).

Lightfoot, Mary Minor: treasurer (1894–1908), vice president (1910–30), director (1908–19).

Lyons, Elizabeth Henry: incorporator, recording secretary (1896–99), director (1899–1900), honorary vice president (1919–20).

Pryor, Sarah Rice: incorporator, vice president (1896), honorary vice president (1898–1913).

Robins, Sally Nelson: director (1896–99), recording secretary (1899–1907), vice president (1924–25).

Stanard, Mary Mann Page Newton: director (1896–1900), historian (1900–1915).

Tazewell, Mary Louisa: incorporator, vice president (1889–96), honorary vice president (1898–1919).

Tyler, Alice M.: director (1898–1908), recording secretary (1908–10).

Valentine, Katherine Cole Friend Mayo: director (1896–98), vice president (1898–1924), honorary vice president (1924–26).

Wilmer, Margaret W.: director (1913–21), corresponding secretary (1921–24), vice president (1924–35), president (1935–45).

Appendix 2

APVA Advisory Board: A Selected List, with Terms of Service

Anderson, Archer (1896–1913): attorney, industrial executive, VHS officer, and leader of the Lost Cause movement.

Brock, Robert Alonzo (1889–1913): historian, VHS officer, and Southern Historical Society secretary.

Bruce, Philip Alexander (1898–1901): historian and VHS officer.

Bryan, John Stewart (1910–41): newspaper publisher, civic booster, and college president.

Bryan, Joseph (1889–1908): newspaper publisher, corporate executive, and VHS officer.

Byrd, Harry F. (1931–41): former governor of Virginia, United States senator.

Cabell, James Alston (1889–1926): attorney and former state legislator.

Carter, Thomas Nelson (1896–99): attorney and bank executive.

Clark, William Meade (1908–13): Episcopal minister and antiquarian author.

Coleman, George P. (1919–41): Williamsburg booster, mayor, bank president, and state highway commissioner.

Curry, J. L. M. (1889–1901): former United States congressman and diplomat, educational reformer, and Presbyterian clergyman.

Ellyson, J. Taylor (1908–19): former Richmond mayor, lieutenant governor, and president of the Confederate Memorial Association.

Henry, William Wirt (1889–1900): former Commonwealth's Attorney, state legislator, and historian.

Hunton, Eppa, Jr. (1913–31): prominent attorney and son of a Confederate general.

Hutzler, Henry S. (1899–1921): bank executive.

Lancaster, Robert A., Jr. (1896–1938): investment banker and businessman.

McGuire, John P., Jr. (1896–1901): master of a Richmond boy's school.

Meredith, Wyndham R. (1896–1910): corporate attorney and president of the Virginia Bar Association.

Mitchell, Samuel Chiles (1899–1908): historian, temperance leader, and educational reformer.

O'Connell, Dennis J. (1913–26): Roman Catholic bishop of Richmond.

Page, Rosewell (1923–38): lawyer and essayist.

Page, Thomas Nelson (1889–1921): attorney, writer, and United States ambassador to Italy.

Randolph, Alfred M. (1889–1913): Episcopal bishop of southern Virginia.

Robinson, Morgan Poitaux (1913–41): state archivist.

Sheppard, William Ludwell (1889–1912): painter of the Lost Cause.

Stanard, William G. (1896–1933): VHS officer and editor of the *Virginia Magazine of History and Biography.*

Tucker, Harry St. George (1908–31): lawyer and United States congressman.

Valentine, Edward Virginius (1889–1927): VHS officer, antiquarian, and sculptor of the Lost Cause.

Yonge, Samuel H. (1908–35): engineer and antiquarian archaeologist.

Appendix 3

Buildings and Ruins Acquired by APVA, 1889–1939

1889	Powder Horn in Williamsburg
1890	Mary Ball Washington house in Fredericksburg
1893	Church ruin, graveyard, and 22½ acres at Jamestown
1897	Capitol foundations in Williamsburg
1897	Monmouth Church ruins in Lexington
1907	Rising Sun Tavern in Fredericksburg
1910	Debtor's prison in Accomac
1911	John Marshall house in Richmond
1912	Old Stone House in Richmond
1913	Courthouse, clerk's office, and debtor's prison in Eastville
1929	Jail in Williamsburg
1930	Cape Henry Lighthouse in Princess Anne County
1933	Smith's Fort plantation in Surry County
1935	Adam Craig house in Richmond
1938	Isle of Wight County Courthouse in Smithfield
1938	Tobacco warehouse in Urbanna
1938	Pulliam house in Richmond

Notes

Abbreviations

APVA	Association for the Preservation of Virginia Antiquities, Richmond
AQ	*American Quarterly*
CCB	Colonial Capital Branch, records kept at Swem Library, College of William and Mary, Williamsburg
CWM	Swem Library, College of William and Mary, Williamsburg
Duke	Perkins Library, Duke University, Durham, N.C.
JAH	*Journal of American History*
LC	Manuscripts Division, Library of Congress, Washington, D.C.
MB	Minute Book of APVA, kept by recording secretary, in APVA archives and Virginia Historical Society
NPL	Kirn Memorial Library, Norfolk
PRM	President's Report of Meetings, in APVA archives
SPNEA	Archives, Society for the Preservation of New England Antiquities, Boston
UVA	University of Virginia Library, Charlottesville
VM	Valentine Museum, Richmond
VHS	Virginia Historical Society, Richmond
VMHB	*Virginia Magazine of History and Biography*
VSL	Virginia State Library and Archives, Richmond
YB	*Year Book of the Association for the Preservation of Virginia Antiquities,* published irregularly in Richmond, 1896, 1898, 1899, 1900, 1901, 1905, 1908, 1910, 1913, 1921, 1924, 1926, 1928, 1931, 1934, 1938

Prologue: The Gospel of Preservation

1. "Fete on the Island," unidentified newspaper, n.d. [May 1895], Organizations file, APVA; "Settlement of Jamestown," *Richmond Times,* 14 May 1895.

2. Hall, *Introductory Address, 1891,* 8; [Bryan], "The Jamestown Anniversary," *Richmond Times,* 14 May 1895.

3. "The Jamestown Pilgrimage," unidentified newspaper, 10 May 1927, PRM 1926–27; Hobsbawm and Ranger, *Invention of Tradition;* Mrs. John B. Lightfoot, "Report of Jamestown Committee," *YB* 1908: 36.

4. Kammen, *Mystic Chords of Memory,* pt. 2; Trachtenberg, *Incorporation of America;* Wiebe, *Search for Order.*

5. Gaston, *New South Creed;* Foster, *Ghosts of the Confederacy.*

6. Geertz, *Interpretation of Cultures;* Turner, *Forest of Symbols.*

7. Hobsbawm, "Mass-Producing Traditions: Europe, 1870–1914," in *Invention of Tradition,* 263–307; Horne, *The Great Museum.*

8. J. S. Ingram, *The Centennial Exposition: Described and Illustrated* (Philadelphia, 1876), 629, 634; Badger, *Great American Fair;* Rydell, *All the World's a Fair,* 38–71.

9. Davies, *Patriotism on Parade;* Plumb, *Death of the Past,* 30, 31; Baltzell, *Protestant Establishment,* 114–16; Lamar, *National Society of Colonial Dames.*

10. Hosmer, *Presence of the Past;* Lindgren, *Preserving Historic New England.*

11. In the mid-twentieth century, it became fashionable for critics to dismiss such longings as a form of escapism. Wilbur Cash charged postbellum Virginians with the offense of withdrawing "from a world grown too dangerous." Richard Hofstadter similarly interpreted the founding of ancestral, patriotic, and cultural preservation associations as part of a status revolution in the country. At a time of social and economic upheaval, old-stock Americans joined such organizations, he said, because they "found satisfying compensation in turning to family glories of the past." J. C. Furnas humorously satirized the preservation movement as one of "atavistic old ladies" who preoccupied themselves with old homes and curios. Such "cults of quill pen and corner cupboard" had acted in Virginia, for example, to maintain Washington's home as a museum. He further dismissed genealogists as "the cult of knee-breeched Colonial forebears" (Cash, *Mind of the South,* 157; Hofstadter, *Age of Reform,* 139n; Furnas, *The Americans,* 604).

Subsequent historians have given the preservation movement more scrutiny. Charles Hosmer has chronicled the movement but gave short shrift to the APVA. Its interest in sentimentalism, memorial plaques, and colonial balls struck him as beyond the preservationist pale. Karal Ann Marling also followed that tack and focused primarily on the APVA's preoccupation with status, high society, and domesticity (Hosmer, *Presence of the Past,* and *Preservation Comes of Age;* Marling, *George Washington Slept Here,* 91–94; Lindgren, *"Pater Patriae,"* 705–13).

Cultural historians have increasingly shown more sensitivity to the role of history in the nation's ceaseless change. Michael Kammen's *Mystic Chords of Memory* tracks the roller-coaster ride of historical consciousness in the United States, thoroughly shows that the control of history can serve powerful interests, but says little about the APVA. On a different note, Jackson Lears interpreted the antiquarianism of the late nineteenth and early twentieth centuries as part of a pervasive antimodernism that tried to accommodate old and new America. As elite moderns energetically pursued industrial progress, they suffered from cultural dislocation and an enervating *angst.* To remedy such anxiety and gain personal therapy, they studied history. As they evoked tradition for modern purposes, Lears thought that those traditions lost meaning. In so doing, however, "WASP elites" became "a unified and self-conscious ruling class." Far from Hofstadter's picture of escapist, status-declining Americans, Lears sees antimodernists actively bidding for cultural hegemony in a restructured America (Kammen, *Mystic Chords of Memory;* Lears, *No Place of Grace,* 301).

12. As Robin Winks described American attitudes, "that which we teach, that which we say, those things which we preserve, must be relevant and invariably relevant to some future point. The past must be usable, it must help define future goals for the nation" (Winks, "Conservation in America," 142).

13. Pryor, *Jamestown,* 352; R. W. B. Lewis, *The American Adam: Innocence, Tragedy, and Tradition in the Nineteenth Century* (Chicago, 1955), 5–8; Edward P. Crapol, *America for Americans: Economic Nationalism and Anglophobia in the Late Nineteenth Century* (Westport, Conn., 1973).

14. Hall, *Organization of American Culture;* Plumb, *Death of the Past,* 40, 41; Karsten, *Patriot-Heroes,* 166.

15. Clifford Geertz saw such a pattern in human societies. "Man is an animal suspended in webs of significance he himself has spun," he said. If culture is that web, artifacts such as those protected by preservationists "draw their meaning from the role they play . . . in an ongoing pattern of life, not from any intrinsic relationships they bear to one another" (Geertz, "Thick Description: Toward an Interpretive Theory of Culture," in *Interpretation of Cultures*, 5, 7; Ward, *Red, White, and Blue*, 8).

16. Ryan quoted in "Address of Mrs. J. Taylor Ellyson," *YB* 1913:14; Thomas J. Wertenbaker, *Norfolk: Historic Southern Port*, 2d ed., ed. Marvin W. Schlegel (Durham, N.C., 1962), 120.

17. Zelinsky, *Nation into State;* Glassberg, *American Historical Pageantry.*

18. Isobel Bryan, "President's Report," *Association for the Preservation of Virginia Antiquities* 1896:27.

19. Cabell, *Let Me Lie,* 74.

1. "The Past Was Severed from the Present"

1. Stanard, *Richmond,* 211; Page, "The Old South," 4; Tyler, *Virginia Principles,* 1.

2. Foner, *Reconstruction.*

3. Curry, *Civil History,* 185.

4. Joseph Bryan to Edward W. James, 31 May 1898, Bryan Letterbook, Bryan Family Papers, VHS; Curry, "Causes of the Power and Prosperity of the United States," oration, 27 June 1889, 26–27, Curry Papers II-10, LC; Mary J. Galt, undated draft of a letter, no heading, Galt Family Papers III, Manuscripts and Rare Books Department, CWM; Maddex, *Virginia Conservatives.*

5. Pulley, *Old Virginia Restored,* 6, 9, 10; Degler, *Other South,* 270.

6. Curry quoted in Rice, *Curry,* 83; Pulley, *Old Virginia Restored,* 38; Degler, *Other South,* 279; Moore, *Two Paths,* 120–21.

7. Curry, *Lessons of Yorktown,* 14; George W. Bagby, *John Brown and Wm. Mahone: An Historical Parallel, Foreshadowing Civil Trouble* ([Richmond, 1880]).

8. Moore, *Two Paths,* 121; Pearson, *Readjuster Movement;* Dabney, *Virginia,* 377–78.

9. Curry, "Recent Tendencies in Free Political Institutions," Curry Papers I-13; Curry, *George Peabody,* 45; Henry, "Speech of William Wirt Henry," *Richmond State,* 20 Dec. 1879, Henry Papers, VHS.

10. Chesson, *Richmond after the War,* 189; Pulley, *Old Virginia Restored,* 41, 50.

11. Cynthia Coleman to Bland, 29 May 1883, Tucker-Coleman Papers, box 57, Manuscripts and Rare Books Department, CWM.

12. Cynthia Coleman to George [Coleman], 13 Nov. 1883, 2 Apr. 1885, ibid.; Munford, *Random Recollections,* 110.

13. Mullen quoted in Fink, *Workingmen's Democracy,* 159, 163, 167, 175; Kammen, *Spheres of Liberty,* 101; [Joseph Bryan], "Closer Relations with White Workingmen," *Richmond Times,* 7 Nov. 1889.

14. Coleman to George [Coleman], 18 Nov. 1889, Tucker-Coleman Papers, box 57; [Joseph Bryan], "Thanksgiving Day," *Richmond Times,* 28 Nov. 1889.

15. Coleman to George [Coleman], 26 Feb. 1884, Tucker-Coleman Papers, box 57; Joseph Bryan to Holmes Conrad, 11 June 1898, Bryan Letterbook; Curry quoted in Rice, *Curry,* 157; Curry quoted in Degler, *Other South,* 306; Page quoted in Friedman, *White Savage,* 67–68; Rabinowitz, *Race Relations,* 339.

16. Rydell, *All the World's a Fair* 87–88; Nuckols, *City of Richmond,* 22.

17. Bryan to Beverley, 28 Mar., 6 June 1894, Bryan Letterbook; Archer Anderson to W. L. Wilson, 31 Oct. 1896, Anderson Family Papers (23881g), Business Records Collection, VSL; Sheldon, *Populism in the Old Dominion,* 135.

18. Bryan quoted in Bryan, *Joseph Bryan,* 259; Mitchell, *Aftermath of Appomattox,* 61; Bryan to William F. Gordon, Jr., 5 June 1903, Bryan Letterbook.

19. Munford, *Random Recollections,* 159; Ann Field Alexander, "Black Protest in the New South: John Mitchell, Jr. (1863–1929), and the Richmond *Planet*" (Ph.D. diss., Duke Univ., 1973), 223; Curry, *Lessons of Yorktown,* 19.

20. Pulley, *Old Virginia Restored,* viii, 58–59.

21. Kousser, *Southern Politics,* 230; Grantham, "Contours of Southern Progressivism," 1044; Tindall, *Persistent Tradition,* 22.

22. Pulley, *Old Virginia Restored,* 155; Bryan to Beverley, 1 Jan. 1894, Bryan Letterbook; Bryan quoted in Bryan, *Joseph Bryan,* 250; Kousser, *Southern Politics,* 257.

23. Kent, *Preservation of the Past,* 4; "The Declaration of Independence," *Richmond Times,* 4 July 1902.

24. Pryor, *Jamestown,* 157.

25. Page, "Old Yorktown," 806; Osterweis, *Myth of the Lost Cause,* 40.

26. Curry, *Lessons of Yorktown,* 20; Curry, *George Peabody,* 82; Samuel C. Mitchell, "The South and the School," 1906, and "The Ethics of Democracy," n.d., Mitchell Papers, box 9, LC.

27. Bruce, *Rise of the New South,* 471; Mary J. Galt to unknown correspondent, n.d., draft, Galt Papers III; Curry, *George Peabody,* 82; L. Moody Sims, Jr., "Philip Alexander Bruce and the Negro Problem, 1884–1930," *VMHB* 75 (1967): 349–62.

28. Kousser, *Southern Politics,* 247; Pulley, *Old Virginia Restored,* 93.

29. Kent, *Preservation of the Past,* 5; Mitchell, *Aftermath of Appomattox,* 38–39.

30. Pulley, *Old Virginia Restored,* 112, 155.

31. Parke Bagby to Mary J. Galt, 17 Apr. 1911, Galt Papers III.

32. Grantham, "Contours of Southern Progressivism," 1040, 1045; Cynthia Coleman to George [Coleman], 6 Feb. 1890, Tucker-Coleman Papers, box 58.

33. "Report of the President for 1903," *YB* 1905:7.

34. Cynthia Coleman, untitled essay on the prophecies of Isaiah, n.d., Tucker-Coleman Papers, box 102; Edward V. Valentine, "My Recollections: Manners and Customs," 14 Dec. 1923, draft, Valentine Papers, VM; Paul A. Carter, *The Spiritual Crisis of the Gilded Age* (DeKalb, Ill., 1971), vii, ix, 146.

35. Green, *America's Heroes,* 110–11; Warren Susman, "'Personality' and the Making of Twentieth-Century Culture," in *New Directions in American Intellectual History,* ed. John Higham and Paul Conkin (Baltimore, 1979), 214; [Joseph Bryan], "Tendencies Unforeseen by the Founders of the Republic," *Richmond Times,* 23 Nov. 1889; Cynthia Coleman to George [Coleman], 22 Mar. 1887, Tucker-Coleman Papers, box 57; Gray, *Writing the South,* 75–121.

36. Valentine, "My Recollections," draft, 14 Dec. 1923, Valentine Papers; Bryan to Moses D. Hoge, 16 Dec. 1892, Bryan Letterbook; Greene, *American Heroes,* 118.

37. Bryan to Judge William McLaughlin, 16 Dec. 1890, Bryan Letterbook; Karsten, *Patriot-Heroes,* 169; Greene, *America's Heroes,* 314.

38. Valentine, "My Recollections," draft, 14 Dec. 1923, Valentine Papers; [Bright], *Memories of Williamsburg,* 12; Persons, *Decline of American Gentility,* 281–82.

39. "History of the Association for the Preservation of Virginia Antiquities," in *Souvenir of The Midsummer Night's Dream* (Richmond, 1899); Stanard, *John Marshall,* 17; Page, "Old Yorktown," 803.

40. Stanard, *John Marshall,* 19; Cynthia Coleman, "The Annals of Williamsburg, Virginia," n.d., Tucker-Coleman Papers, box 101; Fass, *The Damned and the Beautiful.*

41. "A Fine Address by General Roller," *Richmond Times,* 10 Jan. 1899; Goodwin quoted in "Henry Tablet Is Given to Church," *Richmond Times-Dispatch,* 23 Mar. 1911.

42. Pryor, *Jamestown,* 261–62; Rev. W. A. R. Goodwin, *Church Enchained,* 36, 164–65; Grantham, "Contours of Southern Progressivism," 1044; Rodgers, "In Search of Progressivism," 124–25; Green, *Fit for America.*

43. "Nature Study," *Richmond Times,* 9 Nov. 1902; Holman, "Thomas Nelson Page," 136; Stanard, *John Marshall,* 28; Marx, *Machine in the Garden,* 145, 228.

44. Mayo, *Myths and Men,* 45; Pryor, *Mother of Washington,* 181–82; Linda K. Kerber, *Women of the Republic: Intellect and Ideology in Revolutionary America* (Chapel Hill, N.C., 1980), 269–88.

45. Pryor, *Mother of Washington,* 181–82; Julia Cherry Spruill, *Women's Life and Work in the Southern Colonies* (1938; rept. New York, 1972), 60–61.

46. Valentine, "My Recollections," draft, 14 Dec. 1923, Valentine Papers, VM; "History of the Association for the Preservation of Virginia Antiquities," in *Souvenir of The Midsummer Night's Dream;* "Virginia Homes and History," *Richmond Evening Leader,* 13 Jan. 1900; Steven M. Stowe, *Intimacy and Power in the Old South: Ritual in the Lives of the Planters* (Baltimore and London, 1987); Catherine Clinton, *The Plantation Mistress: Woman's World in the Old South* (New York, 1982).

47. McDannell, *Christian Home;* Clarence Cook, *The House Beautiful: Essays on Beds and Tables, Stools and Candlesticks* (New York, 1878); [Joseph Bryan], "Tendencies Unforeseen by the Founders of the Republic," *Richmond Times,* 23 Nov. 1889; Trachtenberg, *Incorporation of America,* 143–44; Michael Pearlman, *To Make Democracy Safe for America: Politicians and Preparedness in the Progressive Era* (Urbana, Ill., 1984), 4; Gilman M. Ostrander, *American Civilization in the First Machine Age: 1890–1949* (New York, 1970), 57–58; William L. O'Neill, *Divorce in the Progressive Era* (New Haven, 1967).

48. Trachtenberg, *Incorporation of America,* 99; Pryor, *Mother of Washington,* 181.

49. Stanard, *Colonial Virginia;* Goodwin, *Historical Sketch.*

50. Bertelson, *Lazy South;* "Nature Study," *Richmond Times,* 9 Nov. 1902; Hall, *Introductory Address, 1891,* 6.

51. Tyler, *South and Germany,* 6; Cynthia Coleman, "Jamestown," n.d., Tucker-Coleman Papers, box 102; Page, *Address at Jamestown,* 17; Elizabeth Henry Lyons, "First American Assembly," *Philadelphia Record,* 11 Aug. 1907, in Elizabeth Henry Lyons Scrapbook 2, VHS.

52. Thomas Nelson Page, "Henry Clay and the Treaty of Ghent," 22 Feb. 1913, corrected copy, Page Papers 20B-35, Duke; Fishwick, *Hero American Style,* 87; Woodward, "The Southern Ethic in a Puritan World," *American Counterpoint,* 42.

53. Joseph Bryan to H. C. Rice, 12 Apr. 1895, to Col. William E. Peters, 5 July 1888, Bryan Letterbook; Wiebe, *Search for Order,* 136; Pocock, *Machiavellian Moment,* 551–52; Cabell, *Patrick Henry;* Williams, *Culture and Society,* 325–26.

54. Bryan cited in Lindgren, "'First and Foremost a Virginian,'" 167; Tyler, *South and Germany,* 9; Page, "Henry Clay and the Treaty of Ghent," corrected copy, Page Papers 20B-35; Sproat, *"Best Men,"* 277; Lyons, "Red Hill, Where Sleeps Patrick Henry, the Patriot," unidentified periodical, n.d., in Elizabeth Lyons Scrapbook 2; Karsten, *Patriot-Heroes,* 166.

55. Pulley, *Old Virginia Restored,* 39; Curry, "Recent Tendencies in Free Political Institutions," 15 Jan. 1901, Curry Papers, I-13; Curry, *Confederate Veterans,* 29; Mitchell, "The Ethics of Democracy," n.d., Mitchell Papers, box 9.

56. Bryan to Bagby, 27 Aug. 1906, Bagby Family Papers 60, VHS; Mitchell, "Five Factors in the Negro Problem" *Hartford Seminary Record,* Nov. 1904, 3–4, Mitchell Papers, box 15.

57. Mitchell, *Aftermath of Appomattox,* 28, 94.

58. "Holds Meeting in Marshall House," *Richmond Times-Dispatch,* 5 Jan. 1913, MB 1908–14; Jean B. Quandt, *From the Small Town to the Great Community: The Social Thought of Progressive Intellectuals* (New Brunswick, N.J., 1970).

59. Kirby, *Darkness at the Dawning,* 58; Grantham, "Contours of Southern Progressivism," 1037.

60. Curry, *George Peabody,* 82; Mitchell, "The South and the School," 1906, "The Ethics of Democracy," n.d., Mitchell Papers, box 9; Curry, *Lessons of Yorktown,* 20.

61. Mitchell, *Aftermath of Appomattox,* 83.

62. "Virginia Homes and History," *Richmond Evening Leader,* 13 Jan. 1900.

63. Meeeting, May 1916, MB; Mrs. J. Enders Robinson to William Sumner Appleton, 11 Apr. 1916, APVA file, SPNEA. SPNEA's *Bulletin* (1910–19) and *Old-Time New England* (1920–   ) were generously illustrated with photographs and line drawings, but both the APVA's *Year Book* and SPNEA's publications decided not to match the detailed, analytical, and often cumbersome reports of the American Scenic and Historic Preservation Society. For the iconographical revolution, see Neil Harris, "Iconography and Intellectual History: The Half-Tone Effect," in *New Directions,* ed. Higham and Conkin, 199.

64. Coleman, untitled essay, n.d., Tucker-Coleman Papers, box 103.

65. Wallace, "Revitalization Movements," 264–81; John F. Wilson, *Public Religion in American Culture* (Philadelphia, 1979), 170–72.

66. Geertz, "Ethos, World View, and the Analysis of Sacred Symbols," in *Interpretation of Cultures,* 127; Geertz, "Religion as a Cultural System," ibid., 123; Bellah, *Broken Covenant;* Edward McNall Burns, *The American Idea of Mission: Concepts of National Purpose and Destiny* (New Brunswick, N.J., 1957); Ernest Lee Tuveson, *Redeemer Nation: The Idea of America's Millenial Role* (Chicago, 1968); Richey and Jones, *American Civil Religion.*

67. Marling, *George Washington Slept Here,* 25–52.

68. Philip S. Foner, ed., *We, the Other People: Alternative Declarations of Independence by Labor Groups, Farmers, Woman's Rights Advocates, Socialists, and Blacks, 1829–1975* (Urbana, Ill., 1976); Philip S. Foner, *American Labor Songs of the Nineteenth Century* (Urbana, Ill., and London, 1975).

69. Byrd, *Public Schools in Williamsburg,* 27; Davies, *Patriotism on Parade,* 219–23; Hobsbawm, "Inventing Traditions," in *Invention of Tradition,* 1–14; "Gilbert," "The Neglect of Our Antiquities," *William and Mary College Monthly* 1 (1891): 161. When the *Youth's Companion* asked every child to recite the "Pledge" on Columbus Day, it evidently tried to limit the Italianness of the celebration in those areas with a large Italian population.

70. Rydell, *All the World's a Fair,* 35, 73.

71. Hartmann, *To Americanize the Immigrants,* 31–35; Gerd Korman, *Industrialization, Immigrants, and Americanizers: The View from Milwaukee, 1866–1921* (Madison, Wis., 1967), 139; Davies, *Patriotism on Parade,* 241.

72. "Gilbert," "The Neglect of Our Antiquities," 161; Yonge, "The Site of Old 'James Towne,'" *VMHB* 11 (1904): 262; Emma L. Crowell, "Building Historic Shrines," n.d., Scrapbook, 1921–35, Daughters of the American Colonists file, VHS.

73. Wecter, *Hero in America;* Warner, *Living and the Dead,* 15, 97. According to

Peter Karsten, antistatist heroes were on the decline at the time. Although the APVA virtually ignored the legacy of antistatist Thomas Jefferson, it essentially reinterpreted the antistatism of men such as Nathaniel Bacon and Robert E. Lee as attempts to establish a separate southern nation (Karsten, *Patriot-Heroes,* 70–71).

74. Pryor, *Mother of Washington,* 355–56; Cabell, *Patrick Henry,* 1, 2; Joseph Bryan to Judge T. R. B. Wright, 27 May 1891, Bryan Letterbook.

75. "President's Report," annual meeting, 4 Nov. 1902, MB; "President's Report Submitted to Virginia Antiquities Group," *Richmond Times-Dispatch,* 9 Jan. 1927.

76. Coleman, untitled address, n.d., Tucker-Coleman Papers, box 103.

77. Bryan to Capt. Richard Irby, 30 Jan. 1897, Bryan Letterbook; Cabell, *Let Me Lie,* 145; Samuel C. Mitchell, "The Vicarious Element in the Character of Lee," 5 Dec. 1911, Mitchell Papers, box 9; Tyler, *Propaganda in History;* Chesson, *Richmond after the War,* 206; Connelly and Bellows, *God and General Longstreet,* 85.

2. "Whatever Is Un-Virginian is Wrong"

1. Coleman, untitled address, draft, n.d., Tucker-Coleman Papers, box 103; Curry, *Lessons of Yorktown,* 22.

2. Mary J. Galt, "Origin of the Association for the Preservation of Virginia Antiquities," *YB* 1913:46. Galt's story bears a uncanny resemblance to that of Ann Pamela Cunningham and the origins of the Mount Vernon Ladies' Association. In both accounts the mother sparks the movement and laments the neglect of historic sites; she predicts that inaction would allow continued ruination and stirs her daughter to act. For the MVLA's founding, see Hosmer, *Presence of the Past,* 45, and Mrs. J. Enders Robinson, "Origins of the A.P.V.A.," *YB* 1901:4.

3. Quoted in Grace King, *Mount Vernon on the Potomac: History of the Mount Vernon Ladies Association of the Union* (New York, 1929), 19–20; Hosmer, *Presence of the Past,* 41–62.

4. Scott, "Women's Perspective," 52; Cunningham quoted in King, *Mount Vernon,* 56, 67; Cunningham quoted in Elswyth Thane, *Mount Vernon Is Ours: The Story of Its Preservation* (New York, 1966), 138.

5. Cunningham quoted in King, *Mount Vernon,* 20–21; Forgie, *Patricide in the House Divided,* 159–75.

6. Cunningham quoted in Mount Vernon Ladies' Association, *Historical Sketch of Ann Pamela Cunningham: "The Southern Matron"* (Queens, N. Y., 1911), 48–49; Marling, *George Washington Slept Here,* 76–89; Lindgren, *"Pater Patriae,"* 705–13; Pryor, "The Mount Vernon Association," 406–20.

7. Galt to Coleman, 26 Oct. 1888, Powhatan's Chimney Research file, APVA; Galt to Robert Alonzo Brock, 14 Jan. 1889, transcript in Galt Papers III.

8. Galt to Robert Alonzo Brock, 14 Jan. 1889, Galt Papers III; "Norfolk Branch," *Association for the Preservation of Virginia Antiquities* 1896:63. Both Galt and Coleman took credit for establishing the organization, and internecine disputes erupted constantly from 1889 until 1923 when a Richmond law firm investigated the extant documentation, partisan and sketchy as it was. Although the 1923 decision credited Galt as the founder and Coleman as the organizer, Galt deserves at least equal credit as organizer. Not only did Coleman shut her out, she revised Galt's draft charter at the first meeting. Galt knew that she lost out in this power play, and their dispute never abated. In 1930 the Norfolk branch dedicated a bronze tablet to Galt at old St. Paul's Church; at the same time a

general meeting in Richmond resolved to place a tablet to Coleman in Williamsburg ("President's Address," and "Report of the Norfolk Branch," *YB* 1931:15, 44.

9. Cabell, *Let Me Lie,* 155; "Mrs. Roger A. Pryor Dead," *New York Times,* 16 Feb. 1912, 9. I am grateful to Edward D. C. Campbell, Jr., Thomas Connelly, and James I. Robertson, Jr., for help in substantiating Cabell's implication of Pryor. One biographer made no mention of this infamy, however (Robert S. Holzman, *Adapt or Perish: The Life of Roger A. Pryor, C.S.A.* [Hamden, Conn., 1976]).

10. "Interesting Publication, *Lynchburg News,* 12 Sept. 1894; Cynthia Coleman, "The Annals of Williamsburg, Virginia," n.d., Tucker-Coleman Papers, box 101.

11. Jeanette S. Kelly, "The First Restoration in Williamsburg," 1933, CCB Papers, box 1, Manuscripts and Rare Books Department, CWM; Committee Reports, 4 Mar. 1924, PRM 1923–24.

12. Newton, "The Association," 10; Cabell to Mrs. George D. Chenoweth, 13 Sept. 1921, Minutes, Yorktown Branch APVA, Manuscripts and Rare Books Department, CWM.

13. Nellie Bernard Lee to Coleman, 20 Dec. 1888, Powhatan Chimney Restoration file, APVA; Mrs. Paul Welles to Col. [H. F.] du Pont, draft, n.d. [June 1923], Galt to Robert Alonzo Brock, 14 Jan. 1889, transcript, Galt Papers III. In 1901 Galt wrote Bagby expressing her surprise that Coleman apparently had doctored the Williamsburg branch records to set its founding in June 1888 (Galt to Bagby, 24 Apr. 1901, Bagby Papers 78).

14. Coleman to Bagby, 23 Sept. 1889, Bagby Papers 67.

15. Bryan to Bagby, n.d., ibid., 59.

16. Cabell, *Let Me Lie,* 135, 138; Bruce, *Rise of the New South,* 418; Francis Butler Simkins and Charles Pierce Roland, *A History of the South,* 4th ed. (New York, 1972), 376.

17. Page, *Address on the South,* 17, 26; Friedman, *The White Savage,* 62; Aaron, *Unwritten War,* 287; Holman, "Thomas Nelson Page"; Hubbell, *The South in American Literature,* 802.

18. Munford, *Random Recollections,* 194; Cash, *Mind of the South,* 130; Hubbell, *The South in American Literature,* 799; Bruce, *Rise of the New South,* 416.

19. Smith, *Killers of the Dream,* 215–16.

20. In 1892 the APVA revised its constitution and dropped its joint-stock provisions so that its property could be held tax-free. Although the original charter limited APVA's preservation work to buildings and tombs, the revised charter added monuments, graveyards, and artifacts (*Constitution and By-Laws of the Society for the Preservation of Virginia Antiquities* [Richmond: Baughman Bros., 1889]). Note the name of the organization and the printer; Baughman Brothers had recently broken a Knights of Labor organizing drive and boycott.

21. *Constitution and By-Laws,* 18; Mary Meares Galt, untitled recollections, n.d., Mary J. Galt to Bagby, 16 Apr. 1895, draft copy, Galt Papers III. Cash described those who glorified the old Virginia heritage "as a sort of closed corporation to which those who had not belonged before could not ever fully penetrate now" (Cash, *Mind of the South,* 129). In the case of the APVA, his interpretation falls considerably short of the evidence. The APVA did represent the FFVs, but it was open to the wealthy and propertied who swore fealty to the ancients.

22. Lee to Coleman, 25 Jan. 1889, Powhatan Chimney Research file; Bryan to

Bagby, 17 Sept. 1889, Galt to Bagby, 14 Apr. 1890, Bagby Papers 59, 78; "President's Report," *YB* 1896:22; "President's Report," 4 Nov. 1902, MB.

23. Lee to Coleman, 14 Jan. 1889, Powhatan Chimney Restoration file; W. Gordon McCabe, "Proceedings," *VMHB* 19 (1911): xix.

24. "To the Women of the South," printed circular, n.d., Mary Custis Lee Scrapbook, VHS; Mary H. Mitchell, *Hollywood Cemetery: The History of a Southern Shrine* (Richmond, 1985).

25. [Joseph Bryan], "Preservation of Our Historical Landmarks," *Richmond Times,* 28 Nov. 1889.

26. Bryan, *Joseph Bryan,* 234, 292–93.

27. Lindgren, "'First and Foremost a Virginian,'" 157–80.

28. Page quoted in "Talk about Old Things," *Richmond Times,* 19 Jan. 1890.

29. Ibid.; for the song's text, see "The Sword of Bunker Hill," in Charles R. Skinner, ed., *Manual of Patriotism: For Use in the Public Schools of New York* (Albany, 1900), 119–20.

30. Bryan quoted in "Talk about Old Things," *Richmond Times,* 19 Jan. 1890.

31. [Joseph Bryan], "The Old Powder Horn," ibid.

32. Valentine, "My Recollections," 14 Dec. 1923, draft, VM; Potter, "The Enigma of the South," in *The Sectional Conflict,* 15–16; Connelly and Bellows, *God and General Longstreet,* 40–41. C. Vann Woodward, on the other hand, saw such sentiments as an attempt by southerners to protect their regional identity against northern domination (Woodward, "The Search for Southern Identity," in *The Burden of Southern History,* 20).

33. Wallace, "Revitalization Movements," 264–81; "Jamestown Annual Reports, 1922–23," unsigned carbon copy, box 5, APVA; Bryan to John B. Henneman, 8 Sept. 1898, Bryan Letterbook; Cabell, *Virginia Municipalities.*

34. Curry, *Lessons of Yorktown,* 21–22.

35. Coleman, untitled essay, n.d., Tucker-Coleman Papers, box 101; *Lower Norfolk County, Virginia, Antiquary* quoted in Craven, *Legend of the Founding Fathers,* 153n.

36. Henry, "Resolutions respecting Independency," speech, 7 June 1876, Henry Papers; "Association for the Preservation of Virginia Antiquities," typescript of 1889 invitation, MB 1889–91, 11; Ernst Cassirer, *The Myth of the State* (New Haven, 1946), 43; Joseph Campbell, *The Power of Myth,* ed. Betty Sue Flowers (New York and London, 1988).

37. Bryan to Thomas Pinckney, 22 May 1897, to Col. John Mosby, 30 Aug. 1902, to Col. John Scriven, 31 July 1889, Bryan Letterbook; Cash, *Mind of the South,* 194; Woodward, *Origins of the New South,* 157; Dabney, *Virginia,* 442; Lears, *No Place of Grace;* Charles Eliot Norton, "The Lack of Old Homes in America," *Scribner's Magazine* 5 (1889): 636–41; Clifford Edward Clark, Jr., *The American Family Home, 1800–1960* (Chapel Hill, N.C., 1986).

38. Dabney, *Richmond,* 244; Connelly and Bellows, *God and General Longstreet,* 43, 45; Osterweis, *Myth of the Lost Cause,* 7, 11.

39. Elson, *Guardians of Tradition,* 8, 173–75, 403–8. The GAR acted as excessively as the UCV when it condemned John Fiske's *History of the United States* (1894) because he used the term "Civil War," instead of "Pro-Slavery Rebellion." At the same time Virginia's UCV castigated Fiske's *Critical Period of American History* (1888) as a "Trojan Horse" for its northern ideas. Fiske joined the APVA and won its friendship because of his staunch Anglo-Saxonism. Once southerners began to publish schoolbooks, General

Stephen Lee of Mississippi headed a UCV committee in 1895 that pressed southern legislatures to abandon the northern texts. By 1904 the Williamsburg schools used Lee's *New Primary United States History* (Davies, *Patriotism on Parade*, 232–40; Hunter McGuire, *Official Report of the History Committee of the Grand Camp C.V., Department of Virginia*, [Richmond, 1899], 14; Byrd, *Public Schools in Williamsburg*, 28; Buck, *Road to Reunion*, 238).

3. "Leaning on Virginia as Children Resting on a Mother"

1. "Interesting Publication," *Lynchburg News*, 12 Sept. 1894; McCarthy, *Women's Culture*, 3–79.

2. *Souvenir of The Midsummer Night's Dream* (Richmond, 1899); *Association for the Preservation of Virginia Antiquities*, printed invitation to Virginians, MB 1889–91; Scott, *Southern Lady*, 213.

3. "APVA Holds Its Annual Meeting," *Richmond Virginian*, 6 Jan. 1915, PRM 1915–16; Bagby to Galt, 17 July 1895, Galt Papers III; Ellyson, note, n.d., inserted in May 1919, PRM; Ginzberg, *Women and Benevolence*.

4. Galt to Bagby, 16 Apr., 12 June 1895, draft, Galt Papers III; Coleman to President and Board of Managers, n.d., MB 1896–97; Pryor, *My Day*, 424; Galt to Bagby, 15 Apr. 1895, Bagby Papers 78; Bryan to T. R. B. Wright, 20 Jan. 1900, Bryan Letterbook.

5. Linda K. Kerber, "Separate Spheres, Female Worlds, Woman's Place: The Rhetoric of Women's History," *JAH* 74 (1988): 9–39, and *Women of the Republic*; Welter, "Cult of True Womanhood," 151–74.

6. Forgie, *Patricide in the House Divided*, 159–99; Page, *Mount Vernon*; Marling, *George Washington Slept Here*, 71–88.

7. Lebsock, *Free Women of Petersburg*; Foster, *Ghosts of the Confederacy*, 31, 173–74; Parrott, "'Love Makes Memory Eternal,'" 219–37.

8. Pryor, *My Day*, 423, 425.

9. Davies, *Patriotism on Parade*.

10. Randolph, "Restoration of Church at Jamestown, Va.," presented at APVA general meeting, 14 May 1906, MB 1902–7; Woodward, *Origins of the New South*, 156.

11. Davies, *Patriotism on Parade*, 24–25; Curry, *North American Colonization*, 12; Hall, *Introductory Address, 1895*, 2; Cash, *Mind of the South*, 131; Holman, "Thomas Nelson Page."

12. Ryan, *Women in Public*; Degler, *At Odds*, 324; Scott, *Southern Lady*, 152, 153, 155.

13. Lears, *No Place of Grace*; George Miller Beard, *American Nervousness, Its Causes and Consequences* (New York, 1881); Green, *Fit for America*, 137–66.

14. Cynthia Coleman to George [Coleman], 26 Feb. 1884, 4 May 1885, Tucker-Coleman Papers, box 57; Kelly, *The First Restoration*; Marjorie S. Mendenhall, "Southern Women of a 'Lost Generation,'" *South Atlantic Quarterly* 33 (1934): 334–53; Degler, *At Odds*, 298; Scott, *Southern Lady*, 147.

15. Cash, *Mind of the South*, 310; Cynthia Coleman, untitled address in Baltimore, March 1896, Tucker-Coleman Papers, box 103; "Mount Vernon Branch," *YB* 1896:72; Bryan, circular letter, Jan. 1903, "Report of the President for 1903," *YB* 1905:8–9.

16. Bryan, "President's Report," *YB* 1900:10; Pryor, *Mother of Washington*, 5–6.

17. Morgan P. Robinson to W. G. Stanard, 20 June 1920, Stanard file, VHS; Fed-

eral Writers' Project, *Virginia,* 517 (Henry's grave remains at Red Hill); Hall, "Ancient Epitaphs and Inscriptions in James City County, Virginia," *VHS* (unidentified periodical), n.d., Hall Papers, CWM.

18. Mitchell, *Hollywood Cemetery,* 101–2; annual meeting, 6 Jan. 1920, MB; William Sumner Appleton to Celeste Bush, 13 Jan. 1915, Thomas Lee House file, SPNEA; "High Indignation at Digging Up of Scores of Bodies," *Richmond News Leader,* 1 June 1923.

19. Coleman to her sister, 18 Feb. 1885, Coleman-Tucker Papers, box 57; meetings of 1896, 1897, "1894–1917 Washington Branch Record Book," APVA; Fishwick, *Virginia,* 269; Blair, *Clubwoman as Feminist,* 27–28; Joseph F. Kett, "Women and the Progressive Impulse in Southern Education," in *The Web of Southern Social Relations: Women, Family, and Education,* ed. Walter J. Fraser, Jr. (Athens, Ga. 1985), 166–80.

20. Trachtenberg, *Incorporation of America,* 145; Henry Steele Commager, *The American Mind: An Interpretation of American Thought and Character since the 1880's* (New Haven, 1950), 23; Lebsock, *Free Women of Petersburg,* 112–45, 212; Lebsock, *"A Share of Honour";* Estelle B. Freedman, "Separatism as Strategy: Female Institution Building and American Feminism, 1870–1930," *Feminist Studies* 5 (1979): 512–29.

21. Lottie C. Garrett, "Report of Colonial Capitol Branch," *YB* 1910:41; Stanard, *Richmond,* 3.

22. Ginzberg, *Women and Benevolence,* 174–213, particularly 190, 193; Kathleen D. McCarthy, *Noblesse Oblige: Charity and Cultural Philanthropy in Chicago, 1829–1929* (Chicago, 1982), 72.

23. Coleman to Bagby, 23 Sept. 1889, Bagby Papers 67; Ellyson to Bagby, 9 Feb. 1903, Bagby Papers; 5 Mar. 1918, MB 1914–21; Degler, *At Odds,* 306.

24. Hall, "The Meeting Place," 8, 12.

25. Bagby, "Universal Suffrage," n.d., Bagby Papers 23; Degler, *At Odds,* 340–50; Foster, *Ghosts of the Confederacy,* 25–35.

26. "W" to editor, *Richmond Times-Dispatch,* 10 Nov. 1911; Cabell to Flora Adams Darling, 17 Jan. 1891, cited in Davies, *Patriotism on Parade,* 283.

27. Mary Johnston, *Hagar* (Boston, 1913), 331; Christian, *Richmond,* 519; meeting, 7 Mar. 1911, PRM 1911–12; general meeting, 4 Apr. 1911, MB; Taylor, "Lila Meade Valentine," 471–87; Walter Russell Bowie, *Sunrise in the South: The Life of Mary-Cooke Branch Munford* (Richmond, 1942).

28. Valentine, "Woman's Suffrage," n.d., VM; Bryan to Mrs. Annie D. Gray, 3 Mar. 1894, Bryan Letterbook; Holman, "Thomas Nelson Page," 212. Norfolk preservationist Conway Whittle Sams dedicated a book "To the Anti-Suffragettes" (Sams, *Shall Women Vote?: A Book for Men* [New York, 1913]).

29. Tyler, "Virginia Antiquities, *William and Mary Quarterly,* 1st ser, 4 (1895–96): 69.

30. Stanard, *Richmond,* 222; Bryan to Bagby, 17 Sept. 1889, Bagby Papers 59.

31. Sheppard to Bagby, 17 Jan. 1890, Bagby Papers 46; Newton, "The Association," 19–20.

32. Munford, *Random Recollections,* 230, 231; Bryan to Bagby, 24 May 1891, Bryan Letterbook.

33. Newton, "The Association," 19–20; Bryan to Rt. Rev. George W. Peterkin, 8 Jan. 1891, Bryan Letterbook.

34. Pryor, *My Day,* 421; Munford, *Random Recollections,* 234; Marling, *George Washington Slept Here,* 91–93.

35. Meetings, 24 Jan., 7 Mar. 1899, MB; "Social and Personal," unidentified newspaper, 22 Apr. 1914, PRM 1913–14.

36. "A.P.V.A. Pageant and Ball at Armory Brilliant Function," *Richmond Times-Dispatch,* 28 Jan. 1923; *The Association for the Preservation of Virginia Antiquities Ball,* six-page pamphlet (n.p., n.d.), in NPL; "Shades of Yesterday," *Discovery* 10 (Fall 1978): 8.

37. Ellen Glasgow, *A Certain Pleasure* (New York, 1943), 203; Edgar E. MacDonald, "Glasgow, Cabell, and Richmond," *Mississippi Quarterly* 27 (1974): 397–98; printed circular, MB 1901–2, 38.

4. "And They Shall Build the Old Wastes"

1. Coleman, "Annals of Williamsburg, Virginia," Tucker-Coleman Papers, box 101; Tyler, *Williamsburg,* 221, 240; Rouse, *Cows on the Campus,* 67.

2. Coleman to George [Coleman], 22 Mar. 1887, Tucker-Coleman Papers, box 5; Newton, "The Association," 10.

3. Cynthia Coleman to George [Coleman], 26 Feb. 1884, Tucker-Coleman Papers, box 57; Kammen, *Mystic Chords of Memory,* 123–24. The Readjusters also carried Norfolk and Petersburg in 1879, 1881, 1882, and 1883 (Moore, *Two Paths,* 52).

4. Curry, *Lessons of Yorktown.*

5. Stevens, *Yorktown Centennial Handbook,* 83.

6. "APVA a Part of Life for Dr. Kimbrough," *Newport News Daily Press,* 21 Jan. 1979; Rouse, *Cows on the Campus,* 154; Kimbrough, "Early History," 68–75.

7. "Interesting Publication," *Lynchburg News,* 12 Sept. 1894; Annie Galt to Molly [Galt], n.d., Galt Papers III; "Resolution of Mrs. Bryan on Mrs. Coleman's Death," MB 1908–14, 37. The one person who could intimidate Coleman, Tyler discovered, was Parke Bagby. Charlie Coleman admitted that "his mother was scared as death of Mrs. Bagby" (Annie Galt to Molly, n.d., Galt Papers III).

8. Cynthia Coleman to George, 29 Jan. 1885, 28 Jan. 1887, Tucker-Coleman Papers, box 57. Whereas Coleman rebelled against the Rev. Mr. Burch, Mary Galt did so in her petition against Bruton rector Rev. W. J. Roberts ("To the Wardens and Vestry of Bruton Parish," n.d., draft, Galt Papers III).

9. C. C. Buel to Cynthia Coleman, 24 Feb. 1891, William H. Payne to Coleman, 21 Feb. 1891, Tucker-Coleman Papers, box 58.

10. Coleman, misc. papers, n.d., and "The Annals of Williamsburg, Virginia," n.d., Tucker-Coleman Papers, box 101; Shi, *The Simple Life,* chap. 7.

11. Coleman to Bagby, 23 Sept. 1889, Bagby Papers 67; Lyon G. Tyler, *Farewell Address* [10 June 1919], (n.p., n.d.), 9, 15, 16; C. Vernon Spratley, transcript, n.d., Oral History Collection, University Archives, CWM.

12. Tyler quoted in "Settlement of Jamestown," *Richmond Times,* 14 May 1895; John Whitehead to Tyler, 19 Dec. 1905, Tyler Papers, box 24.

13. Cynthia Coleman to Belle Bryan, 16 Apr. 1889, APVA Papers, VHS.

14. Coleman to George, 7 Dec. 1881, Tucker-Coleman Papers, box 57; Coleman's letters of this era contain no other reference to her wish to establish a museum in the Powder Horn. In later years Mary Galt accused her of falsifying the records so as to claim priority in the APVA. The authenticity of this 1881 letter cannot be established. For the Powder Horn, see Tyler, *Williamsburg,* 222.

15. Newton, "The Association," 12; Coleman to Bagby, 16 Sept. 1889, Bagby Papers 67.

16. [Joseph Bryan], "The Old Powder-Horn," *Richmond Times,* 19 Jan. 1890; Coleman, "Read before the Washington Club, 3 Mar. 1896," Tucker-Coleman Papers, box 103; Tyler, *Virginia Principles,* 7.

17. [Bryan], "The Old Powder-Horn," *Richmond Times,* 19 Jan. 1890.

18. Coleman to Bagby, 17 Jan. 1890, Bagby Papers 67; Coleman, "Report of Colonial Capital Branch," *Association for the Preservation of Virginia Antiquities* 1896:48; Robert A. Murdock, "The Association for the Preservation of Virginia Antiquities—Pioneer in Saving Virginia's Past," *Southern Antiques and Interiors* 1 (Winter 1973): 6.

19. Mary Galt to Mr. and Mrs. Bryan, 3 Oct. 1908, Mary Galt to Peter H. Mayo, n.d., draft, A[nnie Galt] to Mollie [Galt], 4 Oct. 1908, Galt Papers III; Mrs. J. Taylor Ellyson, "Report of the Associate President," *YB* 1910:18.

20. Report, 15 Apr. 1920, CCB Minutes, box 1; Lottie C. Garrett, "Report of Colonial Capital Branch," *YB* 1910:41.

21. Cynthia Coleman, untitled address at YMCA, Baltimore, Mar. 1896, and circular letter, n.d., Tucker-Coleman Papers, box 103; Mrs. George W. Bagby to Mary J. Galt, 5 July 1895, Galt Papers III; C. B. Orcutt to Mrs. R. M. Smith, 11 Mar. 1897, MB 1896–97; for Ingalls and the 1896 election, see Sheldon, *Populism in the Old Dominion* 136, and Buck, *Road to Reunion,* 181.

22. Quoted in Hosmer, *Presence of the Past,* 276; Winks, "Conservation in America," 144.

23. "Introduction," *YB* 1898:3; "By-Laws," art. 6, sec. 3: "The Landmark Committee shall take care to identify and suitably mark . . . all historical localities made famous in our Capital city and State from infancy to the ever memorable epoch of 1861" (*YB* 1899:20); "Report of the Associate President," *YB* 1910:16.

24. Valentine et al., Report sent to Charles B. Cooke, President, Civic Improvement League, n.d. [c.1904], Robert L. Traylor Papers 3, VHS. The sites mentioned in the report that the APVA marked included Gamble's Hill, Bloody Run Spring, the Old Stone House, St. John's Church, Williamsburg's Capitol, John Marshall's residence, and the Allan house.

25. Kent, *Preservation of the Past,* 14; Appleton quoted in Hosmer, *Presence of the Past,* 68; Ashbee, *A Report to the National Trust,* 5; Wright, *Moralism and the Model Home,* 127–28.

26. Coleman, circular letter, draft, n.d., Tucker-Coleman Papers, box 103; Coleman, meeting, 12 Oct. 1906, CCB Minutes, box 1. They erred in marking the Peyton Randolph house (Vernon M. Geddy to Mrs. A. D. Jones, 5 Aug. 1932, CCB Minutes, box 2). Mary Galt purchased the "Debtor's Prison" in 1903, but after Colonial Williamsburg acquired it in 1946, its research questioned the legend and attribution. It is now called the Greenhow-Repiton brick office.

27. Henry quoted in Elizabeth Henry Lyons, "Report of Recording Secretary for 1897," *YB* 1908:27; Coleman, untitled address at YMCA, Baltimore, Mar. 1896, Tucker-Coleman Papers, box 103.

28. Lottie C. Garrett, "Unveiling of Monument on Site of House of Burgesses," CCB Minutes, box 1; meeting, 19 Oct. 1900, MB; "Report of Washington Branch," *YB* 1905:48–49; Huntley, *Peninsula Pilgrimage,* 182; "Report of Colonial Capital Branch," *YB* 1905:42–43. Tyler wrote the inscription for the tablet.

29. William Wirt Henry, "One Hundredth Anniversary of the Introduction and Adoption of the 'Resolutions respecting Independence,' an address delivered in Philadelphia, 7 June 1876," VHS. Henry endlessly cited his grandfather's famed

oratory, particularly the "Give Me Liberty" and "If This Be Treason" addresses. These speeches were largely constructed, however, by Henry's eulogizing biographer, William Wirt. As Bernard Mayo concluded, "What Parson Weems did for Washington . . . , Wirt did for Henry in his biography of 1817" (Mayo, *Myths and Men*, 14–15, 22–23). W. W. Henry, for that matter, continued as a hagiographer. Philip Alexander Bruce nonetheless claimed that he performed the "pious duty of clearing the great orator's fame from the clouds imposed upon it by jealousy and malice" ("The True Patrick Henry," unidentified newspaper, 19 Jan. 1908, Elizabeth Lyons Scrapbook 2). In 1899 the APVA proposed marking the site of the Wirt home ("Report of Landmark Committee," *YB* 1900:29).

30. Anderson to Mr. Eaton, 24 Feb. 1913, Anderson Letterbook. Virginia rejected the Sixteenth Amendment, as it did the woman's suffrage amendment (Moger, *Virginia*, 295).

31. Elson, *Guardians of Tradition*, 178; Stanard, *Richmond*, 29; Page, *The Old South*, 25, and "Old Yorktown," 814; Curry, *Lessons of Yorktown*, 11–12; William H. Nelson, *The American Tory* (Boston, 1961), 42.

32. Perry, Shaw and Hepburn, report, 6 Nov. 1933, CCB Correspondence, box 2; meeting, 3 May 1898, MB 1898; Yonge to William Ellis Jones, 26 Nov. 1909, Yonge Papers 1299–7, Special Collections, UVA; Beverley B. Munford to J. Taylor Ellyson, 27 Mar. 1909, Ellyson Papers 4130, ibid.; meeting, 1 Mar. 1910, MB 1908–14; annual meeting, 4 Jan. 1910, and April meeting, 1911, CCB, box 1.

33. Coleman, "Annals of Williamsburg, Virginia," Tucker-Coleman Papers, box 101; Robins, "Report of Recording Secretary," *YB* 1901:27; meeting, 10 Apr. 1900, CCB Minutes, box 1.

34. Dorsey, *Early English Churches*, 60.

35. Coleman to her sister, 12 Sept. 1886, and Coleman, "The Annals of Williamsburg, Virginia," n.d., Tucker-Coleman Papers, boxes 57, 101; annual meeting, 4 Jan. 1896, MB; "To Restore Old Bruton Church," *Richmond Times-Dispatch*, 5 Feb. 1905.

36. Coleman, "The Picturesque and Traditional in the Story of a Colonial City," an address delivered under APVA auspices, 20 Mar. 1891, Tucker-Coleman Papers, box 101; Coleman, "Along the Lower James," 323–33.

37. C. W. Coleman, "The Picturesque and Traditional in the Story of a Colonial City"; Cynthia Coleman, "The Annals of Williamsburg, Virginia," n.d., Tucker-Coleman Papers, box 101.

38. Meeting, 10 Nov. 1904, CCB Minutes, box 1; Lottie C. Garrett, "Report of the Colonial Capital Branch," *YB* 1908:46.

39. "Reverend Beverly Dandridge Tucker," in *Eminent and Representative Men of Virginia and the District of Columbia of the Nineteenth Century*, ed. Ainsworth R. Spofford (Madison, Wis., 1893), 579; Rouse, *Cows on the Campus*, 113–14; Tucker, "The Continuity of the Life of the Church," in Goodwin, *Bruton Parish Church Restored*, 149.

40. Goodwin, *Bruton Parish Church Restored*, 90, 175; Beverley B. Munford to J. Taylor Ellyson, 27 Mar. 1907, Ellyson Papers; Whiffen, *The Public Buildings of Williamsburg*, 200; Fishwick, *Virginia*, 245.

41. Goodwin, *Bruton Parish Church Restored*, 33, 51; Goodwin, *Historical Sketch*, 9, 166.

5. "Our Inspiration and Our Goal"

1. Bryan, "Report of the President for 1903," *YB* 1905:6.
2. Quoted in Craven, *Legend of the Founding Fathers*, 85n.
3. Everett quoted in Forman, *Jamestown and St. Mary's*, 25; Bridenbaugh, *Jamestown*.
4. Helene S. Ward to author, 19 Jan. 1989; "Jamestown," *Richmond Dispatch*, n.d. (dateline 15 Dec. 1882), Valentine Scrapbook, VHS.
5. "Norfolk Branch," *Association for the Preservation of Virginia Antiquities* 1896:63; Galt to Bagby, 11 June 1889, Bagby Papers 78.
6. A. Galt to Parke Bagby, copy, 10 Feb. 1890, Mary Galt to unknown correspondent, n.d., draft, [Mary Galt] to Mrs. Hamson, 18 Oct. 1889, Galt Papers III.
7. [Mary Galt] to Mrs. Hamson, 18 Oct. 1889, Henry to Mary Galt, 23 Dec. 1889, A. Galt to Parke C. Bagby, 10 Feb. 1890, Galt Papers III; meeting, 4 Jan. 1890, quarterly meeting, 5 Oct. 1891, executive committee, 28 Oct. 1891, MB; Coleman to Bagby, 5 Oct. 1891, Bagby Papers 67.
8. "President's Report," 15 Feb. 1892, MB; Bryan to Henry, 16 Feb. 1892, Bryan Letterbook; "An Act to grant the Association for the Preservation of Virginia Antiquities all the title and interest of the State in certain portions of Jamestown Island, and to confer upon said Association the power to condemn lands," *YB* 1896:16–17.
9. Bryan to Meredith, 16 Feb. 1892, Bryan Letterbook; 1892 Constitution, art. 2, *YB* 1896:18.
10. Bryan to Lyon G. Tyler, 25 Aug. 1892, Bryan Letterbook; meetings, 1, 7, 21 Mar., 5 Apr. 1893, 5 Feb. 1897, MB.
11. Baltzell, *Protestant Establishment;* Davies, *Patriotism on Parade.*
12. Thad W. Tate, "The Seventeenth-Century Chesapeake and Its Modern Historians," in *The Chesapeake in the Seventeenth Century: Essays on Anglo-American Society and Politics,* ed. Tate and David L. Ammerman (New York and London, 1979), 3–17.
13. Elson, *Guardians of Tradition,* 60–62; Page, *Address at Jamestown,* 11, 12, 28.
14. "President's Report," *Association for the Preservation of Virginia Antiquities* 1896:24; Elson, *Guardians of Tradition,* 120; Crapol, *America for Americans.*
15. Page, *Address at Jamestown,* 3, 27; Pryor, *Jamestown,* 351–52.
16. John Stewart Bryan, "Speech at Blackwall," [1928], Bryan Family Papers; "Virginia's Priorities," *Richmond Times-Dispatch,* 8 Feb. 1924, PRM 1923–24; "Mrs. J. Taylor Ellyson's Address," *Association for the Preservation of Virginia Antiquities* 1919:9.
17. Tyler quoted in "Settlement of Jamestown," *Richmond Times,* 14 May 1895; Mrs. R. W. Watkins, "Circular Used by Membership Committee," *YB* 1908:65; Ellyson to Tyler, 10 May 1930, APVA file, Tyler Papers; Charlotte M. Gradie, "Spanish Jesuits in Virginia: The Mission That Failed," *VMHB* 96 (1988): 131–56. Lyon Tyler was mistaken not only in believing that Jamestown had log cabins but, because St. Augustine was Catholic and Spanish, in ignoring it as America's first European settlement.
18. Hall, *Introductory Address, 1895,* 6, 7.
19. Tyler, *Cavalier in America,* 18.
20. Hall, *Introductory Address, 1895,* 4; "E. H. L.," "Jamestown Island," unidentified newspaper, 3 Feb. 1891, Galt Papers III. She apparently mixed her ruins, for the church to which she referred was erected two decades after 1619.
21. Unidentified clipping, n.d. [Nov. 1911], PRM 1911–12; Bruce to editor, *Rich-*

mond News-Leader, 8 June 1914, proof copy, Blackwall Monument research file, APVA; "Report of the Treasurer," *APVA 1919*, in Galt Papers III.

22. "Report of Norfolk Branch," *YB* 1908:45; Huntley, *Peninsula Pilgrimage*, 330–31, 334.

23. Bryan, "Report of the President for 1903," *YB* 1905:6; Hall, *Introductory Address, 1891*, 5.

24. Yonge, "The Site of Old 'James Towne,'" *VMHB* 11 (1904): 402.

25. Pryor, *Jamestown*, 289, Yonge, "The Site of Old 'James Towne,'" *VMHB* 11 (1904): 402, 12 (1904): 42.

26. Tyler, *Virginia First*, 4; "The Historical Interest of the Settlement at Jamestown," *VMHB* 8 (1901): 416.

27. Yonge, "The Site of Old 'James Towne,'" 11 (1904): 262; Trachtenberg, *Incorporation of America*, 99.

28. Hall, *Introductory Address, 1891*, 3.

29. Newton, "The Association," 10, 19; Hall, *Introductory Address, 1891*, 4.

30. Hall, *Introductory Address, 1891*, 2; Hall, *Introductory Address, 1895*, 6.

31. Hall, *Introductory Address, 1895*, 8; Robert R. Roberts, "Popular Culture and Public Tastes," in *The Gilded Age*, ed. H. Wayne Morgan, rev. enl. ed. (Syracuse, N.Y., 1970), 288; Osterweis, *Myth of the Lost Cause*, 130; Cash, *Mind of the South*, 129.

32. Stanard, *Richmond*, 3; Coleman, "A Bit of Unwritten History," [1887], Tucker-Coleman Papers, box 102; "Virginia Pageant Week, April 24, 1922," PRM 1922–23; Morgan, *American Slavery*, 95, 111, 266–67.

33. Stanard, *Richmond*, 6; Pryor, *Jamestown*, 52; Coleman, untitled address, n.d., Tucker-Coleman Papers, box 103.

34. "Jamestown Island: The Observance There To-Morrow of Founders Day," unidentified newspaper, 12 May 1895, Organizations file, APVA; Kammen, *Mystic Chords of Memory*, 386; Kammen, *Selvages and Biases: The Fabric of History in American Culture* (Ithaca, N.Y., and London, 1987), 287.

35. Goodwin, *Bruton Parish Church Restored*, 183; Hall, "The Meeting Place," 10.

36. Minnie Cook to Eliz. Lyons, 1 Mar. [?], Lyons Papers 36, VHS; "Mrs. Stanard's Colonial Virginia," *Richmond News-Leader*, 10 Dec. 1917.

37. Mrs. George W. Bagby, untitled piece on Gloucester, n.d., Bagby Papers 23; Hall, *Introductory Address, 1895*, 5.

38. Thomas, "The Affairs in Virginia from 1642 to 1660, Showing the Relation That Virginia Bore to the Various Governments of England, Both Regal, and Parliamentary," n.d., APVA.

39. Saveth, *American Historians*, 37; Potter, "The Enigma of the South," in *The Sectional Conflict*, 5; Tate, "The Seventeenth-Century Chesapeake and Its Modern Historians," 3–50.

40. Bagby, untitled piece on Gloucester, n.d., Bagby Papers 23; "Mrs. Stanard's Colonial Virginia," *Richmond News-Leader*, 10 Dec. 1917; Page, "In Virginia Long Ago," *Richmond Times*, n.d. [1893], Elizabeth Lyons Scrapbook 1; Taylor, *Cavalier and Yankee*, 340.

41. Cabell, *Let Me Lie*, 76; Fishwick, *Virginia*, 281.

42. Tindall, "Mythology: A New Frontier in Southern History," in *Ethnic Southerners*, 23.

43. Cabell, *Let Me Lie*, 67; Cash, *Mind of the South*, 144; Gaston, *New South Creed*, 8.

44. Yonge, "The Site of Old 'James Towne,'" 12 (1904): 39: "Jamestown Island: The Observance There Tomorrow of Founders Day," unidentified newspaper, 12 May 1895, Organizations file, APVA; Hall, *Introductory Address, 1891*, 3; "Fine Celebration Fifty Years Ago," *Richmond Times*, 9 Nov. 1902; Lyon Tyler to J. B. C. Spencer, 28 Nov. 1907, Tyler Papers, box 24.

45. "History of the Association for the Preservation of Virginia Antiquities," *Souvenir of The Midsummer Night's Dream*; Lamar, *National Society of the Colonial Dames*, 125; Geertz, "Religion as a Cultural System," in *Interpretation of Cultures*, 112; Warner, *Living and the Dead*, chaps. 4, 5. These rituals were "a mechanism that periodically converts the obligatory into the desirable" and a "process of making public what is private or making social what is personal" (Turner, *Forest of Symbols*, 30, 46, 50).

46. "Fete on the Island," unidentified newspaper, n.d. [May 1895], Organizations file, APVA; "The Jamestown Anniversary," *Richmond Times*, 14 May 1895; Bryan, "President's Report," *Association for the Preservation of Virginia Antiquities* 1896:27.

47. Hall, *Introductory Address, 1895*, 5; J. L. M. Curry, "New Elements and Dangers," n.d. [c.1889], Scrapbook C, Curry Papers II-12; Simkins and Roland, *History of the South*, 391; Hobsbawm and Ranger, *Invention of Tradition*.

48. "Resolutions on Death of Mr. William G. Stanard," YB 1934:36; meeting, 2 Apr. 1895, MB; "Monument to Father of Virginia," unidentified newspaper, n.d., Jamestown Scrapbook, Organizations file, APVA.

49. "In the Jamestown Way on Jamestown Day," unidentified newspaper, 11 May 1927, PRM 1926–27; [Mary Galt], loose note, n.d., MB 1896–99; Bagby to Galt, 15 May 1895, Galt Papers III.

50. Galt to Bagby, 22 May 1902, Bagby Papers 78; Galt, notes, n.d., Galt Papers III.

51. "Report of Norfolk Branch," YB 1899:40; "Report of Jamestown Committee," YB 1908:32; Huntley, *Peninsula Pilgrimage*, 331.

52. Mrs. John B. Lightfoot, "Report of Jamestown Committee," YB 1908:36; Lightfoot, "Report of the Jamestown Committee," in *The Report of the President of the Association for the Preservation of Virginia Antiquities* (Richmond, 1915), 15; central committee meeting, 2 Apr. 1901, meetings, 11 Feb. 1902, 7 Dec. 1915, MB; "Indian Items," *Hampton Student* 5–6 (1913–16): 7.

53. "Coming Pilgrimage to Old Dominion," unidentified newspaper, n.d., MB 1901–2; meetings, 4, 11 Feb., 1 Apr. 1902, MB.

54. Ellen M. Bagby, "Association for the Preservation of Virginia Antiquities," n.d., Miscellaneous Broadsides, Yonge Papers 1299–8; Bagby, "Report of the Jamestown Committee," YB 1931:23; Meeting, 6 Nov. 1916, MB.

55. Page, *The Old South*, 37; Joseph Bryan to J. Henning Nelms, 13 Aug. 1896, Bryan Letterbook. Bryan's claim was frequently cited by Page, Tyler, and others as well. Because Virginia lacked a viable transatlantic shipping industry, it became entrenched in the internal slave trade. Virginians may not have been involved in the African trade, but they certainly were employed in bringing slaves in from the West Indies (Thad W. Tate, *The Negro in Eighteenth-Century Williamsburg* [Charlottesville, Va., 1965], 28; Jordan, *White over Black*, 321; and David Brion Davis, *Slavery and Human Progress* [New York and Oxford, 1984], 235).

56. The legend apparently stemmed from the misidentification of the *Mayflower's* captain. A ship commander of the same family name became not only a pirate but a slave trader (Carolyn Freeman Travers of Plimoth Plantation to author, 25 Aug. 1983).

57. Galt to Bagby, 11 Oct. 1902, Bagby Papers 78; Rouse, *Cows on the Campus,* 147, 186; John Henry Cutler, *"Honey Fitz": Three Steps to the White House: The Life and Times of John F. (Honey Fitz) Fitzgerald* (Indianapolis, 1962), 36–37.

58. "Mrs. G. W. Bagby Funeral Saturday," *Richmond News Leader,* 15 Sept. 1927; "Of Her Generation's Best," unidentified newspaper, 16 Sept. 1927, PRM 1926–27.

59. Galt, "Report," [1901], VHS; Galt to Bagby, n.d., draft [Mar. 1896], Galt Papers III; Galt to Bagby, 3 Mar., 9, 10 Apr. 1896, Bagby Papers 78; Lears, *No Place of Grace;* Green, *Fit for America,* 137–66.

60. Galt to Bagby, n.d. [Mar. 1896], draft, Galt Papers III; Galt to Bagby, 23 Mar. 1896, Bagby Papers 78.

61. Meeting of board of managers, 6 Oct. 1896, MB; Galt to Bagby, 23 May 1901, Bagby Papers 78.

62. Coleman, untitled address, n.d., Tucker-Coleman Papers, box 103.

63. Galt to Bagby, 24 Jan. [?], 24 Apr. 1901, Bagby Papers 78; Bagby to Galt, 22 Jan. 1898, 27 Oct. 1899, Galt Papers III.

64. Forman, *Jamestown and St. Mary's,* 154; Galt, "Report," [1901], VHS; Yonge to Bagby, 14 Nov. 1904, YB 1905:33.

65. "E. H. L.," "Jamestown Island," unidentified newspaper, 3 Feb. 1891, Galt Papers III; Galt to Bagby, 23 May 1901, Bagby Papers 78; Forman, *Jamestown and St. Mary's,* 165–66; George M. LaMonte to Lyon Tyler, 28 Mar. 1908, Jamestown Exposition file, Tyler Papers.

66. Samuel H. Yonge, address to "Phi Beta Kappa, Jamestown," draft, 24 Nov. 1926, Yonge Papers 1299–1. Much is still unknown archaeologically about Jamestown. Some APVA preservationists seemed most interested in what remained of the 1607 fort. Tyler shocked his 1895 audience when he claimed that it had long washed away. Yonge and archaeologist Forman both discounted that claim but acknowledged that the impermanent structure had left few telltale remains. E. E. Barney probably discovered the first statehouse in 1901 on his land, which his heirs sold to the United States government for the present-day park (Noël Hume, *Here Lies Virginia,* 62–65; Harrington, "The Location of James Fort," 36–53).

67. "President's Report," *Association for the Preservation of Virginia Antiquities* 1896:28; Galt to Bagby, undated [Mar. 1896], draft, Galt Papers III; Galt to Bagby, 23 Mar. 1896, 12 Oct. 1900, Bagby Papers 78.

68. Mrs. John B. Lightfoot, "Report of Jamestown Committee," *YB* 1908:33; Lightfoot, "Report of Jamestown Committee," *YB* 1913:30.

69. Bagby to Galt, 10 Jan. 1895, 17 Nov. 1899, 16 Oct. 1900, Galt Papers III.

6. "With Reverence and Due Regard for History"

1. Hall to the editor, "Plans for Jamestown Island," *New York Times,* 28 Feb. 1902; central committee meeting, 4 Mar. 1902, MB.

2. Meeting, 15 Jan. 1903, MB; Bryan to Barney, 28 Jan. 1903, Bryan Letterbook; Barney to Tyler, 19 Apr. 1907, Tyler Papers.

3. "Jamestown National Park Again Proposed," *Seventeenth Annual Report, 1912, of the American Scenic and Historic Preservation Society* (Albany, 1912), 251–54; "Address of Mrs. J. Taylor Ellyson," *YB* 1913:13; meeting, n.d. [May 1916], MB.

4. David L. Moffitt to author, 18 Jan. 1989; Helene S. Ward to author, 19 Jan. 1989.

5. E. S. Brooks, *The Century Book of the American Colonies* (New York, 1909), 73;

Forman, *Jamestown and St. Mary's,* 87, 174; Joseph Bryan to Alexander Brown, 7 Feb. 1891, Bryan Letterbook; meetings, 7 Mar. 1893, 4 Dec. 1894, MB.

6. Galt to Bagby, 14 Jan. 1895, draft, Bagby to Galt, 21 Jan. 1895, Galt Papers III; meeting, 22 Jan. 1895, central committee meeting, 5 Nov. 1901, MB; Galt to Bagby n.d., [1896], Bagby Papers 78.

7. Forman, *Jamestown and St. Mary's,* front-leaf map; Galt to Mrs. Lee, 4 July 1889, draft, to Mrs. Hamson, 18 Oct. 1889, draft, Galt Papers III; quarterly meeting, 3 Oct. 1893, MB. Another estimate put the erosion at as much as four feet per year (Ellen M. Bagby, "Virginia and the Nation's Debt to the A.P.V.A.," n.d., Organizations file, APVA).

8. Bryan to Col. W. P. Craighill, 17 Sept., 29 Oct. 1894, Bryan Letterbook; Rice, *Curry,* 70, 164, 224; Stanard, *Jamestown and APVA;* "A Bill to Appropriate Ten Thousand Dollars," *Association for the Preservation of Virginia Antiquities* 1896:79; *YB* 1898:63; Elizabeth Lyons, "Report of Recording Secretary," *YB* 1899:25.

9. Bagby to Galt, 20 Apr. 1895, Galt Papers III; board of managers meeting, 1 Apr. 1902, MB; Galt to Bagby, 15 Oct. 1900, Bagby Papers 78.

10. Meeting, 3 May 1898, MB; Mrs. George W. Bagby, "Report of Jamestown Committee," *YB* 1899:30; Davies, *Patriotism on Parade,* 322–23; Winslow Warren, "Address of the President," *Proceedings of the Bunker Hill Monument Association* (Boston, 1899), 15–26.

11. Dabney, *Virginia,* 406; Bryan to Thomas Pinckney, 25 Apr. 1898, to J. S. Hernsberger, 24 Sept. 1898, Bryan Letterbook; Mitchell, *Aftermath of Appomattox,* 66; Walter LaFeber, *The New Empire: An Interpretation of American Expansionism, 1860–1898* (Ithaca, N.Y., and London, 1963).

12. Bryan to Moses D. Hoge, 6 May 1898, Bryan Letterbook; Robert Beisner, *Twelve against Empire: The Anti-Imperialists, 1898–1900* (New York, 1968); Curry, "Recent Tendencies in Free Political Institutions," 1901, Curry Papers I-13; Rice, *Curry,* 168.

13. Coleman, misc. papers, n.d., and untitled address, n.d., Tucker-Coleman Papers, boxes 101, 103.

14. Quoted in Sheldon, *Populism in the Old Dominion,* 145n. Wilson biographer Arthur S. Link questions the accuracy of the Richmond *Dispatch* report on this speech but lacks an actual transcript of the address (Arthur S. Link to author, 10 Mar. 1983).

15. Influential in the Nicaraguan Canal Company, president of a failing locomotive company, and fearing the consequences of a troubled economy, Bryan abandoned his anti-imperialism and endorsed economic imperialism by 1899 (James M. Lindgren, "The Apostasy of a Southern Anti-Imperialist: Joseph Bryan, the Spanish-American War, and Business Expansion," *Southern Studies,* n.s., 2 (Summer 1991): 151–78.

16. "Report of Hampton Branch," and "St. Paul, Minn," *YB* 1899:47, 51; meeting, 3 May 1898, MB; Galt, notes on Jamestown, n.d., Galt Papers III.

17. A. MacKenzie to John Lamb, 10 Mar. 1904, Jamestown file, VHS; general meeting, 8 Jan. 1901, MB.

18. "Settlement of Jamestown," *Richmond Times,* 14 May 1895; "Jamestown Island: The Observance There To-Morrow of Founders Day," unidentified newspaper, n.d. [12 May 1895], Organizations file, APVA.

19. Galt to Bagby, 14 May 1895, Bagby Papers 78; Bagby to Galt, 11 May 1895, Galt Papers III.

20. Yonge, "The Site of Old 'James Towne,'" *VMHB* 11 (1904): 404–5; Harrington, "The Location of James Fort," 36–53; Forman, *Jamestown and St. Mary's,*

front-leaf map. What actually washed away was a considerable section of the north-western section of the island, but the most historic section, it is thought, lies to the southeast.

21. Yonge, "Reminiscent of Washington College, Va., under the Presidency of General Robert E. Lee," n.d., corrected copy, Yonge Papers, box 5, Manuscripts and Rare Books Department, CWM; John Stewart Bryan, "Speech at Blackwall," [1928], Bryan Family Papers; Forman, *Jamestown and St. Mary's,* 165–68; W. G. Stanard, "Report of Jamestown Committee, *YB* 1905:25–33.

22. "Patriotism Vindicated," *Richmond News-Leader,* n.d. [Mar. 1920], PRM 1919–20.

23. Craven, *Legend of the Founding Fathers,* 146, 153–54; meeting, 1 Oct. 1901, central committee meeting, 4 Mar. 1902, MB; Rydell, *All the World's a Fair.*

24. Mitchell, *Aftermath of Appomattox,* 87–88; "The Ter-Centenary," unidentified newspaper, 2 Feb. 1901, and "An Act of the 58th Congress," passed 3 Mar. 1905, in Jamestown Tercentennial, box 7, APVA; Williamsburg Businessmen's Association, circular letter, 12 Feb. 1901, VHS. The APVA's resolution supposedly passed on 12 June 1900, yet the minutes disclose no quorum for that day (MB).

25. "Jamestown in the Celebration," *Richmond News,* 12 Dec. 1901; Bryan quoted in Bryan, *Joseph Bryan,* 316.

26. Mrs. J. Taylor Ellyson to Mrs. Dunn, 8 Dec. 1930, Jamestown permanent file, APVA; "An Act of the 58th Congress," passed 3 Mar. 1905, in Jamestown Tercentennial, box 7, APVA. The governor also appointed a commission, which included the APVA's president, to oversee the fair.

27. Galt to Mr. and Mrs. O'Connor, n.d. [1907], Galt Papers III; Carl Abbott, "Norfolk in the New Century: The Jamestown Exposition and Urban Boosterism," *VMHB* 85 (1977): 86–96.

28. William Hayes Ward, "A Race Exhibition," *New York Independent,* 14 Nov. 1907, 1168–72; Giles B. Jackson and D. Webster Davis, *The Industrial History of the Negro Race in the United States* (Richmond, 1908); Lucy Brown Franklin, "The Negro Exhibition of the Jamestown Ter-Centennial Exposition of 1907," *Negro History Bulletin* 38 (1975): 408–14; Dabney, *Richmond,* 272; Rydell, *All the World's a Fair,* 72–104.

29. Alderman quoted in Kirby, *Darkness at the Dawning,* 107; "Hungry Statesmen Quit Jamestown," *New York Times,* 28 Apr. 1907.

30. Loth, *Virginia Landmarks Register,* 294.

31. Mrs. J. Taylor Ellyson, "Report of First Vice President and Acting President," *YB* 1908:17; Sally Nelson Robins to J. Taylor Ellyson, 6 Jan. 1906, Ellyson Papers; meeting, 15 Jan. 1907, MB. In 1906 the General Assembly appropriated $2,500 for the APVA's work at Jamestown Island and the United States government allotted other moneys (central committee meeting, 3 Apr. 1906, MB).

32. Jones to Ellyson, 4 Apr. 1906, Jamestown Tercentennial, box 7, APVA; Bryan to Central Committee, 12 June 1906, in "A.P.V.A. Holds General Meeting," *Richmond Times-Dispatch,* 13 June 1906.

33. Swanson quoted in Ellyson, "Report of First Vice President and Acting President," *YB* 1908:16; James Bryce, *The American Commonwealth,* 3d ed. (New York, 1908).

34. Mrs. John B. Lightfoot, "Report of Jamestown Committee," *YB* 1908:31; Moomaw quoted in "People and Scenes at Jamestown Yesterday," unidentified news-

paper, 14 May 1907, Jamestown Scrapbook, Organizations file, APVA; meetings, 23 Nov. 1906, 15 Jan. 1907, MB; "Mr. Roosevelt's Speech," *New York Times,* 27 Apr. 1907.

35. "Roosevelt Sails Back," *New York Times,* 28 Apr. 1907; Roosevelt quoted in "Make Employers Liable—Roosevelt," *New York Times,* 11 June 1907.

36. General meeting, 10 June 1904, YB 1905:27; Isobel Bryan, "Notes concerning Jamestown Church," [c.1905], Bryan Papers; Yonge and Stanard to Mrs. Joseph Bryan, 15 Nov. 1904, in YB 1905:27–28.

37. Annual meeting, 19 Oct. 1905, general meeting, 14 May 1906, MB; meeting, 8 Apr. 1906, "1894–1917 Washington Branch Record Book," APVA; "Agreement Relative to the Consecration of the Church at Jamestown," 19 Oct. 1906, signed by A. M. Randolph, bishop of Southern Virginia, MB 1902–7; Kate Cabell Cox, "Report of Dedication Services at Jamestown, May 23, 1908," MB.

38. Kammen, *Mystic Chords of Memory,* 194; "Petition of General Convention, Protestant Episcopal Church," YB 1908:43; A. M. Randolph, "Restoration of Church at Jamestown, Virginia," paper delivered at an APVA general meeting, 14 May 1906, MB; unsigned resolution, n.d. [c.1907], misplaced in MB 1889–91.

39. Isobel Bryan, "Notes concerning Jamestown Church," [c.1905], VHS; Yonge, "The Site of Old 'James Towne,'" *VMHB* 12 (1904): 44; Yonge, "Description of Proposed Memorial Building at Jamestown," n.d., in Bryan, "Notes concerning Jamestown Church."

40. Dorsey, *Early English Churches,* 54–55; William H. Pierson, Jr., *American Buildings and Their Architects: The Colonial and Neoclassic Styles* (Garden City, N.Y., 1970), 37; Forman, *Jamestown and St. Mary's.*

41. Ellyson, "Report of First Vice President and Acting President," YB 1905:11; general meeting, 14 May 1906, MB; "Church Will Be under Diocese," unidentified newspaper, n.d., in "1894–1917 Washington Branch Record Book," APVA.

42. M. M. T. to the editor, "Save the Tower at Jamestown," *Richmond Times-Dispatch,* 3 May 1906; Mrs. John B. Lightfoot to Samuel H. Yonge, 30 Aug. 1907, Yonge Papers 1299–7, UVA.

43. M. A. DeWolfe Howe, *Barrett Wendell and His Letters* (Boston, 1924), 196–97. For the demolition, see Lamar, *National Society of Colonial Dames,* 116–31, and general meeting, 4 Dec. 1906, MB. W. G. Stanard reported that 5,000 good glazed bricks were thus acquired for $300. According to his spouse, the APVA's historian, "Part of the walls and a chimney of a small house believed to have been a contemporary of the Jamestown dwellings were to be seen near Hampton until the year 1907, when the bricks—of a fine glazed kind—were used in the restoration of Jamestown Church" (Stanard, *Colonial Virginia,* 60).

44. [John Stewart Bryan], "Lying for Historical Fame," *Richmond News Leader,* 7 Jan. 1920.

45. Curry, *North American Colonization,* 11; resolution, 2 June 1897, in Bryan Letterbook. Curry's views reflected a traditional emphasis on Protestant individualism, but some see a "heavy emphasis upon environmentalism" in the writings of Lost Cause leaders such as Page and Pryor (Connelly and Bellows, *God and General Longstreet,* 65–66). For the hierophant tradition, see Aaron, *Unwritten War,* 282; Elson, *Guardians of Tradition,* 185.

46. Virginia Miller, "Report of Washington Branch," YB 1908:57; President's Re-

port, annual meeting, 4 Nov. 1902, MB; "Monument to Father of Virginia," unidentified newspaper, n.d., in Jamestown Scrapbook, Organizations file, APVA; Blow quoted in unidentified newspaper clipping, n.d., MB 1908–14; Mrs. A. A. Blow, *An Address Delivered before the Daughters of the American Revolution at Their Congress Held in Washington, D.C., April 1905* (n.p., n.d.).

47. Blow cited in unidentified newspaper clipping, n.d., MB 1908–14; Cabell, *Let Me Lie,* 63, 69–70. Blow's wife served as director of the APVA's Gloucester branch until 1915.

48. Henry, "Rescue of Captain John Smith by Pocahontas," [1875], Henry Papers; for a contrary view, see Robert Alonzo Brock, "Prejudication of History," *Richmond Dispatch,* 20 July 1877.

49. "William Wirt Henry," *Chronicle,* Dec. 1900, Henry Scrapbook; Henry, "Rescue of Capt. John Smith," n.d., Henry Papers; Alden T. Vaughan, *American Genesis: Captain John Smith and the Founding of Virginia* (Boston, 1975), 190. The APVA invited Henry to deliver a variation of this lecture in 1894 (Mary M. P. Newton to William Wirt Henry, 8 Oct. 1894, Henry Papers; "Origin of Jamestown," *Richmond Times,* 2 Feb. 1895).

50. Pryor, *Jamestown,* 207, 260–261; Samuel H. Yonge, "Address to Phi Betta Kappa, Jamestown," 24 Nov. 1926, Yonge Papers, box 1, CWM; [Stanard], *Notes on a Journey to Jamestown,* 2; Elson, *Guardians of Tradition,* 187–88.

51. Kammen, *Mystic Chords of Memory,* 75; "Report of Pocahontas Branch," *YB* 1905:62; meeting, 6 Nov. 1900, MB; "Virginia Honors Memory of Pocahontas, Savior of Colony," unidentified newspaper, 3 June 1922, PRM 1922–23. The legend behind "Pocahontas's Basin" is mostly oral tradition and undocumented (directory board meeting, 2 Feb. 1915, MB; Berkhofer, *White Man's Indian*).

52. Jamestown Annual Report, 1922–23, box 5, APVA; Susie P. Nelson to Mrs. J. Taylor Ellyson, 6 Aug. 1920, PRM 1919–20.

53. William Carter Stubbs, "Address Delivered before the A.P.V.A., Gloucester Branch," n.d., Addresses file, APVA; Coleman, "Jamestown," n.d., Tucker-Coleman Papers, box 102.

54. Henry, "Oration of the Day," *Washington [D.C.] Evening News,* 18 Sept. 1893, Henry Scrapbook; Sams, *Conquest of Virginia,* 29; Pryor, *Jamestown,* 59–60; Timothy H. Silver, *A New Face on the Countryside: Indians, Colonists, and Slaves in South Atlantic Forests, 1500–1800* (New York, 1990).

55. Pryor, *Jamestown,* 62–63, 300.

56. Valentine, "At the Opening of the New Building at the University College of Medicine," 24 Nov. 1897, Addresses, VM; annual meeting, 4 Jan. 1922, board meeting, 2 May 1922, meeting, 3 Oct. 1922, MB; Federal Writers' Project, *Virginia,* 293.

57. Federal Writers' Project, *Virginia,* 582; committee on Jamestown Memorial Building, report, 12 Feb. 1908, 4 Jan. 1909, MB; "Foreword," *YB* 1931:5; Huntley, *Peninsula Pilgrimage,* 327.

58. Broadside, n.d., Northampton Branch Correspondence, box 3, APVA; Smith quoted in Federal Writers' Project, *Virginia,* 384; "Report of Northampton Branch," *YB* 1941:64; Coleman, "Jamestown," n.d., Tucker-Coleman Papers, box 102; Slotkin, *Regeneration through Violence,* 5.

59. Cabell, *Let Me Lie,* 46, 51.

60. Page, *The Old South,* 16; Tyler, *Virginia First,* 9.

61. Mrs. Granville Valentine, "Committee Research—Memorial Markers," n.d.

[1925], Trustee Information, box 10, APVA. For the Occaneechee battle, see Federal Writers' Project, *Virginia*, 475–76; Wilcomb E. Washburn, *The Governor and the Rebel: A History of Bacon's Rebellion in Virginia* (Chapel Hill, N.C., 1957), 40–48; Couture, *To Preserve and Protect*, 171; Morgan, *American Slavery*, 259–60.

62. Coleman, "Jamestown," n.d., Tucker-Coleman Papers, box 102; "Williamsburg Report," *Association for the Preservation of Virginia Antiquities*: 1896:55; "Report of Landmark Committee, YB 1900:26; Bright, *Address at Williamsburg;* Stanard, *Bacon's Rebellion*, 9; Wecter, *Hero in America*, 25–30; Washburn, *Governor and the Rebel*, 10.

63. Page, *Address at Jamestown*, 24; Page, "Address," [1919], 28; Coleman, "Annals of Williamsburg, Virginia," n.d., and "Jamestown," n.d., Tucker-Coleman Papers, boxes 101, 102; Stanard, *Richmond*, 13.

64. Washburn, *Governor and the Rebel*, 166; Morgan, *American Slavery*, 269–70.

65. Quarterly meeting, 7 Oct. 1890, central committee meeting, Nov. 1896, meetings, 8 Jan. 1898, 2 Mar. 1915, MB; Newton, "Report of Landmark Committee," YB 1900:27; Stillinger, *The Antiquers*.

7. "Keeping Alive a Proper Veneration for the Past"

1. Annual meeting, 19 Oct. 1898, C. Whittle Sams and Judge Theodore S. Garnett to A.P.V.A., 21 Dec. 1908, meeting, 2 Mar. 1909, MB. A meeting in 1911 rejected attempts by the Norfolk, Williamsburg, and Hampton branches to decentralize the association (YB 1913:59).

2. Rose, *Colonial Houses of Worship*, 475; Loth, *Virginia Landmarks Register*, 455.

3. Meeting, 19 Apr. 1892, MB; "Report of Smithfield Branch," YB 1908:58; "Settlement of Jamestown," *Richmond Times*, 14 May 1895.

4. Meeting, 23 Oct. 1894, MB; Mrs. Richard S. Thomas, "Report of Smithfield Branch," YB 1905:52; Dorsey, *Early English Churches*, 55; Rose, *Colonial Houses of Worship*, 458–60.

5. Elizabeth Henry Lyons, "Report of Recording Secretary for 1897," YB 1898:27; meeting, 6 Apr. 1897, MB; O'Neal, *Architecture in Virginia*, 109; "Report of Kecoughtan Branch, YB 1913:64; "Address of Mrs. J. Taylor Ellyson," ibid., 14; Rose, *Colonial Houses of Worship*, 472, 476, 495, 501–2.

6. Mrs. A. S. Nelson, "Report of Lexington Branch," YB 1898:56–58; Elizabeth Lyons, "Report of Recording Secretary," ibid., 25; Saveth, *American Historians*, 37.

7. Henry, "Virginia of the Revolutionary Period"; Slotkin, *Regeneration through Violence;* "A Fine Address by Gen. Roller," *Richmond Times*, 10 Jan. 1899.

8. Mary Macon Aylett Fitzhugh to Mrs. Lightfoot, 9 May 1922, Northampton Branch Correspondence, box 3, APVA.

9. "Ancient Landmarks Preserved," *Eastville Times Dispatch*, n.d., PRM 1913–14; [Kate Savage], broadside, n.d., PRM 1917–18; "Report of Northampton Branch," YB 1938:79; Moore, *Two Paths*, 125, 127, 129; Moger, *Virginia*, fig. 4, opp. p. 81.

10. "Ancient Landmarks Preserved," *Eastville Times-Dispatch;* William Henry Harbaugh, *Power and Responsibility: The Life and Times of Theodore Roosevelt* (New York, 1961), 420–21.

11. W. B. Fitzhugh to Tyler, 8 Nov. 1913, Kate Savage to Tyler, 4 Dec. 1913, Tyler Papers, box 24; Mary Fitzhugh to Ellyson, 28 Oct. 1914, to Mrs. Lightfoot, 9 May 1922, Northampton Branch Correspondence, box 2; Lora H. Ellyson, *The Report of the President of the Association for the Preservation of Virginia Antiquities, 15 January 1915* (Richmond,

1915), 11; "William Bullitt Fitzhugh," *History of Virginia,* ed. Philip Alexander Bruce and Richard L. Morton (Chicago and New York, 1924), 5:465–66.

12. Kate S[avage] to Mrs. Fitzhugh, 5 July 1917, Northampton Branch Correspondence, box 3; [Kate Savage], untitled appeal, n.d., PRM 1917–18; "A Worth While Effort," *Eastern Shore Herald,* n.d., ibid.

13. Kate S[avage] to Mrs. Fitzhugh, 5 July 1917, Northampton Branch Correspondence, box 3.

14. Kate [Savage] to Ellyson, [?] Feb. 1915, 6 July 1917, and Ellyson to Mrs. Fitzhugh, 29 Mar. 1922, Mrs. Fitzhugh to Mrs. Lightfoot, 9 May 1922, ibid.

15. Savage to Ellyson, 10 Jan. 1922, ibid.; meeting, 6 July 1923, MB.

16. Ellyson to Mrs. Lightfoot, 3 Sept. 1923, Northampton Branch Correspondence, box 3; meeting, 2 Oct. 1923, MB; Loth, *Virginia Landmarks Register,* 303.

17. "Report 1913," Drummondtown Branch, box 2, APVA; Mary T. Fletcher, "Report of Drummondtown Branch," YB 1913:77–78; Loth, *Virginia Landmarks Register,* 3.

18. Meeting, 27 Nov. 1894, MB; Rosa Rountree, "Report of Norfolk Branch," YB 1898:45; Page, "Old Yorktown," 801–16.

19. "Report of Gloucester Branch," YB 1913:63; "Report of Joseph Bryan Branch," YB 1934:80; "Report of Joseph Bryan Branch," YB 1938:83; Ludwell Lee Montague to the Directress, Joseph Bryan Branch, 5 Aug. 1971, Powhatan's Chimney Research file, APVA.

20. Bryan to E. Bergland, 17 Aug. 1894, Cape Henry Lighthouse file, box 7, APVA; quarterly meeting, 2 Oct. 1894, MB; Stilgoe, *Common Landscape,* 110–11.

21. "The Cape Henry Park and Land Company," and John P. Kennedy to Henry Sargeant, 21 Sept. 1905, Lighthouse file, NPL; Mrs. Catesby G. Jones, Jr., and Mrs. Joseph L. McClane, Jr., *The Norfolk Branch, 1888–1984 . . . of the Association for the Preservation of Virginia Antiquities* (Williamsburg, Va., 1989), 15; "Memo," n.d., Norfolk Branch Correspondence, box 3, APVA; "Mrs. Ellyson Emphasizes Year's Work of A.P.V.A.," *Richmond News Leader,* 3 Jan. 1931; "Report of Norfolk Branch," YB 1941:43–44; Loth, *Virginia Landmarks Register,* 466.

22. Coleman to Belle Bryan, 16 Apr. 1889, APVA Papers, VHS; Coleman to Bagby, 13 July 1891, Bagby Papers 67.

23. Meeting, 19 Apr. 1892, MB; Henry to Leland Stanford, 22 Apr. 1892, Henry Letterbook.

24. Page to Bagby, 17 Dec. 1894, Bagby papers 105; Lightfoot to Bagby, 13 June 1895, ibid., 92; meetings, 12 Mar., 16 Apr., 30 Apr., 14 Aug., 1 Oct. 1895, 3 Mar., 17 Mar. 1896, MB; Huntley, *Peninsula Pilgrimage,* 294; Trudell, *Colonial Yorktown,* 109–10; Kent, *Preservation of the Past,* 11; Edith M. Elliott, Clerk of York County Circuit Court, to author, 7 Mar. 1989.

25. "To Burn Henry House," unidentified newspaper, n.d. (dateline, Richmond, Va., 22 Apr. [1908]), Elizabeth Henry Lyons Scrapbook 2, VHS. Montville was not Patrick Henry's home but that of his descendant Colonel William Aylett. It comprised two mirror-image houses; one was demolished, the other still stands in King William County.

26. "From the Jamestown Committee," n.d., MB 1898; Henry James, *The American Scene,* ed. W. H. Auden (New York, 1946), 370, 371, 377.

27. Scott, *Old Richmond Neighborhoods,* figs. 37, 93; Maurice Duke, "Cabell's and Glasgow's Richmond: The Intellectual Background of the City," *Mississippi Quarterly* 27 (1974): 389.

28. Florence S. Peple to Mrs. Stanard, 6 Nov. 1923, Hullihen-Stanard-Kline Papers 6394-1, Special Collections, UVA; Richard M. Dorson, *American Folklore* (Chicago, 1959), 4; Cash, *Mind of the South,* 243,

29. Stanard, *Colonial Virginia,* vii, viii; meeting, 4 Dec. 1917, MB; Kimball to William G. Stanard, 26 Jan. 1920, Hullihen-Stanard-Kline Papers 6394-1.

30. "Mrs. Ellyson Reviews Year's Work of A.P.V.A.," *Richmond Virginian,* 9 Jan. 1911, in "1894–1917 Washington Branch Record Book," APVA; Stanard, *Richmond,* 31–33.

31. Stanard, *Richmond,* xix, xx, 223.

32. Ibid., 219, 220.

33. Dabney, *Richmond,* fig. 42, between pp. 220–21; Scott, *Houses of Old Richmond,* 69–73; Bryan, *Sword over the Mantel,* 116.

34. Bryan quoted in "A.P.V.A. Holds General Meeting," *Richmond Times-Dispatch,* 13 June 1906, "1898–1917 Washington Branch Record Book," APVA. One gentleman at the APVA meeting "expressed the opinion that this historic landmark might as well be destroyed" (meeting, 19 June 1906, MB).

35. The APVA filed resolutions of support from the Colonial Dames, UDC, DAR, Woman's Club, Chamber of Commerce, Business Men's Club, State Medical Association, the Merchant Association, Civic Improvement League, and others (meeting, 20 June 1910, MB; Charles Hutzler to Mrs. Ellyson, 28 Oct. 1910, Marshall House file, APVA).

36. Christian, *Richmond,* 531.

37. Mrs. Walter Christian, "Report of John Marshall House Committee," *YB* 1913:41; Pulley, *Old Virginia Restored,* 27n, 102.

38. Fiske, *Civil Government in the United States* (1890), 195; Curry, "Recent Tendencies in Free Political Institutions," 15 Jan. 1901, Curry Papers I-13.

39. Beveridge to Philip L. Leidy, 29 Dec. 1921, Marshall House Fund Drive, box 6, APVA; Beveridge, *Address on Washington's Birthday, February 22, 1921* (New York, 1921), 27; visitor quoted in meeting, 4 Dec. 1917, MB.

40. Mrs. Walter Christian, "Report of John Marshall House Committee," *YB* 1913:40; meeting, 4 Dec. 1923, MB.

41. Meetings, 2 Mar., 7 Apr. 1915, MB. Marshall was president of the Virginia branch of the American Colonization Society in the year of Nat Turner's Rebellion, 1831. In the early twentieth century, African-Americans owned 75 percent of the real estate in Jackson Ward, the segregated black district (Jackson and Davis, *Industrial History,* 104).

42. Stanard, *John Marshall,* 25–26.

43. Ibid., 19, 24, 27, 30; Elson, *Guardians of Tradition,* 208–9; "Opening of the Marshall House," unidentified newspaper, 27 Mar. 1913, PRM 1913–14.

44. Page, "To the People of Richmond," 12 Jan. 1910, Marshall House file, APVA.

45. "Hold Meeting in Marshall House," *Richmond Times-Dispatch,* 5 Jan. 1913.

46. Meetings, 4 Nov. 1919, 3 Feb. 1920, MB; Tyler, *Virginia Principles,* 18–19; Higham, *Strangers in the Land,* 173–74.

47. Julian Ralph, "How a Tourist Sees Richmond," *Harper's Weekly* 38 (24 Feb. 1894): 179; Patricia C. Click, *The Spirit of the Times: Amusements in Nineteenth-Century Baltimore, Norfolk, and Richmond* (Charlottesville, Va., 1989), 25–27.

48. J. Thompson Brown to Mrs. B. S. Bryan, 5 Sept. 1895, APVA Papers, VHS; Valentine, "At the Opening of the New Building at the University College of Medicine," 24 Nov. 1897, Addresses, VM; quarterly meeting, 1 Oct. 1895, MB.

49. "The Edgar Allan Poe Shrine," *VMHB* 31 (1923): 168; advisory board meeting, 9 Dec. 1911, meeting, 4 May 1920, MB.

50. Meetings, 21 Oct. 1921, 4 Jan., 22 May 1922, MB; Loth, *Virginia Landmarks Register,* 381–82.

51. Cabell, *Let Me Lie,* 126–27; Smith, *Killers of the Dream,* 214; Wendell quoted in Hubbell, *The South in American Literature,* 548.

52. Page, "The First American Man of Letters," n.d., Page Papers 20B-36; "Report of the Landmark Committee," *YB* 1908:41; Federal Writers' Project, *Virginia,* 287; Edward V. Valentine to Charles B. Cooke, Report of Committee on Marking Historic Spots, n.d., Robert L. Traylor Papers 3.

53. "Poe Celebration Reaches a Climax," *Richmond Times-Dispatch,* 20 Jan. 1909; Edward V. Valentine, "My Reminiscences of Richmond," [1912], and "Final Opening of Edgar Allan Poe Shrine," [1922], Addresses, VM; Cabell, *Let Me Lie,* 127.

54. Meeting, 9 Apr. 1907, MB; "Report of Fredericksburg Branch," *YB* 1908:49–50. Both Kenmore and the Mary Washington house also had been built before the American Revolution.

8. "To Capitalize Some of Its Historic Assets"

1. Cash, *Mind of the South,* 183.

2. Bryan to Bagby, 27 Aug. 1906, Bagby Papers 106; Bryan to Thomas Pinckney, 22 May 1897, Bryan Letterbook; Henry Sydnor Harrison, "An Ideal Newspaperman," *American Magazine,* July 1914, 61, John S. Bryan Scrapbook, 1903–19, VHS; Tindall, "Bourbons" and "Progressives," in *The Persistent Tradition.*

3. Bryan to Judge W. O. Harris, 22 Feb. 1900, to Col. Thomas L. Brown, 15 May 1900, Bryan Letterbook; Bryan, *Sword over the Mantel,* 62; [Joseph Bryan], "What It Is to Be 'Intensely Southern,'" *Richmond Times,* 17 May 1901; John A. Cutchins, *Memories of Old Richmond (1881–1944)* (Verona, Va., 1973), 174.

4. Curry, *Lessons of Yorktown,* 7.

5. Mitchell, *Aftermath of Appomattox,* 2, 22.

6. Ibid., 22; Mitchell to Curry, 4 Nov. 1902, Curry Papers I-14.

7. "Oration of the Day," *Washington [D.C.] Evening News,* 18 Sept. 1893, in Henry Scrapbook; "Mount Vernon Branch," *Association for the Preservation of Virginia Antiquities* 1896:79; Bryan quoted in Bryan, *Sword over the Mantel,* 118.

8. Mitchell, "The South and the School," [1906], Mitchell Papers 9; "Virginia First State to Denounce Slavery," unidentified newspaper, n.d., PRM 1923–24; Dabney, *Virginia,* 404.

9. Curry, *Civil History,* 242–43.

10. Merle E. Curti, *The Roots of American Loyalty* (1946; rept. New York, 1967), 177, 178.

11. "Report of the Landmark Committee," *YB* 1900:28. The APVA only placed the memorial in the mid-1920s (Couture, *To Preserve and Protect,* 169–70); W. W. Henry, "Patrick Henry," n.d., Henry Essays; Bryan to Col. John S. Mosby, 13 Nov. 1899, Bryan Letterbook.

12. Hall, "The Meeting Place," 8; Tyler, *Propaganda in History,* 1 (not coincidentally, the timing of this publication counteracted the Pilgrim Tercentennial in 1920); Cash, *Mind of the South,* 146.

13. Tyler to Ellyson, 14 Feb. 1924, PRM 1923–24.

14. Page quoted in Aaron, *Unwritten War,* 287; Page, *Address on the South;* Bruce to

Editor of the *Richmond News-Leader,* proof copy, 8 June 1914, Blackwall Monument Research file.

15. Bruce to Editor, *Richmond News Leader,* proof copy, 8 June 1914, to Ellyson, 3 Aug. 1914, Blackwall Monument Research file.

16. Cabell, *Let Me Lie,* 158; Tyler, *Propaganda in History,* 10–19; Tyler, *Confederate Catechism,* 27.

17. Anderson to Daniel, 4 June 1890, Anderson Letterbook.

18. Foster, *Ghosts of the Confederacy;* Parrott, "'Love Makes Memory Eternal,'" 219–38; John J. Winberry, "'Lest We Forget': The Confederate Monument and the Southern Townscape," *Southern Geographer* 23 (1983): 107–21; Dulaney, *Architecture of Historic Richmond,* 164–65.

19. Quoted in Dabney, *Richmond,* 276; Parrott, "'Love Makes Memory Eternal,'" 226–27.

20. "Report of Landmark Committee, *YB* 1901:37; Belle Bryan and her mother donated the Stewarts' family home, in which Lee had lived during the war, to the Virginia Historical Society in 1893 with the proviso that the APVA use it for its headquarters. Some preservationists thought that the association's constitution should have been heeded and the placement of this Confederate memorial to Lee be left to other organizations, but they were outvoted (central committee meeting, 2 Jan. 1900, MB).

21. "Address of Mrs. J. Taylor Ellyson," *YB* 1913:10; general meeting, 6 Nov. 1916, MB; James M. Lindgren, "Arlington," *Encyclopedia of the Confederacy,* ed. Richard N. Current (forthcoming).

22. Meetings, 4 Dec. 1918, 10 June 1919, MB.

23. Connelly and Bellows, *God and General Longstreet,* 45; Wilson, *Patriotic Gore,* 613; Chesson, *Richmond after the War,* 171–72; Osterweis, *Myth of the Lost Cause.*

24. Craven, *Legend of the Founding Fathers,* 84; Wecter, *Hero in America,* 25–30; Page, *Address at Jamestown,* 24; Valentine, "At the Opening of the New Building at the University College of Medicine," 24 Nov. 1897, Addresses, VM. Conveniently for the APVA, Marshall's early twentieth-century biographer repeated Page's estimation of Bacon (Albert J. Beveridge, *The Life of John Marshall* [Boston and New York, 1916], 1:6).

25. [Stanard], *Notes on a Journey to Jamestown;* "Report of Yorktown Branch," *YB* 1938:74.

26. William H. Payne to Coleman, 21 Feb. 1891, Tucker-Coleman Papers, box 58; Coleman to Bagby, 9 Nov. 1892, Bagby Papers 67; Galt to [Bagby], fragment of a draft letter, n.d, Bagby to Galt, 23 Apr. [1896], Galt Papers III.

27. Page quoted in Clement Eaton, *The Waning of the Old South Civilization, 1860–1880's* (Athens, Ga., 1968), 166.

28. Page, *Address on the South,* 17; Page quoted in Pulley, *Old Virginia Restored,* 61. C. Vann Woodward has argued that the New South swallowed its "bitter mixture of recantation and heresy" in the Old South's "syrup of romanticism." While calling the Old South myth "a cult of archaism," he downplayed its political usage (Woodward, *Origins of the New South,* 154, 158, and "The Southern Ethic in a Puritan World," *American Counterpoint,* 44; Gaston, *New South Creed,* 6–7).

29. Bryan to J. Henning Nelms, 13 Aug. 1896, Bryan Letterbook. The historical record extant in 1896 proved otherwise (Robert McColley, *Slavery and Jeffersonian Virginia,* 2d ed. [Urbana, Ill., 1973], 163; Jordan, *White over Black,* 320, 324).

30. Page, *Address on the South,* 15; Goodwin, "Three Hundred Years of Church Life and Influence in Virginia," in *Bruton Parish Church Restored,* 167.

31. Howells, "The South in Recent Literature," *Literary Digest* 17 (29 Oct. 1898):

518; Du Bois, "The Southerner's Problem," *Dial* 38 (1 May 1905): 316; Jackson and Davis, *Industrial History*, 22.

32. Tyler, *Virginia Principles*, 6.

33. C. Vann Woodward, "The Strange Career of a Historical Controversy," in *American Counterpoint*, 250; Eugene D. Genovese, "The Slave South: An Interpretation," in *The Political Economy of Slavery: Studies in the Economy and Society of the Slave South* (New York, 1965), 35; Page, *The Negro;* Rabinowitz, *Race Relations*, 334.

34. Hall, *Introductory Address, 1891,* 6; Bryan to R. H. Nelson, 17 Oct. 1902, Bryan Letterbook; Mary Newton, "Report of Landmark Committee," *YB* 1900:25–26; Patrick J. Hearden, *Independence and Empire: The New South's Cotton Mill Campaign* (DeKalb, Ill., 1982).

35. Lindgren, "'First and Foremost a Virginian,'" 157–80; David R. Goldfield, "The Urban South: A Regional Framework," *American Historical Review* 86 (1981): 1024–25; Grantham, *Southern Progressivism*.

36. "Virginia Homes and History," *Richmond Evening Leader*, 13 Jan. 1900; Page, "The Old South," in *The Old South,* 7.

37. Page, *Address at Jamestown*, 14–16; Coleman, "Jamestown," n.d., Coleman-Tucker Papers, box 102; John Stewart Bryan, "Speech at Blackwall," 1928, Blackwall Monument file, APVA; Goodwin, *Bruton Parish Church Restored,* 159.

38. Pryor, *Jamestown,* 334–35; "Oration of the Day," *Washington [D.C.] Evening News,* 18 Sept. 1893, Henry Scrapbook; Thomas P. Abernethy, *Three Virginia Frontiers* (University, La., 1940), 24.

39. Lawrence Goodwyn, *Democratic Promise: The Populist Moment in America* (New York, 1976); Milton A. McLaurin, *The Knights of the Labor in the South* (Westport, Conn., 1978).

40. General meeting, 4 May 1915, MB; Couture, *To Preserve and Protect,* 171.

41. Tyler quoted in "Settlement of Jamestown," *Richmond Times*, 14 May 1895.

42. Anderson, "Address before the Washington Literary Society," [25 June 1873], 5, VHS; Page, *Address on the South*, 24; Tyler, *South and Germany*, 9; Tyler, *Virginia Principles*, 23; Cash, *Mind of the South,* 140. Apparently the 1890s depression and merger mania dramatically affected Richmond. Bruce reported that the number of manufacturing establishments there declined from 966 to 763, but the total capital grew (Bruce, *Rise of the New South*, 236). As Richmond businesses were bought out by northerners, wealth increased, but local control diminished. As local power declined, Virginians insisted more strenuously on old cultural standards.

43. Cabell, *Virginia Municipalities;* Pryor, *My Day,* 424; Hofstadter, *Age of Reform,* 139.

44. Glassberg, *American Historical Pageantry*, 252.

45. Hosmer, *Preservation Comes of Age,* 232–74, 290–306.

46. Brownell, *Urban Ethos*, 196, 212, and chap. 7, "The Uses of Local History"; Kent, *Preservation of the Past*, 3; Meredith quoted in Christian, *Richmond,* 502.

47. "Mrs. Ellyson Indorses Movement for Pageant," unidentified newspaper, 26 Nov. 1920, PRM 1919–20; meeting, 2 May, 10 June 1922, MB; "Virginia Pageant Work," unidentified newspaper, 24 Apr. 1922, PRM 1922–23; David Glasberg, "History and the Public: Legacies of the Progressive Era," *Journal of American History* 73 (1987): 957–80.

48. "President's Report Submitted to Virginia Antiquities Group," *Richmond Times-Dispatch*, 9 Jan. 1927.

49. "A Strange Neglect," *Richmond Times-Dispatch,* 3 Mar. 1926; Cabell, *Let Me Lie,* 92; Loth, *Virginia Landmarks Register,* 480–81.

50. Fishwick, *Virginia,* 280; meetings, 4 May, 10 June, 1920, annual meeting, 4 Jan. 1922, MB; Lindgren, "'A Constant Incentive to Patriotic Citizenship,'" 594–608.

51. "Mrs. Ellyson Reviews Year's Work of A.P.V.A.," *Richmond Virginian,* 9 Jan. 1911, in "1894–1917 Washington Branch Record Book," APVA; Peters, *Virginia's Historical Markers,* ix; Fishwick, *Virginia Tradition,* 83, and *Virginia,* 280; Carson, *Historic Shrines.*

52. "Peninsula Pilgrimages," unidentified newspaper, n.d. [1924], PRM 1923–24; Huntley, *Peninsula Pilgrimage;* "Excursion a Success," unidentified newspaper, in letter from Nell Nottingham to Mrs. Lightfoot, 9 Nov. 1922, Northampton Branch Correspondence, box 3, APVA; Coleman, "Along the Lower James," 328–31.

53. "Jamestown Stands for 'Closed Sunday,'" unidentified newspaper, 19 May 1921, PRM 1920–21; "Felt He Was Treading on Hallowed Ground," unidentified newspaper, n.d. (dateline 7 May 1922), PRM 1922–23; Scott, "A.P.V.A.," 26.

54. Annual meetings, 4 Jan. 1910, 6 Jan. 1920, meetings, 6 Apr. 1920, 3 July 1922, MB.

55. [Joseph Bryan], "Preservation of Our Historical Landmarks," *Richmond Times,* 28 Nov. 1889.

56. Stanard, *Richmond,* xvii, xviii, 218, 223.

57. "Good Progress Shown in Preserving Relics," unidentified newspaper, 5 Jan. 1916, PRM 1915–16; Munford, *Random Recollections,* 199; Dabney, *Richmond,* 286.

58. Meeting, 10 June 1912, MB; Massie and Christian, *Homes and Gardens,* 219; Loth, *Virginia Landmarks Register,* 468.

59. Lightfoot to Bagby, 15 July 1907, Bagby Papers 72; [APVA], *Souvenir of The Midsummer Night's Dream* (Richmond, 1899); Yonge, Memorandum for Remarks at Jamestown, Oct. 1923, Yonge Papers, box 1F4, CWM.

60. Bruce et al., *Virginia: Rebirth of the Old Dominion* (Chicago, 1919), 2:332–33; L. Moody Simms, Jr., "History as Inspiration: Philip Alexander Bruce and the Old South Mystique," *McNeese Review* 18 (1967): 3–10; Charles Washington Coleman, "The Picturesque and Traditional in the Story of a Colonial City, an address delivered to the APVA 20 Mar. 1891," Tucker-Coleman Papers, box 101; Hawthorne, *Rambles in Old College Towns,* 54–55.

61. Bruce, *Virginia* 2:333; Rouse, *Cows on the Campus,* 106–10; Tyler to Yonge, 27 Sept. 1910, Yonge Papers 1299-7, UVA.

62. Galt to Bagby, 17 July 1895, Bagby Papers 78; Coleman quoted in Janet Kimbrough, "The Early History of the APVA," Colonial Capital Branch files, APVA.

63. "Mrs. Ellyson Reports on Work of Society," *Richmond Times-Dispatch,* 7 Jan. 1917; Cash, *Mind of the South,* 227.

9. "Upholding the Standards of Liberty"

1. Page, "Has Civilization Failed?" 1914 address, Page Papers 20B–35, Duke; Tyler, *Pocahontas,* 7–8, 14.

2. John S. Bryan, "Our World War," speech at YMCA, Bryan Scrapbook 1903–19; Baker to Maj. Gen. James W. McAndrew, 30 Dec. 1918, F. P. Keppel to Officers Commanding All Training Camps, 11 Sept. 1918, Bryan Scrapbook 1916–20; David S. Patterson, *Toward a Warless World: The Travail of the American Peace Movement, 1887–1914* (Bloomington, Ind., 1976), 250.

3. Directory board meeting, 1 Feb. 1916, board of managers meeting, 7 Apr. 1914, MB.

4. Bruce to Editor, *Richmond News-Leader,* proof copy, 1914, Bruce to [R. S.] Thomas, 23 Apr. 1914, Blackwall Monument Research file; Bruce, "Monument to Voyagers of 1606," *Richmond Times-Dispatch,* n.d., PRM 1915–16; Mary Newton, "Report of Landmark Committee," YB 1900:30; Bryan, "Speech at Blackwall," 1928, Bryan Scrapbook; annual report 1912–13, Norfolk Branch Annual Reports, box 3, APVA; meeting, 1 April 1913, MB; "Annual Report A.P.V.A.," unidentified newspaper, 11 Jan. 1914, in "1894–1917 Washington Branch Record Book," APVA.

5. Bruce to Editor, *Richmond News-Leader,* proof copy, 1914, Blackwall Monument Research file; Bruce, "Monument to Voyagers of 1606," *Richmond Times-Dispatch,* n.d., PRM 1915–16.

6. "Mrs. James Lyons Presented Cannon to Winchester," unidentified newspaper, 28 May 1915, Elizabeth Lyons Scrapbook 2.

7. Meetings, 13 Mar., 3 Apr. 1917, MB.

8. General meeting, 1 May 1917, PRM 1917–18; "In Honor of Jamestown," unidentified newspaper, n.d. (dateline 13 May 1917), PRM 1917–18.

9. "Barton Myers Making Address," *Norfolk Ledger-Dispatch,* 26 Oct. 1917; "La-Fayette Tablet and Its Unveiler," *Norfolk Ledger-Dispatch,* 25 Oct. 1917; meeting, 6 Nov. 1917, MB.

10. *Virginia Gazette* quoted in Mabel B. Friend, "Williamsburg and James City County in War Time," in *Virginia Communities in War Time,* ed. Arthur Kyle Davis, Publications of the Virginia War History Commission, 6 (Richmond, 1926), 601; Tyler, *South and Germany,* 3, 11. Wilson had personally courted Tyler by visiting his college earlier that month.

11. Quoted in Hawthorne, *Rambles in Old College Towns,* 49; "Miss Lee Abhors Thought of Great War," unidentified newspaper, n.d., in "1894–1917 Washington Branch Record Book," APVA; meeting, 1 May 1917, MB.

12. "Mrs. J. Taylor Ellyson's Address," *Association for the Preservation of Virginia Antiquities 1919* (Richmond, 1919), 9, 14.

13. Page, "Address" [1919], 30–32; Page, "Address to New England Manufacturers Association," 5 Sept. 1919, Page Papers 20B–36, Duke; Tyler, *Confederate Catechism,* 59.

14. John S. Bryan to Stewart, 6 Jan. 1919, Bryan Scrapbook 1916–20. After the U.S. Senate again rejected entry into the league in 1923, Mitchell helped form the "Friends of the League" with Bryan as its president (Mitchell, *Aftermath of Appomattox,* 223).

15. "Anglo-Saxon Unity Stressed as Hope of the Whole World," *Richmond Times-Dispatch,* 7 Oct. 1920; Laura Drake Gill to Mrs. J. Taylor Ellyson, n.d., PRM 1919–20; W. B. Southall, "Acclaim Virginia as Real Cradle of the Republic," *Richmond Times-Dispatch,* 8 Oct. 1920; meeting, 10 June 1920, MB; David I. Kertzer, *Ritual, Politics, and Power* (New Haven and London, 1988), chaps. 6, 9; Mrs. John B. Lightfoot, "Jamestown Annual Report, 1927–28," box 5, APVA.

16. Mary Newton, "Report of Landmark Committee," YB 1900:30; Bryan, "Speech at Blackwall," 1928, Bryan Scrapbook.

17. Ellyson to Bruce, 3 Feb. 1916, unsent, Blackwall Monument Research file; unidentified clippings, *Norfolk Virginian-Pilot* and *Norfolk Landmark,* 28 July 1927, Serpell Scrapbook, APVA; Bryan, "Speech at Blackwall," 1928, Bryan Scrapbook.

18. Bryan, "Speech at Blackwall," 1928, Bryan Scrapbook; "The Goodspeed," *Lon-*

don Times, 2 July 1928, "Girl to Unveil a Memorial," *London Evening Standard,* 25 June 1928, Serpell Scrapbook; for the text of the monument, see *YB* 1931:36–37.

19. Page, *Address on the South,* 3; meeting, 5 Apr. 1921, MB; Wesley Frank Craven, *The Virginia Company of London, 1606–1624* (Williamsburg, Va., 1957), 12.

20. "Report of Recording Secretary for 1896," *YB* 1898:23; "Report of Landmark Committee," *YB* 1901:37; "Report of First Vice President and Acting President," *YB* 1908:15; Mary Newton, "Report of Landmark Committee," *YB* 1900:25–26.

21. For proposed Washington markers, see "Report of Landmark Committee," *YB* 1900:29–30; Marling, *George Washington Slept Here,* chaps. 4–7.

22. Wecter, *Hero in America,* 99–147; Mayo, *Myths and Men,* 37–60; Karsten, *Patriot-Heroes,* 89; Cunliffe, *George Washington;* Schwartz, *George Washington;* quarterly meeting, 2 June 1896, MB.

23. Karsten, *Patriot-Heroes,* 95, table 5.3; meeting, 4 Dec. 1918, MB; W. E. Woodward, *George Washington: The Image and the Man* (1926; rept. New York, 1946), 8, 453–54.

24. Meetings, 6 Feb., 6 Mar., 3 Apr. 1923, MB; "Open Letter from Father Byrd to the A.P.V.A.," unidentified newspaper, n.d., PRM 1922–23; Coolidge quoted in Wecter, *Hero in America,* 144; Marling, *George Washington Slept Here,* chap. 8.

25. Daniel quoted in Pryor, *Mother of Washington,* 359–60.

26. Wallace, "Visiting the Past," 137–99.

27. Quarterly meeting, 3 Oct. 1889, MB; George Washington Ball to Mrs. John B. Lightfoot, 19 Aug. 1889, APVA Papers, VHS. The fate of the Virginia Relics Association is unknown, but five years later Ball donated the burial ground of his ancestor Colonel Burgess Ball, including more than ten graves, to the APVA; such a donation would not have occurred had the VRA still existed (Belle S. Bryan, "Report of the President," *YB* 1896:26).

28. Ball to Mrs. John B. Lightfoot, 19 Aug. 1889, Carmichael to Bryan, 13 Mar. 1890, APVA Papers, VHS; Newton, "The Association," 10; "Report 1893," Mary Washington Branch Correspondence, box 2, APVA. According to a later account, Chicagoans tried to purchase anything historic to enhance their fair. They removed from Richmond, for example, the notorious Libby Prison of the Confederacy ("Home of Washington's Mother Was Saved by Richmond Women," *Richmond Times-Dispatch,* n.d., PRM 1922–23).

29. Meeting, 3 Mar. 1891, MB; Joseph Bryan to J. L. Margue, 22, 25 Apr. 1890, Bryan Letterbook; Belle Bryan quoted in 7 May 1890 meeting, MB 1889–91; Lily Lykes Shepard, "Fredericksburg Landmark Restored," *DAR Magazine* 65 (1931): 273–78; Hosmer, *Presence of the Past,* 67; Mrs. Marshall C. Hall, "Report 1893," Mary Washington Branch Correspondence, box 2, APVA.

30. Elizabeth Coalter Carmichael, "Report of Fredericksburg Branch," *YB* 1900:40; Newton, "The Association," 16; Carmichael, "Report of Fredericksburg Branch," *YB* 1905:46–47; Mrs. C. M. Fleming, "Report of Fredericksburg Branch," *YB* 1910:46; Pryor, *Mother of Washington,* 181.

31. Pryor, *Mother of Washington,* 4–8.

32. Ibid., 3–8.

33. "Mrs. Ellyson's Address," *Fredericksburg Daily Star,* 14 June 1917, PRM 1917–18.

34. Russell to Ellyson, 20 May 1929, Properties file 9, APVA; Stillinger, *The Antiquers,* 212. The Mary Washington house drew 1,068, the Rising Sun Tavern 409, and Jamestown 1,024 (annual meeting, 6 Jan. 1920, MB).

35. Fleming to Ellyson, 14 Feb. 1931, Properties file 9.
36. Appleton, Notes concerning the Home of Washington's Mother at Fredericksburg, n.d., Virginia file, SPNEA.
37. Russell to Ellyson, 16 Feb. 1931, Fleming to Ellyson, 20 Feb. 1931, Properties file 9.
38. Marling, *George Washington Slept Here,* chap. 11; "Report of Mary Washington Branch," *YB* 1931:50, *YB* 1934:58–59.
39. Appleton to Ellyson, 1 Aug. 1922, Appleton to Wendell, 24 Nov. 1922, Virginia file; Federal Writers' Project, *Virginia,* 223–24.
40. Ann Flanders, "Forts Norfolk and Nelson Built to Withstand the Test of Time," *Norfolk Compass* 10–11 (Oct. 1984) Fort Norfolk file, NPL; Loth, *Virginia Landmarks Register,* 293; "A.P.V.A. Opposes Proposed Razing of Old Fort Norfolk," *Richmond Times-Dispatch,* 2 May 1923; general meeting, 1 May 1923, and Dwight F. Davis to Mrs. Arthur P. Wilmer, 28 May 1923, MB.
41. Meetings, 6 Feb., 6 Mar., 2 Oct. 1923, MB; Loth, *Virginia Landmarks Register,* 52; Ronald F. Lee, *The Antiquities Act of 1906* (Washington, D.C., 1970), 94.
42. Walter Muir Whitehill, "The Right of Cities to Be Beautiful," in *With Heritage So Rich: A Report of a Special Committee on Historic Preservation under the Auspices of the United States Conference of Mayors,* ed. Albert Rains and Laurance G. Henderson (New York, 1966), 48; Harbaugh, *Power and Responsibility,* 33.
43. Meeting, 6 Nov. 1923, MB; Loth, *Virginia Landmarks Register,* 234; Lora H. Ellyson, "The A.P.V.A., " 8, VHS.
44. Joseph Bryan to Dr. W. P. Palmer, 7 Apr. 1892, Bryan Letterbook; central committee, 7 Feb. 1906, MB.
45. Anderson to Gov. Andrew J. Montague, 3 Apr. 1903, Anderson Letterbook; meetings, 2 May, 10 June 1922, MB; Mrs. J. Taylor Ellyson to editor, *Richmond Times-Dispatch,* 23 Aug. 1925; Kopper, *Colonial Williamsburg,* 187.
46. General meeting, 1 May 1923, MB; Hosmer, *Presence of the Past,* chap. 8; "Speech of W. W. Henry," *Richmond State,* 20 Dec. 1879, Henry Scrapbook.
47. Page, "Thomas Jefferson: Apostle of Liberty," address, n.d., Page Papers 20B–36; Mayo, *Myths and Men,* chap 3.
48. Grantham, "Contours of Southern Progressivism," 1054.
49. "Saving Virginia's History," *Richmond Times-Dispatch,* 8 Jan. 1925; "Few Realize How Much Has Been Done in These Six Years," *Richmond News-Leader,* 18 Feb. 1929.
50. Appleton to Kimball, 16 Apr. 1923, APVA file, SPNEA. Appleton mentioned the courthouses in Chesterfield, Stafford, Prince George, Westmoreland, and Shenandoah counties. The first three had been pulled down, the fourth lost in an enlarged structure, and the last modernized (Federal Writers' Project, *Virginia,* 348, 421, 547, 572, 575).
51. Appleton to Ellyson, 13 June 1923, Kimball to Appleton, 7 July 1923, APVA file.
52. Ellyson to Appleton, 19 June 1923, Appleton to Kimball, 16 Apr. 1923, ibid.; Appleton to Kimball, 27 June 1923, Kimball file, SPNEA.
53. Ellyson to Appleton, 19 June 1923, APVA file.
54. "Virginia's Court-Houses," *Richmond Times,* 3 Feb. 1900.
55. Henry, "Virginia of the Revolutionary Period," 29 Dec. 1891, Henry Speeches.

10. "A Spirit That Fires the Imagination"

1. Meetings, 1 May 1917, 4 Jan. 1918, MB.
2. "The Tragedy of Jamestown," Mrs. J. Taylor Ellyson to the editor, *Richmond Times-Dispatch,* 2 June 1925.
3. Meetings, 6 Apr. 1920, Oct., Nov. 1921, 4 Dec. 1923, MB; "Foreword," *YB* 1931:4.
4. "Anniversary Service Held at Jamestown," *Richmond Times-Dispatch,* 21 Jan. 1915; meetings, Oct. 1921, 10 June 1922, MB. A decade later the fact that Colonial Williamsburg was open on the Sabbath sparked some controversy, however (Kammen, *Mystic Chords of Memory,* 365–66).
5. Coleman to Messrs. Phipps, Slocum & Co., 8 Nov. 1895, Coleman-Tucker Papers, box 58; meetings, 16 Oct. 1905, 15 Mar. 1906, CCB Minutes 1900–1934, CWM; Jamestown Annual Report, 1922–23, box 5, APVA; Bishop Alfred M. Randolph to Mrs. Joseph Bryan, 27 July 1909, Bryan Family Papers 12; Mrs. J. Taylor Ellyson, acceptance address, 15 June 1922, MB. For the destroyed mill and the role of the Colonial Dames, see Jamestown Annual Report, 1922–23, box 5, APVA.
6. William W. Old, *Robert Hunt Memorial* (n.p.: Episcopal Church, n.d. [c.1906]), in Jamestown vertical file, VM; Goodwin, *Bruton Parish Church Restored,* 198; Huntley, *Peninsula Pilgrimage,* 332.
7. Tyler, *Virginia First,* 11; Crunden, *Ministers of Reform.*
8. Goodwin, "The Spiritual and Ideal Significance of Bruton Parish Church, Restored," *Bruton Parish Church Restored,* 188; Bryan, "Speech before Episcopal Assembly," n.d. (1897), Bryan Letterbook; Bagby, untitled essay on Gloucester, n.d., Bagby Papers 23.
9. "Report of the Kicotan Branch," *YB* 1908:54–55.
10. "A Bill for the Purchase and Preservation of Jamestown Island," 62d Cong., 1st sess., HR 12423, 12 July 1911, APVA.
11. Ellyson, "President's Address," *YB* 1931:11–12; "Mrs. Ellyson Emphasizes Year's Work of A.P.V.A.," *Richmond News-Leader,* 3 Jan. 1931.
12. David L. Moffitt, Superintendent of Colonial National Park, to author, 18 Jan. 1989; Helene S. Ward, James City County Clerk of Circuit Court, to author, 19 Jan. 1989; "Report of Jamestown Committee," *YB* 1938:28–30; "Report of Jamestown Committee," *YB* 1941:29; Federal Writers' Project, *Virginia,* 494–95; Kammen, *Mystic Chords of Memory,* 367.
13. Board of managers meeting, 6 Oct. 1896, annual meeting, 4 Jan. 1897, general meeting, 19 Oct. 1900, central committee meeting, 6 May 1902, MB.
14. Loth, *Virginia Landmarks Register,* 98; Trudell, *Colonial Yorktown,* 18, 25–26; McGuire quoted in "Yorktown Campaign," *Richmond Dispatch,* 16 Jan. 1897; meeting, 18 Feb. 1921, Minutes, Yorktown Branch APVA, CWM.
15. Meeting, 3 Feb. 1920, MB; meeting, 10 June 1921, Minutes, Yorktown Branch APVA; "Planning Park for Yorktown," *Richmond News-Leader,* n.d. (dateline 2 Feb. 1923), PRM 1922–23; William J. Murtagh, *Keeping Time: The History and Theory of Preservation in America* (Pittstown, N.J., 1988), 173–74.
16. Appleton to Kimball, 12 June 1924, Yorktown file, SPNEA.
17. Jean Henri Clos, *Yorktown Country Club* (New York, 1924), 2, 10, 12, 14.
18. Ibid., 16, 25.

19. Appleton to Secretary, Yorktown Country Club, 17 Dec. 1924, Yorktown file, SPNEA.

20. Swanson to Mrs. George D. Chenoweth, 3 Nov. 1921, Chenoweth to Bland, 1 Nov. 1921, Bland to Chenoweth, 26 Nov. 1921, Minutes, Yorktown Branch APVA; Raymond W. Smilor, "Creating a National Festival: The Campaign for a Safe and Sane Fourth, 1903–1916," *Journal of American Culture* 2 (1980): 611–22.

21. Trudell, *Colonial Yorktown,* 149–50.

22. Goodwin, *Church Enchained,* 36, 67.

23. Ibid., 19, 20, 21, 56.

24. Goodwin, *Bruton Parish Church Restored,* 33; Hosmer, *Preservation Comes of Age,* 11–12; Stillinger, *The Antiquers,* 272–79.

25. Rouse, *Cows on the Campus,* 164–65; Fishwick, *Virginia,* 245.

26. Hawthorne, *Rambles in Old College Towns,* 44, 48, 67.

27. Central committee meeting, 2 May 1911, MB; Ellyson to the City Council of Williamsburg, 12 Apr. 1911, PRM 1911–12; Whiffen, *Public Buildings of Williamsburg,* 199.

28. Central committee meeting, Apr. 1919, MB; Mrs. J. Enders Robinson to the Honorable School Board, 22 Mar. 1919, in Byrd, *Public Schools in Williamsburg,* 53.

29. Quoted in Byrd, *Public Schools in Williamsburg,* 54, 57.

30. Wecter, *Hero in America,* 49; W. G. Stanard to editor, 25 Mar. 1925, *Richmond Times-Dispatch,* n.d., PRM 1924–25; "Valuable Statue of Botetourt Is Moved at W & M," *Richmond News Leader,* 24 Mar. 1925; Linwood Norman, "Confederate Still Causes a Problem," *Newport News Daily Press,* 11 Apr. 1982.

31. Meetings, 1 Dec. 1916, 17 Apr. 1922, CCB Minutes, box 1; central committee meeting, 5 Dec. 1916, MB.

32. Meetings, 20 Apr. 1923, 14 Nov. 1925, CCB Minutes, box 1; Richard L. Morton, Report, 2 July 1925, CCB, box 2; "Save the 'Powder Horn,'" *Richmond News Leader,* n.d., PRM 1924–25.

33. Ellyson to Coleman, 28 Nov. 1925, CCB, box 2; Coleman to Ellyson, 15 Apr. 1926, PRM 1926–27.

34. Meetings, Jan. 1924, 12 Feb. 1925, CCB Minutes, box 1. Later Goodwin also hunted for antiques to fill the buildings of reconstructed Williamsburg and readily used northern furniture.

35. Meeting, 1 Dec. 1924, CCB Minutes, box 1; *Baltimore Sun* quoted in Noël Hume, *Here Lies Virginia,* 85. Hall would serve as Williamsburg's mayor from 1934 to 1947 and oversee the early years of Colonial Williamsburg.

36. Goodwin quoted in Yetter, *Williamsburg,* 51–52.

37. Hosmer, *Preservation Comes of Age,* 15, 22; Yetter, *Williamsburg,* 51–55.

38. "Mrs. Ellyson Reports on Work of Society," *Richmond Times-Dispatch,* 7 Jan. 1917; Noël Hume, *Here Lies Virginia,* 85; Colonial Williamsburg Foundation, *Official Guidebook* (Williamsburg, Va., 1972), 51–52.

39. Meeting, 1 Dec. 1924, CCB Minutes, box 1.

40. Murray McGuire to Mrs. J. Taylor Ellyson, 1 Nov. 1927, copy, Yonge Papers 1299-7, UVA; meeting, 29 Dec. 1927, CCB Minutes, box 1; Goodwin cited in Kopper, *Colonial Williamsburg,* 165, 168. Goodwin appeared before the advisory board in November and the central committee in December 1927.

41. Ellyson to Members, 15 May 1928, APVA file, VHS; Bryan quoted in Kopper,

Colonial Williamsburg, 165. APVA later donated the land outright to the Williamsburg Holding Corporation ("Foreword," *YB* 1931:4).

42. Byrd, *Public Schools in Williamsburg,* 65; Rouse, *Cows on the Campus,* 186–87; Yetter, *Williamsburg,* 55; Freeman quoted in Kopper, *Colonial Williamsburg,* 164.

43. Cabell, *Let Me Lie,* 134; Kopper, *Colonial Williamsburg,* 204, 208; Ada Louise Huxtable, "Lively Original versus Dead Copy," and "Where Did We Go Wrong?" *New York Times,* 9 May 1965, 14 July 1968; Wallace, "Visiting the Past," 147; Zelinsky, *Nation into State,* 95.

44. Swem, "Report of the Capitol Committee," *YB* 1934:41; Yonge, Appendix A, ibid., 42–43.

45. [Bright], *Memories of Williamsburg,* 22–23.

46. Mitchell, *Aftermath of Appomattox,* 221.

47. Ellyson, "President's Address," *YB* 1931:15.

48. "Report of the Committee on the Publick Prison," *YB* 1931:39–41; "Final Report of the Committee on the Publick Prison," *YB* 1934:47–48; "President's Address," ibid., 14; "A.P.V.A. to Get and Restore Jail at Williamsburg," *Richmond News-Leader,* 25 June 1924; "Seek Exchange of Cottage for Jail," ibid., 27 May 1929; Report of Colonial Capital Branch, 3 Jan. 1934, APVA; Lora Ellyson, "The A.P.V.A.," VHS.

49. Meeting, 5 Dec. 1911, MB; "Historical Society Says 'Smith's Fort' Was Not Discovered by Bishop," unidentified newspaper, PRM 1923–24; "Seek Exchange of Cottage for Jail," *Richmond News-Leader,* 27 May 1929; "President's Address," *YB* 1934:14; "Report of Thomas Rolfe Branch," ibid., 84.

50. Cabell, *Let Me Lie,* 90. Further investigation has discovered that "Smith's Fort Plantation" has no links with Warren either. It was probably built in the mid-eighteenth century (Loth, *Virginia Landmarks Register,* 457–58).

51. For the courthouse, see N. P. Dunn, "Foreword," *YB* 1941:5, and Loth, *Virginia Landmarks Register,* 210; for the bridge, see "Report of Rockbridge Branch," *YB* 1938:95, 97, and Carrington C. Tutwiler, *The Ruth Anderson McCulloch Branch of the Association for the Preservation of Virginia Antiquities* (Williamsburg, Va., 1989), 1.

52. Scott, *House of Old Richmond,* 45, 76–77, 118–19.

53. Scott, "A.P.V.A.," 27; Dulaney, *Architecture of Historic Richmond,* 39.

54. Scott, "A.P.V.A.," 28.

55. Ibid., 30–31.

56. Ibid., 31; Scott, "Report of William Byrd Branch," *YB* 1938:91–92; Scott, *Old Richmond Neighborhoods.*

57. Dulaney, *Architecture of Historic Richmond,* 50–51, 136, 143; "Report of the Pulliam House," *YB* 1941:38. Years later the APVA sold the Glasgow house, as it did the Hancock-Wirt-Caskie house, with restrictive covenants to protect the building's appearance.

58. Appleton to Donald Millar, 21 Mar. 1928, Virginia file, SPNEA; Appleton to Kimball, 16 Apr. 1923, APVA file, SPNEA; Appleton to E. J. Frothingham, 14 Sept. 1918, Hazen Garrison file, SPNEA; Ellyson, "President's Address," *YB* 1934:14.

59. "Holland Article on Preservation Causes Comment: Group Formed in 1910 Is Placed Ahead of A.P.V.A.," unidentified newspaper, n.d., and Holland to Ellyson, 16 Nov. 1933, Organizations file, APVA.

60. Holland quoted in "President Roosevelt Leader in Movement to Halt Destruction of Nation's Landmarks," unidentified newspaper, n.d. [May 1933], ibid.; Hosmer,

Preservation Comes of Age, 548–62; "Consolidated Report of the John Marshall House Committee," *YB* 1938:32.

Epilogue: The Hegemony of Traditionalism

1. Fishwick, *Virginia,* 267, 279, and *Virginia Tradition.*
2. Bryan, "Report of the President for 1903," *YB* 1905:6; "Foreword," *YB* 1938:6.
3. Lears, "Concept of Cultural Hegemony," 567–93.
4. Jamestown Annual Report, 1922–23, unsigned carbon copy, box 5, APVA.
5. Dearing, *Veterans in Politics;* Davies, *Patriotism on Parade;* Foster, *Ghosts of the Confederacy.*
6. Wallace, "Visiting the Past," 137–61; Carroll Van West and Mary S. Hoffsch- welle, "'Slumbering on Its Old Foundations': Interpretation at Colonial Williamsburg," *South Atlantic Quarterly* 83 (1984): 157–75.
7. Rex M. Ellis, "Presenting the Past: Education, Interpretation, and the Teaching of Black History at Colonial Williamsburg" (Ed.D. diss., College of William and Mary, 1989); Barbara J. Howe, "Women in Historic Preservation: The Legacy of Ann Pamela Cunningham," *Public Historian* 12 (1990): 31–61; McCarthy, *Women's Culture,* 111–45.

Select Bibliography

Aaron, Daniel. *The Unwritten War: American Writers and the Civil War.* The Impact of the Civil War, ed. Harold M. Hyman. New York: Knopf, 1973.

Albanese, Catherine L. *Sons of the Fathers: The Civil Religion of the American Revolution.* Philadelphia: Temple Univ. Press, 1976.

Ashbee, C[harles] R. *A Report to the Council of the National Trust for Places of Historic Interest and Natural Beauty, on His Visit to the United States on the Council's Behalf, October 1900 to February 1901.* London: Essex House Press, 1901.

Badger, R. Reid. *The Great American Fair: The World's Columbian Exposition and American Culture.* Chicago: Nelson-Hall, 1979.

Bailey, Kenneth K. *Southern White Protestantism in the Twentieth Century.* New York: Harper & Row, 1964.

Baltzell, E. Digby. *The Protestant Establishment: Aristocracy and Caste in America* New York: Random House, 1964.

Bellah, Robert N. *The Broken Covenant: American Civil Religion in Time of Trial.* New York: Seabury Press, 1975.

Berkhofer, Robert F., Jr. *The White Man's Indian: Images of the American Indian from Columbus to the Present.* New York: Knopf, 1978.

Bertelson, David. *The Lazy South.* New York: Oxford Univ. Press, 1967.

Blair, Karen J. *The Clubwoman as Feminist: True Womanhood Redefined, 1868–1914.* New York and London: Holmes and Meier, 1980.

Bridenbaugh, Carl. *Jamestown, 1544–1699.* New York: Oxford Univ. Press, 1980.

Bright, Robert S. *The Address at the Unveiling of the Memorial Window to Nathaniel Bacon on the Powder Horn at Williamsburg, Virginia, November 14, 1901.* Richmond, 1941.

——. *Memories of Williamsburg and Stories of My Father.* Richmond: Garrett & Massie, 1941.

Brownell, Blaine A. *The Urban Ethos in the South, 1920–1930.* Baton Rouge: Louisiana State Univ. Press, 1975.

Bruce, Philip Alexander. *The Rise of the New South.* The History of North America, ed. Guy Carleton Lee, vol. 17. Philadelphia: G. Barrie, 1905.

Bryan, John Stewart. *Joseph Bryan: His Times, His Family, His Friends.* Richmond: Whittet & Shepperson, 1935.

Bryan, J[oseph], III. *The Sword over the Mantel: The Civil War and I.* New York: McGraw Hill, 1960.

Buck, Paul H. *The Road to Reunion, 1865–1900.* Boston: Little, Brown, 1937.

Byrd, Rawls. *History of Public Schools in Williamsburg.* Williamsburg, Va.: privately printed, 1968.

Cabell, J. Alston. *An Address to the League of Virginia Municipalities.* Richmond: Wm. Ellis Jones, 1907.

———. *Patrick Henry: An Address.* Richmond: Everett Waddey Co., 1902.

Cabell, James Branch. *Let Me Lie: Being in the Main an Ethnological Account of the Remarkable Commonwealth of Virginia and the Making of Its History.* New York: Farrar, Straus., 1947.

Carson, William E. *Historic Shrines of Virginia.* Richmond: State Commission on Conservation and Development, 1933.

Cash, W. J. *The Mind of the South.* 1941. Rept. New York: Vintage Books, 1969.

Chesson, Michael B. *Richmond after the War, 1865–1890.* Richmond: Virginia State Library, 1981.

Christian, W. Asbury. *Richmond: Her Past and Present.* Richmond: L. H. Jenkins, 1912.

Coleman, Charles Washington. "Along the Lower James." *Century Magazine* 41 (1891): 323–33.

Connelly, Thomas L., and Barbara L. Bellows. *God and General Longstreet: The Lost Cause and the Southern Mind.* Baton Rouge: Louisiana State Univ. Press, 1982.

Couture, Richard T. *To Preserve and Protect: A History of the Association for the Preservation of Virginia Antiquities.* Dallas: APVA, 1984.

Craven, Wesley Frank. *The Legend of the Founding Fathers.* Ithaca, N.Y.: Cornell Univ. Press, 1956.

Crunden, Robert M. *Ministers of Reform: The Progressives' Achievement in American Civilization, 1889–1920.* New York: Basic Books, 1982.

Cunliffe, Marcus. *George Washington, Man and Monument.* Boston: Little, Brown, 1958.

Curry, J. L. M. *Address before the Association of Confederate Veterans, Richmond, Virginia, July 1, 1896.* Richmond: B. F. Johnson, 1896.

———. *A Brief Sketch of George Peabody, and a History of the Peabody Education Fund through Thirty Years.* Cambridge, Mass.: Harvard Univ. Press, 1898.

———. *Civil History of the Government of the Confederate States with Some Personal Reminiscences.* Richmond: B. F. Johnson, 1900.

———. *Lessons of the Yorktown Centennial: An Address Delivered in Richmond on 22 October 1881.* Richmond: Dispatch Steam Printing House, 1881.

———. *North American Colonization, with Particular Reference to Virginia and the Carolinas.* Washington, D.C., 1896.

Dabney, Virginius. *Richmond: The Story of a City.* Garden City, N.Y.: Doubleday, 1976.

———. *Virginia: The New Dominion.* Garden City, N.Y.: Doubleday, 1971.

Davies, Wallace Evan. *Patriotism on Parade: The Story of Veterans' and Hereditary*

Organizations in America, 1783–1900. Cambridge, Mass.: Harvard Univ. Press, 1955.

Dearing, Mary R. *Veterans in Politics: The Story of the G.A.R.* Baton Rouge: Louisiana State Univ. Press, 1952.

Degler, Carl N. *At Odds: Women and the Family in America from the Revolution to the Present.* New York: Oxford Univ. Press, 1980.

———. *The Other South: Southern Dissenters in the Nineteenth Century.* New York: Harper & Row, 1974.

Dorsey, Stephen P. *Early English Churches in America, 1607–1807.* New York: Oxford Univ. Press, 1952.

Dulaney, Paul S. *The Architecture of Historic Richmond.* 2d ed. Charlottesville: Univ. Press of Virginia, 1976.

Ellyson, Mrs. J[ames] Taylor [Lora H.]. *The First Permanent Settlement in America.* Richmond: APVA, [1926?].

Elson, Ruth M. *Guardians of Tradition: American Schoolbooks of the Nineteenth Century.* Lincoln: Univ. of Nebraska Press, 1964.

Fass, Paula S. *The Damned and the Beautiful: American Youth in the 1920's.* New York: Oxford Univ. Press, 1977.

Federal Writers' Project. *Virginia: A Guide to the Old Dominion.* New York: Oxford Univ. Press, 1941.

Fink, Leon. *Workingmen's Democracy: The Knights of Labor and American Politics.* Urbana and Chicago: Univ. of Illinois Press, 1983.

Fishwick, Marshall W. *The Hero, American Style.* New York: David McKay Co., 1969.

———. *Virginia: A New Look at the Old Dominion.* New York: Harper & Brothers, 1959.

———. *The Virginia Tradition.* Washington, D.C.: Public Affairs Press, 1956.

Foner, Eric. *Reconstruction: America's Unfinished Revolution, 1863–1877.* New York: Harper & Row, 1988.

Forgie, George B. *Patricide in the House Divided: A Psychological Interpretation of Lincoln and His Age.* New York: Norton, 1979.

Forman, Henry C. *Jamestown and St. Mary's: Buried Cities of Romance.* Baltimore: Johns Hopkins Univ. Press, 1938.

Foster, Gaines M. *Ghosts of the Confederacy: Defeat, the Lost Cause, and the Emergence of the New South, 1865–1913.* New York and Oxford: Oxford Univ. Press, 1987.

Friedman, Jean E. *The Enclosed Garden: Women and Community in the Evangelical South, 1830–1900.* Chapel Hill and London: Univ. of North Carolina Press, 1985.

Friedman, Lawrence J. *The White Savage: Racial Fantasies in the Postbellum South.* Englewood Cliffs, N.J.: Prentice-Hall, 1970.

Furnas, J. C. *The Americans: A Social History, 1587–1914.* New York: G. P. Putnam's Sons, 1969.

Gaston, Paul M. *The New South Creed: A Study in Southern Mythmaking*. New York: Knopf, 1970.

Geertz, Clifford. *The Interpretation of Culture: Selected Essays*. New York: Basic Books, 1973.

Ginzberg, Lori D. *Women and the Work of Benevolence: Morality, Politics, and Class in the Nineteenth-Century United States*. New Haven and London: Yale Univ. Press. 1990.

Glassberg, David. *American Historical Pageantry: The Uses of Tradition in the Early Twentieth Century*. Chapel Hill and London: Univ. of North Carolina Press, 1990.

Goodwin, William A. R. *Bruton Parish Church Restored and Its Historic Environment*. Petersburg, Va.: Franklin Press, 1907.

———. *The Church Enchained*. New York: E. P. Dutton, 1916.

———. *Historical Sketch of Bruton Church, Williamsburg, Virginia*. Petersburg, Va.: Franklin Press, 1903.

Grantham, Dewey W. "The Contours of Southern Progressivism." *American Historical Review* 86 (1981): 1035–59.

———. *Southern Progressivism: The Reconciliation of Progress and Tradition*. Knoxville: Univ. of Tennessee Press, 1983.

Gray, Richard. *Writing the South: Ideas of an American Region*. Cambridge: Cambridge Univ. Press, 1986.

Green, Harvey. *Fit for America: Health, Fitness, Sport, and American Society*. New York: Pantheon Books, 1986.

———. *The Light of the Home: An Intimate View of the Lives of Women in Victorian America*. New York: Pantheon Books, 1983.

Green, Theodore. *America's Heroes: The Changing Models of Success in American Magazines*. New York: Oxford Univ. Press, 1970.

Hall, John Lesslie. *Half-Hours in Southern History*. Richmond: B. F. Johnson, 1907.

———. *Introductory Address at the Jamestown Celebration, Held May 13th 1895*. Richmond, 1895.

———. *Introductory Address at the Jamestown Celebration, May 13th, 1891*. Richmond: J. L. Hill, 1891.

———. "The Meeting Place of the First Virginia Assembly." In *Exercises and Addresses at the Celebration of the 300th Anniversary of the First Law Making Body on the Western Hemisphere Which Convened at Jamestown, July 30, 1619*. Richmond, 1919.

Hall, Peter Dobkin. *The Organization of American Culture, 1700–1900: Private Institutions, Elites, and the Origins of American Nationality*. New York: New York Univ. Press, 1982.

Harrington, Virginia S. "Theories and Evidence for the Location of James Fort." *Virginia Magazine of History and Biography* 93 (1985): 36–53.

Hartmann, Edward G. *The Movement to Americanize the Immigrants*. New York: Columbia Univ. Press, 1948.

Hawthorne, Hildegarde. *Rambles in Old College Towns*. New York: Dodd, Mead, 1917.

Higham, John. *Strangers in the Land: Patterns of American Nativism, 1860–1925*. New York: Atheneum, 1978.

Hobsbawm, Eric, and Terence Ranger, eds. *The Invention of Tradition*. Cambridge: Cambridge Univ. Press, 1983.

Hofstadter, Richard. *The Age of Reform: From Bryan to F.D.R.* New York: Knopf, 1955.

———. *Anti-Intellectualism in American Life*. New York: Knopf, 1963.

Holman, Harriet R. "The Literary Career of Thomas Nelson Page, 1884–1910." Ph.D. diss., Duke Univ., 1947.

Horne, Donald. *The Great Museum: The Re-Presentation of History*. London and Sydney: Pluto Press, 1984.

Hosmer, Charles B., Jr. "The Broadening View of the Historic Preservation Movement." In *Material Culture and the Study of American Life*, ed. Ian M. G. Quimby. New York: Norton, 1978.

———. *Presence of the Past: A History of the Preservation Movement in the United States before Williamsburg*. New York: G. P. Putnam's Sons, 1965.

———. *Preservation Comes of Age: From Williamsburg to the National Trust*. Charlottesville: Univ. Press of Virginia, 1981.

Hubbell, Jay. *The South in American Literature, 1607–1900*. Durham, N.C.: Duke Univ. Press, 1954.

Huntley, Elizabeth Valentine. *Peninsula Pilgrimage*. Richmond: Whittet & Shepperson, 1941.

Jackson, Giles B., and D. Webster Davis. *The Industrial History of the Negro Race in the United States*. Richmond: Virginia Press, 1908.

James, Henry. *The American Scene*, ed. W. H. Auden. New York: Charles Scribner's Sons, 1946.

Jordan, Winthrop D. *White over Black: American Attitudes toward the Negro, 1550–1812*. Chapel Hill: Univ. of North Carolina Press, 1968.

Kammen, Michael. *Mystic Chords of Memory: The Transformation of Tradition in American Culture*. New York: Knopf, 1991.

———. *People of Paradox: An Inquiry concerning the Origins of American Civilization*. New York: Knopf, 1972.

———. *A Season of Youth: The American Revolution and the Historical Imagination*. New York: Knopf, 1978.

———. *Spheres of Liberty: Changing Perceptions of Liberty in American Culture*. Madison: Univ. of Wisconsin Press, 1986.

Karsten, Peter. *Patriot-Heroes in England and America: Political Symbolism and Changing Values over Three Centuries*. Madison: Univ. of Wisconsin Press, 1978.

Kasson, John F. *Civilizing the Machine: Technology and Republican Values in America, 1776–1900*. New York: Grossman Publishers, 1976.

Kelly, Jeannette S. *The First Restoration in Williamsburg: A Brief Review of the Cath-*

arine Memorial Society and Early Activities of the Association for the Preservation of Virginia Antiquities. Richmond: APVA, 1933.

Kent, Charles W. *The Preservation of the Past: An Address Delivered before the Association for the Preservation of Virginia Antiquities in the House of Delegates, Richmond, Va., on March 14, 1901.* Richmond: Wm. Ellis Jones, 1901.

Kimbrough, Janet C. "The Early History of the Association for the Preservation of Virginia Antiquities: A Personal Account." *Virginia Cavalcade* 30 (1980): 68–75.

Kirby, Jack Temple. *Darkness at the Dawning: Race and Reform in the Progressive South.* Philadelphia: J. B. Lippincott, 1972.

Kopper, Philip. *Colonial Williamsburg.* New York: Harry N. Abrams, 1986.

Kousser, J. Morgan. *The Shaping of Southern Politics: Suffrage Restriction and the Establishment of the One-Party South, 1880–1910.* New Haven: Yale Univ. Press, 1974.

Lamar, Mrs. Joseph R. *A History of the National Society of Colonial Dames of America from 1891 to 1933.* Atlanta: Walter R. Brown, 1934.

Lancaster, Robert A., Jr. *Historic Virginia Homes and Churches.* Philadelphia and London: J. B. Lippincott, 1915.

Lears, T. J. Jackson. "The Concept of Cultural Hegemony: Problems and Possibilities." *American Historical Review* 90 (1985): 567–93.

——. *No Place of Grace: Antimodernism and the Transformation of American Culture, 1880–1920.* New York: Pantheon Books, 1981.

Lebsock, Suzanne. *The Free Women of Petersburg: Status and Culture in a Southern Town, 1784–1860.* New York and London: Norton, 1984.

——. *"A Share of Honour": Virginia Women, 1600–1945.* Richmond: Virginia Women's Cultural History Project, 1984.

Leon, Warren, and Roy Rosenzweig, eds. *History Museums in the United States: A Critical Assessment.* Urbana and Chicago: Univ. of Illinois Press, 1989.

Lindgren, James M. "APVA: Uniting Town and Gown," *William and Mary Magazine* 57 (Summer 1989): 30–31.

——. "'A Constant Incentive to Patriotic Citizenship': Historic Preservation in Progressive-Era Massachusetts," *New England Quarterly* 64 (1991): 594–608.

——. "'First and Foremost a Virginian': Joseph Bryan and the New South Economy." *Virginia Magazine of History and Biography* 96 (1988): 152–80.

——. "'For the Sake of Our Future': The Association for the Preservation of Virginia Antiquities and the Regeneration of Traditionalism," *Virginia Magazine of History and Biography* 97 (1989): 47–74.

——. "Pater Patriae: George Washington as Symbol and Artifact." *American Quarterly* 41 (1989): 705–13.

——. *Preserving Historic New England: Yankee Preservation and Traditionalism in the Early Twentieth Century* (forthcoming).

——. "'Virginia Needs Living Heroes': Historic Preservation in the Progressive Era," *Public Historian* 13 (1991): 9–24.

——. "'Whatever Is Un-Virginian Is Wrong': The APVA's Sense of the Old Dominion," *Virginia Cavalcade* 38 (1989): 112–23.

Loth, Calder, ed. *The Virginia Landmarks Register.* 3d ed. Charlottesville: Univ. Press of Virginia, 1986.

Lowenthal, David. *The Past Is a Foreign Country.* Cambridge and New York: Cambridge Univ. Press, 1985.

McCarthy, Kathleen D. *Women's Culture: American Philanthropy and Art, 1830–1930.* Chicago and London: Univ. of Chicago Press, 1991.

McDannell, Colleen. *The Christian Home in Victorian America, 1860–1900.* Bloomington: Indiana Univ. Press, 1986.

Maddex, Jack P., Jr. *The Virginia Conservatives, 1867–1879: A Study in Reconstruction Politics.* Chapel Hill: Univ. of North Carolina Press, 1970.

Marling, Karal Ann. *George Washington Slept Here: Colonial Revivals and American Culture, 1876–1986.* Cambridge, Mass., and London: Harvard Univ. Press, 1988.

Marx, Leo. *The Machine in the Garden: Technology and the Pastoral Idea in America.* New York: Oxford Univ. Press, 1964.

Massie, Susanne Williams, and Frances Archer Christian eds., *Homes and Gardens in Old Virginia.* Richmond: Garrett and Massie, 1931.

Mayo, Bernard. *Myths and Men: Patrick Henry, George Washington, Thomas Jefferson.* New York: Harper & Row, 1959.

Mitchell, Samuel Chiles. *Aftermath of Appomattox: A Memoir.* Atlanta: privately printed, 1954.

Moger, Allen W. *Virginia: From Bourbonism to Byrd, 1870–1925.* Charlottesville: Univ. Press of Virginia, 1968.

Moore, James Tice. *Two Paths to the New South: The Virginia Debt Controversy, 1870–1883.* Lexington: Univ. Press of Kentucky, 1974.

Morgan, Edmund S. *American Slavery, American Freedom: The Ordeal of Colonial Virginia.* New York: Norton, 1975.

Munford, Beverley B. *Random Recollections.* Richmond: privately printed, 1905.

Munford, Robert Beverley, Jr. *Richmond Homes and Memories.* Richmond: Garrett and Massie, 1936.

Newton, Mary M. P. "The Association for the Preservation of Virginia Antiquities." *American Historical Register,* Sept. 1894, 8–21.

Noël Hume, Ivor. *Here Lies Virginia: An Archaeologist's View of Colonial Life and History.* New York: Knopf, 1963.

Nuckols, R. R. *A History of Government of the City of Richmond, Virginia, and a Sketch of Those Who Administer Its Affairs.* Richmond: Williams Printing Co., 1899.

Nutting, Wallace. *Virginia Beautiful.* Garden City, N.Y.: Garden City Publishing, 1935.

O'Neal, William B. *Architecture in Virginia: An Official Guide to Four Centuries of Building in the Old Dominion.* New York: Walker & Co., 1968.

Osterweis, Rollin G. *The Myth of the Lost Cause, 1865–1900.* Hamden, Conn.: Archon Books, 1973.

Page, Thomas Nelson. "Address." In *Exercises and Addresses at the Celebration of the 300th Anniversary of the First Law Making Body in the Western Hemisphere Which Convened at Jamestown, July 30, 1619.* Richmond, 1919.

———. *Address at the Three Hundredth Anniversary of the Settlement at Jamestown* [1907]. Richmond: Whittet & Shepperson, 1919.

———. *Address on the Necessity for a History of the South.* Roanoke, Va.: William Watts Camp, 1892.

———. *Mount Vernon and Its Preservation: 1858–1910.* 1910. Rept. New York: Knickerbocker Press, 1932.

———. *The Negro: The Southerner's Problem.* New York: Charles Scribner's Sons, 1904.

———. *The Old Dominion: Her Making and Her Manners.* New York: Charles Scribner's Sons, 1908.

———. "The Old South," in *The Old South: Essays Social and Political.* New York: Charles Scribner's Sons, 1908.

———. "Old Yorktown." *Scribner's Monthly* 22 (1881): 801–16.

Parrott, Angie. "'Love Makes Memory Eternal': The United Daughters of the Confederacy in Richmond, Virginia, 1897–1920." In *The Edge of the South: Life in Nineteenth-Century Virginia,* ed. Edward L. Ayers and John C. Willis. Charlottesville and London: Univ. Press of Virginia, 1991.

Pearson, Charles C. *The Readjuster Movement in Virginia.* New Haven: Yale Univ. Press, 1935.

Persons, Stow. *The Decline of American Gentility.* New York: Columbia Univ. Press, 1973.

Peters, Margaret T., comp. *A Guidebook to Virginia's Historical Markers.* Charlottesville: Univ. Press of Virginia, 1985.

Plumb, J. H. *The Death of the Past.* Boston: Houghton Mifflin, 1970.

Pocock, J. G. A. *The Machiavellian Moment: Florentine Political Thought and the American Republican Tradition.* Princeton, N.J.: Princeton Univ. Press, 1975.

Potter, David M. *The South and the Sectional Conflict.* Baton Rouge: Louisiana State Univ. Press, 1968.

Pryor, Mrs. R. A. *The Birth of the Nation, Jamestown, 1607.* New York: Grosset & Dunlap, 1907.

———. *The Mother of Washington and Her Times.* New York: Macmillan, 1903.

———. "The Mount Vernon Association." *American Historical Register,* Jan. 1895, 406–20.

———. *My Day: Reminiscences of a Long Life.* New York: Macmillan, 1909.

Pulley, Raymond H. *Old Virginia Restored: An Interpretation of the Progressive Impulse, 1870–1930.* Charlottesville: Univ. Press of Virginia, 1968.

Rabinowitz, Howard N. *Race Relations in the Urban South, 1865–1890.* New York: Oxford Univ. Press, 1978.

Rice, Jessie Pearl. *J. L. M. Curry: Southerner, Statesman, and Educator.* New York: King's Crown Press, 1949.

Richey, Russell E., and Donald G. Jones, eds., *American Civil Religion.* New York: Harper & Row, 1974.

Rodgers, Daniel T. "In Search of Progressivism." *Reviews in American History* 10 (1982): 113–32.

Rose, Harold Wickliffe. *The Colonial Houses of Worship in America: Built in the English Colonies before the Republic, 1607–1789, and Still Standing.* New York: Hastings House, 1963.

Rouse, Parke, Jr. *Cows on the Campus: Williamsburg in Bygone Days.* Richmond Dietz Press, 1973.

Ryan, Mary P. *Women in Public: Between Banners and Ballots, 1825–1880.* Baltimore and London: Johns Hopkins Univ. Press, 1990.

Rydell, Robert W. *All the World's a Fair: Visions of Empire at American International Expositions, 1876–1916.* Chicago and London: Univ. of Chicago Press, 1984.

Sams, Conway Whittle. *The Conquest of Virginia: The Forest Primeval.* New York and London: G. P. Putnam's Sons, 1916.

Saveth, Edward N. *American Historians and European Immigrants, 1875–1925.* 1948. Rept. New York: Russell & Russell, 1965.

Schwartz, Barry. *George Washington: The Making of an American Symbol.* New York: Free Press, 1987.

Scott, Anne Firor. *The Southern Lady: From Pedestal to Politics, 1830–1930.* Chicago and London: Univ. of Chicago Press, 1970.

———. "Women's Perspective on the Patriarchy in the 1850s." *Journal of American History* 61 (1974): 52–64.

Scott, Mary Wingfield, "A.P.V.A. Tries to Save Old Richmond." *Journal of American Society of Architectural Historians* 3 (1943): 26–31.

———. *Houses of Old Richmond.* Richmond: Valentine Museum, 1941.

———. *Old Richmond Neighborhoods.* Richmond: privately printed, 1950.

Sheldon, William DuBose. *Populism in the Old Dominion: Virginia Farm Politics, 1885–1900.* Princeton, N.J.: Princeton Univ. Press, 1935.

Shi, David E. *The Simple Life: Plain Living and High Thinking in American Culture.* New York: Oxford Univ. Press, 1985.

Slotkin, Richard. *Regeneration through Violence: The Mythology of the American Frontier, 1600–1860.* Middletown, Conn.: Wesleyan Univ. Press, 1973.

Smith, John David. *An Old Creed for the New South: Proslavery Ideology and Historiography, 1865–1918.* Westport, Conn., and London: Greenwood Press, 1985.

Smith, Lillian. *Killers of the Dream.* New York: Norton, 1949.

Spofford, Ainsworth R., ed. *Eminent and Representative Men of Virginia and the District of Columbia of the Nineteenth Century.* Madison, Wis.: Brand and Fuller, 1893.

Sproat, John G. *"The Best Men": Liberal Reformers in the Gilded Age*. New York: Oxford Univ. Press, 1968.

Stanard, Mary Newton. *Colonial Virginia: Its People and Customs*. Philadelphia: J. B. Lippincott, 1917.

——. *Jamestown and the A.P.V.A.* Richmond: Wm. Ellis Jones, [1904].

——. *John Marshall and His Home, Read before A.P.V.A. at Opening of the John Marshall House, March 27, 1913*. Richmond: Wm. Ellis Jones, 1913.

——. *Richmond: Its People and Its Story*. Philadelphia: J. B. Lippincott, 1923.

——. *The Story of Bacon's Rebellion*. New York: Neale Publishing Company, 1907.

Stanard, William G. "The Homes of the Virginia Historical Society: Past, Present, and Future." *Virginia Magazine of History and Biography* 34 (1926): 1–19.

——, comp. *Notes on a Journey on the James Together with a Guide to Old Jamestown*. [Richmond: APVA, 1907].

Stevens, John Austin. *Yorktown Centennial Handbook: Historical and Topographical Guide to the Yorktown Peninsula, Richmond, James River, and Norfolk*. New York: C. A. Coffin & Rogers, 1881.

Stilgoe, John. *Common Landscape of America, 1580 to 1845*. New Haven and London: Yale Univ. Press, 1982.

Stillinger, Elizabeth. *The Antiquers: The Lives and Careers, the Deals, the Finds, the Collections of the Men and Women Who Were Responsible for the Changing Taste in American Antiques, 1850–1930*. New York: Knopf, 1980.

Taylor, Lloyd C., Jr., "Lila Meade Valentine: The FFV as Reformer." *Virginia Magazine of History and Biography* 70 (1962): 471–87.

Taylor, William R. *Cavalier and Yankee: The Old South and American National Character*. New York: Harper & Row, 1961.

Tindall, George Brown. *The Ethnic Southerners*. Baton Rouge: Louisiana State Univ. Press, 1976.

——. *The Persistent Tradition in New South Politics*. Baton Rouge: Louisiana State Univ. Press, 1975.

Trachtenberg, Alan. *The Incorporation of America: Culture and Society in the Gilded Age*. New York: Hill & Wang, 1982.

Trudell, Clyde F. *Colonial Yorktown*. Old Greenwich, Conn.: Chatham Press, 1971.

Turner, Victor. *The Forest of Symbols: Aspects of Ndembu Ritual*. Ithaca, N.Y.: Cornell Univ. Press, 1967.

Tyler, Lyon G. *Bruton Church*. Richmond: Whittet & Shepperson, 1895.

——. *The Cavalier in America*. Richmond: Whittet & Shepperson, 1913.

——. *A Confederate Catechism: The War for Southern Self Government*. 6th ed. enl. Holdcroft, Va., 1931.

——. *Pocahontas; Peace and Truth: An Address Read in the Memorial Church at Jamestown, October 24, 1914, on the Occasion of the Unveiling of a Tablet Presented to the Association for the Preservation of Virginia Antiquities by the Washington Branch*. Richmond: Whittet & Shepperson, 1915.

——. *Propaganda in History.* Richmond: Richmond Press, 1920.

——. *The South and Germany.* Richmond: Whittet & Shepperson, 1917.

——. *Virginia First.* 2d enl. ed. Richmond: Colonial Dames of America, 1921.

——. *Virginia Principles.* Richmond: Richmond Press, 1928.

——. *Williamsburg: The Old Colonial Capital.* Richmond: Whittet & Shepperson, 1907.

Vaughan, Alden T. *American Genesis: Captain John Smith and the Founding of Virginia.* Boston: Little, Brown, 1975.

Wallace, Anthony F. C. "Revitalization Movements." *American Anthropologist* 58 (1956): 264–81.

Wallace, Michael. "Visiting the Past: History Museums in the United States." In *Presenting the Past: Essays on History and the Public,* ed. Susan Porter Benson et al. Philadelphia: Temple Univ. Press, 1986.

Ward, John William. *Red, White, and Blue: Men, Books, and Ideas in American Culture.* New York: Oxford Univ. Press, 1969.

Warner, W. Lloyd. *The Living and the Dead; A Study of the Symbolic Life of Americans.* New Haven: Yale Univ. Press, 1959.

Wecter, Dixon. *The Hero in America: A Chronicle of Hero-Worship.* Ann Arbor: Univ. of Michigan Press, 1966.

Welter, Barbara. "The Cult of True Womanhood: 1820–1860." *American Quarterly* 18 (1966): 151–74.

Whiffen, Marcus. *The Eighteenth-Century Houses of Williamsburg: A Study of Architecture and Building in the Colonial Capital of Virginia.* Rev. ed. Williamsburg: Colonial Williamsburg Foundation, 1984.

——. *The Public Buildings of Williamsburg: Colonial Capital of Virginia.* Williamsburg: Colonial Williamsburg, 1958.

Weibe, Robert H. *The Search for Order, 1877–1920.* New York: Hill & Wang, 1967.

——. *The Segmented Society: An Introduction to the Meaning of America.* New York: Oxford Univ. Press, 1975.

Williams, Raymond. *Culture and Society, 1780–1950.* New York: Harper & Row, 1958.

Wilson, Charles Reagan. "The Religion of the Lost Cause: Ritual and Organization of the Southern Civil Religion." *Journal of Southern History* 46 (1980): 219–38.

Wilson, Edmund. *Patriotic Gore: Studies in the Literature of the American Civil War.* New York: Oxford Univ. Press, 1962.

Winks, Robin. "Conservation in America: National Character as Revealed by Preservation." In *The Future of the Past: Attitudes to Conservation, 1174–1974,* ed. Jane Fawcett. New York: Watson-Guptill, 1976.

Woodward, C. Vann. *American Counterpoint: Slavery and Racism in the North-South Dialogue.* Boston: Little, Brown, 1971.

——. *The Burden of Southern History.* Rev. ed. New York and Toronto: New American Library, 1968.

———. *Origins of the New South, 1877–1913*. Baton Rouge: Louisiana State Univ. Press, 1971.

Wright, Gwendolyn. *Moralism and the Model Home: Domestic Architecture and Cultural Conflict in Chicago, 1873–1913*. Chicago and London: Univ. of Chicago Press, 1980.

Wynes, Charles E. *Race Relations in Virginia, 1870–1902*. 1961. Rept. Totowa, N.J.: Rowman and Littlefield, 1971.

Yetter, George Humphrey. *Williamsburg Before and After: The Rebirth of Virginia's Colonial Capital*. Williamsburg, Va.: Colonial Williamsburg Foundation, 1988.

Yonge, Samuel H. "The Site of Old 'James Towne,' 1607–1698." *Virginia Magazine of History and Biography* 11 (1904): 257–76, 393–414, 12 (1904): 3–53, 113–33.

———. *The Site of Old 'James Towne' 1607–1698: A Brief Historical and Topographical Sketch of the First American Metropolis*. 1904. Rept. Richmond: L. H. Jenkins, 1927.

Zelinsky, Wilbur. *Nation into State: The Shifting Symbolic Foundations of American Nationalism*. Chapel Hill and London: Univ. of North Carolina Press, 1988.

Index

Abingdon Church, Gloucester County, 63

Adam Craig house, Richmond, 236–37

Adam Thoroughgood house, Princess Anne County, 192, 210

Adams, Henry, 130, 131

Adams, John, 85

African-Americans: and colonial buildings, 80, 153, 154; and Emancipation, 15, 17, 108; and Jamestown, 95, 109–10, 119; in Northampton County, 156; in politics, 15, 18–19, 20, 21; and progressivism, 21; in Richmond, 19, 166, 191, 235–37; and slavery, 102, 110, 156, 172, 173, 181, 182, 202; at the tercentennial, 124; and white fears, 19, 23, 33–34, 45, 70, 125, 183, 240; in Williamsburg, 17–18, 76, 194

Alderman, Edwin A., 86, 124, 184

American Revolution: popular-class interpretation of, 18; traditionalist interpretation of, 85–86, 87, 90, 135, 163. *See also* New England, and the American Revolution

American Scenic and Historic Preservation Society (ASHPS), 6, 63, 82; and Jamestown, 116, 117, 220

Ampthill, Chesterfield County, 211

Anderson, Archer: on advisory board, 253; on Capitol, 212; on Lee statue, 178; on moral decline, 186; on politics, 19, 85–86

Anglophobia, 8, 95

Anglo-Saxonism: and Great Britain, 177, 197–98, 201–2; and imperialism, 183; and Jamestown, 1–2, 91, 95, 107, 118, 123, 125, 130, 132, 218, 220, 234; and Virginia, 8, 20, 31, 134, 155, 168, 235, 243; and Wilson, 120, 198

Ann Carrington house, Richmond, 237

Antimodernism: and agrarianism, 28–29, 56; and APVA balls, 72, 74; and Jamestown, 100–101, 108, 114, 129, 193;

and Mary Washington house, 209; and Mount Vernon, 43–45; in the North, 258; and Williamsburg, 77, 85, 90, 193, 226; and Yorktown, 27, 222–23

Antiquities Act, 210–11. *See also* United States government

Antiradicalism: and APVA origins, 14–21, 185; and civil religion, 36, 38–39; and Curry, 55; in 1896 election, 19–20, 82; expressed symbolically, 67, 131, 135, 165, 216; and Jamestown, 98–99; and Jefferson, 33, 213; and 1920s, 168; and Red Scare, 98, 122, 166–67, 218. *See also* Culture, as mechanism to control popular classes

Appleton, William Sumner, Jr.: and the APVA, 214–15, 216, 235, 238–39, 247–48; on graveyards, 65; and Kenmore, 210; and Mary Washington house, 208–9; on memorials, 83–84; and neurasthenia, 63; and Paul Revere, 189; and World War I, 200; on Yorktown, 221–23. *See also* Society for the Preservation of New England Antiquities

Archaeological Institute of America, 211

Architectural symbolism, 55, 105, 241, 243; and Bruton Parish Church, 87, 90; and Cape Henry Lighthouse, 159–60; and Capitol (Richmond), 24, 212; and courthouses, 215–16; and Eastville colonial block, 156–57; and family home, 55–56; and HABS, 239; and Jamestown, 1–2, 40, 53, 95–101, 112, 129, 134; and John Marshall house, 164–68; and Mary Washington house, 207–9; and Mount Vernon, 43–45; and the Powder Horn, 80–81; and the Rising Sun Tavern, 170–71; and the White House of the Confederacy, 51; and Williamsburg, 78, 90, 233